International Financial Instability

Global Banking and National Regulation

World Scientific Studies in International Economics
(ISSN: 1793-3641)

2 World Scientific
Studies in
International
Economics

International Financial Instability

Global Banking and National Regulation

Editors

Douglas D Evanoff
Federal Reserve Bank of Chicago, USA

George G Kaufman
Loyola University Chicago, USA

John R LaBrosse
International Association of Deposit Insurers, Switzerland

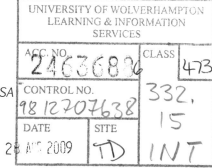
World Scientific

NEW JERSEY · LONDON · SINGAPORE · BEIJING · SHANGHAI · HONG KONG · TAIPEI · CHENNAI

Published by

World Scientific Publishing Co. Pte. Ltd.

5 Toh Tuck Link, Singapore 596224

USA office: 27 Warren Street, Suite 401-402, Hackensack, NJ 07601

UK office: 57 Shelton Street, Covent Garden, London WC2H 9HE

British Library Cataloguing-in-Publication Data
A catalogue record for this book is available from the British Library.

World Scientific Studies in International Economics — Vol. 2
INTERNATIONAL FINANCIAL INSTABILITY
Global Banking and National Regulation

ISBN-13 978-981-270-763-5
ISBN-10 981-270-763-8

Typeset by Stallion Press
Email: enquiries@stallionpress.com

Printed in Singapore by B & JO Enterprise

Acknowledgements

Both the conference and this resulting volume represent a joint effort of the Federal Reserve Bank of Chicago and the International Association of Deposit Insurers. Numerous people at both organizations aided in their preparation and successful execution. The three editors served as the principal organizers of the conference program and are indebted to the assistance of many people who contributed at various stages of the endeavor. At the risk of omitting some, they wish to thank John Dixon, Ella Dukes, Jennie Krzystof, Hala Leddy, Loretta Novak, Elizabeth Taylor, Julia Baker and Wempy (Ping) Homeric.

Special mention must be accorded Regina Langston and Pam Suarez, who shared primary responsibility for administrative duties, and Kathryn Moran, who compiled the information for both the program and this conference volume.

Preface

Cross-border banking in the form of international branches or subsidiaries is increasing rapidly, but prudential regulation of banking — supervision, deposit insurance, lender of last resort facilities, insolvency resolution — remains primarily national. This mismatch raises concerns about the ability of regulators to stem banking crises and financial instability both from being ignited and from spreading rapidly across national boundaries. The papers published in this volume describe the existing structure of both cross-border banking and prudential regulation, identify the vulnerabilities in that structure, analyze the implications for the safety, soundness and efficiency of the international banking system, and make recommendations on how to improve the existing structure to enhance the safety and soundness of the banking system without reducing efficiency. Should there be greater emphasis on international cooperation, harmonization of regulations and supranational regulatory agencies, or is the current system, with minor country-specific regulatory adjustments, sufficient to avoid financial crises?

These issues were explored at a conference cosponsored by the Federal Reserve Bank of Chicago and the International Association of Deposit Insurers at the Federal Reserve Bank on October 5–6, 2006. The conference was the ninth in a series of annual international banking conferences sponsored by the Federal Reserve Bank of Chicago that focus on important current issues in global economics, finance, and banking. Keynote speakers, paper presenters and discussants are internationally recognized experts in their areas. Speakers and audience members combined represented a wide array of countries, philosophies, experiences and affiliations, including bankers, bank regulators, and academics. In total, more than 40 countries were represented, reinforcing the term "international" in the title of the conference series.

The papers in this volume, as well as the comments of the discussants of the papers, are intended to bring the ideas that were discussed at the conference to the attention of a larger and more diverse audience. In the process, this may contribute both to increasing attention to some of the problems identified in the papers and to searching for solutions. Thus, we hope this volume will contribute to enhancing global financial stability.

Douglas D. Evanoff
Federal Reserve Bank of Chicago

George G. Kaufman
Loyola University Chicago and
Federal Reserve Bank of Chicago

John Raymond LaBrosse
International Association of Deposit Insurers

Contents

I. SPECIAL ADDRESSES

Cross-Border Banking Regulation — A Way Forward: The European Case

Stefan Ingves*
Sveriges Riksbank

1. Introduction

It is an honor for me to address this distinguished audience on a very timely topic. I have spent many years dealing with distressed banks in my own and, by now, a large number of other countries. One conclusion I have drawn from this rather odd line of work is that efficient banking regulation is needed both to reduce the risk that banks run into problems and to minimize the externalities that arise if banks actually fail. At the national level, many countries — including my own — still need to implement regulations to ensure that these risks are fully mitigated.

Let me also take this opportunity to congratulate the organizers on their choice of subject for this conference. The importance of the international dimension of the regulatory setup is growing steadily. It is only now that many banks are becoming truly cross-border, with substantial retail activities in several countries. At the same time, banking regulation, in terms of supervision, oversight, deposit guarantee schemes and responsibility for financial stability, remains predominantly national. This imposes additional challenges for financial regulators. These challenges are particularly acute in Europe given the rapid growth of cross-border banks on that continent. However, the issues raised are of global concern.

With this in mind, let me start out by stating my main message, but, before doing so, let me stress that these are my personal views and do not represent the official opinion of any institution. In my view we need to plan for a special body — let us call it a European Organization for Financial Supervision (EOFS) — to gather information and produce a

*Stefan Ingves is Governor of Sveriges Riksbank (the Central Bank of Sweden).

coherent and consistent assessment of the risks in the major cross-border banks in Europe.

As you all know, a separate regulatory framework for banks is based both on consumer protection arguments and on financial stability considerations. Banks provide fundamental services to the economy but could be subject to bank runs. There are also large contagion risks in banking activities so that problems in one bank could easily spread to other banks. Here, I will concentrate on the financial stability perspective.

2. Banking Developments in the European Union

Until not so long ago, most banks had a clear national (or local) character with most of the activities limited to one country. Sure, many banks have had international operations for many decades but that has typically been limited to wholesale markets and services to large corporations. Financial services to retail customers and small- and medium-sized companies (SMEs) have been provided on a national or local basis. In this setting, the national character of the regulatory framework has been appropriate. Now this is rapidly changing, not only in Europe — but also elsewhere.

First, banks in different countries are increasingly merging and creating some genuinely cross-border banking groups, targeting retail customers and SMEs in several countries. There are now about 40 banking groups with substantial activities in more than three countries in Europe. Just to take few examples: Unicredit Group has, after the merger with Germany's HypoVereinsbank, a market share of at least 5 percent (in terms of total assets) in Italy, Germany, Austria, Bulgaria, the Czech Republic, Hungary, Poland, Luxembourg, Slovenia, as well as Slovakia. Barclays and Grupo Santander are major players in both Spain and the UK. Fortis and ING are both important in the Benelux region. Erste Bank is large in Austria, the Czech Republic, Slovakia and Hungary; KBC in Belgium and a number of eastern European countries. Nordea is central to the banking market in Sweden, Denmark, Finland and Norway.

Second, banks are increasingly dependent on the international financial markets for funding, risk management, etc. The inter-linkages and contagion risk between banks are probably increasing even for the banks that stick to a purely national focus.

Third, many of the cross-border banks are progressively concentrating various functions, such as funding, liquidity management, risk management, internal controls, compliance, credit decision-making, auditing, etc., to various centers of competence. As a consequence, cross-border linkages are rising.

Fourth, with the increased cross-border specialization, the distinction between a branch and a subsidiary is becoming increasingly blurred. Subsidiaries are becoming less self-contained. If the parent bank of a cross-border banking group defaults, it is getting more and more unrealistic to assume that the foreign subsidiaries could continue their business as usual. It takes time to establish all the necessary competencies to transform such a subsidiary to an independent bank. Also, the possibilities for the host country to successfully ring-fence the assets are diminishing, given the speed at which funds can be transferred across borders. When there still is a clear legal difference between branches and subsidiaries with clear consequences for supervision, the distinction becomes less important both in practical and in economic terms.

Fifth, and as a consequence of this merger activity, the banking market in some countries is dominated by foreign banks. In the 10 new European Union (EU) member states, about 70 percent of the banking sectors are foreign owned. In Estonia, foreign groups account for more than 90 percent of all lending.

My worry is that the next financial crisis in Europe could have serious cross-border implications and not be bounded by national borders. As a central banker, I see it as a major responsibility to be prepared for such an event, both in terms of handling the acute problem and in finding more long-term solutions.

One reason why this cross-border development is more pronounced in Europe than in many other parts of the world is the long-term project of creating a single market for financial services in Europe. Let me be clear here. I strongly support this project. It has freed banking from its national restrictions and fostered a more efficient financial sector. It has created an environment to support greater economic growth. Cross-border banking should not be seen as an economic problem but rather a challenge for the regulators and supervisors. The problem is that the regulatory framework for ensuring financial stability has not adapted as quickly and as thoroughly as needed.

Let me stress that historically, regulatory and supervisory convergence across borders has taken time. It cannot be expected that the optimal regulatory setup will emerge immediatly when market conditions change. The single market for financial services in Europe has definitely changed the market environment for financial firms. Now, it is up the regulators to do their bit.

3. Regulatory Challenges

The question is then how the regulatory and supervisory framework could be adapted to face up to a situation where some banks play important roles in providing banking services in several countries.

Let me — for the sake of argument — assume that a problem occurs in a major cross-border bank under the present framework in Europe. Apart from the challenges to solve a problem in a purely national bank, it becomes both more important and more complicated to address such a crisis in an international framework. There are a number of challenges.

The first challenge concerns the sharing of relevant information. For a cross-border banking group, the number of authorities involved multiplies. As a consequence, information sharing may be slowed down. Also, compared to purely national banks, many cross-border banking groups have a more complex structure. This makes the analysis and information gathering more difficult. The functional specialization of cross-border banks also complicates supervision and information gathering. If a cross-border banking group concentrates all its credit assessments in one country, it will be difficult for the supervisor in another country to assess the risk of the bank in that country without efficient supervisory cooperation and exchange of information. Further, if the bank puts all its liquidity management in a third country, extensive information sharing will be needed in order for any supervisor to get the full picture of the group's total risks. In principle, the parent bank — and therefore the parent bank's supervisor — should have a full overview, but in a crisis, positions may change quickly and thus complicate the collection of all relevant information. Such extensive information sharing becomes acute in a crisis but is also necessary in the day-to-day supervision.

A second challenge is that conflicts of interest multiply. Banking problems can be very costly and the ultimate guarantee for financial stability can only be given by the government, since only the government has the power to tax. In most countries, the deposit guarantee schemes are only able to finance the problem if it is confined to minor banks. For systemic problems, the government would have to intervene. With predominantly national banks, how this is done is fairly straightforward.

With the emergence of truly cross-border banks the question is how to share the burden. To what extent would the taxpayers in one country be willing to support the depositors in another country? And to what extent would the depositors in the second country be willing to rely on the potential future support of the taxpayers in the first country?

A similar problem applies when a central bank considers providing emergency liquidity assistance to a cross-border bank. Such funding is inherently risky. If it were not, the market would typically be able to provide the funding. Such assistance is also likely to affect the entire banking group. What happens if a bank is systemically important in one smaller country but not in another perhaps larger country? The smaller country will probably have greater incentive to save the bank but may end up paying for the entire group, if the larger country refuses.

Also, there are conflicts of interest if the bank is reconstructed. Any such reconstruction is risky and it is therefore uncertain whether the taxpayers would be willing to take these risks in another country.

A third challenge is how to achieve joint assessments. In Europe, there is an agreement to share views and assessments if there is a crisis. However in my opinion, that is not sufficient. In a crisis, most countries are likely to present assessments that support their national interests. With the present supervisory setup, there is, unfortunately, a risk that it will be time-consuming to achieve joint assessments, and time is a scarce resource, especially in crisis management.

A fourth challenge is how to coordinate decisions by the authorities. The central bank must decide whether to grant emergency liquidity assistance or not and occasionally a bank may have to be placed under public administration. All of these decisions have to be made at short notice and typically with limited information. For this to be effective, there is a need for a clear line of command. For cross-border banks where many supervisors, many central banks and many ministries of finance are involved, this is complicated to achieve. Without prior agreements on responsibilities, this is going to be even more complicated, and may very well lead to suboptimal solutions.

The potential inefficiencies are probably enhanced by the differences in language and legal structure. The problem is further inflated by the interdependencies between the different countries. The decisions by one authority will typically have repercussions in many other countries.

To alleviate these problems there are today many Memoranda of Understanding (MoUs) between the authorities in the different countries — both regional and on an EU basis. Such MoUs are important to foster cooperation and information sharing but are, in my view, not sufficient. They are not legally binding and address neither the need for joint assessments nor the underlying conflicts of interest. Instead they should be seen as an important first step in facilitating the handling of cross-border institutions. However, we need to go further.

4. Potential Solutions

To address these challenges four potential solutions have been discussed in various fora.

The first is to establish supervisory colleges. The idea is to create specific standing committees for each individual cross-border banking group with representatives from the relevant supervisors. The recently proposed operational networks of the Committee of European Banking Supervisors (CEBS) can be seen as a first step in this direction. This is a good start but also generates a series of problems. The supervisory framework becomes very complex and scattered. Which supervisors should be part of which college? It could also undermine the likelihood of equal treatment among banks.

The second is to enhance the home country's responsibility by giving the home supervisor additional powers not only for the group but also for all its foreign subsidiaries. One agency would thus get the responsibility for assembling information, formulating a joint assessment and coordinating decisions for all subsidiaries as well as the group level. A general problem with this solution is that it does not address the conflicts of interest. Will the home country authorities take the situation in the host countries fully into account in their decisions? How will host countries that do not share the assessment or disagree with the decision act? Also, will the authorities in a host country be willing to delegate such responsibilities to an authority in another country?

A third proposed solution is an extension of the second alternative. In addition, the home country will get an explicit EU-mandate to take the interest of the other relevant countries into account in its assessments and decisions, but it is not clear how this will work in practice. There is also an accountability problem with this solution. National authorities are both appointed by and accountable to the national governments and in extension to the national electorate. It may be difficult for a host country to hold the authorities in a home country responsible for a specific decision, even if its main effect is in the host country.

A fourth possibility is the pan-European solution where both the mandate and responsibility for supervision are transferred from the national level to the EU-level. This would imply the creation of a European Financial Services Authority (FSA), as well as granting the European Central Bank (ECB) a role as lender of last resort for cross-border banks. This solution raises a number of difficult political considerations. It basically means handing over a part of the sovereignty to the EU-level. Also, at present the EU has no supra-national taxing power, so some other formula on burden sharing would have to be found. Presumably the political obstacles for this solution are large. At least in the short run, this fourth solution is not realistic.

5. Another Approach

With this background, I draw three conclusions. First, the present situation with a growth of cross-border banks — with some clear examples in the European region — combined with national responsibility for supervision and financial stability is not satisfactory. If we are hit by a critical crisis in one or more of the major financial institutions today, the regulatory and supervisory framework is not sufficient. Second, we need to move forward and find a modified framework before problems arise. My experience is that if a crisis hits an unprepared authority, the choice of solution will suffer. Third, we should move ahead gradually, since there are obvious political difficulties and it is uncertain what the first-best solution would look like. In a political world, it is difficult to achieve first-best directly. Instead we have to move stepwise and ensure that we have our compass firmly in our hands to ensure a move in the right direction.

To solve some of the problems of coordination of information and assessments, I propose the establishment a new pan-European body, a European Organization for Financial Supervision (EOFS). The idea is to create a separate agency to follow the major cross-border banking groups in Europe. The EOFS should only focus on the presently about 40 truly cross-border banking groups and not deal with some 8,000 European banks with a predominately national character. The EOFS should have three tasks: It should gather information about the banking groups and their activities in different countries. Importantly, it should also create unified risk-assessments of each cross-border banking group. Finally, it should also oversee the activities and risks of these banking groups.

To achieve these tasks, there is a need for a separate agency, staffed with a sufficient number of competent employees. Initially, these employees could, of course, be recruited from the existing national supervisors. Also, the staff of the EOFS would have to cooperate with the national supervisors.

I also want to stress that the EOFS should be an independent agency. This independence is important to achieve a division of labor and power. It should not be part of the European Commission and not of the ECB. One possible solution is therefore that EOFS is established directly by the EU countries and with an obligation to report to the European Parliament.

My proposal is therefore quite different from the existing CEBS-structure which is part of the Lamfalussy regulatory framework in the EU. Although some of the EOFS's tasks would overlap with those of CEBS, the focus is different. CEBS's main tasks are to advise the EU Commission, to enhance supervisory cooperation, and to contribute to convergence of Member States' supervisory practices. CEBS is therefore a regulator and not a supervisory agency. The EOFS would be much more of a supervisor with as main task to produce coherent assessments of the risks and vulnerabilities of cross-border banking groups.

In my view and to start out with, the EOFS need not have formal powers, with the exception that it should have the right to require cross-border banks to submit information. Formal supervision could still rest with the national supervisors according to the existing home–host arrangements and potential sanctions be decided by the national supervisors. In this respect, the EOFS should be limited to suggesting actions to the national supervisors. Furthermore, the work conducted by the EOFS does not replace the oversight by the national central banks. They still need to oversee the banks as a part of their mandate on financial stability.

The creation of an EOFS could, if the organization is successful, be seen as the embryo to a full-fledged European supervisor — a future European FSA. It is much too early to tell whether such a development is feasible. First the EOFS would have to prove that it can produce added-value in terms of information gathering and assessments with real supervisory resources beyond that of a talk shop.

To be honest, my approach is not without problems either. It would make the regulatory structure somewhat more complex, and it would increase the regulatory burden on the cross-border banks by adding a new agency for reporting. However, in my view, we need to achieve a greater coordination of the information gathering and assessments. Sometimes, you need to settle for the second-best solution when the best is not possible.

Given the problems that I have sketched, a natural question is why my proposed solution has a purely European focus. The growth of cross-border banking is not unique to Europe, even if the development of truly cross-border banks is accelerating fast in Europe — perhaps faster than in other regions. The reason for my European focus is that there is, within the EU, a common regulatory framework, which includes the establishment of joint organizations. One example is the European Monetary Institute, which was the forerunner to the ECB. There is also a tradition of using a gradual approach. One of the underlying long-term principles in the EU is the ever-increasing integration through small successive steps. Therefore Europe is likely to be a good starting point for the establishment of such a supranational supervisory framework for cross-border banks. In my view though, the underlying challenge is of global nature. My forecast is therefore that the timely subject of this conference will be relevant also for future conferences.

Thank you.

Remarks Before the Conference on International Financial Instability

Sheila C. Bair*
Federal Deposit Insurance Corporation

Good evening. It is a pleasure to be here tonight. I would like to thank President Moskow and Chairman Sabourin for inviting me to speak this evening. I would also like to thank Doug Evanoff and George Kaufman for putting together an excellent program.

The topics of this conference — cross-border banking and national regulation — affect financial stability and public confidence, two things the Federal Deposit Insurance Corporation (FDIC) stands for at home and seeks to foster abroad. Tonight I would like to talk about three areas the FDIC views as critical for ensuring global stability and confidence: strong international capital standards, credible deposit insurance systems and an international strategy for large bank resolution.

Significant progress has been made in improving international standards for effective prudential supervision. These improvements have not, however, eliminated the potential for banking crises to occur. When crises arise, such as the Asian crisis of 1998, the economic costs and dislocation are significant, with implications for growth and stability not just in the region, but around the globe. For example, in Indonesia, the country perhaps the hardest hit by the Asian crisis, 83 out of their 228 banks were closed and, by the end of 1998, nonperforming loans peaked at 57 percent of total loans. As a consequence, Indonesia experienced a 7-percent decline in its gross domestic product (GDP).

In addition, banking crises in one country can spill over to others. For example, in 2001, the financial system in Uruguay was not initially affected by the exchange rate crisis in neighboring Argentina. However, when severe withdrawal restrictions were imposed on bank customers

*Sheila C. Bair is chairman of the Federal Deposit Insurance Corporation.

in Argentina, many turned to their accounts in Uruguay, precipitating a bank run there. The subsequent collapse of the banking system in Uruguay ultimately led to widespread unemployment and a 20 percent decline in the country's GDP.

As these experiences illustrate, banking crises have very real effects on domestic economies and the global marketplace. Crisis prevention and containment depends on strong national regulation and international cooperation and coordination. The first place to start is with capital.

1. Basel II and the Importance of an International Capital Standard

For the past three days, I have been in Mexico attending the biennial conference of national banking supervisors. The conference focused on the core principles for effective banking supervision and their importance in protecting banking safety nets worldwide. So of course, we spent a lot of time talking about capital.

As you know, on September 5, the FDIC board of directors, along with the other federal banking regulators, voted to publish the Basel II Notice of Proposed Rulemaking (NPR) for public comment. In conjunction with Basel II, US bank and thrift regulators also are developing a more risk-sensitive capital framework for non-Basel II banks, known as Basel IA, which we hope to publish for comment in the near future.

It is appropriate and necessary that we move forward with the Basel II process. While views and opinions differ about the changes that may be needed, there is one area where I believe there is much common ground: The implementation of Basel II must not result in significant reductions in capital or in the creation of competitive inequities among different types of insured depository institutions.

I look forward to receiving the comments on the NPR, and I will approach them with an open mind. I am particularly interested in comments on the question of whether the regulators should allow alternatives to the advanced approach. The US is the only country proposing to make the advanced approaches mandatory for some banks. Several large banks have asked to be allowed to use the Basel standardized approach for calculating their requirements.

The standardized approach links risk weights to external ratings and includes a greater array of risk classes than are included in the current rules. It is simpler and less costly to implement than the advanced approach. In addition, because there is a floor for each risk exposure, it does not provide the same potential for dramatic reductions in capital requirements and therefore would not pose the same issues about competitive inequity. On the other hand, there is the argument that only the advanced approach provides an adequate incentive for strengthening risk-measurement systems at our largest banks. Whether our largest banks should be required to use the advanced approach is an important policy issue.

I will support implementing the advanced approach only if I can develop a comfort level that strong capital levels will be preserved. In addition, I have an open mind regarding the possibility of allowing a US version of the standardized approach as an alternative option for implementation of Basel II in the US.

In my view, no discussion of capital can be complete without a few words about the leverage ratio. The FDIC has consistently supported the idea that the leverage ratio — a simple tangible capital to assets measure — is a critically important component of our regulatory capital regime. I am pleased that all the US bank regulators have expressed their support for preserving the leverage ratio. I appreciate that banks in most other Basel Committee countries are not constrained by a leverage ratio and that effective capital standards around the world vary widely as a result. Indeed, if large European banks were subject to the leverage ratio mandated by US prompt corrective action standards, several would be categorized as undercapitalized.

For this reason, in testimony before the Senate Banking Committee and during the meetings this past week in Mexico, I raised with my colleagues the issue of international supplemental capital measures, such as a leverage ratio. The leverage ratio provides US supervisors with comfort that banks will maintain a stable base of capital in both good and bad times. I appreciate that other countries have different approaches to supplemental capital measures, and I look forward to learning more about them. Several countries face the prospect of double digit drops in risk-based capital for many of their large banking organizations under Basel II's advanced approaches. As Basel II moves forward, the question of supplemental capital measures such as a leverage ratio will assume greater importance. I look forward to further discussions with the Basel Committee and the larger international community on this question. Deposit insurers, in particular, should be part of this debate, given the importance of capital as a first line of defense against bank failures. We need a minimum cushion of capital for safety-and-soundness throughout the global banking system.

2. The Importance of Establishing a Deposit Insurance System

While capital can help prevent a financial crisis, an effective deposit insurance system can mitigate its effects. The lessons of past banking crises have demonstrated the importance of developing legal procedures for efficiently closing banks and having a system in place for paying off depositors and creditors. These are some of the most important and least recognized benefits of establishing an explicit, limited coverage deposit insurance system. Countries without systems in place tend to resort to ad hoc strategies when banks fail. In these cases, countries are often faced with unfortunate options, such as providing guarantees to all depositors and creditors, usually at 100 percent; delaying problem bank resolution to the point where a single bank failure is transformed into a larger event; or forbearing on problem bank resolutions and thereby increasing moral hazard and the likelihood of future crises.

3. Coordination and Cooperation among Deposit Insurers

When it comes to designing and maintaining effective and efficient deposit insurance systems, countries can benefit from the collective knowledge and experience of two important groups: the International Association of Deposit Insurers (IADI) and the European Forum of Deposit Insurers. Both were formed in 2002 to enhance deposit insurance effectiveness and promote cooperation among deposit insurers and other safety net players. Currently, these associations have a combined membership of 94 deposit insurers.

Over its short existence, IADI has set out much useful guidance — taking into account each country's different circumstances, settings, and structures. It has facilitated the sharing and exchange of expertise and information on deposit insurance issues through training, development, and educational programs. And IADI has undertaken specialized research on operational issues relating to deposit insurance.

As you can see, what IADI brings to our efforts on crisis prevention and response is unique: the collective experience and hands-on learning of the world's deposit insurance practitioners. This is scarce knowledge that we cannot afford to ignore.

4. Cross-Border Risks and Resolution Issues

The final key to global stability and confidence is an international strategy for large bank resolution. I would like to take a few minutes to talk about the challenges involved in resolving large bank failures and our efforts to address them.

Banks are taking advantage of technology and increasing international trade to expand their businesses and geographically diversify their risks. As many speakers at this conference have noted, this increase in cross-border banking could present significant deposit insurance and bank resolution issues.

Currently, there are few formal agreements between countries on how to deal with the failure of a large international bank. If a failure occurs, an "every country for itself" scenario could easily be envisioned. Legally binding multilateral agreements on the treatment of failed bank creditors could be useful in a crisis but may be difficult to attain. Progress can be made by working cooperatively at the staff level of relevant agencies within each country. These discussions can be used to acquaint each party with the relevant laws and procedures in other countries and, potentially, to yield agreements between countries regarding the exchange of information and protocols that can be used during a crisis.

5. Concluding Remarks

Financial stability and public confidence are two things that are easy to take for granted until they are tested. Strong and fair international capital regulation, well-constructed deposit insurance systems, and an orderly and collaborative approach to a large international bank failure are three cornerstones to preserving stability and confidence on the global stage. I look forward to working with all of you to reduce the likelihood of a banking crisis and to improve our collective ability to respond to one.

Benign Financial Conditions, Asset Management, and Political Risks: Trying to Make Sense of Our Times

Raghuram G. Rajan*
International Monetary Fund

Good afternoon. The Dow Jones Industrial Average has been scaling new heights recently. Risk premia and measures of risk aversion are at extremely low levels. All this, even while the housing market is slowing sharply, and the US economy is slowing. With the equity markets anticipating strong earnings growth, credit markets foreseeing low defaults, and the bond markets expecting little inflation, one has to ask: Isn't anyone pricing in risks? If not, what is going on?

In what follows, I will argue that we might be seeing the confluence of two strong forces — first, a widespread surge in productivity across the world, with the associated domestic demand varying country by country based on the strength of domestic financial markets; and second, the increasing institutionalization of, and competition within, advanced financial markets for savings. While the world has grown strongly as a result of both these forces in recent years, risks have built up, and there is no guarantee that the future will be as rosy as the recent past. Some of the risks are cross-border, and financial — central to the theme of this conference — but I will focus, not so much on the risks to financial stability, which have been widely discussed, but the associated political risks.[1] Given the limited time, I will start by skipping the lunchtime jokes.

*Raghuram G. Rajan is economic counselor and director of research at the International Monetary Fund. The following reflects his views only and are not meant to represent the views of the International Monetary Fund, its management, and its board. The author thanks Charles Collyns and Laura Kodres for helpful comments.

[1] See, for example, Borio, Claudio, 2006, "Monetary and Prudential Policies at a Crossroads: New Challenges for a New Century", BIS, working paper; White, William, 2006, "Is Price Stability Enough?", BIS working paper; Rajan, Raghuram, 2006, "Has Financial Development Made the World Riskier", NBER, working paper.

1. The Productivity Revolution

We are now in the fourth year of strong world growth, growth that has been maintained in the face of headwinds such as soaring commodities prices. In my view, productivity growth, fostered in part not only by the revolution in information technology, but also in part by the rationalization of production through the creation of global supply chains, has played a critical role in this expansion. While much attention has been focused on the extraordinary surge in US productivity since 1995, equally impressive productivity growth in emerging markets has been little commented upon. Taken together, rapid, and largely unexpected, worldwide productivity growth can explain why the demand for commodities is so strong, how emerging markets have weathered commodity price increases without a serious slowdown in investment, why inflation is still largely contained despite the unprecedented rise in raw material costs, and why both household incomes and corporate profits are buoyant at the same time.

The reaction of domestic demand to rising productivity growth has varied across countries, in part based on the sophistication of their financial sector. In the United States, for example, the surge in productivity led to a boom in investment in the late 1990s, financed by deep financial markets. Not all the investment was wise, but the debris created by the bust was quickly cleared by the financial markets. Growth and investment picked up again. In addition, though, the United States' strong arm's-length financial system allowed consumers to borrow against future incomes and consume immediately. Indeed, the expectation of higher future incomes coupled with accommodative monetary policy and low interest rates may have fueled the housing boom, which expanded consumption even more as the financial system allowed borrowing through vehicles such as home equity loans. Thus, the United States' financial system translated productivity growth into strong domestic demand and a large current account deficit (also see International Monetary Fund, *World Economic Outlook*, September 2006).

Emerging markets countries with less sophisticated financial systems did not have the capacity to reallocate resources effectively to the newly productive areas. Some, for example in East Asia, allocated resources indiscriminately, leading to investment booms and very severe busts. Experience brought more circumspection in investment. Others, realizing their limitations, were more circumspect from the outset. Regardless of the path, barring some notable exceptions like China, investment in emerging markets has been relatively muted in recent years (see International Monetary Fund, *World Economic Outlook*, 2005) even in the face of strong growth. Moreover, because of the limited availability of housing and retail finance, households in these countries have not been able to expand consumption through borrowing. Thus, domestic demand in these countries has been relatively muted, and these countries have generated net savings or current account surpluses.

Finally, to complete this sketch, a number of advanced countries like Germany have not experienced much increase in productivity. Given low expectations of wage growth, impending population aging and safety nets that are likely to prove inadequate absent reform, consumption has remained muted and savings high.

2. The Savings Investment Imbalance

So for the world as a whole, despite widespread strong productivity growth, investment has remained relatively weak, while desired savings is strong. Call this a "savings glut" as did Chairman Bernanke or "investment restraint" as did the International Monetary Fund (IMF), the net effect is an imbalance between desired savings and realized investment. Consequently, real long-term interest rates have been low for some time. Interestingly, even as the Federal Reserve has raised policy rates, long-term interest rates have fallen further — in slowing domestic demand in the United States, markets may believe the Fed is aggravating the world-wide excess of desired savings over realized investment further.

Current conditions are unlikely to be permanent, though a quick look at history [see Catao and Mackenzie (2005),[2] for example] would suggest that the low real interest rates of the present period are more representative than the high interest rates of the previous three decades. Given aging populations in developed countries though, one would presume that the rebalancing of worldwide investment to desired savings will have to take place primarily in nonindustrial countries. Investment will increase partly through foreign direct investment, but partly mediated by the financial systems in emerging markets, which will have to develop further. Increases in consumption, as safety nets improve and retail finance becomes widely

---

[2] Catao, Luis and G. A. Mackenzie, 2006, "Perspectives on Low Global Interest Rates", IMF, working paper, March, No. 06/76.

available, will also help reduce desired savings. Certainly, the seemingly perverse pattern of net capital flows, from poor to rich countries, will have to change, if for no other reason than to accommodate demographics.

I now want to turn to my second issue — the increasing institutionalization of, and competition within, advanced financial markets. The link between the issues will soon be clear. The break-up of oligopolistic banking systems and the rise of financial markets has expanded individual financial investment choices tremendously. While individuals don't deposit a significant portion of their savings directly in banks anymore, they don't invest directly in the market either. They invest indirectly via mutual funds, insurance companies, pension funds, venture capital funds, hedge funds, and other forms of private equity. The managers of these financial institutions, whom I shall call "investment managers", have largely displaced banks and "reintermediated" themselves between individuals and markets.

As competition among these various institutional forms for the public's investment dollar increases, each one attempts to assure the public that they will offer superior performance. But what does superior performance mean?

3. Performance Management

The typical manager of financial assets generates returns based on the systematic risk he takes — the so-called beta risk — and the value his abilities contribute to the investment process — his so-called alpha. Shareholders in any asset management firm are unlikely to pay the manager much for returns from beta risk — for example, if the shareholder wants exposure to large traded US stocks, she can get the returns associated with that risk simply by investing in the Vanguard S&P 500 index fund, for which she pays a fraction of a percent in fees. What the shareholder will really pay for is the manager beating the S&P 500 index regularly, that is, generating excess returns while not taking more risk. Indeed, hedge fund managers often claim to produce returns that are uncorrelated with the traditional market (the so-called market neutral strategies) so that all the returns they generate are excess returns or alpha, which deserve to be well compensated.

In reality, there are only a few sources of alpha for investment managers. One comes from having truly special abilities in identifying undervalued financial assets — Warren Buffet certainly has these, but study after academic study shows that very few investment managers do, and certainly not in a way that can be predicted before the fact by ordinary investors.

A second source of alpha is from what one might call activism. This means using financial resources to create, or obtain control over, real assets and to use that control to change the payout obtained on the financial investment. A venture capitalist, who transforms an inventor, a garage and an idea into a full-fledged profitable and professionally managed corporation, is creating alpha. A private equity fund that undertakes a hostile corporate takeover, cuts inefficiency and improves profits is also creating alpha. So is a vulture investor who buys up defaulted emerging market debt and presses authorities through various legal devices to press the country to pay more.

A third source of alpha is financial entrepreneurship or engineering — investing in exotic financial securities that are not easily available to the ordinary investor, or creating securities or cash flow streams that appeal to particular investors or tastes. Of course, if enough of these securities or streams are created, they cease to have scarcity or diversification value and are valued like everything else. Thus, this source of alpha depends on the manager constantly innovating and staying ahead of the competition.

Finally, alpha can also stem from liquidity provision. For instance, investment managers, having relatively easy access to finance, can hold illiquid or arbitrage positions to maturity: If a closed end fund is trading at a significant premium to the underlying market, the manager can short the fund, buy the underlying market and hold the position till the premium eventually dissipates. What is important here is that the investment managers have the liquidity to hold till the arbitrage closes.

4. Illiquidity Seeking

This discussion should suggest that alpha is quite hard to generate since most ways of doing so depend on the investment manager possessing unique abilities — to pick stock, to identify weaknesses in management and to remedy them, or undertake financial innovation. Unique ability is rare. How then do the masses of investment managers justify the faith reposed in them by masses of ordinary investors? The answer is probably liquidity provision, which is the activity that depends least on special managerial ability and could be termed the poor manager's source of alpha.

The problem when the world has excess desired savings relative to investment, and when central banks are accommodative, is that it is awash in liquidity. Many investment managers can enter the business of liquidity provision, and even as they take ever more illiquid positions, they compete away the returns from doing so. The point is that current benign conditions engender "illiquidity seeking" behavior. But they could have worse effects.

5. Tail Risk and Herding

What is the manager with relatively limited ability to do when central banks flood the market with liquidity and the rents from liquidity provision are competed away? He could hide risk — that is, pass off returns generated through taking on beta risk as alpha by hiding the extent of beta risk. Since additional risks will generally imply higher returns, managers may take risks that are typically not in their comparison benchmark (and hidden from investors) so as to generate the higher returns to distinguish themselves.

For example, a number of hedge funds, insurance companies and pension funds have entered the credit derivative market to sell guarantees against a company defaulting. Essentially, these investment managers collect premia in ordinary times from people buying the guarantees. With very small probability, however, the company will default, forcing the guarantor to pay out a large amount. The investment managers are thus selling disaster insurance or, equivalently, taking on "peso" or "tail" risks, which produce a positive return most of the time as compensation for a rare very negative return.[3] These strategies have the appearance of producing very high alphas (high returns for low risk) so managers have an incentive to load up on them, especially when times are good and disaster looks remote.[4] Every once in a while, however, they will blow up. Since true performance

---

[3] Peso risk is named after the strategy of investing in Mexican pesos while shorting the US dollar. This produces a steady return amounting to the interest differential between the two countries, although shadowed by the constant catastrophic risk of a devaluation. Another example of a strategy producing such a pattern of returns is to short deep out-of-the money S&P 500 put options. See Chan, Nicholas, M. Getmansky, S. Haas and A. Lo, 2005, "Systemic Risk and Hedge Funds", MIT, working paper, August.

[4] Certainly, the pattern of returns of hedge funds following fixed income arbitrage strategies suggested they were selling disaster insurance. The worst average monthly return between 1990 and 1997 was a loss of 2.58 percent, but losses were 6.45 percent in September 1998 and 6.09 percent in October 1998.

can only be estimated over a long period, far exceeding the horizon set by the average manager's incentives, managers will take these risks if they can.

One example of this behavior was observed in 1994, when a number of money market mutual funds in the United States came close to "breaking the buck" (going below a net asset value of $1 per share, which is virtually unthinkable for an ostensibly riskless fund). Some money market funds had to be bailed out by their parent companies. The reason they came so close to disaster was because they had been employing risky derivatives strategies in order to goose up returns, and these strategies came unstuck in the tail event caused by the Federal Reserve's abrupt rate hike.

While some managers may load up on hidden "tail risk" to look as if they are generating alpha, others know that for the more observable investments or strategies for their portfolio, there is safety in mimicking the investment strategies of competitors — after all, who can be fired when everybody underperforms? In other words, even if they suspect financial assets are overvalued, they know their likely underperformance will be excused if they herd with everyone else.

Both the phenomenon of taking on tail risk and that of herding can reinforce each other during an asset price boom, when investment managers are willing to bear the low probability tail risk that asset prices will revert to fundamentals abruptly, and the knowledge that many of their peers are herding on this risk gives them comfort that they will not underperform significantly if boom turns to bust.

6. Risk Seeking

Times of plentiful liquidity not only induce investment managers to seek illiquidity and tail risk, as well as to herd, since they are also times of low interest rates that may induce more familiar risk-seeking behavior. For example, when an insurance company has promised premium holders returns of 6 percent, while the typical matching long-term bond rate is 4 percent, it has no option if it thinks low interest rates are likely to persist, or if it worries about quarterly earnings, but to take on risk, either directly or indirectly through investments in alternative assets such as hedge funds. Similarly, a pension fund that has well defined long dated obligations will have a greater incentive to boost returns through extra risk when risk-free returns are low. All manner of risk premia are driven down by this search for yield and thus risk.

So, let me summarize. We are experiencing a widespread phenomenon of high productivity growth but low investment relative to desired savings, which has pushed down interest rates and pushed up asset prices. With plentiful liquidity, investment managers have reduced the premia for risk as they search for yield. In an attempt to generate alpha, many managers may be taking on beta risk, and even underpricing it. Of course, low interest rates and plentiful access to credit will, for a time, result in low default rates, which will appear to justify the low risk premia. The search for yield and for illiquidity knows no borders as oceans of capital spread across the globe, and asset prices across the globe are being pumped up. As one says in French, "Pourvu que ça dure! (Provided that that lasts!)"

7. Consequences

What could go wrong? Our hope is of a "soft" landing in the real sector where the factors that led to the current real sector imbalances reverse gently — for instance, domestic demand picks up in the nonindustrial world, and growth recovers in Europe and Japan, even while tighter financial conditions slow consumption in the United States. As a better balance between desired savings and investment is achieved, interest rates move up slowly, credit becomes less easy (aided by central bank tightening), and illiquidity seeking and risk-seeking reverse gently without major blow-ups.

Of course, if any of this happens more abruptly, the consequences could be uglier. Since many of you are banking experts, I will not belabor the possible risks to the banking system, about which you are well aware. Indeed, I do think the greater concern has to be about the rest of the financial system, the 80 percent of value added by the financial sector that is outside the banking system. The nonbank sector is increasingly central to economic activity and is not just a passive holder of assets. Moreover, some nonbanks, such as insurance companies, and some hedge funds are subject to runs. But most important, risks to financial stability are invariably compounded by political risk.

Let me explain this last concern. As you know, there has always been a constituency in American politics that has viewed Wall Street as preying on Main Street. In Jacksonian times, this expressed itself as the concern that the East Coast bankers were holding back the frontier, in the time of William Jennings Bryan, it was the worry that the bankers' adherence to the Gold Standard was crucifying the indebted farmer. During the depression, it was the view that universal banks had exploited the ordinary firm and investor. This anti-finance constituency typically gains power in the aftermath of a financial crisis, and while some of the constraints it imposes on finance may be warranted, some like the Glass–Steagall Act are neither justified by the evidence nor, by most counts, welfare enhancing.

It may well be that today's financial sector comes out of a future political investigation smelling like roses. But as you will guess from this talk, I see some ingredients that have me more concerned.

First, the general public's money is being invested in some of the more risky ventures, a fact highlighted by the revelation that a number of state pension funds were invested in a risky hedge fund like Amaranth. Diversification into such alternative investments can be a valuable component of an overall investment strategy if it is carefully thought out. The problem is that, all too often, it takes place as a form of herding and late in the game — after lagging pension managers see the wonderful returns in energy or from writing credit derivatives made by their more competent or lucky competitors, so there is pressure on them to enter the field. They do so late, when the good hedge or commodity funds are closed to investment and when the cycle is nearer peak than trough. Myriad new unseasoned hedge or commodity funds are started precisely to exploit the distorted incentives of the pension or insurance fund managers who queue like lemmings to dutifully place the public's money. Thus far, losses from isolated failures have been washed away in diversified portfolios and the public has not noticed. Will this always continue?

Second, the fees charged by investment managers like hedge funds and private equity cannot but arouse envy. It is surprising that despite the furor over chief executive officer (CEO) pay, very little angst has been expressed over investment manager pay, even though Kaplan and Rauh (2006) suggest that investment manager pay growth has probably exceeded CEO pay growth.[5] My sense is that there is a belief amongst the public that many investment managers are following sophisticated investment strategies — in other words, that the managers are generating alphas and earning returns for their talents — hence their pay is not questioned.

Yet, investigations of collapsed funds such as LTCM don't seem to indicate terribly sophisticated strategies — indeed more beta than alpha.

---

[5] Steve Kaplan and J. Rauh, 2006, "Wall Street and Main Street: What Contributes to the Rise in the Highest Incomes?", working paper, University of Chicago.

While there is a selection bias in examining failed funds — they are likely to have more beta — it is also likely that large funds with unsophisticated strategies became that size through a series of lucky bets that paid off. So their managers will have taken home enormous sums of money before it is realized that they had simply been gambling with other people's money. Large losses, "greedy" managers and an angry public — this is a perfect scenario for a muck-raking politician to build a career on. The regulatory impediments that could be imposed on the investment managers who add value, and on the financial sector as a whole, could be debilitating.

Third, and accentuating the political problem, is that while it is clear to the public how a bank making a loan benefits the real economy or "Main Street", it is less clear to it how an investment manager who spreads and allocates risk, improves governance, or reveals information through his trading, helps. We economists know these are very important functions in the economy but they are not so easily sold politically.

And finally, since capital has spread across borders, any sudden future retrenchment could not only inflict pain on recipient countries but also generate foreign political pressure seeking to impede the free flow of capital.

Let me conclude. The last few years have been, in many ways, the best of times for the world economy. The financial sector has contributed immensely. However, the current conjuncture has led to some practices that deserve examination. In particular, I worry whether compensation structures give too much incentive to take risk and, relatedly, whether pay is sufficiently linked to performance. Much of the debate has been over whether these are systemic concerns. My point today is that even if the consequences are not collectively important enough to stress an enormous economy like the United States, if questionable practices are numerous enough, they could stress the political system, which then may react in a way that has systemic consequences. To avoid the risk of possibly excessive political reaction, it is important that the issues that I have just alluded to be discussed by the financial sector itself, and where necessary, and possible, adjustments made. It would be a shame if sparks from the red-hot financial sector set off a conflagration that destroyed the very real gains finance has made in the last few decades. Indeed, history suggests abundant caution. Thank you.

International Financial Instability:
Cross-Border Banking and National Regulation
Chicago — Dinner Remarks

Jean Pierre Sabourin*

International Association of Deposit Insurers

and

Malaysia Deposit Insurance Corporation

Ladies and gentlemen, good evening!

First, on all your behalf, allow me to thank and congratulate the Federal Reserve Bank of Chicago for organizing this excellent conference and for inviting the International Association of Deposit Insurers (IADI) to co-host the event. As chairman and president of IADI, I extend our members sincere appreciation for having been given this great opportunity.

After two days of highly interesting discussions and dialogue, I find myself in a situation of having to provide some stimulating and provocative views and delivering them in an interesting manner while I stand between you and the beginning of a long weekend.

Given this almost impossible task, please bear with me.

Allow me to say a few words on our conference topic. We all agree that while cross-border issues are complex, they are of great importance and need to be addressed. It is a topic is of high interest, and the level of participation at the conference certainly confirms that point.

I won't get into the specifics of the issues this evening, but I do want to comment on the realities of the matter. Cross-border issues can only be appropriately addressed if there is political will to do so. National interest will always override international ones when it comes to protecting a country's safety net and constituents. Cross-border issues are also compounded by the existence of different legal frameworks including

*Jean Pierre Sabourin is the chair of executive council and president of the International Association of Deposit Insurers, and the chief executive officer of the Malaysia Deposit Insurance Corporation.

insolvency regimes. And political support is required for laws to be amended and agreements to be executed between agencies and between jurisdictions.

How can cross-border issues be advanced? What will it take to place them on the political agenda? In my opinion, this will only happen with a failure of a large international financial institutional, or a near miss, to warrant action. Action might also be possible if someone with enough economic interest is able to push the political agenda. I can only see one group that has the economic interest to do so — large international banks. In my view, they have the capability to put cross-border issues on the political agenda, since they contribute to funding the costs of each national financial safety net by paying fees to regulators and supervisors and premiums to deposit insurance agencies. The argument can be advanced that, although there has been convergence in the global financial system, there has been little movement in the national regulatory and supervisory regimes. As an example, if there is little collaboration in assessing the type of information required, how data is collected, reported, and shared between safety net players nationally or between jurisdictions, they pay for those inefficiencies. And we know that the cost of a failure of a large international bank will be borne in large part by the surviving banks doing business nationally and internationally.

I wonder if any large international bank has done an analysis of the overall annual costs they pay globally for fees, premiums and reporting requirements.

However cynical I am about the political will to drive this agenda today, I do believe we can contribute to the discussion by continuing to hold conferences on this subject. In my mind, we need to raise awareness by studying and discussing the issues thereby slowly chipping away at resistance. And we do need to start looking at potential solutions well before the next crisis occurs.

Allow me now to give you an overview on what IADI has accomplished since its establishment and what are our future challenges and initiatives. IADI will be celebrating its fifth anniversary next May, and it has become the strong voice for deposit insurers internationally. There is now a greater awareness and interests in IADI and its activities globally. We have made great strides and have set for ourselves a number of important objectives and initiatives to enhance the effectiveness of deposit insurers around the work.

We built IADI from level zero, and we have grown from the initial 25 member countries to 45 member deposit insurers, six associates, four observers (Bearing Point, Deloitte and Touche, Goodmans LLP, and KPMG) and seven partners (Asian Development Bank, the Center for American Monetary Policies, the European Forum of Deposit Insurers, the European Bank for Reconstruction and Development, International Monetary Fund, SEACEN, and the Toronto Center). In total so far, we have 62 organizations participating in our association's activities. And we're growing every year!

Our achievements: During the last four years, we have focused on building IADI's institutional foundation and governance structure. The executive council, the governance body of IADI, has been of one mind in adopting high governance standards for IADI that are on par with best practices followed by leading organizations. Simply put, we believe we cannot provide international guidance to our members without walking the talk!

Our standing committees have significantly added to our impact as a global organization. Our committees have been established to ensure the sound functioning of our Association and to ensure that we can demonstrate that we are well governed and well managed. We have established governance, finance and planning, audit, training and development, membership and conferences, and research and guidance committees. They have contributed collectively in enhancing our organizational effectiveness and advancing our corporate vision globally.

For instance, the approach of the research and guidance committee (RGC) has been to build deposit insurance effectiveness through the promotion of guidance materials and international cooperation. This is achieved through various forums, dialogues and training opportunities.

We have also undertaken extensive research on important areas affecting deposit insurers as part of IADI's ongoing efforts to improve deposit insurance arrangements nationally and globally. In this area, the RGC has developed guidance materials on a range of key issues, such as differential premiums, bank resolutions and interrelationships.

These papers have been issued by IADI as guidance for those interested in building effective deposit insurance systems.

Next month, at our annual conference in Rio de Janeiro, we shall introduce four new consultative guidance papers on corporate governance, funding, mandates, and claims and recoveries.

Each guidance topic is developed by a committee specifically established to complete the work. Different executive council members are charged with chairing a committee and developing a business plan that outlines the process, deliverables and timing to getting the job done. Every committee follows an open, transparent and consultative process. These committees include a number of other members and participants who are specifically interested in the guidance topic.

As part of ensuring a quality product, we include a consultative process whereby interested parties can provide their views and comments before the guidance papers are completed and issued as actual guidance. We also issue research papers and newsletters to highlight our work. All of our papers and newsletters are available on our website (iadi.org).

Our guidance provides reference for our members seeking to benchmark or remodel their systems and to advance the effectiveness of their organizations.

In implementing our vision of "sharing deposit insurance expertise with the world", IADI follows a policy of inclusiveness.

We practice inclusiveness by inviting nonmembers of IADI, other safety net players and any other interested parties to join with us at our conferences, seminars and workshops, and we request feedback on our guidance papers. Our co-hosting of this conference is yet another example of our approach to reaching out.

We also encourage our members to seek views of seasoned deposit insurers in order to share experiences on operational and policy matters.

As individual members, we are often called upon to provide assistance and advice to members on various deposit insurance matters including general operating matters, and we also provide advice and assistance to country policymakers who are studying or wish to develop an effective deposit insurance system in their own country.

Allow me to stop here to acknowledge two specific deposit insurers who have contributed greatly to helping build effective deposit insurers around the globe. Canada Deposit Insurance Corporation (CDIC) and the Federal Deposit Insurance Corporation (FDIC) have been and continue to be major contributors to sharing knowledge to those in need.

They have vast experiences from which we can all reduce our learning curve. We hope that we can continue to count on them to provide their assistance and expertise in future. Because those that don't learn from history or from the experience of others, are bound to repeat it!

And, I should add, IADI members have been actively consulting and sharing knowledge. In many instances, IADI has brought different perspectives to deposit insurance discussions, and, in many instances, it has been prominent in helping policymakers draft effective legislation for new deposit insurance systems or in amending current legislation to enhance existing systems.

This augers well for IADI as it positions itself to be a repository for deposit insurance expertise and information.

The IADI also receives great benefit from its regional committees that provide the opportunities for regional exchange of ideas and information through holding regional seminars, conferences, meetings, and discussions. We currently have seven regional committees established. Latin America — chaired by Mexico; Asia — chaired by Japan; Europe — chaired by the Czech Republic; the Balkans — chaired by Bulgaria; Euro-Asia — chaired by Ukraine; North African and Middle East — chaired by Jordan; and Africa — chaired by Nigeria! We cover the globe and we get everyone involved!

Next steps: Going forward, IADI is preparing for the future and will be defining our future strategic direction and we shall set the agenda for our future growth over the next three to five years.

IADI will continue to enhance efficiency and effectiveness of deposit insurers as part of our higher level vision of protecting the public interest.

We accept that much work is still required to build internal organizational effectiveness in all our members. Therefore, our focus in the near to medium term, is to continue to build the strength of our members by promoting good governance standards.

For deposit insurers, governance is important. Good governance builds institutional credibility. Credibility builds depositor confidence. Confidence builds stability in the financial system, which in turn promotes economic growth.

Governance distinguishes the excellent deposit insurers from amongst the good ones. Seen from this perspective, good governance is the corner stone that forms the base upon which our members can build institutional capacity and competency.

On this matter, IADI will work toward introducing high level principles as well as specific governance initiatives that may be adopted by members.

Strategic planning and organizational readiness are aspects of good governance. Hence, we have and will continue to organize seminars and workshops in these areas. As an example, two weeks ago we held an Enterprise Risk Management (ERM) Seminar in Kuala Lumpur sponsored by the Malaysia Deposit Insurance Corporation (MDIC) to enhance sound risk management in MDIC's member institutions, deposit insurers and Central Banks in the Asian Region.

We had over 200 participants. The following day we held an ERM workshop specifically for deposit insurers where we featured the CDIC and the FDIC approach to enterprise risk management.

For those that are not so familiar with the term, ERM is an approach and a strategy that emphasizes the identification, assessment and management of all risks inherent in one's business depending on the organization's risk appetite.

One can no longer simply look at individual stove-pipe risks but one must understand how risks can be a byproduct of other risks or how risks can be compounded.

Since our job is to insure banks whose business is to take risks, we need to understand and manage all of our risks, individually and organizational wide.

This is critical for deposit insurers, and I should add for any safety net player.

Sadly, I expect one could count on two hands those safety net players who have implemented an ERM approach or strategy to ensure that they are optimally managing and mitigating their risks and can demonstrate that they are in control.

A few more words on risks inherent in providing deposit insurance. It is important for deposit insurers to demonstrate that they understand and manage the risks inherent in their business.

Deposit insurers have internal as well as external risks — some they can manage and mitigate and others they cannot. Cross-border issues are among the external risks not currently being addressed.

During this conference we have heard many reasons why managing cross-border risk is difficult and maybe impossible. But that does not mean we should not try! Indeed, it is highly relevant to deposit insurers and we have to address these issues.

And ladies and gentlemen, IADI will play its part.

We have already established a research and guidance committee to research this topic and with the objective of developing a guidance paper on cross-border issues as it relates to the provision of deposit insurance. This is already on our agenda and this conference will help us kick off our work.

Furthermore, IADI is pleased to announce that it will be organizing a conference on cross-border deposit insurance issues on May 3, 2007, at the Bank for International Settlements where IADI and the European Deposit Insurance Forum members will come together to start addressing some of these issues. We are indeed looking forward to having our European colleagues play an important role given the specific European issues and approaches. We know there is some urgency in this matter.

For those of you interested in our guidance work, please speak to Fred Carns of the FDIC who is chairing the committee.

As one would expect, training will remain a key focus of IADI. We are working to put in place a comprehensive training program designed specially for deposit insurers. This will be a unique program.

We know that we lack training programs specifically suited to our business. And, I should add, that contrary to some understanding, many deposit insurers are not just pay-boxes with a narrow mandate to reimburse depositors when banks fail. A number of deposit insurers have much wider mandates and fill many other highly important functions.

Deposit insurers have many functions and they can be in many businesses. One function is promoting and contributing to public confidence in the stability of the financial system, another is to promote sound risk management in member banks. Another is to be prepared to deal with problem banks before they fail working in collaboration with supervisors. And when banks get into trouble, find least cost resolutions.

Deposit Insurers can also act as receiver-managers and liquidators and provide policy advice to governments.

Furthermore, deposit insurers are in the advertising and education business since they must provide public awareness and education to the depositing public. Thus, there is a need to develop a comprehensive training program, including the study of best practices in interrelationships between safety net participants — an area that must continue to receive special attention.

While we have been discussing cross-border issues, as a matter of priority, there is much work left to address many national safety net issues, such as information sharing and collaboration between supervisors and deposit insurers.

Our training program will also need to provide the necessary broad perspective that will make a well-rounded deposit insurer. This program should also cover technical and leadership skills.

As an example, a module will need to be developed to build up leadership skills of senior officers with potential to take over top management posts at their deposit insurance corporations.

The objective is to develop strong policy thinkers able to adapt, innovate and lead their corporations towards our common goal of building effective organizations and achieving sounder financial systems.

We shall also be looking to export the deposit insurance module into training programs of central banks.

We have been told that it would not be easy to develop and deliver such a program. We are mindful that some also questioned our capability to establish IADI and have it make a worthwhile contribution. I am optimistic that IADI can do it with everyone's support.

The IADI is also hard at work looking at innovative ways in which it can fund itself in future. As you may know, IADI charges its members an annual fee that it uses to fund its operations.

Our annual fee has never been increased since our objective is to ensure that fees do not preclude any deposit insurer from joining and participating on our activities. With that in mind, we need to increase our revenues. A task force has been established and we're hopeful that we shall also find a solution in short order.

And finally, IADI also owes its success to other supporters. We acknowledge the great contribution of the Bank of International Settlements, where IADI's head office resides, and Canada Deposit Insurance Corporation who provides support to our Secretary-General. Without their continuing support, IADI could not have hoped to achieve its successes in the past four years and to look to the future.

Ladies and Gentlemen, I shall conclude my remarks by thanking you for taking time from your busy schedule to join with us at this very interesting conference. I am certain that this has been an enriching learning experience — and I bid you a safe return home! Thank You!

II. LANDSCAPE OF INTERNATIONAL BANKING AND FINANCIAL CRISES

Current State of Cross-Border Banking

Dirk Schoenmaker* and Christiaan van Laecke
Vrije Universiteit Amsterdam and Ministry of Finance (NL)

1. Introduction

Recent years have witnessed increased merger and acquisition activity in banking. At the same time, deregulation has enabled banks to increase the scale and scope of their business. In the US, the Riegle-Neal Act of 1994 removed barriers interstate banking and the Gramm-Leach-Bliley Act of 1999 removed barriers between banks, securities- and insurance companies (Barth *et al.*, 2000). At the regional level, the North American Free Trade Agreement (NAFTA) was created to promote economic integration in North America (the US, Canada, and Mexico). In Europe, the Single Market Program Act created an environment in the early 1990s allowing banks in any member country of the European Union (EU) to open branches anywhere else in the EU (Dermine, 2006). The introduction of the euro in 1999 further strengthened the linkages between financial markets. The Asian-Pacific region, however, follows without significant regional economic ties.

Consolidation is mainly a domestic affair and involves the merger or acquisition of small and medium-sized banks. In the US, for example, the number of banks was reduced from 12,392 in 1990 to 7,491 in 2006

*Dirk Schoenmaker teaches at Vrije Universiteit Amsterdam and is deputy director, financial markets policy, at the Ministry of Finance (NL). Christiaan van Laecke was MSc student at the University of France and now works as policy advisor at the financial markets policy directorate at the Ministry of Finance. Paper presented at the International Banking Conference on *International Financial Instability: Cross-Border Banking and National Regulation* organized by the Federal Reserve Bank of Chicago, October 5–6, 2006. We would like to thank Jean Dermine, Douglas Evanoff, George Kaufman, Luc Laeven, Sander Oosterloo and Alexander Tieman for discussions and comments. The opinions in the chapter are those of the authors and not necessarily those of the Netherlands Ministry of Finance. Correspondence to: d.schoenmaker@minfin.nl.

(FDIC). In the EU-15, the number of banks came down from 11,937 in 1990 to 7,045 in 2006 (ECB). At the same time, some of the larger banks have been involved in domestic as well as cross-border expansion.

The goal of this chapter is to explore the current state of cross-border banking. In this chapter, the level of cross-border penetration is measured using the Transnationality Index (TNI) developed by Sullivan (1994). The TNI is an unweighted average of three indicators (assets, revenues and employees) and measures foreign activity of a bank as a percentage of total activity of that bank. The TNI provides a relatively full and stable measure of cross-border activity. We will contrast the level and trend of cross-border banking in the three main economic regions: the Americas, Asia-Pacific and Europe. Examining the sixty largest banks, we find that banks headquartered in the Americas and Asia-Pacific have a domestic orientation (defined as more than 50 percent of business in the home country). Citigroup is the only bank in these regions with truly international aspirations. The picture in Europe is different. Distinguishing between regional expansion (that is, within Europe) and global expansion, we find that 11 banks operate on a European scale and a further three banks on a global scale. Our figures indicate that the long expected cross-border merger wave in Europe has started.

The observed cross-border banking patterns seem to follow non-financial trade patterns. The influence of regional trade pacts is strong. The EU's Single Market has been successful in promoting cross-border trade including banking. The regional component in European banking amounts to 23 percent in 2005. NAFTA is far less wide-ranging than the EU's Single Market. This is also the case for banking. The regional banking component in the Americas is 9 percent. Turning to the Asia-Pacific region, there are no real trade pacts (except for the southern sub-region of Trans-Tasmania). The regional component for Asian-Pacific banks is only 5 percent. The global banking component follows the same pattern: 25 percent for European banks, 13 percent for American banks and 9 percent for Asian-Pacific banks.

We examine the appropriate supervisory response to cross-border banking. Do informal coordination arrangements between national supervisors suffice to deal with cross-border banks? An example of such an arrangement is a supervisory college consisting of the main supervisors of an international bank. Or do we need to create more binding transnational arrangements to internalize the externalities of cross-border banking? An example would be the establishment of a European system of financial supervisors to deal with the emerging pan-European banks. That would reflect the experience of the US, where federal systems of supervision (for example, the Federal Reserve System and the OCC) emerged alongside state supervisors

2. Measuring Cross-Border Banking

2.1 *Literature*

The literature on the internationalization of financial services is extensive (see Moshirian, 2006, for an overview). A first line of research examines the patterns of foreign direct investment (FDI) in banking. How large are the flows into banks in (emerging) economies and what is the impact on the banking system of these economies? Soussa (2004) reports that most of the FDI in banking in emerging economies was directed to Latin America and Eastern Europe over the 1990–2003 period. The focus of this research is on the recipient countries. A second line of research looks at the cross-border expansion of individual banks. Internationalization can be measured by examining a specific aspect of international banking. Berger *et al.* (2003), for example, investigate the geographic reach of banks' cash management services. How many countries do banks cover? Internationalization is then measured by the amount of countries in which a bank is active.

A separate approach would be to look at the full set of activities of banks. In the literature on multi-nationals, Sullivan (1994) reviews 17 studies estimating the degree of internalization based on a single item indicator. Using just a single indicator increases the possibility for errors, as the indicator could, for example, be more susceptible to external shocks. Sullivan develops the Transnationality Index, which is based on three indicators (see below). The Transnationality Index provides a full and stable measure of internationalization.[1] Slager (2004) and Schoenmaker and Oosterloo (2005) have applied this Index to banking. Extending earlier work, we follow this approach in this chapter.

Finally, there is a body of research focusing on the determinants of cross-border banking (for example, Buch and DeLong, 2004; Focarelli and Pozzolo, 2001) and the performance of cross-border banks (for example,

---

[1] The Index is multidimensional. It concentrates on the demand side (captured by income) as well as the supply side (captured by assets and employees) (Ietto-Gillies, 1998).

Berger *et al.*, 2000). We do not discuss this research. The purpose of our chapter is to examine the patterns in internationalization and not the strategy behind internationalization or the outcome.

2.2 *Transnationality Index*

We use the Transnationality Index to investigate the degree of cross-border banking. This Index is calculated as an unweighted average of 1) foreign assets to total assets, 2) foreign income to total income, and 3) foreign employment to total employment.

While our earlier study focused on Europe (Schoenmaker and Oosterloo, 2005), this chapter examines the degree of internationalization of banks in the three main economic regions: the Americas, Asia-Pacific and Europe. It is interesting to distinguish between regional expansion (for example, within the Americas) and global expansion of banks. The data on the Transnationality Index is therefore broken down into activities in the home market (h), the rest of the region (r), and the rest of the world (w).

2.3 *Classifying banks*

Following the geographical breakdown of activities, banks are classified as domestic, regional or global banks in this chapter. Domestic banks are defined as follows:

> *1) More than 50 percent of their business is conducted in the home market ($h > 0.5$).*

This first criterion makes a distinction between domestic and international banks. Banks that conduct the majority of their business in their home country are regarded as domestic banks. International banks are divided into regional and global banks. Regional banks are defined as:

> *1) 50 percent or more of their business is conducted abroad ($h \leq 0.5$).*
> *2) 25 percent or more of their business is conducted within the region ($r \geq 0.25$).*

The second criterion identifies regional banks among the international ones. International banks that have a sizeable part of their business in the rest of the region (for example, Europe) are regarded as regional banks

("European banks"). The total business of a bank in the region is a sum of the home activities and the activities in the rest of the region $(h + r)$.

Global banks are then defined as:

1) *50 percent or more of their business is conducted abroad (h $\leq$ 0.5).*
2) *Less than 25 percent of their business is conducted within the region (r < 0.25).*

The remaining group of banks is of a global nature. These banks have no gravity of business at home nor in the rest of the region. They operate on a truly global scale. Our classification only distinguishes between domestic, regional and global banks. A further distinction could be made by counting the number of countries in which international banks are operating (Sullivan, 1994). As the focus of this chapter is on domestic versus international banking, we do not include this further breakdown.

3. Data on Cross-Border Banking

Most of the empirical studies on cross-border banking find a positive relationship between the size of banks and the degree of internationalization (for example, Focarelli and Pozzolo, 2001). We therefore focus our empirical study of cross-border banking on the large banks. The 60 largest banks are selected on the basis of Tier 1 Capital (*The Banker*, July 2005). As the European banks compromise about 50 percent of assets of *The Banker's* Top 1,000 world banks, the dataset also consists of more European than American or Asian-Pacific banks. The dataset is divided into three samples: top 15 American banks, top 15 Asian banks and top 30 European banks.

Looking at the names of the banks in Tables 1 to 3, it is clear that *The Banker's* Top 1,000 is a ranking of the world's commercial banks, which have a significant retail base.[2] Retail business is often combined with investment banking (for example, Citigroup, HSBC, JP Morgan Chase & Co, Barclays). Fully fledged investment banks, like Merrill Lynch, Goldman Sachs and Morgan Stanley, are not included in *The Banker's* Top 1,000.

---

[2] Under the catchy title "Bring Me Your Consumers, Your Unbanked Mass", *The Banker* (June, 2006) talks of a retail banking revolution whereby large parts of the world's population, previously unbanked, are entering a new world of available financial services. *The Banker* considers retail as the next frontier of cross-border expansion, both in developed and in emerging markets. Retail banking offers sustainable revenues at a low risk. In contrast, wholesale banking generates more volatile revenues.

Table 1. Index for the cross-border business of top 15 American banking groups

Banking Groups	2000			2001			2002			2003			2004			2005			Capital Strength ($bn)
	h	r	w	h	r	w	h	r	w	h	r	w	h	r	w	h	r	w	
1 Citigroup	61	7	32	59	8	33	57	9	34	59	14	28	54	15	31	53	16	31	74.4
2 JP Morgan Chase & Co	65	3	32	68	2	30	74	2	24	72	3	25	77	2	22	79	2	20	68.6
3 Bank of America Corp	92	1	7	92	1	7	93	1	6	94	0	6	94	2	4	93	2	5	64.3
4 Wells Fargo & Co	97	3	0	97	3	0	97	3	0	97	3	0	97	3	0	97	3	0	29.1
5 Wachovia Corporation	98	1	1	98	1	1	98	1	1	98	1	1	98	1	1	98	1	1	28.6
6 Metlife	97	1	1	97	1	1	95	2	2	95	3	3	95	3	3	94	3	3	21
7 Washington Mutual	100	0	0	100	0	0	100	0	0	100	0	0	100	0	0	100	0	0	16.4
8 U.S. Bancorp	95	3	3	95	3	3	95	3	3	95	3	3	95	3	3	95	3	3	14.7
9 Scotiabank	61	27	13	55	32	13	56	32	12	60	29	12	62	26	11	63	25	12	14.1
10 MBNA Corp	87	2	11	85	2	13	80	2	17	78	3	19	75	3	22	73	3	25	14
11 Royal Bank of Canada	76	10	14	68	17	15	62	24	14	59	24	17	60	23	17	62	22	16	13.3
12 Bank of Montreal	63	30	8	61	32	8	63	32	5	65	30	5	67	27	6	69	26	6	11
13 Toronto-Dominion Bank	62	24	14	65	19	17	66	18	17	68	18	15	70	16	14	67	21	12	10.4
14 Countrywide Financial Corporation	100	0	0	99	0	0	97	2	2	97	1	1	96	2	2	97	1	1	10.3
15 Canadian Imperial Bank of Commerce	59	33	8	61	30	9	68	24	8	74	21	5	74	20	6	75	20	5	10
Weighted average (to total assets)	77	8	15	76	8	16	77	8	15	78	9	13	78	9	13	78	9	13	
Number of domestic banking groups	15			15			15			15			15			15			
Number of American banking groups	0			0			0			0			0			0			
Number of global banking groups	0			0			0			0			0			0			

Sources: Annual reports over 2000–2005 and own calculations for the index (see the Annex for underlying data); *The Banker* (July, 2005) for capital strength. Notes: "Home" is defined as a bank's business in its home country (denoted by *h*); "Rest of the region" is defined as a bank's business in other countries in the region (denoted by *r*); "Rest of world" is defined as a bank's business in countries outside the region (denoted by *w*). The three categories add up to 100%. Banks are ranked according to "capital strength" (Tier 1 capital as of year-end 2004) as reported by *The Banker*. The abbreviation "*n.a.*" means "*not available*." "–" means this bank has been acquired by another bank.

Table 2. Index for the cross-border business of top 15 Asian-Pacific banking groups

Banking Groups	2000			2001			2002			2003			2004			2005			Capital Strength ($bn)
	h	r	w	h	r	w	h	r	w	h	r	w	h	r	w	h	r	w	
1 Mitsubishi Tokyo Financial Group	59	7	34	62	7	32	64	5	30	68	4	28	69	5	26	69	5	26	39.9
2 Mizuho Financial Group	75	5	20	75	5	20	79	3	17	85	2	13	83	3	14	85	3	12	38.9
3 Bank of China	93	3	3	92	4	4	94	3	3	94	3	3	94	3	3	95	3	2	34.9
4 Sumitomo Mitsui Financial Group	82	6	12	80	5	14	87	3	10	90	3	7	90	3	7	90	3	7	30.4
5 China Construction Bank	95	3	3	95	3	3	95	3	3	95	3	3	95	3	3	95	3	3	23.5
6 UFJ Holdings	76	7	17	82	6	12	87	4	10	90	3	8	89	2	9	87	4	9	21.6
7 Industrial and Commercial Bank of China	95	3	3	95	3	3	95	3	3	95	3	3	95	3	3	95	2	3	20.2
8 Norinchukin Bank	76	8	16	79	7	14	80	8	12	82	7	11	83	6	12	84	7	9	18.5
9 Agricultural Bank of China	100	0	0	100	0	0	100	0	0	100	0	0	100	0	0	100	0	0	16.7
10 National Australia Bank	51	10	38	53	12	35	56	12	32	58	12	30	61	12	26	65	12	24	15
11 Resona Holdings	95	3	3	95	3	3	95	3	3	95	3	3	95	3	3	95	3	3	11.1
12 ANZ Banking Group	65	23	12	71	20	9	73	20	7	75	19	6	66	30	4	66	31	4	9.7
13 Commonwealth Banking Group	85	12	3	84	12	4	81	14	4	82	14	3	81	15	4	81	16	3	8.7
14 Sumitomo Trust & Banking	100	0	0	100	0	0	100	0	0	100	0	0	100	0	0	100	0	0	8
15 Kookmin Bank	100	0	0	99	0	1	100	0	0	100	0	0	99	0	1	99	0	1	7.8
Weighted average (to total assets)	80	6	15	81	5	14	84	4	12	87	3	10	86	4	10	86	5	9	
Number of domestic banking groups	15			15			15			15			15			15			
Number of Asian-Pacific banking groups	0			0			0			0			0			0			
Number of global banking groups	0			0			0			0			0			0			

Sources: Annual reports over 2000–2005 and own calculations for the index (see the Annex for underlying data); *The Banker* (July, 2005) for capital strength. Notes: "Home" is defined as a bank's business in its home country (denoted by *h*); "Rest of the region" is defined as a bank's business in other countries in the region (denoted by *r*); "Rest of world" is defined as a bank's business in countries outside the region (denoted by *w*). The three categories add up to 100%. Banks are ranked according to "capital strength" (Tier 1 capital as of year-end 2004) as reported by The Banker. The abbreviation "n.a." means "not available". "–" means this bank has been acquired by another bank.

Table 3. Index for the cross-border business of top 30 European banking groups

Banking Groups	2000			2001			2002			2003			2004			2005			Capital Strength ($bn)
	h	r	w	h	r	w	h	r	w	h	r	w	h	r	w	h	r	w	
1 HSBC	33	6	61	36	7	57	31	5	64	24	6	70	26	9	65	25	9	65	67.3
2 Crédit Agricole Groupe	61	19	20	59	20	21	60	18	22	61	19	20	74	11	15	83	9	8	63.4
3 Royal Bank of Scotland	76	7	17	74	6	20	74	6	20	77	5	18	72	7	21	77	7	16	43.8
4 HBOS	94	3	3	93	4	3	92	4	4	91	5	4	87	6	6	90	5	5	36.6
5 BNP Paribas	48	21	31	46	24	30	45	25	30	47	25	28	49	24	27	55	21	24	35.7
6 Santander Central Hispano	28	10	62	34	10	56	38	14	48	45	16	39	41	25	34	40	26	34	33.3
7 Barclays	76	7	17	78	6	16	79	7	14	80	8	12	78	7	15	50	16	34	32.2
8 Rabobank	80	7	13	76	8	16	76	9	15	75	9	16	72	17	11	73	14	13	30.8
9 ING Group	36	19	45	27	23	50	26	23	51	29	24	47	24	30	46	23	29	48	28.8
10 UBS	35	30	35	32	19	49	32	21	47	31	21	48	28	25	47	25	28	47	27.4
11 ABN AMRO	34	33	33	33	34	33	31	35	34	28	36	36	37	25	38	34	30	36	27
12 Deutsche Bank	41	29	30	39	30	31	35	33	31	31	37	32	30	36	34	28	36	36	25.5
13 Groupe Caisse d'Epargne	n.a.	n.a.	n.a.	n.a.	n.a.	n.a.	70	26	4	50	38	12	44	42	13	40	47	13	25.1
14 Société Générale	68	11	21	64	13	23	60	18	22	56	21	23	56	23	21	57	21	21	25
15 Crédit Mutuel	100	0	0	100	0	0	100	0	0	100	0	0	100	0	0	100	0	0	24.8
16 Lloyds TSB	84	8	8	87	6	7	88	6	6	94	3	3	94	3	3	95	3	3	22.6
17 Credit Suisse Group	29	32	39	28	32	40	30	34	36	32	37	31	30	27	43	32	34	34	21.7
18 HypoVereinsbank	62	34	3	48	43	8	49	47	4	51	46	3	48	50	2	—			21.4
19 Banca Intesa	66	19	15	67	14	19	73	13	14	78	10	12	77	15	8	76	15	9	21.2
20 Banco Bilbao Vizcaya Argentaria	31	2	67	35	5	60	39	3	58	44	3	53	45	3	52	40	3	57	20
21 Fortis Group	45	27	28	41	43	16	42	28	30	44	28	28	51	44	5	48	47	6	19.5
22 Groupe Banques Populaires	98	1	1	97	1	2	93	4	3	92	4	4	92	5	4	92	4	3	18.3
23 UniCredit	74	8	18	74	8	18	70	8	22	71	13	16	71	20	9	24	72	4	16.8
24 Dexia	52	48	0	56	40	4	53	40	7	54	37	9	55	36	8	51	37	12	15

(Continued)

Table 3. (*Continued*)

Banking Groups	2000			2001			2002			2003			2004			2005			Capital Strength ($bn)
	h	*r*	*w*	*h*	*r*	*w*	*h*	*r*	*w*	*h*	*r*	*w*	*h*	*r*	*w*	*h*	*r*	*w*	
25 SanPaolo IMI	82	12	6	79	17	5	85	12	3	89	8	3	92	6	1	92	7	2	14.8
26 Nordea Group	22	76	2	18	79	3	23	74	3	28	71	1	28	72	0	25	75	0	14.4
27 Commerzbank	77	13	10	72	21	7	74	16	10	75	15	10	70	24	6	71	25	5	14.3
28 KBC Group	45	36	19	45	36	19	40	38	22	40	40	20	46	32	22	50	29	21	13.4
29 Bayerische Landesbank	63	18	19	65	19	16	71	17	12	76	15	9	77	16	7	78	14	7	12.8
30 Caja de Ahorros y Pen. de Barcelona	98	2	0	98	2	0	98	2	0	98	2	0	98	2	0	98	2	0	11.5
Weighted average (to total assets)	55	20	25	53	21	26	54	21	25	55	21	24	54	22	24	53	23	25	
Number of domestic banking groups		18			17			17			17			17			15		
Number of European banking groups		7			7			8			8			10			11		
Number of global banking groups		5			6			5			5			3			3		

Sources: Annual reports over 2000–2005 and own calculations for the index (see the Annex for underlying data); *The Banker* (July, 2005) for capital strength. Notes: "Home" is defined as a bank's bus ness in its home country (denoted by *h*); "Rest of the region" is defined as a bank's business in other countries in the region (denoted by *r*); "Rest of world" is defined as a bank's business in countries outside the region (denoted by *w*). The three categories add up to 100%. Banks are ranked according to "capital strength" (Tier 1 capital as of year-end 2004) as reported by The Banker. The abbreviation "n.a." means "not available". "-" means this bank has been acquired by another bank.

These investment banks would be classified as global banks, as investment banking is a global business.

To calculate the Transnationality Index, data are gathered from the consolidated income statements and balance sheets of the 60 largest commercial banks (see Schoenmaker and van Laecke, 2006, FMG Special Paper sp168 for a description of the data analysis). The results are reported in Tables 1 to 3. At the bottom of the tables, the weighted average of the Transnationality Index for each region is calculated. To test whether there is a statistically significant trend (downwards or upwards) in the data, a statistical test proposed by Lehmann (1975) will be applied.[3] However, we should be careful with interpreting trends as we have only data for a six year period.

American commercial banks have a strong domestic orientation with a domestic component of about 77 percent in Table 1. The regional component is rather small (around 8 percent), while the global component is slightly larger (13 to 16 percent). While there is no clear up- or downward trend in the regional component, there is a statistically significant downtrend trend in the global component at the 10 percent level ($p = 0.0514$) over the 2000–2006 period.

Asian-Pacific banks also have a strong domestic orientation within the range from 80 to 87 percent in Table 2. Regional business is very minor (around 5 percent) and global business somewhat larger (10 to 15 percent). The trend has a particular shape. International business decreased up to 2003 and has been slowly increasing since 2004. One explanation is that international business is squeezed in the aftermath of the severe recession in the nineties in Japan (the infamous decade of lost growth). When banks face difficulties and make losses, they tend to reduce foreign business first (even when investment opportunities abroad are more favorable than at home).[4] Now that the Japanese economy is growing, banks are slowly expanding their foreign business. Over the full 2000–2005 period, the overall downward trend of international (regional and global) business is statistically significant at the 5 percent level ($p = 0.0292$).

---

[3] This test statistic is $D = \sum_{i=1}^{n}(T_i - i)$, where i indicates the year and T_i is the rank of the score of year i.

[4] Internationalization can thus be explained by the capital strength of a bank. When profits are accumulating and capital is increasing through retained earnings, banks use the extra capital to expand internationally. When the capital base is eroding through losses, banks first cut their foreign business. This is a free interpretation of the capital crunch. See Peek and Rosengren (1995) on the general working of the capital crunch.

European banks have a far smaller domestic orientation with a domestic component of about 54 percent in Table 3. Both regional business (20 to 23 percent) and global business (about 25 percent) is rather large. While there is no clear up- or downtrend in the domestic component, there is a clear increase in regional business at the expense of global business. The increase of regional business in Europe from 20 percent in 2000 to 23 percent in 2005 is statistically significant at the 1 percent level ($p = 0.0014$). The decrease of global business is statistically significant at the 10 percent level ($p = 0.0875$). It is remarkable that regional business has been growing over the last six years, while most European countries have experienced a recession during this period (with the exception of Spain and the UK which have had a major economic expansion during this period).

Figure 1 indicates that the European countries have a more international orientation than any of the countries from the Americas or Asia-Pacific.

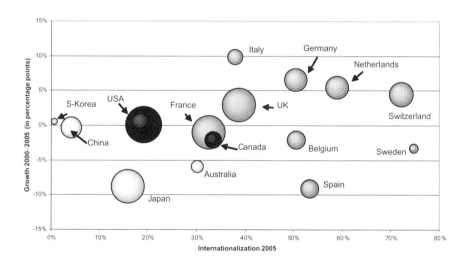

Figure 1. The degree and trend of cross-border banking of 15 countries over 2000–2005

Source: Tables 1,2, 3 and own calculations.

Notes: The circles, degree of internationalization (x-axis) and growth-trend (y-axis) represent the sixty banks aggregated on country level. The aggregates are weighted-averages to total assets of the banks. The degree of internationalization represents the international business (both regional and global) of banks headquartered in the respective countries in 2005. The growth trend represents the growth in internationalization from 2000 to 2005.

The large banks head-quartered in Sweden and Switzerland even conduct most of their business abroad, but hardly become more or less international over these six years. Italy and Spain on the other hand, are less international but show a substantial increase and decrease, 10 percent and 9 percent respectively, in their degree of cross-border banking. All European countries except France show a shift in their level of internationalization. This is not the case in the Americas, where the US remain domestic over the period observed. The internationalization of the Asian-Pacific countries differs quite a lot. China and South-Korea are almost completely domestic, while Japan and especially Australia conduct some business abroad. Japan, however, shows a large cross-border divestment over 2000–2005.

International banks

Table 4 reports the international banks in the top 60 banks. Using our classification for the different types of banks, we find that all banks in the Americas and Asia-Pacific are domestic. This reflects the overall domestic orientation of the banks in the two regions. In Europe the number of domestic banks decreased from 18 in 2000 to 15 in 2006. So, half of the banks can currently be classified as international. The number of regional banks (that is, "European" banks) increased from 7 to 11, even at the expense of the number of global banks coming down from 5 to 3. Using the Lehmann test, the upward trend of "European" banks and the downward trend of global banks are significant at the 1 percent level ($p = 0.0028$ and $p = 0.0097$).

4. Comparing Cross-Border Banking across the Continents

The intensity of cross-border banking is very different on the three continents. Figure 2 illustrates the geographic segmentation of banks in Europe, the Americas and the Asia-Pacific for the year 2005. The graph ranges from the most international to the least international region. European banks are far more international than their American and Asian counterparts. Both the regional and the global component of business are large in Europe (over 20 percent). The influence of regional trade pacts seems to be strong. The large regional component in Europe (23 percent)

Table 4. Categories of international banks

Continent	International Banks	2000	2001	2002	2003	2004	2005
Americas	American banks	—	—	—	—	—	—
	Global banks	—	—	—	—	—	—
Asia-Pacific	Asian-Pacific banks	—	—	—	—	—	—
	Global banks	—	—	—	—	—	—
Europe	European banks	10 UBS 11 ABN AMRO 12 Deutsche Bank 17 Credit Suisse 21 Fortis 26 Nordea 28 KBC	11 ABN AMRO 12 Deutsche Bank 17 Credit Suisse 18 HypoVereinsbank 21 Fortis 26 Nordea 28 KBC	5 BNP Paribas 11 ABN AMRO 12 Deutsche Bank 17 Credit Suisse 18 HypoVereinsbank 21 Fortis 26 Nordea 28 KBC	5 BNP Paribas 11 ABN AMRO 12 Deutsche Bank 13 Groupe Caisse 17 Credit Suisse 21 Fortis 26 Nordea 28 KBC	6 Santander 9 ING 10 UBS 11 ABN AMRO 12 Deutsche Bank 13 Groupe Caisse 17 Credit Suisse 18 HypoVereinsbank 26 Nordea 28 KBC	6 Santander 9 ING 10 UBS 11 ABN AMRO 12 Deutsche Bank 13 Groupe Caisse 17 Credit Suisse 21 Fortis 23 Unicredit 26 Nordea 28 KBC
	Global banks	1 HSBC 5 BNP Paribas 6 Santander 9 ING 20 BBVA	1 HSBC 5 BNP Paribas 6 Santander 9 ING 10 UBS 20 BBVA	1 HSBC 6 Santander 9 ING 10 UBS 20 BBVA	1 HSBC 6 Santander 9 ING 10 UBS 20 BBVA	1 HSBC 5 BNP Paribas 20 BBVA	1 HSBC 7 Barclays 20 BBVA

Sources: Tables 1 to 3.

Notes: International banks (less than 50% of business at home) are divided into regional banks (25% or more of business in the region) and global banks (less than 25% of business in the region).

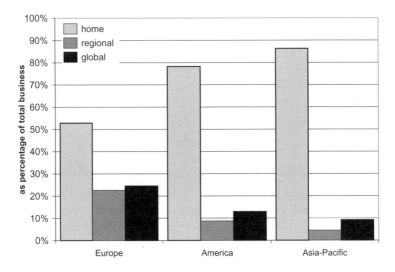

Figure 2. Geographical segmentation of banks in 2005
Source: Tables 1, 2 and 3.

can by explained by the existence of the Single Market of the European Union. The North American Free Trade Agreement (NAFTA) of 1994 is far less wide-ranging than the EU's Single Market. This seems to be also the case for banking. The regional component in the Americas is only 9 percent.

Turning to Asia, there are no real trade pacts. The Association of Southeast Asian Nations (ASEAN), for example, aims to promote regional cooperation but has no common market. Moreover, the large countries in the Asian-Pacific region, such as China, Japan and Australia,[5] are not part of ASEAN. The regional component for Asia-Pacific banks is 5 percent. It is noteworthy that regional component (5 percent) is substantially lower than the global component (9 percent) for these banks. This contrasts with the picture for European and American banks, where regional and global businesses are more balanced.

While the picture of the three continents is very different, there is one common finding. The largest bank on each continent is also the most international bank of that continent. In the Americas, the largest bank is

[5] In the southern sub-region, Trans-Tasmania forms an exception to the lack of trade pacts in the Asian-Pacific region. The Australia New Zealand Closer Economic Relations Trade Agreement (CER) of 1983 provides for free trade in services, including financial services.

Citigroup with 47 percent of its business abroad, both regional and global. The largest Asia-Pacific bank is Mitsubishi Tokyo Financial Group with 31 percent of its business abroad. Finally, HSBC is the largest European group with 75 percent of its business abroad. The global component of these banks outstrips the respective regional component, so one can truly speak of large international players.

When comparing the regions, it is clear that there are no regional banks in the Americas and Asia-Pacific. Citigroup is on its way becoming a global bank. This finding is very different from Europe. The European banking scene is populated by 11 regional banks and three global banks. Intra-European business is thus an important feature of banking in Europe.

4.1 *Individual regions*

Turning to the individual regions, Table 1 illustrates that the US banks are very domestic (80 to 90 percent) with Citigroup being the exception. The lifting of limits on interstate banking by the Riegle-Neal Act in 1994 has spurred a domestic consolidation drive (Stiroh and Strahan, 2003). Banking consolidation took place among small and medium-sized banks as well as large banks. An example of the latter is Bank of America, which is the result of a merger between BankAmerica and NationsBank in 1998 and further mergers with Fleet Boston in 2004 and MBNA in 2006. Bank of America has truly national coverage in the US and is close to holding 10 percent of national deposits. Federal law prevents any bank from gaining more than 10 percent of national deposits through acquisition. In contrast, Citigroup provides an example of both domestic and cross-border consolidation. Within the US, Citigroup grew out of a merger between Citibank and Travelers (insurance) in 1998 Citigroup has, however, divested most of its insurance underwriting business over the last few years. Before the merger, Travelers acquired Salomon Brothers (investment banking) in 1997. A major foreign acquisition of Citigroup is Banamex, the second largest bank in Mexico (see below), in 2001.

Canadian banks have less domestic business (60 to 70 percent), while regional business is sizeable (20 to 30 percent). This can of course be explained by the fact that Canada is a smaller country. Finally, Mexico provides an interesting example of a banking system that is dominated by foreign banks. After the banking crisis of 1995, foreign banks were allowed to enter in order to recapitalize Mexican banks (Ortiz, 2006).

Table 5. Foreign ownership of the Mexican banking system

Mexican banks	Assets (%)	International Bank	Foreign (%)
Bancomer	23.0	BBVA (Spain)	23.0
Banamex	20.5	Citigroup (US)	20.5
Serfin	16.1	Santander (Spain)	16.1
Bital	11.3	HSBC (UK)	11.3
Mercantil del Norte	8.2	—	
Inverlat	5.2	Scotiabank (Canada)	5.2
Inbursa	3.7	—	
Other banks	12.0	—	
Total	**100.0**		**76.1**

Source: Boletin Estadistico, Banca Múltiple, Comisión Nacional Bancaria y de Valores, March 2006.
Notes: Five out of the seven largest Mexican banks are foreign owned. The column international banks contains the names of the foreign owners.

Table 5 illustrates that five out of the seven largest Mexican banks are owned by foreign banks. This amounts to about 75 percent of Mexican banking assets. It is noteworthy that not only banks from the region (Citi and Scotia) but also European banks (BBVA, Santander and HSBC) are active players in Mexico.

In the Asia-Pacific region, cross-border banking within the region is very limited. Japanese banks are domestically oriented (70 to 90 percent) with a very tiny regional component (less than 5 percent). Consolidation has been a domestic affair. In line with the spectacular growth of the economy, Chinese banks have been rising in the ranks of The Banker's Top 1000 over the last few years. The major, (formerly) state-owned, banks were recently privatized or are in the process of privatization. The Chinese banks are still operating on an almost fully domestic scale (95 to 100 percent). Only the Australian banks have a meaningful regional component (10 to 30 percent). The Australian banks dominate the banking system of New Zealand. The Australian banks own more than 90 percent of New Zealand banking assets (Ortiz, 2006).

In Europe, cross-border banking is very intensive. Almost half of the European top 30 banks are international banks. In 2005, we find 11 regional banks and three global banks in Europe. As reported earlier, the increase from seven European banks in 2000 to 11 in 2005 is statistically significant at the 1 percent level. It is interesting to note that consolidation in Italy has really started. In addition to the three large cross-border deals, Banca Intesa (nr. 2) and Sanpaolo IMI (nr. 3) have announced their plans for a domestic merger in August 2006. It should however be noted that not all the "European" banking groups in Table 4 are the same. There are some European banks that focus on a specific region within Europe and can be regarded as "regionally active" European banks. Fortis, for example, primarily operates in Belgium and the Netherlands. Similarly, the Nordea Group primarily operates in the Nordic countries. Other European banks operate Europe-wide and can be labeled as "pan-European" banks, examples are ABN AMRO and Deutsche Bank. The group of global banks in Europe consists of HSBC (UK), BBVA (Spain) and Barclays (UK). Global banks are a heterogeneous group. On the one hand, one can distinguish global banks like HSBC and Citigroup, which are present in most countries across the three continents. On the other hand, there are global banks with a more limited reach such as BBVA and Santander, which cover part of Europe and Latin America.

4.2 *Overall picture of cross-border banking*

The picture emerging is that cross-border banking is diverse. First, the number of truly global players in the commercial banking field is very limited. The main players are HSBC and BBVA from Europe and Citigroup from the US. Furthermore, some large European banks, such as the Dutch banks (ABN AMRO and ING) and Swiss banks (Credit Suisse and UBS), have a significant global reach. Although the number of global players is limited, these banks are super-size banks. HSBC and Citigroup, for example, have each total assets of $1.5 trillion at the end of 2005. Second, cross-border banking at the regional level is very uneven across the continents. In Europe, cross-border banking is clearly present and still growing. The current level of regional business is close to 25 percent within Europe. Regional banking is far less important in the Americas and Asia-Pacific (both less than 10 percent). Third, the global component, outside the region, is also larger for European banks than American and Asian-Pacific banks. Fourth, the banking systems of some smaller countries, such as Mexico, New Zealand and the new member states in the EU, are dominated by foreign banks. In some cases, the stake of foreign banks is up to 80 or 90 percent.

5. Public Policy Issues

The focus of this chapter is on commercial banking. Commercial banking is more relevant for policy purposes than investment banking. Prudential supervision to protect retail depositors is aimed at commercial banks (retail) and less so at investment banks (wholesale). Moreover, commercial banks play a key role in the financial system (lending, payments). Problems with large parts of the commercial banking system could threaten financial stability. Major problems in the commercial banking system could also have an impact on the wider economy, as the lending capacity to small and medium-sized business would be disrupted (Goodhart, 1987). Of course, investment banks (and also some commercial banks) are dominant players on financial markets, both cash and derivatives, and therefore important for the well-functioning of financial markets.

5.1 *Financial supervision*

The challenge for the effective supervision of an international bank is to get an overall view of the financial soundness of the bank (consolidated supervision), which is also based on a good knowledge of local conditions in the different markets in which the bank operates (host country perspective). Cooperation between the consolidated home supervisor and the host supervisors is therefore crucial. Given the limited number of global banks, supervisors have opted for informal arrangements. Supervisory colleges have been established to bring together the most important supervisors for the large international banks. A case in point is the cooperation between the Swiss EBK, the FSA and the New York Fed on Credit Suisse and UBS (McCarthy, 2006). The three supervisors meet half yearly to share concerns and to form a view on the overall risk profile of these banks. A wide network of bilateral and multilateral Memoranda of Understanding (MoUs) exists to support information exchange and coordination between national supervisors. It should be noted that these MoUs are not legally binding (Mayes, 2006).

Our assessment is that these arrangements for global banks suffice as only a handful of banks are involved (though this small group of global banks comprise the world's largest banks such as Citigroup and HSBC). Moreover, there is no international jurisdiction available to go further.

Supervision is related to political sovereignty (Herring and Litan, 1994). The assessment for Europe is different. First, a jurisdiction to establish formal, binding arrangements can be made available with the EU. Second, our figures indicate that there are already 11 banks with significant cross-border business within Europe, and this number is still growing.

The current European structure of supervision consists of a fairly harmonized regulatory framework based on EU Directives and coordination between supervisors. In the so-called Lamfalussy approach, regulatory and supervisory committees are established to speed up the regulatory process and to foster supervisory convergence. The main aim of the supervisory committees is to coordinate policies by developing common guidelines. At the sub-regional level, supervisors have established institution specific MoUs (for example, for Nordea and Fortis) to arrange for cooperation in the day-to-day supervision of cross-border banks. As noted before, these MoUs may put a moral obligation on supervisors to cooperate (in terms of game theory, there is a setting of repeated play), but does not pose a formal obligation on supervisors (Mayes, 2006).

The newly emerging European financial landscape confronts the home and host authorities with complex coordination issues. In the face of these challenges, it is questionable whether the current level of cooperation between different national authorities (with a patchwork of bilateral and multilateral MoUs) will be an adequate arrangement in an integrating market. Different proposals have been put forward to enhance the supervisory structure in Europe. A key proposal for bringing home and host supervisors together is to establish some form of a European System of Financial Supervisors (for example, Vives, 2001, and Schoenmaker and Oosterloo, 2006). A new central agency would be created to work in tandem with the national supervisors.[6] The role of the central agency is to foster cooperation and consistency among members of the System, but leaves the day-to-day supervision of cross-border financial groups with the consolidating or lead supervisor. This is a decentralized version of a European System of Financial Supervisors.

Notwithstanding the possible creation of new legal structures in Europe, it is important that European supervisory agencies keep on cooperating with supervisors outside Europe, notably those in the US. Figure 2 illustrates that EU banks have a strong global component in their business.

---

[6] Examples of such structures are the European System of Central banks with the ECB in the center and the Federal Reserve System with the Board of Governors in Washington DC.

5.2 *Financial stability*

The second challenge for public policy is related to financial stability. How can national authorities foster the stability of their financial system when the players in the system are operating cross-border? There are two sides to this problem: home and host. Home country authorities have currently neither an incentive nor a legally binding obligation to incorporate cross-border externalities. When a bank is in difficulties, the home authorities will focus on the impact on the home financial system and ignore the potential impact in foreign countries. This raises the issue who should bear the burden of any proposed recapitalization should failures occur in large cross-border banks. A recapitalization is efficient if the social benefits (preserving systemic stability) exceed the cost of recapitalization. If not, the bank should be closed.

Using a multi-country model, Freixas (2003) shows that *ex post* negotiations on burden sharing lead to an underprovision of recapitalizations. Countries have an incentive to understate their share of the problem in order to have a smaller share in the costs. This leaves the largest country, almost always the home country, with the decision whether to shoulder the costs on its own or to let the bank close, and possibly be liquidated. Freixas (2003) labels this mechanism, which reflects the current arrangements in Europe, as improvised cooperation. Schoenmaker and Oosterloo (2005) provide an empirical assessment of the intensity of cross-border externalities in Europe. This issue is not confined to Europe but to any cross-border banking setting.

Host country authorities do not have the tools to manage financial stability when foreign banks dominate their financial system. Foreign banks are in some countries allowed to enter in order to recapitalize national banks after a banking crisis (for example, Mexico, see Table 5) or to privatize national banks after opening the economy (for example, the Eastern European countries). The entry of foreign banks can have a positive impact on the efficiency of the financial system (see Ortiz, 2006; and De Haas and van Lelyveld, 2006). But foreign entry comes at the expense of financial stability management. Host country authorities have no effective mechanism to influence the parent banks — and the respective home country authorities - in case of a crisis. Host authorities are dependent on the action, or lack of it, by the home authorities. A case in point is the Argentine banking crisis in the early 2000s. At the height of the crisis, some of the nine foreign banks abandoned their branches and subsidiaries in Argentina and were allowed (or encouraged?) by the respective home supervisors to do so.[7]

The effectiveness of crisis management depends on the degree of (binding) cooperation between home and host authorities (see Evanoff and Kaufman, 2005, for an overview). The underlying challenge in crisis management is the readiness of home and host authorities to share the burden if needed (that is the social benefits exceed the costs of intervention). We define crisis management here in a broad sense: lender of last support, deposit insurance and recapitalization. Goodhart and Schoenmaker (2006) explore different *ex ante* burden sharing mechanisms.

The European banking scene would provide a fertile ground for such an *ex ante* burden sharing mechanism. Cross-border banking in Europe is mainly confined to European banks. The foreign banks in Eastern Europe are mostly West European banks. Moreover, the intensity of cross-border banking is strong: the regional component of the large European banks within Europe is 25 percent. So, solidarity is easier to organize within Europe. Finally, legally binding arrangements can be established within the EU, though it should be noted that the political appetite for new European arrangements is not very large at the moment. In the previous section, we discussed the search for an appropriate division of labor between home and host supervisors in the EU.

Outside Europe, the picture is different. At the global level, we find a very limited number of truly international banks spanning the different regions. So, there is no particular need for extensive arrangements at the global level. In addition, we have seen that regional business is limited (less than 10 percent) both in the Americas and Asia-Pacific. However, we have identified a few banking systems that are dominated by foreign players. The large foreign banks in Mexico are from the Americas [Citi (US) and Scotia (Canada)] and Europe [HSBC (UK) and BBVA and Santander (Spain)]. Effective cooperation for crisis management (and financial supervision) with foreign authorities from four countries and two regions is very challenging. Moreover, there is no possibility for Mexico to create a single jurisdiction with these countries.

Building on European and Trans-Tasman experience, the governor of the Banco de México (Ortiz, 2006) proposes to conduct crisis simulation exercises with American and European authorities. So far, the main

---

[7] Scotiabank from Canada, Crédit Agricole from France and Banca Intesa from Italy abandoned their activities in Argentina.

mechanism has been to require a separate, locally incorporated subsidiary in case the Mexican activities of foreign banks are significant. Although the subsidiary structure has drawbacks (parent banks may influence local management; parent banks may shift assets around; subsidiaries are dependent on the parent for risk models, etc), host authorities have a handle on a subsidiary as they are responsible for licensing, supervising and, if needed, closing a subsidiary.

When effective cooperation for financial supervision and crisis management is difficult to achieve, the main alternative for host authorities appears to be imposing a subsidiary structure. Such structures foster the prospect of uncoordinated and improvised solutions during a crisis, likely to result in an undersupply of recapitalizations (see Freixas, 2003). The risk of national solutions (including ring fencing of assets) could even worsen the problems. Moreover, a subsidiary structure will partly reverse the process of international financial integration. Internationally operating banks face additional burdens (for example, host country requirements and reporting) and may not be allowed to fully realize synergies from integrated operations (for example, risk management, asset management, back-office operations).

6. Conclusions

Cross-border banking appears to be uneven across the regions. Business within the region is large for European banks (about 25 percent of their total business). For American and Asian-Pacific banks the regional component is not very important (less than 10 percent). Similarly, global expansion of European banks (also close to 25 percent) appears to be larger than their American and Asia-Pacific counterparts (less than 15 percent). The result is that American and Asia-Pacific banks can be characterized as domestic banks with more than 50 percent of their business in the home country. The only exception is Citigroup, which has truly international aspirations. We conclude that the consolidation process in banking has been primarily a domestic event in the Americas and Asia-Pacific.

The picture is different in Europe. Our findings indicate that 11 banks currently operate on a European scale and a further three banks on a global scale. It is remarkable that the number of banks operating on a European scale increased from seven in 2000 to 11 in 2005, while most European countries witnessed a recession during this period. This increase is statistically significant. We conclude that the long expected cross-border merger wave in Europe has started. European banking is finally arriving.

What are the implications for public policy? Public policy issues focus on home-host cooperation for financial supervision and crisis management. The limited number of global banks (one from the US and three from Europe) suggest that there is no need for global solutions. Informal supervisory colleges consisting of the main supervisors are sufficient for this handful of banks, though this small group of global banks embrace the world's largest banks like Citigroup and HSBC. The strong cross-border penetration within Europe suggests that a formal supervisory structure may be beneficial to enhance legally binding cooperation between home and host authorities. We explore the idea of a European System of Financial Supervisors, where national supervisors work in tandem with a central agency. The fairly harmonized regulatory framework in the EU is a good starting point for such a system. Cooperation in good times (supervision) also requires cooperation in bad times (crisis management). The latter raises the thorny issue of burden sharing between countries when a systemically large cross-border bank fails.

The picture on cross-border banking and banking supervisory policy mirrors the more general picture on trade and exchange rate policy. The US have relatively low export (7 percent of GDP (OECD)), so US policymakers do not see much need for coordinating exchange rates. Put more strongly, exchange rates are considered as a useful mechanism for adjustment. European countries have relatively high export (28 percent of GDP for EU-25; 9 percent of GDP when intra EU-25 trade is excluded (OECD and Eurostat)), so European policymakers do see the need for having a coordinated exchange rate policy. As known, the latter resulted in a single currency for Europe.

References

Barth, J., D. Brumbaugh and J. Wilcox (2000). The repeal of glass-steagall and the advent of broad banking. *Journal of Economic Perspectives*, 14, 191–204.

Berger, A., R. DeYoung, H. Genay and G. Udell (2000). Globalization of financial institutions: Evidence from cross-border banking performance. *Brookings-Wharton Papers on Financial Services*, 3, 23–120.

Berger, A., Q. Dai, S. Ongena and D. Smith (2003). To what extent will the banking industry be globalized? A study of bank nationality and reach in 20 european nations. *Journal of Banking & Finance*, 27, 383–415.

Buch, C. and G. DeLong (2004). Cross-border bank mergers: What lures the rare animal?. *Journal of Banking & Finance*, 28, 2077–2102.

Dermine, J. (2006). "European banking integration: Don't put the cart before the horse. *Financial Markets, Institutions & Instruments*, 15, 2, 57–106.

Evanoff, D. and G. Kaufman, eds. (2005). *Systemic Financial Crises: Resolving Large Bank Insolvencies*. Singapore: World Scientific.

Focarelli, D. and A. Pozzolo (2001). The patterns of cross-border bank mergers and shareholdings in OECD countries. *Journal of Banking & Finance*, 25, 2305–2337.

Freixas, X. (2003). Crisis management in Europe. In *Financial Supervision in Europe*, J. Kremers, D. Schoenmaker and P. Wierts (eds.), pp. 102–119. Cheltenham: Edward Elgar.

Goodhart, C. (1987). Why do banks need a central bank?. *Oxford Economic Papers*, 39, 75–89.

Goodhart, C. and D. Schoenmaker (2006). Burden sharing in a banking crisis in Europe. *Economic Review*, 2, 34–57.

Haas, de, R. and I. van Lelyveld (2006). Foreign banks and credit stability in Central and Eastern Europe: A panel data analysis. *Journal of Banking & Finance*, 30, 1927–1952.

Herring, R. and R. Litan (1994). *Financial Regulation in a Global Economy*. Washington DC: Brookings Institution.

Ietto-Gillies, G. (1998). Different conceptual frameworks for the assessment of the degree of internationalization: An empirical analysis of various indices for the top 100 transnational corporations. *Transnational Corporations*, 7, 17–39.

Kane, E. (2006). Confronting divergent interests in cross-country regulatory arrangements. In *Cross-Border Banking: Regulatory Challenges*, G. Caprio, D. Evanoff and G. Kaufman (eds.), pp. 265–285. Singapore: World Scientific.

Kroszner, R. (2006). The effect of removing geographic restrictions on banking in the United States: Lessons for Europe. Speech at the Conference on the Future of Financial Regulation. London: London School of Economics.

Lehmann, E. (1975). *Nonparametrics: Statistical Methods Based on Ranks*. San Francisco: Holden Publisher Inc.

Mayes, D. (2006). Cross-border financial supervision in Europe: Goals and transition paths. *Economic Review*, 2, 58–89.

McCarthy, C. (2006). The Future Regulation of Financial Services. Speech at the Smith Institute Breakfast Seminar, London.

Moshirian, F. (2006). Aspects of international financial services. *Journal of Banking & Finance*, 30, 1057–1064.

Ortiz, G. (2006). Cross-border banking and the challenges faced by host country authorities. In *Cross-Border Banking: Regulatory Challenges*, G. Caprio, D. Evanoff and G. Kaufman (eds.), pp. 11–19. Singapore: World Scientific.

Peek, J. and E. Rosengren (1995). The capital crunch: Neither a borrower nor a lender be. *Journal of Money, Credit and Banking*, 27, 625–638.

Schoenmaker, D. and S. Oosterloo (2005). Financial supervision in an integrating Europe: Measuring cross-border externalities. *International Finance*, 8, 1–27.

Schoenmaker, D. and S. Oosterloo (2006). Financial Supervision in Europe: Do We Need a New Architecture?. *Cahier Comte Boël*, no. 12. Brussels: European League for Economic Cooperation.

Slager, A. (2004). *Banking Across Borders*. Rotterdam: Erasmus Research Institute of Management.

Soussa, F. (2004). A note on banking FDI in emerging markets: Literature review and evidence. Working Paper. London: Bank of England.

Stiroh, K. and P. Strahan (2003). The competitive dynamics of competition: Evidence from US banking deregulation. *Journal of Money, Credit and Banking*, 35, 801–828.

Sullivan, D. (1994) Measuring the degree of internationalization of a firm. *Journal of International Business Studies*, 25, 325–342.

Vives, X. (2001). Restructuring financial regulation in the European monetary union. *Journal of Financial Services Research*, 19, 57–82.

Actual and Near-Miss Cross-Border Crises

Carl-Johan Lindgren*
Consultant

1. Introduction and Conclusions

This chapter reviews incidences of cross-border financial crises, both actual crises and what could be considered near-miss crisis events. As all major financial crises have involved crises in the banking sector, the analysis has been simplified to focus on banking crises. Although financial crises typically also involve problems in other financial institutions and markets — to the extent such institutions and markets exist and function — crises typically center on countries' banking systems.

A cross-border crisis is defined as a crisis in one country with a significant enough impact on another country to cause a crisis in that second country. It should be stressed that, although financial crises typically have many similar causes and features, each crisis is defined by a complex set of country-specific policy and institutional circumstances.

A review of some 170 banking crises cases included in the World Bank's *Banking Crises Database* shows remarkably few cross-border crisis cases over the last 30 years and equally few cases of near-miss cross-border crises.[1] There are no simple explanations for near-misses not becoming crises; they seem to be the result of unique combinations of market, macroeconomic and political dynamics that affect expectations as well as policy responses.

---

*Carl-Johan Lindgren is a private consultant and a former senior official of the International Monetary Fund. carl_lindgren@msn.com

[1] The World Bank *Banking Crisis Database* is included in Patrick Honohan and Luc Laeven (eds.), (2005), *Systemic Financial Crises, Containment and Resolution*, Cambridge, UK: Cambridge University Press.

This chapter will first review five cases of cross-border crisis followed by six cases that could be considered near-misses and a discussion of common features or causes of cross-border crises.

The chapter concludes that cross-border crises seldom are caused by individual bank failures or even by systemic national banking problems or crises alone. Most cross-border financial crises arise from unsustainable macroeconomic policies and changing expectations of macro-financial sustainability. They are often are triggered by liquidity shocks, exchange rate adjustments, and/or debt defaults that swiftly are transmitted across borders through national and international financial markets. The presence of deposit insurance or blanket guarantees does not seem to affect cross-border transmittal once other fundamental forces are at play.

2. Five Cross-Border Crisis Cases

A gleaning of recorded banking crises in *Banking Crisis Databank* shows 169 banking crises cases in 130 countries over the last three decades (see Table 1). Two thirds of those crises were systemic and one third nonsystemic. Most of the crises took place in Africa, Latin America and the transition

Table 1. Worldwide incidence of banking crises, 1975–2005

Type of Crises/ Geographical Area	Systemic	Non Systemic	Total	Systemic	Non Systemic	Total
	(Number of Crises)			(Percent of Total Crises)		
Africa	43	13	56	25	8	33
Americas	26	7	33	15	4	20
Asia[2]	14	15	29	8	9	17
Europe	4	9	13	2	5	8
Middle East and North Africa[3]	9	5	14	8	5	3
Transition[4]	21	3	24	12	2	14
Total	**117**	**52**	**169**	**67**	**33**	**100**

Source: Banking Crisis Databank.

[2] Includes Australia and New Zealand.

[3] Includes Israel and Turkey.

[4] Includes countries in Central and Eastern Europe and of the former Soviet Union.

countries of Central and Eastern Europe and of the former Soviet Union. Some countries experienced repeated crises, including systemic ones, in the period under review.

Few of those crisis cases involved cross-border contagion. Only four cross-border crises cases were identified in the *Databank*: Mexico and Argentina in 1994–95, Thailand and the Asian region in 1997–2000, Russia and several countries in the Western Hemisphere 1998–99 and Argentina/Uruguay in 2001–02. In addition, the failure of the Meridien BIAO group and the crises this caused in some African countries in 1995 is included as a fifth cross-border case.[5]

Not included as cross-border crises — even though they involved a range of cross-border crisis issues — are the unique crises in the financial systems of the countries of Central and Eastern Europe and the former Soviet Union during their initial transitions and consolidations from centrally planned to market based banking systems in the late 1980s and early 1990s. There were subsequent banking crises in most of these countries but they did not have major cross-border effects or cause cross-border crises — with the exception of the 1998 crisis in Russia.

Neither does the analysis include the banking crises in the Nordic countries in the late 1980s and early 1990s. These crises roughly coincided in time but were largely home-grown and not transmitted across borders. The financial sector problems in Norway, Sweden and Finland were due to poorly managed liberalizations as well as careless and excessive lending by banks and near-banks. The Finnish crisis intensified due to the real sector effects of the collapse of the Soviet Union, which did involve cross-border causes but not of a financial kind.

Finally, banking crises triggered or aggravated by the failure of offshore units of domestic banks are not included. Off-shore units are here considered extensions of domestic banking institutions and problems in offshore units — although they involve cross-border issues — are considered failures of domestic banks and of domestic regulation and supervision.

2.1 *Mexico–Argentina, 1994–95*

The Mexican "Tequila" crisis in late 1994 brought an end to a fixed exchange rate regime and unsustainable short-term US dollar borrowing by banks and the government in Mexico. A major devaluation of the Mexican

---

[5] The *Databank* mentions this case only as part of a crisis in Swaziland in 1995.

peso exposed banks and bank borrowers to large losses and led to a major banking crisis. A near default on the public debt further unnerved markets.

The greatest cross-border impact of this crisis was felt in Argentina, where depositors started to test the fixed exchange rate or "convertibility" regime introduced in 1991. Additional features of that regime were legal limitations on the central bank's ability to act as lender of last resort and the absence of deposit insurance. During the "Tequila" crisis, the Argentine banking system lost 18 percent of its deposit base within a few months in early 1995. Several banks failed but the government was able to defend the convertibility /fixed exchange rate regime with the help of special liquidity support facilities to banks organized outside the central bank.[6] There was no direct financial contagion in this case — only a contagion of market perceptions.

2.2 *Meridien BIAO Bank and several African countries, 1995*

Bank subsidiaries of Luxemburg-based holding company Meridien BIAO SA (MBSA) in Zambia, Kenya and Swaziland were closed in early 1995 after facing acute liquidity shortages, as funds were transferred to other parts of the failing MBSA network and to their Bahamas-based parent bank Meridien International Bank Ltd. MBSA had operations in seventeen additional African countries and had substantial market shares in several African countries. The failure of the MBSA network of banks caused systemic crises not only in Zambia and Swaziland, but also in Cameroon and the Central African Republic.

The effects of the failure of the Meridien BIAO network of banks are largely unrecorded in the literature, as it was a bank operating almost exclusively outside major banking markets. It has been overshadowed by the far better known failure of the larger UK-based Bank of Credit and Commerce International (BCCI). But the failure of MBSA had four more severe cross-border effects in Africa than the failure of BCCI.

2.3 *Thailand and the Asian region, 1997–2000*

The suspension of 16 Thai finance companies in June 1997 and the floating of the Thai baht in early July 1997 triggered the largest and best

---

[6] Limited deposit insurance was reintroduced in 1995.

known recent cross-border crises. The Thai crisis exposed major balance sheet weaknesses of banks and corporations. Balance sheets had been inflated during years of exuberant foreign capital inflows and increasingly poor investment decisions by companies and lending decisions by banks and near-banks.

As investors reassessed their earlier assumptions about the soundness of corporate and financial sector entities in the entire Asian region, they started to withdraw funds. The crisis rapidly spread through the markets to other Asian countries, as investors and creditors withdrew not only from Thailand but also from Indonesia, Korea, Malaysia, Hong Kong SAR, the Philippines, Singapore and Taiwan ROC.

The crisis led to major capital outflows in all the countries and to large currency depreciations in those most affected. No government defaulted on its debt but there were widespread corporate debt defaults and subsequently financial and corporate sector failures. There were output losses in all affected countries, especially in Thailand, Indonesia, Korea and Malaysia, and the crises had a negative impact on financial markets and trade worldwide.

2.4 *Russia and several other countries, 1998–99*

In August 1998, Russia defaulted on its public debt. This caused hundreds of private banks to fail in Russia.

The public debt default sent shockwaves through the international markets for emerging market borrowers and led to a sudden and general hardening of borrowing terms in international financial markets. Economic and banking sector crises in Ecuador, Brazil and Argentina were partly explained by the fallout of the Russian default — with different time lags. In the industrialized world, the widening of market spreads following the Russian default mainly showed up in the failure a major US hedge fund, Long Term Capital Management (LTCM).

2.5 *Argentina and Uruguay, 2001–02*

In 2001, the Argentine convertibility regime was (again) severely tested, as the fixed exchange rate was perceived to be overvalued and the public external debt burden increasingly unsustainable. A deteriorating confidence in economic management showed up as massive deposit withdrawals in the second half of 2001; this was sustained with massive liquidity support from the central bank. An introduction of capital/exchange controls and a deposit freeze in early December 2001 did not succeed in stopping the deposit outflow — the banking system lost altogether 22 percent of its deposit base in 2001.

Following the sovereign debt default in late December 2001 and a series of other unprecedented measures highly damaging to the banking system in early 2002, the crisis intensified and the deposit outflow accelerated; the deposit base was not stabilized until the second half of 2002. By end 2002, the system has lost 66 percent of its end 2001 deposit base in US dollars terms although it remained largely unchanged in peso terms, as the currency had depreciated to about a third of its end 2001 value.

Neighboring Uruguay was heavily affected by the crisis in Argentina. In late 2001, Argentine depositors in Uruguay had started to withdraw their deposits and in the first half of 2002 the severe Argentine crisis spread to Uruguay, where the banking system experienced massive systemwide deposit withdrawals. By end 2002, the Uruguayan banking system had lost 54 percent of its end 2001 deposit base in US dollars terms and several banks had failed.

3. Near-Miss Cross-Border Crises

Near-miss cross-border crisis cases seem to be as rare as full-fledged crises and more difficult to identify. Perhaps every major national crisis could be considered a potential cross-border crisis and therefore a near-miss crisis. But a review of the crisis cases in the *Databank* indicates that most crises are national without features or dynamics that make them likely to be near-misses across borders. The selection of near-misses below is the subjective assessment of the author taking into account perceptions of market participants and policymakers at the time of each crisis; it does not pretend to be scientific or exhaustive.

The following six cases might be considered near-misses: The less developed countries' (LDC) debt crisis of the early 1980s, Japan after 1992, Long Term Capital Management in 1998, Ecuador in 1998–99, Brazil in 1998–99 and Turkey in 2000–02.

3.1 *LDC debt crisis*

The LDC debt crisis of the early 1980s caused major cross-border problems to banks in industrialized countries with common exposures. At the peak of the crisis, the LDC exposures of several major banks in the US and in some other industrialized countries exceeded their capital bases. Open crises was avoided through a combination of debt renegotiation, forbearance by supervisors as well as higher interest rates and improved bank profitability over time.

3.2 *Japan*

Since the early 1990s Japan experienced a slow-moving banking crisis that forced head offices, branches and subsidiaries of Japanese banks to curtail their lending in the Asian region. In none of the affected Asian countries did this cause a crisis.

3.3 *Long Term Capital Management*

As discussed above, LTCM became illiquid and failed as a result of sharply rising interest rate spreads in 1998. Although LTCM was not a bank, major US banks were highly exposed to it. A private sector bail-in organized by the Federal Reserve Bank of New York prevented wider systemic repercussions in the US banking system and possible cross-border contagion.

3.4 *Ecuador*

In 1998–2000, Ecuador experienced a major banking crisis accompanied by a large currency depreciation and public debt default. At the time, the debt default was feared to trigger a change investor attitudes and threaten the financial stability of some of the major Latin American countries. In the event, the Ecuador crisis did not affect other countries.

3.5 *Brazil*

In 1998–99, Brazil experienced a banking crisis. Despite the weight of the Brazilian economy and the presence of Brazilian banks in neighboring countries, there were no significant cross-border effects of the Brazilian banking crisis, as major banks were recapitalized. The banking systems in neighboring countries were not affected.

3.6 *Turkey*

In 2000–02, there was a major banking crisis in Turkey. The need to support the large public banks and compensate depositors of failed private banks stretched the capacity of the government to roll over its already large debt. A successful program of bank restructuring and recapitalization avoided a public debt crisis, which could have had major cross-border effects.

4. What Causes Cross-Border Crises?

4.1 *Crisis originating in individual banks*

It is rare that crises in individual banks cause cross-border crises. The only case known to the author is the MBSA case in Africa. This Luxemburg/ Bahamas-based group had a large market share in several African countries and its failure created major problems in several countries and systemic crises in at least four countries. In comparison, the earlier failure of BCCI had caused problems in several developing countries but in no country did it cause an outright crisis.

In the Argentina/Uruguay case the problems of Argentine *Banco de Galicia y Buenos Aires* initially contributed to the crisis in Uruguay but these effects were soon dwarfed by the cross-border effects of the massive systemic crisis in the Argentine banking system.

Despite increasing cross-border ownership of banks and other financial institutions it is not clear that the risk of major cross-border contagion has increased. The extent of such contagion would depend on a failing institution's market share and exposure in another country, the strength of other financial institutions and counterparties in that country, the liquidity effects of a failure as well as the responses of home and host authorities.

4.2 *Crisis originating in systemic banking crisis*

It is also rare that a systemic national banking crisis alone will spill over into a crisis in another country. The only clear case in which a pure banking crisis crossed a border is Argentina/Uruguay in 2001–02. It is not clear that the size of the banking system in the country where the crisis originates is a determining factor, although the aggregate size of financial linkages clearly does matter. Deposits of Argentine residents (households and companies) represented a large share of the deposit base in Uruguay. When these deposits started to be withdrawn first from Argentine bank subsidiaries and subsequently from other local and foreign banks in Uruguay it created a massive liquidity and banking crisis in Uruguay.

The traditional closeness and physical proximity of these two banking markets in the Southern Cone made transmission strong and immediate, especially after the introduction of the deposit freeze in Argentina in late 2001. In Argentina, the systemic banking crisis was the result of the broader macroeconomic crisis that not only swept that country, but also fed back into a deterioration of macroeconomic conditions and confidence in general.

4.3 *Crisis due to unsustainable macroeconomic policies*

Changed expectations of macroeconomic sustainability appear to be the major cause for cross-border transmittal, i.e. in Mexico (1994–95), Asia (1997–2000) and Russia (1998). In these cross-border crises, unsustainable macroeconomic policies and conditions were the main underlying reasons. In particular, changing expectations surrounding exchange rates, combined with unsustainable public or private debt dynamics or outright defaults, were the driving forces. Political meltdowns aggravated expectations and cross-border crises in cases like Indonesia in 1997–98 and Argentina in 2001–02.

In the Mexican "Tequila" crisis, Argentine depositors started to question the fixed exchange rate/convertibility regime and the lack of a lender of last resort and deposit insurance — even though there were no significant financial or banking connections between the two countries — only a contagion of market perceptions.

In Asia, there were few financial links between countries in the region. The floating of the Thai baht revealed signs that many of the country's financial and corporate institutions were insolvent and its banking system generally was overextended. This caused investors and creditors to reassess their excessively positive views not only of Thailand but of the entire region. Massive capital outflows put further pressures on most of the countries in the region. The result of the Thai crisis was a forceful and swift cross-border contagion.

Changed investor expectations and tightening market conditions also explain the cross-border transmission following the Russian debt default of 1998.

4.4 *Market transmission of crisis*

Most cross-border crises are triggered by liquidity crises due to deposit withdrawals and associated capital flight or the shocks of debt defaults. This typically leads to a sudden and major tightening of liquidity, rise in interest rates and/or depreciation of the exchange rate. The liquidity shocks directly affect national money and foreign exchange markets and are quickly transmitted abroad.

The effects of Mexican, Asian, Russian and Argentine crises were largely transmitted across borders through money and foreign exchange markets.[7] As fixed exchange rate regimes crumble and interest rates rise, bank and corporate insolvencies emerge, and public and/or private debt defaults become evident, financial markets transmit and often exaggerate exchange and interest rate effects.

4.5 *The effects of depositor and creditor protection schemes*

Given that the International Association of Deposit Insurers was a co-sponsor of the conference, the role of depositor and creditor protection schemes in cross-border crisis cases also was considered. In Mexico and Asia depositors had implicit protection, which was converted into explicit legal protection during the crises. In Asia, legal depositor and creditor guarantees reassured domestic depositors and investors but worked less well with foreign creditors and investors. In the Meridien BIAO Bank case, the affected countries had no depositor protection, and in Russia,

---

[7] In the case of the Meridien BIAO Bank, liquidity shortages and the absence of a lender of last resort led to the bank's failure and transmitted the crisis across borders.

depositors and creditors in private banks had no protection. From 2001–02, Argentina had a limited depositor protection scheme in place but withdrawals were limited as most deposits were frozen.

Blanket guarantees of depositors and creditors and limited deposit insurance may play an important role in managing domestic crises and their resolution but the evidence from the above cases is that such schemes have no significant impact on cross-border transmittal of crises once other fundamental forces of contagion are at play.

A Review of Financial Stability Reports

Sander Oosterloo*
University of Groningen and Ministry of Finance, The Netherlands

Jakob de Haan
University of Groningen, The Netherlands and CESifo Munich, Germany

Richard Jong-A-Pin
University of Groningen, The Netherlands

1. Introduction

The growing interest of central banks in monitoring and analyzing risks and threats to the stability of the financial system has spurred the publication of so-called Financial Stability Reports (FSRs). It therefore seems appropriate to reflect upon this development. Why do central banks publish these reports? What information is made public? Does the content of the reports differ? Is there a relationship between the information provided in a FSR and the soundness of the financial system? The aim of this study is to examine these questions in some detail.

Our main findings are as follows. There are three motives for publication of a FSR: increasing the transparency of authorities responsible for financial stability, contributing to financial stability, and strengthening cooperation between the various authorities involved in maintaining financial stability. The occurrence of a systemic banking crisis in the past, gross domestic product (GDP) per capita, and European Union membership are

*Sander Oosterloo is on the faculty of economics at the University of Groningen and Financial Markets Policy Directorate at the Ministry of Finance, both in the Netherlands. Jakob de Haan is on the faculty of economics at the University of Groningen, the Netherlands, and on staff at CESifo in Munich, Germany. Richard Jong-A-Pin is on the faculty of economics at the University of Groningen, the Netherlands. The corresponding author is Jakob de Haan, Faculty of Economics, University of Groningen. The Netherlands. jakob.de.haan@rug.nl. The views expressed in this chapter are those of the authors only and not necessarily those of the Netherlands Ministry of Finance.

positively related to the likelihood that a FSR is published. The content of FSRs differs widely; on average only 33 percent of the indicators as suggested by the International Monetary Fund is actually published. The level of information provided in a FSR seems unrelated to the health of the banking system.

The remainder of this chapter is organized as follows. Section 2 provides an overview of central banks that publish a FSR and examines the motives of central banks for doing this. Section 3 offers an empirical analysis examining factors that are related to the publication of a FSR, while Section 4 compares the content of the various FSRs, following the list of financial stability indicators suggested by the International Monetary Fund (2004). As the informational content of the reports varies, it is examined in Section 5 whether there is any relationship between the degree of transparency of the FSR and the soundness of the financial system. The final section offers some concluding comments.

2. Central Banks That Publish a FSR

Central banks may provide information on financial stability in various ways. Gai and Shin (2003) argue that the format of the central bank's communication is critical to its ability to convey its intentions to the public. A FSR aims to provide clear and coherent information to its audience in order to achieve common knowledge of its main propositions. As a result, each individual in the audience is able to understand the content and can be reasonably confident that the audience as a whole has grasped the main propositions. A communication strategy that relies more heavily on speeches and testimonies of policymakers made at different times may convey a coherent message, but the fragmented nature of the communication leaves open the possibility that some market observers may fail to capture the intended picture with its emphases and qualifications. Furthermore, even those market participants who have understood the full picture may be uncertain whether everyone else has grasped it. So the FSR offers a univocal framework for communicating to the public on the role, policies, decisions, performance, and operations of the central bank related to financial stability.

Nowadays, a growing number of central banks (CBs) publish a FSR as shown in Table 1. During the last decade, the number of CBs that publish a FSR has increased rapidly from 1 in 1996 to 40 in 2005 (see Figure 1).

Table 1. Central banks that publish a financial stability report[a]

Jurisdiction	First FSR Publication	Half Yearly or Yearly?
1. Argentina	2004	Half-yearly
2. Australia	2004	Half-yearly
3. Austria	2001	Half-yearly
4. Belgium	2003	Yearly
5. Brazil	2002	Half-yearly
6. Canada	2002	Half-yearly
7. Chile	2004	Half-yearly
8. Czech Republic	2005	Yearly
9. Denmark	2002	Yearly
10. Estonia	2003	Half-yearly
11. European Central Bank	2004	Yearly
12. Finland	1998[b]	Yearly
13. France	2002	Half-yearly
14. Germany	2005	Yearly
15. Hong Kong	2003	Half-yearly
16. Hungary	2000	Half-yearly
17. Iceland	2000	Yearly
18. Indonesia	2003	Half-yearly
19. Ireland	2001	Yearly
20. Israel	2004	Yearly
21. Japan	2005	Yearly
22. Korea	2005	Half-yearly
23. Latvia	2003	Yearly
24. Luxembourg	2002	Yearly
25. Netherlands	2004	Yearly
26. New Zealand	2004	Half-yearly
27. Norway	1997	Half-yearly
28. Poland	2003	Unclear (3 different periods up to now)
29. Portugal	2005	Yearly
30. Russia	2001	Yearly
31. Singapore	2004	Half-yearly
32. Slovakia	2004	Yearly
33. Slovenia	2004	Yearly
34. South Africa	2004	Half-yearly
35. Spain	2002	Half-yearly

(*Continued*)

Table 1. (*Continued*)

Jurisdiction	First FSR publication	Half yearly or yearly?
36. Sri Lanka	2005	Yearly
37. Sweden	1997	Half-yearly
38. Switzerland	2003	Yearly
39. Turkey	2005	Yearly
40. United Kingdom	1996	Half-yearly

[a] At the time of writing it was not possible to download the FSR of Chile, therefore this document will not be used in this analysis. The same goes for the FSR of Luxembourg, as it is not available in English. After we stopped gathering the data on which the analysis in this chapter is based, Germany also published a FSR. Most FSRs can be found at: www.jdawiseman.com/papers/finmkts/financial-stability-reviews.html
[b] Since 1998, the Bank of Finland has published a half-yearly report on financial stability in broader publications; as of 2003 it published a separate FSR yearly.
Source: Oosterloo *et al.* (2007)

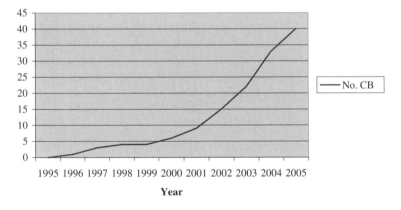

Figure 1. Number of CBs that publish an FSR, 1996–2005

What is the purpose of publishing a FSR? On the basis of a survey among central bankers, Oosterloo and de Haan (2004) conclude that there are three main reasons for publishing the assessment of financial stability:

- *Contribute to the overall stability of the financial system*;

The FSR can be seen as an instrument designed to safeguard financial stability. One of the most important instruments that a CB has at its disposal is the ability to publicly acknowledge and openly discuss developments in the financial sector. By informing the public on both the state of the financial system and the judgment of the CB regarding the system's stability, publishing a FSR can promote better-informed decision-making and can contribute to the stability of the financial system. This can be seen as a form of "moral suasion", that is, benevolent compulsion or making others conform without enforcing rules directly.

According to Haldane *et al.* (2005) surveillance serves as a form of long-range radar on incipient instabilities. Its role is to spot shocks before they occur — or at least before the deleterious effects begin to take hold. Detection of, and transparency about, those shocks may itself help engineer an orderly, pre-emptive response by private market participants. This, in turn, should lower the probability of a full blown banking crisis. The authors argue that this, in essence, is the rationale behind the central banks publishing FSRs.

However, it is also argued that too much transparency about potential shocks can create a "self-fulfilling prophecy", that is, by pointing out potential risks CBs could foster instability rather than prevent it from occurring. So, there is an area of tension between openly discussing certain developments in order to guarantee the stability of the financial system and the risk of creating imbalances by being too transparent.

- *Increase the transparency (and accountability) of the financial stability function.*

The provision of information on the financial stability function can be seen as an element of accountability. As Lastra (2001, p. 72) argues, "the provision of information in the context of accountability, whether in an *ex ante* investigation or an *ex post* requirement of disclosure, facilitates transparency. On the other hand, a transparent economic and political environment enhances the effectiveness of accountability. The two concepts are therefore mutually enforcing, and they both share the provision of information as a common requirement". However, it needs to be mentioned that the role of the monetary authority in financial stability poses some quite different issues of conduct and accountability than monetary policy does (see Garcia Herrero and Del Río, 2005; and Oosterloo and de Haan, 2004). First of all, there is no unambiguous definition of financial stability. Even if there would be an explicit definition of financial stability, it will generally be less easy to quantify than, for example, price stability. As a result, the CB is not bound to very specific financial stability objectives and it becomes difficult to evaluate its performance. Second, because of the multilateral nature of financial stability (with different aspects such as prudential supervision, monetary policy, financial markets and payment- and settlement systems) the objective of maintaining financial stability is more difficult to measure than is the case for monetary policy. Third, the instruments used by the CB to maintain financial stability predominantly have an indirect (rather than direct) influence on financial stability. Therefore the impact of these instruments is difficult to measure and makes the accountability process even more difficult. Moreover, instruments can have a different purpose (for example, on the one hand an instrument can have micro-prudential or monetary purposes, and on the other hand it can have financial stability purposes).

- *Strengthen cooperation on financial stability issues between the various relevant authorities.*

The FSR should stimulate the discussion between the relevant authorities and financial institutions, and foster cooperation between these parties. In this respect, the Banque de France (2002, p. 6) argues that "in a globalized and increasingly complex financial environment, assessing and fostering financial stability require strengthened cooperation between the various relevant authorities, governments, central banks, market regulators and supervisors. They also presuppose that a close dialogue be maintained with all financial sector professionals. It is in this spirit that the Banque de France, like several other central banks, has decided to publish a periodic Financial Stability Report".

3. Which Factors Influence Publication of a FSR?

The group of countries that publish a FSR have common characteristics. First, many have a relatively high GDP per capita, which suggests a relation between the level of development of a country and the publication of a FSR. This may be explained as follows. Higher income and financial development are closely related and a more developed financial system may, in turn, imply a stronger need to focus on financial stability. Another explanation might be that high-income countries simply have more resources available to analyze and publish on financial stability.

Second, many of these countries suffered from a banking crisis since 1990 (the UK, the Nordic countries, and various countries in Asia and

Southern America). This suggests that the occurrence of a banking crisis may affect the likelihood that a FSR is published.

Third, many countries that publish a FSR are (candidate) members of the European Union (EU). This is because countries in the euro area have transferred their monetary responsibilities to the European Central Bank (see de Haan *et al.*, 2005). These central banks can therefore redirect their attention to maintaining financial stability. This revised focus has set the standard for other European Countries.

Fourth, the legal origin of a country may also affect the likelihood that a country publishes a FSR. In a large cross-section of countries, it is found that legal origin is one of the most important variables for explaining different levels of regulatory intervention (World Bank, 2004). Likewise, the inclination of public authorities to be transparent on their policies may be related to legal origin.

By means of a simple cross-country probit model we examine whether the aforementioned factors are related to a central bank's decision to publish a FSR. As we employ a cross-country model, "herd behavior" of central banks cannot be captured. Still, Figure 1 suggests that "herd behavior" may be relevant, as there is an acceleration in the number of banks that publish a FSR. Apparently, it becomes more difficult for central banks to refrain from publishing a FSR once other central banks start doing so.

Our sample consists of 154 countries covering the period 1996–2005. Our dependent variable is a dummy that is one when the CB publishes a FSR and zero otherwise. The following explanatory variables have been included:

- GDP per capita (source: World Bank);
- A dummy variable reflecting whether a systemic banking crisis has occurred after 1990 (source: Honahan and Laeven, 2005);
- A dummy variable reflecting whether a non-systemic banking crisis has occurred after 1990 (source: Honahan and Laeven, 2005);
- Dummies reflecting EU membership (or candidate membership); and
- Dummies for various legal systems (source: La Porta *et al.*, 1998).

Inclusion of the dummies for legal systems reduces the number of observations to 44.

The probit estimation results are presented in Table 2. The coefficients reported are marginal effects, that is, the change in the probability for an infinitesimal change in each independent, continuous variable (here only GDP per capita). By default, they report the discrete change in

Table 2. Factors determining whether a central bank publishes a FSR

Explanatory Variable: FSR	I	II	III	IV
GDP per capita (thousands)	0.02	0.02	0.02	0.02
	(5.91)*	(4.84)*	(1.79)**	(1.79)**
Systemic bank crisis after 1990	0.28	0.24	−0.20	−0.20
	(3.11)*	(2.63)*	(−0.09)	(−0.09)
Nonsystemic bank crisis after 1990	0.16	0.13	−0.14	−0.14
	(1.34)	(1.10)	(−0.63)	(−0.63)
EU29 (members + candidates)		0.25	0.10	0.10
		(2.51)*	(0.42)	(0.42)
Legal Origin UK			0.11	
			(0.56)	
Legal Origin France				−0.11
				(−0.56)
Legal Origin Germany			0.14	−0.09
			(0.04)	(−0.28)
Mc-Fadden R-squared	0.35	0.39	0.16	0.16
Number of observations	154	154	44	44

Note: t-statistics are shown in parentheses. *=significant at the 5 percent significance level, **=significant at the 10 percent significance level. The Scandinavian legal origin dummy is dropped from the regressions because all countries with Scandinavian legal origin publish a FSR.

the probability for dummy variables. Column (I) shows the outcomes if only income and the occurrence of banking crises are taken up as explanatory variables, while in column II EU membership is added. In columns III and IV the legal family dummies are also included, reducing the number of observations.

Based on the results shown in Table 2 we reach four conclusions. First, income per capita has a significant impact on the likelihood that a central bank publishes a FSR. Secondly, the occurrence of a systemic banking crisis in the past also increases this probability. Interestingly, this relationship is absent for the occurrence of a nonsystemic banking crisis. Thirdly, membership of the European Union is also positively related to our dependent variable. Finally, there is no relationship between the legal system in place and our dummy variable.

4. The Content of the FSRs: A Comparison

As pointed out by Schinasi (2005), financial systems face endogenous and exogenous risks. Endogenous risks may arise in any of the financial system's three main components, that is, institutions, markets and infrastructure. Problems in a financial institution may subsequently spread to other parts of the financial system, or several institutions may be affected simultaneously because they have similar risk exposures. Markets are subject to various risks including counter party risk, asset price misalignments, runs and contagion. Problems originating in financial institutions may lead to problems in the clearing and settlement systems or other parts of the financial infrastructure that have broader repercussions for the financial system. Likewise, weaknesses originating in the infrastructure may cause business failures.

Exogenous risks stem from problems outside the financial system. Financial stability is susceptible to external shocks, like natural catastrophes, abrupt swings in market sentiment or a sovereign default by a neighboring country. Microeconomic events, such as the failure of a large company, may create imbalances that affect the whole financial system.

As pointed out by Schinasi, financial stability analysis needs to cover all of the above sources of risks and vulnerabilities which require systematic monitoring of individual parts of the financial system, as well as their relationships, and the real economy. The analysis of financial stability therefore requires a broad set of indicators, such as balance sheet data reflecting sector financial positions, ratios between net debt and income, measures of counter party risk (such as credit spreads) and of liquidity and asset quality (such as nonperforming loans), open foreign exchange positions, and exposures per sector with special attention to measures of concentration. Likewise, indicators monitoring conditions in important markets — including the interbank money, repo, bond, equity and derivatives markets — are required.

For a long time, central banks had no standard framework to analyze financial stability. This resulted in ad hoc assessments and the publication of data that was at hand. In an effort to improve the quality and comparability of data, the International Monetary Fund (IMF) has developed a set of Financial Soundness Indicators (FSIs) that it hopes will be calculated on an internationally harmonized basis, and be released quarterly by most countries. These indicators are divided into two sets. The so-called core set includes statistics on the health and performance of the deposit-taking sector. The second, encouraged, set includes additional statistics on deposit-taking institutions as well as statistics relating to the household and corporate sectors, real estate markets and nonbank financial institutions.

As pointed out by the IMF, there are limitations to relying solely on FSIs. Different sources of information need to be combined to adequately analyze the health and stability of the financial system. Still, the core and encouraged FSIs prove a coherent framework for analyzing the content of the FSRs. Oosterloo *et al.* (2007) analyze whether the most recently available issue of the FSR at the time of data gathering (October 2005) provides information on a long list of stability indicators as suggested in the IMF's Financial Soundness Indicators (IMF, 2004).

It appears that the actual content of the various FSRs differs considerably. Table 3 offers a summary of these differences. It follows from Table 3 that FSRs offer much information on deposit-takers, while they provide less information on other financial corporations and nonfinancial corporations. This is illustrated in more detail in Figure 2 (reproduced from Oosterloo *et al.*, 2007) that shows the percentage of particular indicator classes (deposit takers, other financial corporations, nonfinancial corporations, households, markets liquidity and real estate market) that is published in a FSR. On average, a central bank publishes 53 percent of the core FSIs. Furthermore, 37 percent and 40 percent of the suggested indicators for households and real estate markets are published, respectively. The percentage for the other indicator classes lies between 14 percent and 20 percent.

As the core set, which covers all the main categories of banks risk, is most widely available, we pursue a further analysis of these 12 indicators. As shown in Table 3, the core set can be divided into five different categories: indicators on capital adequacy (CA), asset quality (AQ), earnings and profitability (E&P), liquidity (L) and market risk (MR). Because these indicators are relatively easy to compile and are meaningful in most country circumstances, the core set enables central banks to compare their national situation with the stability of financial systems around the world (that is, peer group analysis).

How transparent are central banks on the core set of 12 FSIs? Figure 3 shows that 78 percent of the central banks that publish a FSR make both core indicators on capital adequacy available to the public, while 19 percent publishes one of the two indicators and 3 percent does not publish any indicator on capital adequacy. With respect to the asset quality of the banking

Table 3. Informational content of FSRs: A comparison

Financial Soundness Indicators	Number of FSRs Providing Information on	As Percentage
Core Set: Deposit-Takers		
Regulatory capital to risk-weighted assets (CA)	35	92
Regulatory Tier 1 capital to risk-weighted assets (CA)	25	66
Non-performing loans net of provisions to capital (AQ)	6	16
Non-performing loans to total gross loans (AQ)	27	71
Sectoral distribution of loans to total loans (AQ)	25	66
Return on assets (E&P)	29	76
Return on equity (E&P)	29	76
Interest margin to gross income (E&P)	17	45
Non-interest expenses to gross income (E&P)	22	58
Liquid assets to total assets (liquid asset ratio) (L)	18	47
Liquid assets to short-term liabilities (L)	8	21
Net open position in foreign exchange to capital (MR)	5	13
Encouraged Set: Deposit-Takers		
Capital to assets ratio	5	13
Large exposures to capital	2	5
Geographical distribution of loans to total loans	6	16
Gross asset and liability position in financial derivatives to capital	2	5
Trading and foreign exchange gains and losses to gross income	3	8
Personnel expenses to non-interest expenses	2	5

(Continued)

Table 3. (*Continued*)

Financial Soundness Indicators	Number of FSRs Providing Information on	As Percentage
Spread between reference lending and deposit rates	25	66
Spread between highest and lowest interbank rates	2	5
Customer deposits to total (non-interbank) loans	13	34
Foreign-currency-denominated loans to total loans	8	21
Foreign-currency-denominated liabilities to total liabilities	3	8
Net open position in equities to capital	1	3
Encouraged Set: Other Financial Corporations		
Assets to total financial system assets	6	16
Assets to GDP	5	13
Encouraged Set: Nonfinancial Corporations		
Total debt to equity	9	24
Return on equity	7	18
Earnings to interest and principal expenses (Debt service coverage)	5	13
Net foreign exchange exposure to equity	0	0
Number of applications for protection from creditors	18	47
Encouraged Set: Households		
Household debt to GDP	12	32
Household debt service and principal payments to income	17	45

(*Continued*)

Table 3. (*Continued*)

Financial Soundness Indicators	Number of FSRs Providing Information on	As Percentage
Encouraged Set: Market Liquidity		
Average bid-ask spread in the securities market	5	13
Average daily turnover ratio in the securities market	7	18
Encouraged Set: Real Estate Markets		
Real estate prices	22	58
Residential real estate loans to total loans	18	47
Commercial real estate loans to total loans	7	18

Source: Oosterloo *et al.* (2207)

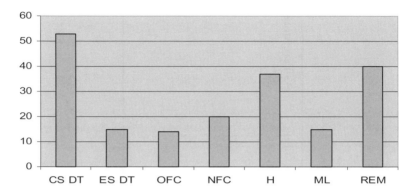

Figure 2. Publication of financial soundness indicator classes (average)
Note: CS DT = Core Set Deposit Takers, ES DT = Encouraged Set Deposit
Takers, OFC = Other Financial Corporations, NFC = Non-Financial Corporations,
H = Households, ML = Market Liquidity, and REM = Real Estate Market.

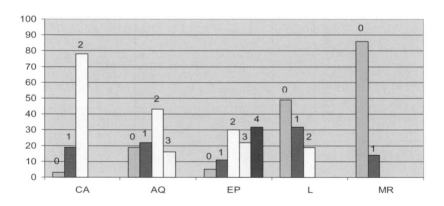

Figure 3. Publication of core set financial soundness indicators
Note: CA = Capital Adequacy, AQ = Asset Quality, E&C = Earning and
Profitability, L = Liquidity Indicators, and MR = Market Risk.

sector, 43 percent publishes two and 16 percent publishes all three indicators. Figure 3 (reproduced from Oosterloo *et al.*, 2007) also shows that
most banks provide very little information on liquidity and/or market risk:
49 percent does not publish any indicator on liquidity and 86 percent does
not publish data on the net open position in foreign exchange to capital.
This analysis therefore suggests that central banks have some scope to

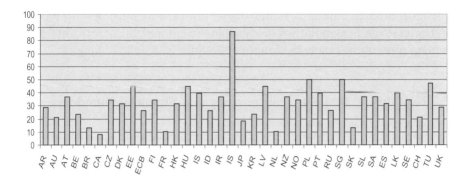

Figure 4. Percentage of financial soundness indicators published per central bank

improve upon the public availability of FSIs. This is further illustrated by Figure 4, which shows the total percentage of FSIs published per CB.

As Oosterloo *et al.* (2007) show, a central bank publishes on average 33 percent of the FSIs suggested by the IMF. In total 17 banks score above average. Especially, the central banks of Israel, Poland and Singapore are relatively transparent. The first makes 87 percent of the suggested indicators available and the latter two 50 percent. The level of public availability of FSIs is expected to rise, as the IMF is organizing a Coordinated Compilation Exercise in order to promote and support the compilation of FSIs.[1]

All in all, these results suggest that central banks have some scope to improve the content of the FSRs. This is supported by Čikák (2006), who assesses the different elements of FSRs on the basis of three characteristics: clarity, consistency, and coverage. The author finds that FSRs provide useful insights into how central banks analyze financial stability, but he also stresses there are areas for improvement. According to Čikák, these include clarifying the aims of the reports, providing an "operational definition" of financial sector soundness; clarifying the "core analysis" that is presented in FSRs consistently across time; making available the underlying data; discussing more openly risks and exposures in the financial system; making greater use of disaggregated data; focusing more on

---

[1] The more than 60 participating countries are required to compile the core indicators and as many of the second set of indicators as possible. Data for end December 2005 are to be submitted by the end of July 2006, and the IMF hopes to publish the results by the end of 2006.

forward-looking measures rather than backward-looking description of indicators; and presenting stress tests that are comparable across time, and among other things include scenarios, liquidity risks and contagion.

5. Relationship between Transparency and Financial Soundness

In this section, we explore the relationship between transparency of the FSR and soundness of the financial system. This relationship is of interest because many central banks argue that one of the rationales for publication of a FSR is that it promotes better-informed decision-making and can contribute to the stability of the financial system. Transparency about detection of potential shocks may trigger market-led actions to stabilize the financial system (see also Haldane *et al.*, 2005).

For the soundness of the financial system, we use two indicators: Moody's weighted average bank financial strength index (IMF, Global Financial Stability Report[2]) and the financial system soundness indicator of Das *et al.* (2004).[3] Both indicators are limited to the banking system. However, Das *et al.* (2004) argue that limiting the analysis to the banking system is not a major drawback from an analytical point of view since banking sector soundness has a predominant impact on the financial system. Our indicator for transparency is the sum of all items indicated in Table 3 on which information is presented in the FSR of the country concerned.

Figures 5 and 6 (reproduced from Oosterloo *et al.*, 2007) show the relationship between indicators of financial soundness and our FSR transparency indicator. It is clear that there is no relationship between the indicators of financial soundness and our indicator of transparency.[4] There are

[2] Moody's define this index as follows: "Factors considered in the assignment of Bank Financial Strength Ratings include bank-specific elements such as financial fundamentals, franchise value, and business and asset diversification. Although Bank Financial Strength Ratings exclude the external factors specified above, they do take into account other risk factors in the bank's operating environment, including the strength and prospective performance of the economy, as well as the structure and relative fragility of the financial system, and the quality of banking regulation and supervision."

[3] We thank Marc Quintyn for providing these data.

[4] The pair wise correlation coefficients between Moody's indicator and our transparency index ($n = 32$) and between the indicator of Das *et al.* (2004) and our transparency index ($n = 20$) are -0.05 and -0.16, respectively. Both correlation coefficients are insignificant at the 5 percent significance level.

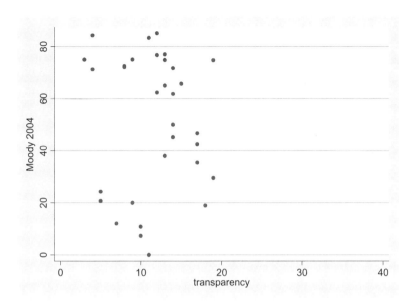

Figure 5. Transparency and financial soundness (Moody's Indicator)

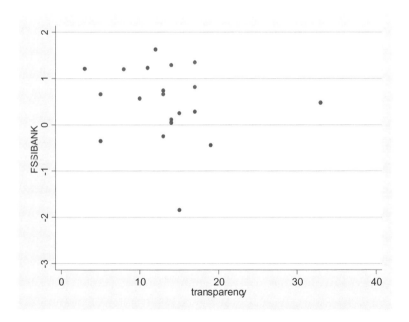

Figure 6. Transparency and financial soundness (indicator of Das *et al.*)

various explanations for this finding. First, most FSRs have only recently been published, and as a result the influence of the FSRs on the stability of the financial system may take more time. Secondly, because of the multilateral nature of financial stability, the stability of the financial system is influenced by a broad set of different factors. As a result, it is difficult to filter out the impact of the publication of a FSR. Thirdly, perhaps these results show that we should not overstate the influence of this kind of communication on the soundness of the financial system.

6. Concluding Comments

The objective of financial stability has gained importance over the last decades. Many central banks have obtained a mandate to pursue financial stability, in addition to their monetary stability mandate. Nowadays, a large number of central banks publish an annual or semi-annual Financial Stability Report (FSR). The aim of this chapter is to get a better understanding of why central banks publish a FSR and to compare the various reports in terms of the topics that are addressed. It is also examined whether the informational content of a FSR is related to the soundness of the financial system.

Our main findings are that the number of central banks that publish a FSR has increased from one in 1996 to 40 in 2005. The publication of a FSR may serve three aims: increasing the transparency (and accountability) of authorities responsible for financial stability; contributing to the overall stability of the financial system; and strengthening cooperation on financial stability issues between the various relevant authorities.

It is found that income per capita has a significant impact on the likelihood that a central bank publishes a FSR. Furthermore, the occurrence of a systemic banking crisis is positively related to the likelihood that a central bank publishes a FSR; this relationship is absent for the occurrence of a nonsystemic banking crisis. Membership of the European Union is positively related to our dependent variable, while the legal system in place does not affect the likelihood that a FSR is published.

With respect to the objectives of publishing a FSR it is found that the content of FSRs differs widely; on average only 33 percent of the indicators as suggested by the IMF is actually published. In general, the FSRs provide more information on deposit-takers, the household sector and the real estate market, than on the other indicator classes. Our results therefore suggest that central banks have some scope to improve the public availability of financial stability indicators.

Finally, based on a very simple bi-variate analysis, we find that the amount of information provided in a FSR is not related to the health of the banking system. However, more data and a more in-depth analysis are needed to further analyze whether a FSR contributes to the stability of the financial system.

References

Čikák, M. (2006). How do central banks write on financial stability?. IMF Working Paper No 06/163. Washington: International Monetary Fund.

Crockett, A. (1997). Why is financial stability a goal of public policy? In *Maintaining Financial Stability in a Global Economy*, pp. 7–36. Federal Reserve Bank of Kansas City.

Das, U., M. Quityn and K. Chenard (2004). Does regulatory governance matter for financial system stability? An empirical analysis. IMF Working Paper, No. 04/89.

De Bandt, O. and P. Hartmann (2000). Systemic risk: A survey. ECB Working Paper, No. 35.

De Haan, J., S.C.W. Eijffinger and S. Waller (2005). *The European Central Bank Credibility, Transparency, and Centralization*. Cambridge, MA: MIT Press.

De Haan, J. and S. Oosterloo (2006). Transparency and accountability of central banks in their role of financial stability supervisor in OECD countries. *European Journal of Law and Economics*, 22, 255–271.

Gai, P. and H.G. Shin (2003). Transparency and financial stability. *Bank of England Financial Stability Review*, December, 91–98.

Garcia Herrero, A. and P. del Rio (2005). Financial stability and the design of monetary policy. Banco d'España, Working Paper No. 0315.

Haldane, A.G., G. Hoggarth, V. Saporta and P. Sinclair (2005). Financial stability and bank solvency. In *Systemic Financial Crises*, D. Evanoff and G. Kaufman (eds.), pp. 83–113. Singapore: World Scientific Publishing.

Honohan, P. and L. Laeven eds. (2005). *Systemic Financial Crises: Containment and Resolution*. Cambridge, UK: Cambridge University Press.

Houben, A., J. Kakes and G. Schinasi (2004). Towards a framework for financial stability. De Nederlandsche Bank, Occasional Study, Vol. 2, No. 1.

International Monetary Fund (2001). Financial soundness indicators. Policy paper. Washington, DC: IMF.

International Monetary Fund (2004) *Compilation Guide on Financial Soundness Indicators*. Washington, DC: IMF.

La Porta, R., F. Lopez-de-Silanes, A. Shleifer and R. Vishny (1998). Law and finance. *Journal of Political Economy*, 106, 1113–1155.

Oosterloo, S. and J. de Haan (2004). Central banks and financial stability: A survey. *Journal of Financial Stability*, 1, 257–273.

Oosterloo, S., J. de Haan and R. A.-P. Jong (2007). Financial stability reviews: A first empirical analysis. *Journal of Financial Stability*, 2, 337–355.

Nier, E.W. (2005). Bank stability and transparency. *Journal of Financial Stability*, 2, 342–354.

Schinasi, G.J. (2005). Preserving financial stability. IMF Economic Issues, No. 36.

World Bank (2004). *Doing Business in 2004. Understanding Regulation.* Washington, DC: The World Bank.

Discussion of Landscape of International Banking and Financial Crises

Luc Laeven*
International Monetary Fund

The past 25 years has been a period of intensified financial deregulation and increased financial development. Interest rate controls have been removed in many countries, state ownership of banks has decreased substantially, capital flows are at a historically high level, stock markets have been mostly liberalized, and financial systems have become increasingly integrated, albeit to various degrees. Yet at the same time, this period coincides with a historically large number of financial crises. Figure 1 shows that a systemically important financial crisis was in progress in at least 20 countries during each year of the 1990s. Not only does it appear that crises have become more frequent, they also seem to have increased in intensity. Crises have become increasingly complex, with shocks to macroeconomic stability coinciding with distress in the banking and corporate sectors of the economy. When observing these trends, the following important questions come to mind: Do financial liberalization and internationalization of financial services cause financial crises? Or do they promote financial stability and sound financial systems, as originally intended by those governments that liberalized and opened up their financial systems?

The chapters in this volume fit nicely in a broader literature that explores the pros and cons of financial liberalization and internationalization of financial services. Before I offer my comments on these papers, let me first clarify what I mean by the internationalization of financial services. I consider financial services to be internationalized when 1) any

*Luc Laeven is a senior economist in the Research Department of the International Monetary Fund: The views expressed here are those of the author and do not necessarily represent those of the International Monetary Fund. llaeven@imf.org

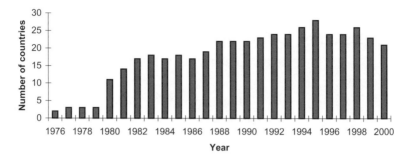

Figure 1. Systemic financial crises in progress worldwide, 1976–2000
Note: This figure shows for each year the number of countries in crisis. Transition economies and countries with incomplete data on the timing of the crisis are excluded. Data refer to systemic financial crises only. Source: Honohan and Laeven (2005).

discrimination in the treatment between foreign and domestic financial services providers has been eliminated, and 2) any barrier to the cross-border provision of financial services has been removed. Spurred by increased trade and migration, financial markets have become increasingly global since the 1960s. This is reflected, among others, in an increase in offshore deposits, increasingly large and volatile portfolio flows, and an increase in cross-border listings. These changes pose new challenges for all countries but especially for countries with small national financial systems. About 40 percent of countries around the world have a banking system with total assets of not even $1 billion (Hanson *et al.*, 2006), less than a moderately sized credit union in the United States. Financial systems and their underpinnings in such countries are ill equipped to deal with the increasingly volatile financial markets and may find it hard to adapt to an increasingly sophisticated and competitive environment for banking. Not surprisingly, foreign banks have increasingly penetrated such markets. Today, foreign banks on average hold about 20 percent of banking system assets in industrial countries and about 25 percent of bank assets in developing countries (Micco *et al.*, 2005). At the same time, we experience the creation of mega banks totaling over one trillion dollars in assets with operations spanning the globe.

With banks becoming increasingly international, national regulators of banking systems face new, complex challenges on a host of issues that arise from the fact that the same bank operates in different markets and regulatory environments. To date, however, a lack of comprehensive data on cross-border banking activities has made it hard to assess the extent to which multinational banks conduct business in host countries. Schoenmaker and van Laecke (2007) make an important contribution by collecting the most comprehensive global dataset of cross-border banking to date. Their data is collected at the bank level and aggregated at the country level. They show that banks in all industrial countries have become increasingly international, with European banks operating the most outside their home markets. By the year 2005, foreign business conducted by US banks amounts to about 22 percent of total activities, while European banks conducted about 48 percent of their business abroad. It is important to make one distinction though. Much of the foreign business conducted by European banks is within other European countries, so if one considers all of as a single market, then strictly speaking the difference between European and US banks is not that large. Schoenmaker and van Laecke construct their measure of internationalization based on rankings of a combination of variables (including total assets, total revenues and employees of the bank), depending on data availability. It would be useful to report rankings based on different measures as well (for example, total loans or deposits) and to show that the rankings and results do not depend on the measure used. As a next step, it would be interesting to analyze which bank characteristics are correlated with foreign activity, and investigate whether geographic factors play a role in determining to location of foreign activity. For example, do European banks operate mostly in other European countries because of language barriers, or does physical distance play a role?

From a theoretical perspective, it is not *a priori* clear that the benefits of internationalization of financial services outweigh the costs. While many countries have had successful experiences, financial liberalization and internationalization pose new risks. Some countries that have experienced financial crises following financial deregulation have put the blame of the crisis on too rapid financial liberalization. Countries with successful experiences (for example, Spain, Ireland and Portugal) tend to have in common that they opened up to foreign banks while also engaging in a process of domestic deregulation. The European Union experience in particular suggests that internationalization and domestic financial deregulation can coincide and be mutually reinforcing. The net benefits of internationalization depend on the regulatory and supervisory framework, which often needs to be adapted. Experience shows that it is vital to strengthen the supporting institutional framework in parallel with deregulation and internationalization (Claessens and Jansen, 2000).

The evidence so far shows that, while there have been many financial crisis of systemic importance, cross-border banking crises (crises that involve banks operating in at least two different markets) have been few thus far. The paper by Carl-Johan Lindgren on cross-border financial crises shows that most financial crises are local in nature. He identifies only five crisis episodes that were cross-border in nature. These include the Mexican crisis of 1994–1995 that spread to countries elsewhere in Latin America; the Meridien Bank default and the resulting crisis in Africa in 1995; the East Asian financial crisis of 1997–2002 that started in Thailand but quickly spread to other countries in the East Asian region; the Russian debt default crisis of 1998–1999 that led to financial turmoil in global financial markets; and the Argentine crisis of 2001–2002. It is interesting to note though that if one considers all countries affected by these five cross-border episodes separately, the number of countries that have faced a cross-border banking crisis in recent years is actually quite large. For example, the Asian crisis started in Thailand but then spread to seven other East Asian countries. As a result, in 1998, more than half of all countries around the world undergoing financial crisis would be considered cross-border crises. Equally interesting is the fact that most of the cross-border banking episodes stem from recent years. This again raises the question to what extent increased financial deregulation and internationalization have been responsible for some of these failures.

Lindgren also makes another important point, often neglected in the banking crisis literature. There are many "near-miss" crises, that is, there have been many shocks to financial systems that did not grow into full-fledged financial crises. It is important to include such non-events into any analyze of what drives financial crisis. Otherwise, the analysis would suffer from selection bias. Charles Goodhart made a similar point during a conference on Systemic Financial Crises that I organized a couple of years ago at the World Bank, so let me refer to this selection bias as the "Goodhart" bias. As a next step, it would be interesting to distinguish between different types of cross-border crises, for example, those arising from financial contagion (including panic) and those related to ownership links between banks in different countries, such as the incident where a failure of a subsidiary in a host country could result in distress of the parent bank in the home country. Fortunately, thus far there have not been many such cases, although with the increase in internationalization of banks such cases may have become increasingly likely. While cross-border crises may not have been common thus far, this may change in the coming years as rapid internationalization is putting increasing pressure on local banking markets, with many banks struggling to survive under increased competition from abroad. These pressures call for the need to further harmonize rules and practices and to improve international cooperation on the exchange of information and oversight of banks.

An important step towards regulatory harmonization has been the set of principles and guidelines developed by the Basel Committee. In 1999, the Bank for International Settlements (BIS) and the Basel Committee on Banking Supervision jointly established the Financial Stability Institute (FSI) to develop best-practice supervision and to assist financial sector supervisors around the world in improving and strengthening their financial systems. Around the same time, the World Bank and the International Monetary Fund (IMF) started to assess the vulnerabilities and development needs of financial sectors under a program known as the Financial Sector Assessment Program (FSAP). The IMF has also introduced a standard set of indicators to measure various dimensions of financial stability, the so-called Financial Soundness Indicators (FSIs), and has made an effort to harmonize data dissemination by collecting data from countries' Central Banks and regulatory bodies through its Special Data Dissemination Standards (SDDS). These efforts and assessments not only point to the need for increased harmonization of rules and standards, but also showcase that supervisory agencies in many countries do not have sufficiently skilled and independent staff to function effectively. Other areas for action raised by these international organizations include, among others: 1) harmonization of accounting standards and disclosure requirements for both banks and corporations; 2) harmonization of securities laws, tax laws and bankruptcy laws; 3) harmonization of the design of financial safety nets, including bank resolution and deposit insurance systems; and 4) anti-trust regulation to make banking markets more contestable.

In line with these new initiatives to introduce standards and codes and publish detailed and internationally comparable statistics on the stability and performance of financial systems, several central banks now publish Financial Stability Reviews (FSRs). Oosterloo and de Haan (2007) compare recent FSRs published by central banks from various countries. They report that many central banks have started to publish FSRs, but that despite efforts to harmonize and standardize data, on average only one-third of the FSIs proposed by the IMF are actually published by central banks. This is not a good record, the more so given that the IMF is about to add new FSIs to the core set of indicators. These findings reinforce the need for a strengthening of the enforcement of such international standards. Standard setting is important but can be rather ineffective without the enforcement of such rules. Oosterloo and de Haan could shed further light on the important question of whether greater disclosure of information enhances financial stability by using regression analysis to analyze which country characteristics are correlated with poor disclosure of FSIs.

Differences in the quality of information and disclosure need not be unintentional. Regulators and supervisors in many countries are captured by local elite. To better understand the effectiveness of a country's regulatory and supervisory framework, one cannot neglect the political economy of bank regulation. This is the theme of a new and controversial book by Caprio *et al.* (2006). This book echoes the idea in Boot and Thakor (1993) that central bankers and regulators are generally not angels but self-interested human beings, like most of us. That such political considerations are not unique to developing countries but also affect banking in developed countries like the United States is clear from the work by Kroszner and Strahan (1999), who show that politics was the main driving force of the relaxation of bank branching restrictions in the United States. To promote checks and balances on regulators and supervisors, Basel II places emphasis on improving the market discipline of banks. The idea is to empower the market through greater disclosure. Greater disclosure, while a prerequisite, need not be a sufficient mechanism for improving the functioning of the market, especially in countries where vested interests or corruption make it hard to enforce rules. In countries where market discipline is hampered by the countervailing force of an incumbent elite, foreign entry can bolster the financial system by creating a constituency for improved regulation and supervision, better disclosure rules, and improvements in the legal and regulatory framework for the provision of financial services (Rajan and Zingales, 2003). National interests can be another force blocking foreign entry, but foreign pressure can change the rules of the game, as Italy has recently shown.

While openness and the removal of barriers and restrictions to banking should generally be encouraged, recent research also shows that the benefits of financial liberalization and integration do not come without some risks. These risks need to be carefully monitored and managed. As restrictions on the activities banks can engage in are lifted, bank will diversify in activities other than banking, such as insurance, investment banking, and real estate. While such diversification allows banks to reap the benefits from economies of scope, a recent paper by Laeven and Levine (2006) shows that much of diversification is value-destroying, as bank managers pursue their own interests, and is more interested in empire-building than in maximizing shareholder value. Of course, activity restriction on banks are no solution, because they tend to limit financial development (Jayaratne and Strahan, 1996) and reduce bank stability (Laeven and Levine, 2006), but supervisors need to watch out for these risks as banks engage in increasingly diverse and complex activities. Also, while foreign bank entry should be encouraged, the benefit may depend on the quality and type of banks that enter. Research shows that entry of "quality" foreign banks can promote competition and improve bank performance by eroding domestic vested interests and reducing corruption in lending (Barth *et al.*, 2004; and Ongena and Giannetti, 2006). It may be necessary to set some minimum standards to safeguard the quality of entrants. Furthermore, in countries with small financial systems, financial integration through foreign bank ownership may lead to a high concentration of foreign ownership, which poses potential negative implications for banking and payment system stability in case of failure of the foreign parent bank, including uncertainty about repayment of depositors arising from differences in deposit insurance schemes. An example is the recent entry of Austrian and Italian banks in Eastern Europe. These banks now dominate many of the banking markets in these countries but their foreign operations are still small compared to the operations in their home countries. In such cross-border cases, it is crucial to agree to loss-sharing arrangements between the taxpayers of both countries in case of bank failures.

Financial integration may also increase the risk of financial contagion, that is, the spread of country-specific shocks to the financial systems of other countries. The East Asian financial crisis of 1997–1998 has spurred a large literature on financial contagion in the East Asian countries. While most financial contagion tends to be regional, there have several recent cases where one could argue that contagion has spread across the globe. For example, Lindgren (2007) shows that the Russian financial crisis of 1998 caused banking sector problems in far away Ecuador, Brazil, and Argentina. One wonders whether such phenomena are at least in part driven by increased integration of world financial markets.

What are solutions to these new global problems? A global regulatory and supervisory authority? As long as financial systems are still predominantly local in nature, it may be more effective to improve the cooperation between existing institutions. Such cooperation and exchange of information should be encouraged both at a global and at a regional level to avoid financial contagion. Of course, laws and regulations need, as much as possible, to be harmonized at a global level, and much has been done in this regard. Multilateral organizations can help through multilateral surveillance and by initiating multilateral and regional agreements to provide prompt financial assistance subject to certain conditions.

In conclusion, internationalization of financial services can offer countries important benefits, but these benefits do not come without risks. Internationalization can help build more robust and efficient financial systems by 1) introducing international practices and standards, 2) by improving the quality, efficiency, and breadth of financial services, and 3) by allowing more stable sources of funds. The extent of these benefits depend on how internationalization is phased in with other types of financial reform, particularly domestic financial deregulation and capital account liberalization.

References

Barth, J., G. Caprio and R. Levine (2004). Bank regulation and supervision: What works best?. *Journal of Financial Intermediation*, 12, 205–248.

Barth, J., G. Caprio and R. Levine (2006). *Rethinking Bank Regulation: Till Angels Govern*. Cambridge University Press.

Boot, A. and A. Thakor (1993). Self-interested bank regulation. *American Economic Review*, 83(2), 206–212.

Caprio, G., L. Laeven and R. Levine (2006). Governance and bank valuation. *Journal of Financial Intermediation*, forthcoming.

Claessens, S. and M. Jansen (2000). The internationalization of financial services: Issues and lessons for developing countries: overview. In *The Internationalization of Financial Services: Issues and Lessons for Developing Countries*, S. Claessens, and M. Jansen (eds.). The Hague: Kluwer Law International.

Giannetti, M. and S. Ongena (2006). Financial integration and entrepreneurial activity: Evidence from foreign bank entry in emerging markets. Mimeo, Tilburg University, November.

Hanson, J., P. Honohan and G. Majnoni (2006). Globalization and national financial systems: Issues of integration and size. In *Globalization and National Financial Systems*, J. Hanson, P. Honohan and G. Majnoni (eds.). The World Bank and Oxford University Press.

Hawkins, J. and P. Turner (2001). International financial reform: Regulatory and other issues. In *International Financial Contagion*, S. Claessens and K. Forbes (eds.). Kluwer Academic Publishers.

Honohan, P. and L. Laeven (2005). *Systemic Financial Crises: Containment and Resolution*. Cambridge, UK: Cambridge University Press.

Jayaratne, J. and P.E. Strahan (1996). The finance-growth nexus: Evidence from bank branch deregulation. *Quarterly Journal of Economics*, 101, 639–670.

Kroszner, R. and P. Strahan (1999). What drives deregulation? Economics and politics of the relaxation of bank branching restrictions. *Quarterly Journal of Economics*, 114(4), 1437–1467.

Laeven, L. and R. Levine (2006). Corporate governance, regulation, and bank risk-taking. Mimeo, Brown University and International Monetary Fund.

Laeven, L. and R. Levine (2007). Is there a diversification discount in financial conglomerates?. *Journal of Financial Economics*, forthcoming.

Lindgren, C.-J. (2007). Actual and near-miss cross-border crises. In *International Financial Instability: Global Banking and National Regulation*, D. Evanoff, G. Kaufman and J.R. LaBrosse (eds.), Singapore: World Scientific Publishing.

Micco, A., U. Panizza and M. Yañez (2005). Bank ownership and performance. Mimeo, Inter-American Development Bank.

Oosterloo, S., J. de Haan and R.A.P. Jong (2007). A review of financial stability reports. In *International Financial Instability: Global Banking and National Regulation*, D. Evanoff, G. Kaufman and J.R. LaBrosse (eds.). Singapore: World Scientific Publishing.

Rajan, R. and L. Zingales (2003). The great reversals: The politics of financial development in the twentieth century. *Journal of Financial Economics*, 69(1), 5–50.

Schoenmaker, D. and C. van Laecke (2007). Current state of cross-border banking. In *International Financial Instability: Global Banking and National Regulation*, D. Evanoff, G. Kaufman and J.R. LaBrosse (eds.). Singapore: World Scientific Publishing.

III. CAUSES AND CONDITIONS FOR CROSS-BORDER INSTABILITY TRANSMISSION AND THREATS TO STABILITY

Cross-Border Contagion Links and Banking Problems in the Nordic Countries

Bent Vale*
Norges Bank

1. Introduction

In Europe, the banking directives issued by the European Commission have facilitated much more cross-border banking inside the European Union than was the case ten to fifteen years ago. Through cross-border activities and mergers banks can realize both diversification benefits and scale economies. However, as the pace of cross-border banking has increased, there have also been more discussions among policymakers concerning the potential costs of cross-border banking, including the potential for cross-border contagion. In this chapter, we will discuss how contagion can take place with different cross-border banking structures, and depending on where the problems originate, in the home country of the banking group or in a host country. Cross-border banking, both within a subsidiary structure and within a branch structure, has become quite extensive between the four large Nordic countries during the last five years. Much of the discussion in this chapter will therefore explicitly or implicitly refer to the Nordic banking structure. However, most of the discussion of bank problems will be about potential problems, as there have been very few critical situations for banks in the Nordic countries over the last 10 years. We will not discuss how to meet the challenges facing national financial authorities regarding crisis resolution involving

*Bent Vale is head of research for the banking and finance group of the Research Department in Norges Bank (central bank of Norway). During the work with this chapter, the author benefited from discussions with and comments from Arild J. Lund, Pål Håvard Martinsen, Thorvald G. Moe, Kjell Bjørn Nordal, Roberto Rigobon, and Garry J. Schinasi. Pål Mathiesen has provided research assistance. Views and conclusions in this chapter are those of the author and cannot be attributed to Norges Bank nor to any of the persons mentioned.

inter-Nordic banks. This chapter solely aims at describing how cross-border contagion can take place when there are large transnational banks.

The chapter is organized as follows: First, we present briefly the major economic reasons for organizing banks across national borders. This is followed by a short description of the banking structure among the Nordic countries and a discussion of contagion during the Nordic banking crises in the early 1990s. Next, we discuss how country specific bank problems in a subsidiary and then in the parent bank can affect banking activities of the whole banking group. Then, we look at how country specific loan losses that lead to a bank failure can be transmitted across borders in a banking group. Throughout these discussions of contagion we will also consider the difference between a branch structure and a subsidiary structure.

2. Why Cross-Border Banking?

One obvious reason for cross-border bank mergers in small countries like the Nordic ones is the possibility of realizing economies of scale in operating costs without creating national banks with monopoly power.[1] Secondly, there are benefits of diversification regarding credit risk as long as the countries in question do not have the same industry structure. This potential for diversification is present among the Nordic countries. Whereas Finland has developed a large manufacturing sector of consumer electronics (Nokia) and has considerable pulp industries, Sweden also has considerable production of machinery and vehicles, Denmark has a relatively diversified industry, and finally Norway is heavy in production of energy, shipping and fisheries. This diversification can then be combined with the expertise in certain industries that the subsidiaries or branches of each country have gained.

3. The Nordic Banking Structure

In the Nordic countries banking has over the last decade become a true inter-Nordic business. The second largest Nordic banking group in terms of total assets, Nordea with large subsidiaries in the four Nordic countries

---

[1] The existence of economies of scale in banking has been somewhat controversial in the academic literature. See Berger and Humphrey (1997) for an overview, and Humphrey and Vale (2004) regarding bank mergers and economies of scale.

Denmark, Finland, Norway and Sweden, was based on merger between large nationwide banks in these four countries. Nordea's parent bank and head office is in Stockholm. In terms of lending, it is by far the largest bank in Finland and among the three largest in Denmark, Norway and Sweden. Similarly Den Danske Bank, which is now (June 2006) the largest Nordic banking group and the largest in Denmark, acquired in 1999 Norway's No. 4 bank, Fokus Bank as a subsidiary. Den Danske Bank also has a considerable branch network in Sweden. Handelsbanken, No. 2 in Sweden, has significant branch networks in Denmark, Finland and Norway. Finally, Glitnir Bank in Iceland acquired BNbank as a subsidiary in Norway in 2005, the 8th largest bank in Norway.

To summarize, among the largest Nordic banks Handelsbanken has a branch structure, whereas Nordea has its parent bank in Sweden and operates through large subsidiaries in Denmark, Finland and Sweden. Den Danske Bank operates both through subsidiaries (Norway) and through branches (Sweden). Nevertheless, the day to day operations of the two latter banking firms are highly similar to those of a pure branch structure.[2]

Some figures can serve to illustrate the scope of inter-Nordic banking. As of 2004, branches and subsidiaries from other Nordic countries constituted 59.1 percent of the total banking sector assets in Finland, 23.4 percent in Norway,[3] 13.8 percent in Denmark, but only 5.6 percent in Sweden and 0 percent in Iceland. In all the European Union (EU) countries combined only 12.6 percent of total banking assets belonged to branches and subsidiaries from other European Economic Area[4] countries.

Before going into the issue of contagion with the present cross-border banking structure, it can be useful to dwell a little on the banking crises that hit the Nordic countries in the early 1990s.

4. The Nordic Banking Crises in the Early 1990s[5]

When first Norway and then Finland and Sweden were hit by systemic banking crises in 1991 and 1992 respectively, there were no Nordic

---

[2] Nordea wants to reorganize into a branch structure, while Den Danske Bank has applied to transform Fokus Bank from a subsidiary into a branch.

[3] Does not include Glitnir's acquisition of BNbank, which took place in April 2005.

[4] The European Economic Area consists of the EU plus Iceland, Liechtenstein, and Norway.

[5] A comparison of the banking crises in the three Nordic countries can be found in Sandal (2004).

banks with any significant cross-border operation in the other Nordic countries. Nevertheless, the crises in the three countries took place within the same two-year period. For the purpose of this conference it may therefore be of interest to consider briefly whether there was any cross-border contagion at work in spite of little cross-border banking activities between the countries concerned. The causes of the crises were similar but domestic factors, such as deregulation of the banking system without adequate attention to credit risk, neither in the banks, nor among supervisors; lending and asset price booms; and finally bursting of these booms when the domestic demand had to consolidate. Several large banks had huge credit losses bringing them into failure. In Finland's case this was aggravated by the collapse of the Soviet Union.

At this time all the three countries had their national currencies pegged to the Deutsche Mark, and all cross-border capital controls had been lifted, that is, the three currencies were fully convertible. Hence all the three countries had to raise their interest rates in response to the German interest rate hike in connection with German reunification in 1990. In that year Norway was in a recession, and if interest rates could have been set according to domestic considerations they should have dropped.

During the fall of 1992, when the banking crises had unfolded both in Sweden and Finland, the Swedish krona and the Finnish Mark were deemed as overvalued, and a speculative attack on the two currencies started. Given the fixed exchange rate regime in place interest rates in Finland and Sweden reached extremely high levels during the fall of 1992.[6] Although the fundamentals in Norway at that time were better than in Sweden, the Norwegian krone was also attacked. Traders in the forex market expected that Norway, having Sweden as its largest trading partner, would have to let the Norwegian krone depreciate if Sweden devalued or depreciated. This effect was aggravated by the fact that the banks in all the three countries had funded a large part of their expansion in the boom period abroad. Foreign investors grouped the three countries together and tried to reduce their exposure to all of them. Hence, Norway also had to keep interest rates extremely high during the fall of 1992. This deepened the credit losses and the banking crisis in Norway. In this way one could say there was a contagion from Sweden's banking crisis to Norwegian banks: the run against the Swedish krona, partly caused by the Swedish banking crisis, also implied an interest rate

---

[6] In Sweden, the overnight rate set by the Riksbank was for a time as high as 500 percent.

hike in Norway, further worsening conditions for the already troubled Norwegian banks.

5. Potential Contagion Links under Nordic Cross-Border Banking

How will cross-border banking affect the contagion links among countries? This is difficult to tell before a new crisis has hit. Fortunately, conditions in the Nordic banking sector are currently very good. However, it may be instructive to develop some hypothetical cases in order to review the potential contagion links under cross-border banking. Nevertheless, I will use one rather undramatic situation in the Nordea Banking Group to illustrate some points. In most of this chapter, the focus will be on what might happen if an inter-Nordic bank group suffers country specific severe loan losses in one country. In particular, we want to analyze the effects on the banking activities in the other Nordic countries. What would be the difference compared to a situation with only national banks? Much of the reasoning below is common to both a subsidiary structure and a branch structure. In cases where the contagion mechanism would be different depending on the structure, this will be discussed.

6. Country Specific Bank Problems in a Subsidiary but Not Failure

6.1 *The case with only independent nationwide banks*

Consider a small group of, say, four countries. At first, let us assume there is at least one large *independent nationwide bank* in each country, that is, there are no significant cross-border banking activities between the countries, neither as subsidiaries nor as branches. Then, let the bank in one country be subject to country specific severe loan losses. The losses raise doubt about the bank's capital adequacy and its overall future.

Now the bank will be subject to corrective actions by its money market creditors and uninsured depositors.[7] Indeed, the short-term funding from money market creditors may be completely shut off. Money market lenders have less information than the bank itself about the quality of its

---

[7] Even insured depositors may start withdrawing deposits when news of severe problems at a bank occur. See Davenport and McDill (2006) for empirical evidence.

loan portfolio. Having observed one recent incidence of severe loan losses, they may fear that there is more to come, and the bank may be considered a "lemon" in the money market. For the same reason, the bank may not be able to raise sufficient equity in the market to ensure that it satisfies the capital requirements with the current size of its loan portfolio. Consequently, the bank will be forced to curb its lending. This may have detrimental effects also on its sound borrowers.[8] These are the main real economic costs in the wake of the problems of the large bank in this country.

6.2 *The case with a cross-border banking group*

Now, assume instead that the large bank in that specific country is a *subsidiary of a bank group* consisting of similarly large banks in all the four countries, one of which is home to the parent bank of the group. The three subsidiaries are 100 percent owned by the parent bank. Although the bank group has a subsidiary structure, the activities of the subsidiaries are assumed to be tightly controlled by and integrated with the head office or the parent bank of the group, as if the group was just one bank. This situation is fairly similar to the present situation of the inter-Nordic banking group Nordea. Let the subsidiary in one of the host countries, we label the country B, suffer the same country specific loan losses as we assumed in the previous case, and assume there are no particular shocks occurring in the other three countries. Although the losses are sufficiently large to raise doubt about capital adequacy in the subsidiary, we assume that there is no question about capital adequacy for the consolidated group. In this situation the subsidiary in B will need fresh funding, and possibly have to raise new equity or reduce its loan portfolio.

However, as regards the ability to raise equity, the funding situation in the money market, or in the market for uninsured deposits, the situation is

---

[8] Slovin *et al.* (1993) document how the share prices of corporate borrowers at Continental Illinois suffered on the news of the bank's huge problems. Chava and Purnanandam (2006) find similar results for bank dependent firms during the Russian debt crisis. Both these studies indicate that borrowers to some extent are stuck with their present bank. These findings can be explained by the switching costs borrowers face if they switch bank. Kim *et al.* (2003) estimate borrower switching costs to be as high as one third of the interest rates on bank loans. These costs may partly be due to borrowers being informationally locked in at their borrowing bank that has obtained private information about borrower quality through the bank-borrower relationship.

likely to be quite different from what it was in the case where the bank was an independent bank only in country B.

The parent bank would be the obvious source of new funding or equity in this situation. Would that bank be more willing to supply the funds than outside investors were in the previous case? There are three reasons why the answer is yes: Firstly, in a tightly governed and integrated banking group the parent bank will have more precise information about the actual quality of the loan portfolio in its country B subsidiary than external money market lenders or stock market investors would have had if the subsidiary had been an independent bank. Hence, the parent bank needs not to worry about the country B subsidiary being a "lemon" to the same extent as outside investors would do.[9] Secondly, and related to the first point, the parent bank will, unlike outside investors, have the full control of the capital they invest. Thirdly, to maintain the reputation of the banking group, the parent bank would not want to see sound borrowers in one of its subsidiaries being credit constrained due to lack of funding or capital in the subsidiary.[10] Hence, the asymmetric information or principal agent problems that could shut off money market funding or new equity finance for an independent bank will not be present when the bank is a subsidiary.

Regarding funding in the money market, in a banking group with a subsidiary structure, the money market funding of the subsidiaries may for the most part be supplied by the parent bank or other subsidiaries in the group. To illustrate, by year-end 2004, 80 percent of Nordea Norway's interbank funding was supplied by the rest of the Nordea group.

To conclude the comparison of an independent bank and a subsidiary in case of severe losses but not failure: When the bank is independent both problems in the money market and problems in raising new equity can cause a curb in lending also to sound borrowers of the bank. However, if the bank is part of a banking group, additional funding or the injection of new capital after severe losses would be much easier. Detrimental effects following a country specific loan loss shock in subsidiary B is dampened through the intervention of the rest of the banking group.

---

[9] Myers and Majluf (1984) is the "classic" paper regarding the principal agent problem between outside investors and incumbent investors when new equity is issued.

[10] One could argue that the same considerations would be made by the bank owners of a large national independent bank. However, in such banks ownership is likely to be rather dispersed. Therefore, there would be a coordination problem among the owners if it was suggested that existing owners should inject new equity.

From the point of view of the other banks in the group, there may be a slight contagion from country B. The parent bank may be subject to slightly more risk by putting up more equity for subsidiary bank B. Furthermore, money market lenders may be worried that the problems in bank B is a symptom of problems elsewhere in the bank group. This being a bank group tightly controlled by the parent bank, investors could fear that loan loss problems in one subsidiary may be due to mistakes by the management of the parent bank and be a signal of problems in the whole bank group. Hence, the bank group may be subject to stricter conditions for funding in the money market. In that way, problems in bank B are partly transmitted to the other group members. On the other hand, should there be a country specific shock in either of these countries, they will also benefit from being part of a diversified group.

With a branch structure the situation would have been much the same, except, of course, that there would not be the question of separate money market funding or raising equity for a branch.

The mechanism described above is an example of the working of the diversification that follows from being part of a larger group. The detrimental effects to a subsidiary from a country specific shock are lower than they would have been had the same shock occurred if the bank was an independent bank. Such diversification is one of the advantages that can be achieved by cross-border banking. A premium to pay for this diversification is the somewhat stricter money market conditions the whole group may face if one of its subsidiaries experience problems in its home market.

It may, however, be the case that a severe loss situation in a subsidiary is an indication that this subsidiary in general has an unsound loan portfolio. If so, the parent bank would not and should not be interested in investing more equity in the subsidiary. Curbing its lending activity in such a situation would actually be socially desirable.

6.3 *Some experience so far regarding the Nordea group*

As mentioned earlier, there have not been any serious banking problems in the Nordic countries since the emergence of strong cross-border banking groups about five to six years ago. Nevertheless, in 2003, there were large loan losses in Nordea Norway. In the fall of 2002, several other smaller Norwegian banks also had severe loan loss problems. Comparing the Nordea case to one of these other banks can to some extent illustrate the benefits to a country of having a bank as a subsidiary in a larger international bank group.

For 2003, Nordea Norway reported annual loan losses that amounted to 1.17 percent of its gross lending. The corresponding figure for all banks in Norway (including foreign subsidiaries and branches) was only 0.53 percent. However, Nordea Norway's capital ratio never fell to a critically low level. In the quarterly statements through 2003 its tier 1 capital ratio was never reported below 8.1 percent and its total capital ratio (tier 1 plus tier 2) was never below 10.0 percent. It did not experience problems in the short-term money market or interbank market, mainly because it had most of its interbank borrowing from the rest of the Nordea group. For the Nordea Group as such, the losses of Nordea Norway in 2003 were a non-event, with no effect on the interest rate the group had to pay to external creditors in the market. The reported loan losses of the consolidated group were negligible in all quarters of 2003.

However, had Nordea Norway instead been an independent bank, reports of the large loan losses relative to the rest of the industry would most likely have caused some difficulties in the short term money market and the bank would have had to pay an extra premium. Some evidence supporting this hypothesis could be the following: In mid-2002 there were rumors in the press that an independent Norwegian regional bank, Nordlandsbanken, (its size was about one eighth of Nordea Norway) had relatively large loans to a high-flying factoring company whose solvency was questionable. As a result of these rumors, Nordlandsbanken had to pay an extra premium in the money market. By end-2002, the rumors had proven correct and the bank recorded loan losses sufficient to bring its capital below the required minimum. Nordlandsbanken was then acquired by Norway's largest bank, DnB.

7. Severe Problems, but Not Failure in the Parent Bank

Assume now the parent bank is hit by country specific loan losses similar to those subsidiary B suffered in the previous section. The other banks of the group do not suffer loan losses. After the losses there will be uncertainty in the market about the parent bank's and the consolidated banking group's ability to satisfy the capital requirements. Hence, the parent bank will have problems regarding its short-term funding in the money market. External uninsured creditors of the banking group may require it either to raise new equity or to curb its lending. The parent bank or the consolidated banking group would now face the same problem as any independent bank in raising new external equity from the market. How would this affect the banking activities of its subsidiaries? As separate legal entities, whose abilities to satisfy the capital requirements are not questioned, the subsidiaries should not meet any new problems from external creditors in the money market. However, if the evaluation of borrowers and credit decisions in the banking group are tightly controlled by the parent bank, money market lenders may fear that the apparently country specific problems of the parent bank also may be a sign of poor credit evaluation that can affect the subsidiaries. In that case also the subsidiaries would face problems in the money market.

If the parent bank cannot at any reasonable cost raise sufficient new external equity to meet the capital requirements both for the parent bank and for the consolidated banking group, it may be forced to curb some lending. Where would lending activity be reduced, mainly in the parent bank or in the subsidiaries? How would the situation be if instead of a subsidiary structure there were a branch structure?

Empirics from the US in the early 1990s may give us some clue. Peek and Rosengren (1997) study the effects on lending by Japanese bank subsidiaries and branches in the US when Japanese parent banks no longer could meet their domestic capital requirements due to losses in Japan in the early 1990s. In particular, Peek and Rosengren find that branches significantly and strongly reduced their lending, whereas they cannot detect any significant reduction in lending by the subsidiaries. They attribute this result partly to the capital regulation in place in Japan at that time, where capital requirements were in force only for the parent bank but not for the consolidated banking group.

What lesson can be drawn from this study to the Nordic case? In Europe, the capital requirements have to be met both by a parent bank and by the consolidated banking group. To meet both these requirements, the most effective approach would be just to reduce the lending at the parent bank, as long as there is a subsidiary structure. Curbing loans at the subsidiaries would not affect the capital ratio of the parent bank, unless it is combined with similarly reduced interbank lending from the parent bank to the subsidiaries. Hence, in this situation it is most likely that reduction in lending mainly will happen at the parent rather than at the subsidiaries.

In a branch structure this could be quite different. Then, the parent bank and the consolidated banking group are the same. Hence, to meet the capital requirement after a negative shock in the home country the bank would be much more likely to curb lending across the board, that is, also across the foreign branches.[11]

8. Diversification: Branches versus Subsidiaries

In the discussion above, we have assumed that the subsidiaries are tightly controlled by and integrated with the parent bank, as tight as if it was one bank. That is exactly how it would be in a branch structure. But, what is then the difference between a subsidiary and a branch structure? The important difference for the issues discussed in this chapter is that a subsidiary is a separate legal entity with its own capital and supervised by the supervisors of the host country. With a branch structure, there is only one legal entity, the bank in the home country, with all its activities, at home and abroad, in principle supervised by the supervisors of the home country.

Since a subsidiary is a separate legal entity, it can fail alone due to loan losses in its own loan portfolio, without the parent bank or the rest of the banking group failing. A branch, however, cannot fail unless the bank in the home country fails. The viability of a branch depends on the soundness of the whole banking group, whereas a subsidiary is more dependent on the quality of its own loan portfolio. In that sense, a branch structure provides more diversification benefits than does a subsidiary structure.

From the point of view of a host country, having a foreign bank as a branch relative to a subsidiary implies that one "imports" the financial stability or instability from the home country. Consider a country with a poorly diversified economy and relatively high probability of failure among its domestic banks. Hosting a large branch from a country with a well-diversified economy and low probability of banking problems would reduce the probability of a bank failure in the host country. Conversely, hosting a large bank from a country with relatively high probability of bank failures would increase the probability of bank failures in the host country.

---

[11] In the case with the lending reduction by Japanese bank branches in the US, Peek and Rosengren attribute their strong results to the reluctance by Japanese banks to curb the lending to their long term domestic borrowers. Instead, they shift their loan shrinkage to their overseas branches. The larger extent of common business culture between the Nordic countries than between Japan and US though, would make such a strong effect on branches in other Nordic countries less likely.

9. Country Specific Problems That Cause Failure of a Cross-Border Bank

In this section, I will extend the previous discussions to situations where loan losses are so large that the bank in question loses its entire capital, that is, it fails. First, assume a huge and severe country specific shock in the home country of the parent bank that causes it to fail. However, at the same time the loan portfolios of the subsidiaries in the countries not directly hit by the shock are still sound and their capital is intact.

Next, I will consider a situation with huge loan losses in a subsidiary causing it to fail but not large enough to cause the parent bank or the consolidated banking group to fail.

Finally, I consider a situation with severe loan losses in all the banks belonging to the group. In this case the losses are assumed large enough to make all the banks in the group fail. Of course, there could also be cases where two or three of the banks in the group fail but the remaining part is healthy. In principle, these latter cases would be rather similar to the case where the fatal loan losses occur in just one bank. In the three cases, I assume there is no immediate government rescue operation.

9.1 *Failure of the banking group due to the parent bank*

In the period just prior to these loan losses and failure occurring, there may have been indications about the problem in the parent bank of the group. Hence, at least the parent bank may face difficulties with its money market funding. So far, the situation is similar to the case described above with non-fatal problems in the parent bank. Similarly, the banking group as such may face stricter conditions from external money market lenders.

Once the failure of the parent bank has occurred, creditors and uninsured depositors in that bank will face some losses. The uninsured depositors and creditors in the subsidiaries should not suffer any losses. These banks can still meet their claims. The agency or institution that handles the remainder of the parent bank will immediately become the owner of the subsidiaries. But how will the banking activities of those subsidiaries be affected after the failure of their parent bank?

The answer to this question will depend on how tightly the three subsidiaries were integrated with and controlled by the now failed parent bank. If the control had been rather loose, and the subsidiaries were operated more or less as potential stand-alone units, it would be relatively easy to sell off the subsidiaries and let them continue as separate banks or a new banking group. Potential buyers of the subsidiaries would consider them more or less as independent solvent banks that are up for sale.

However, the more difficult case would arise if the parent bank had had a fairly tight control of the lending decisions in its subsidiaries, and their operations were strongly integrated with the parent bank. In that case, potential buyers of the subsidiaries may have reason to fear that some of the credit evaluation failures which brought down the parent might have been transmitted into the subsidiaries. Furthermore, buyers may suspect that the assets have been switched between the parent bank and the subsidiaries, that is, the parent bank may have off-loaded some of its bad loans to the subsidiaries in a failed attempt to avoid failure. Both this fear of "lemons" among the subsidiaries, and the tight integration of the subsidiaries' infrastructure with the failed parent bank would make it harder to sell the subsidiaries. Hence, stakeholders, like for instance borrowers, in these subsidiaries could be negatively affected.

Note that in this case of failure by the parent bank, what was a blessing when there were non-fatal losses at a subsidiary, namely the strong integration and the tight control of the whole group by its parent bank, has now become a curse.

Next, consider the situation with a branch structure. If the same country specific shock in the home country topples the bank, disentangling the sound pieces of its foreign branches would be even harder than in the case with tightly controlled and integrated subsidiaries. In a branch structure, there is no way in which particular parts of the portfolio of a branch legally belongs to that branch, since it is not a legal entity. Hence, the process of separating the sound parts of the bank's loan portfolio and trying to sell off the branches as stand-alone banks, may take longer time. Consequently, the banking activities of the failed bank even in the host countries where the fatal shock did not happen can be severely hampered for a while.

As mentioned previously, a branch structure can provide more benefits of diversification compared to a subsidiary structure in more or less normal times. However, a branch structure can turn out to be a disadvantage in the more extreme case of a failure of a large cross-border bank.

In general, the economic costs of a bank failure will depend on how swift the resolution of the bank failure can be handled. When a large bank fails a swift resolution will usually require government intervention. If the large failing bank is the parent in a cross-border banking group, the need for coordination of the resolution efforts between the different national governments is likely to reduce the swiftness of a resolution implying larger economic costs of the bank failure.

9.2 *Failure of a subsidiary*

Prior to such a failure, the subsidiary in question and the parent bank and the other subsidiaries may experience problems in the money market as described in the section where we considered non-fatal problems in one subsidiary. Much of the discussion in that section will also be valid here.

Once the failure of the subsidiary has occurred, how might that be handled inside the group assuming there is no immediate government rescue operation? Had the failed subsidiary been an independent bank, there would not have been any agent outside the government which would have had an interest in somehow rescuing the bank and making it continue its banking operations. However, when the failed bank is a subsidiary inside a banking group, and it is not large enough to topple the parent bank or the consolidated group, things may be different. The interest of the other banks in the group in maintaining the group's reputation may give them an incentive to rescue the failed subsidiary, provided of course they can put up the necessary capital. In a banking group with tight control of the subsidiaries, the parent bank will be better informed than any outside investor, including the government, about the future prospects of the failed subsidiary after injection of new equity.

From the point of view of the host country of the failed subsidiary, this would be an example of the diversification benefits from cross-border banking. A failed bank can be rescued without involving government money. For the other countries, however, infusion of new equity in the failed subsidiary is an example of potential contagion from that subsidiary.

9.3 *A common shock: Failure of all banks in the group*

This situation is not really different from the case with independent national banks failing at the same time. The main difference would be that with the failure of a transnational banking group, the resolution process would be complicated by the need to coordinate government interventions.

10. Concluding Remarks

Diversification across countries reduces the probability of a bank failure. Credit losses in one country that otherwise could have detrimental effects on an independent national bank can to some extent be diluted in the larger transnational banking group. However, what appears as the benefits of diversification for one country can be considered as more or less serious contagion by other countries in which the banking group operates. In the extreme case of a transnational bank failing due to problems in its home country, there can be contagion to stakeholders in branches or subsidiaries that by themselves are financially sound. To what extent contagion can be reduced by coordinated resolution efforts between countries remains a matter for future discussions.

References

Berger, A.N. and D.B. Humphrey (1997). Efficiency and financial institutions: International survey and directions for future research. *European Journal of Operational Research*, 98, 172–212.

Chava, S. and A. Purnanandam (2006). The effect of banking crisis on bank-dependent borrowers. Paper presented at the 2nd FIRS conference in Shanghai, June.

Davenport, A.M. and K.M. McDill (2006). The depositor behind the discipline: A micro-level case study of hamilton bank. *Journal of Financial Services Research*, 30, 93–109.

Humphrey, D.B. and B. Vale (2004). Scale economies, bank merger, and electronic payments: A spline function approach. *Journal of Banking and Finance*, 28, 1671–1696.

Kim, M., D. Kliger and B. Vale (2003). Estimating switching costs: The case of banking. *Journal of Financial Intermediation*, 12, 25–56.

Myers, S. and M. Majluf (1984). Corporate financing and investment decisions: When firms have information that investors do not have. *Journal of Financial Economics*, 13, 187–221.

Peek, J. and E.S. Rosengren (1997). The international transmission of financial shocks: The case of Japan. *American Economic Review*, 87, 495–505.

Sandal, K. (2004). The nordic banking crises in the early 1990s — Resolution methods and fiscal costs. In *The Norwegian Banking Crisis*, T.G. Moe, J.A. Solheim and B. Vale (eds.). Norges Bank Occasional Papers No. 33. Oslo: Norges Bank.

Slovin, M.B., M.E. Sushka and J.A. Polonchek (1993). The value of bank durability: Borrowers as bank stakeholders. *Journal of Finance*, 48, 247–266.

Currency Crises, (Hidden) Linkages and Volume

Max Bruche*
CEMFI

Jon Danielsson
London School of Economics

Gabriele Galati[†]
Bank for International Settlements

1. Introduction

The transmission of shocks across countries via the currency markets — both for fundamental as well as for seemingly unexplained reasons — is an important concern for policymakers. While financial globalization has been the catalyst for significant economic benefits, it also has the potential to increase the likelihood of spillovers of market turbulence and uncertainty across countries. These may occur even between countries that do not share any obvious close linkages, such as geography, trade or development levels. An extensive body of literature has documented country linkages via capital markets, most prominently during the Asian crisis. Considerable anecdotal evidence of contagion in foreign exchange markets exists, which has attracted considerable attention of policymakers and market analysts. Nonetheless, formal analysis of such events has been relatively scarce compared to contagion in equity markets. This lack of formal modeling

*Max Bruche is an assistant professor of economics at CEMFI. Jon Danielsson is a reader in accounting and finance at the London School of Economics. Gabriele Galati is on staff at the Bank for International Settlements. The authors thank the discussant and the conference audience for excellent comments and suggestions. All errors are their responsibility. This paper, and subsequent updates can be downloaded from their website, www.Risk Research.org. This paper is based on the conference presentation and summarizes the results in Bruche et al. (2006). The corresponding author is Jon Danielsson, j.danielsson@ lse.ac.uk. The views expressed in this article are those of the authors and do not necessarily reflect those of the BIS.

[†]The views expressed in this article are those of the authors and do not necessarily reflect those of the Bank for International Settlements.

provides the motivation for our work. We propose two extensions to the extant literature on contagion. First, we extend and adopt extant contagion models to currency markets. Second, we introduce foreign exchange market turnover, or volume, as a key variable to capture country linkages.

A number of models of contagion have been proposed in the literature, most of which were developed with the Asian crisis of 1997 in mind.[1] Tests for contagion are frequently based on changes in correlations, where the significance of the test statistic is adopted to allow for asynchronous volatility levels. As argued by Bruche *et al.* (2007), some common tests lack robustness for small sample sizes and are therefore unable to recognize contagious episodes unless the change in correlations is unrealistically large or the contagious episode is long-lasting. While this may not be a concern in episodes such as the Asian crisis in 1997, currency crises typically tend to be short-lived, lasting often days or weeks rather than months, and thus are too short for most available tests. Consequently, applying these techniques might lead to a possibly erroneous conclusion of interdependence rather than contagion.

Bruche *et al.* (2007) propose an extension of the literature in two main directions. First, they develop a factor structure specific to currency markets by adopting extant models to currency markets. Second, they consider the specific importance of trading volume for currency trading, both during tranquil and crisis periods. This enables them to document linkages in currency markets based on both price and quantity movements.

Their model is in part motivated by the extensive research on informational asymmetries in foreign exchange markets, such as the market microstructure models surveyed in Lyons (2002). In such a context, linkages may arise, for example, through trading activity by hedge funds and proprietary trading desks of commercial banks whose portfolios span many emerging market countries. As a result, when embedded within a contagion model, trading volume has the potential to provide useful information on a number of issues important to policymakers, such as the identification of fragility, examination of crises and near-crises, identification of cross-country linkages and, in particular, the danger of contagious failure. One possible channel, which has received much attention recently, is the spreading of market pressure through the unwinding of carry trade

---

[1] Surveys of this literature can be found, for example, in Claessens *et al.* (2001), Forbes and Rigobon (2001), Moser (2003), and Claessens and Forbes (2004). See, for example, Forbes and Rigobon (2002), Corsetti *et al.* (2005), and Dungey *et al.* (2005) for specific models.

position held in different currency markets. The focus of the paper is on the relationship between volume, volatility and liquidity, and, in particular, on how it changes during times of stress.

One important innovation is the augmentation of factor models of contagion estimated with publicly available data with a unique data set on foreign exchange trading volumes that a selected number of central banks has made available to the BIS. Since foreign exchange trading volume is generally not publicly available, it can have a first moment effect on exchange rates even in a context of efficient markets. The information content of this variable might be important for example in cases where the central bank's activity in the foreign exchange market prevents — at least temporarily — speculative pressure from being reflected in sizable exchange rate changes. In such a case, the various moments of the distribution of exchange rates may fail to reveal important changes in market conditions and linkages across markets.

Considering the considerable literature on contagion during the Asian crisis, Bruche *et al.* (2007) elect to focus on currency crisis and contagion only after the Asian crisis. Their sample starts in 1998, and thus importantly includes the Russia and LTCM crises and their repercussions during 1998.

Bruche *et al.* (2007) sidestep the issue of the causes of currency crisis, such as the realization of underlying macroeconomic weaknesses. Rather, they confine the attention to identifying linkages between financial markets, regardless of whether they arise from fundamentals. In fact, a key part of the approach is to attempt to understand linkages between currency markets where, at least superficially, fundamentals do not indicate strong linkages between the underlying economies. In the context of financial markets that are integrated across the globe, apparently unrelated markets may be linked through their role in international investors' portfolios. The spreading of turbulence across markets in 1998 is a striking example of how trading strategies spanning many markets create a fertile ground for contagion. Another recent example is the widely reported transmission of market pressure from Iceland to a number of emerging markets in early 2006, which, given the relatively small size of Iceland's economy, can hardly reflect linkages driven by fundamentals. Market commentary suggested that one mechanism for spreading contagion in this episode was the use of carry trades by investors that were simultaneously exposed to multiple emerging market economies. In this case, a loss on one country, or even just uncertainty about possible sizeable future losses, can affect trading decisions on other countries in the portfolio, perhaps through risk limits or margin calls. The recent turbulence in foreign exchange markets highlighted how the sudden closing of carry trade positions can spread quickly and affect currencies around the world.

Bruche *et al.* (2007) find general support for the presence of increased country linkages during high turbulence periods. They find that focusing only on correlation-derived tests would lead to erroneously rejecting the presence of contagion in currency markets in most, if not all cases. By contrast, their factor model does identify the presence of contagion in some of the crisis periods. By further employing volume as an explanatory variable, they find strong evidence of interlinkages between currency markets, where volume serves as a strong conduit for the transmission of contagion. During tranquil times, volume provides, at best, weak evidence of linkages between countries, but during crisis episodes its impact increases significantly. These linkages exist even in cases where there are no obvious fundamentals linking the countries. One possible underlying mechanism could be the presence of portfolios spanning financial assets from a number of emerging market countries.

2. Background

A number of approaches for modeling contagion have been proposed in the literature. For a survey, see, for example, Claessens and Forbes (2001), Dungey *et al.* (2003), and Dungey and Tambakis (2003). Contagion is generally considered to be a propagation of a crisis across countries that are not necessarily characterized by geographical proximity, similar economic structures, or trade linkages. There is no agreement, however, on what this means in practice. Eichengreen *et al.* (1996) define contagion narrowly as the association of excess returns in one country with excess returns in another country once the effect of fundamentals has been controlled for. A broader definition of contagion centers instead on the vulnerability of a country to events that occur in another country.

Following Claessens and Forbes' (2001) categorization, the literature on the drivers of contagion typically distinguishes fundamental causes and the behavior of international investors. The former include common shocks (the "monsoonal effect" in Masson, 1998; trade linkages in Glick and Rose, 1999; and financial linkages in Goldfajn and Valdes, 1997). The latter include informational asymmetries (Calvo and Mendoza, 2000), liquidity needs (Kaminski and Schmukler, 1999), benchmarking in international portfolios, or changing views on external support to countries in trouble.

The most common approach followed in the empirical literature to test for the presence of contagion is the testing of changes in the correlation of asset prices across countries (see, for example, King and Wadhwani, 1990; and Baig and Goldfajn, 1999). A common finding is that correlation between markets is higher when volatility increases (see, for example, Ang and Bekaert, 2002, on equity markets).

One variant of this approach consists in analyzing conditional correlations or the probability of crisis in country A conditional on fundamentals in country B (for example, Eichengreen, Rose, and Wyplosz, 1996; Glick and Rose, 1999; Kaminsky and Reinhardt, 2000; De Gregorio and Valdes, 2001; and van Horen *et al.*, 2006). A significant increase in correlations among different countries' markets, after controlling for the fundamentals, is considered evidence of contagion.

Another variant focuses on the second moment of exchange rates and examines the co-movements in volatility across markets, typically represented by ARCH-type models (see, for example, Edwards and Susmel, 2001). An alternative line of research has explored co-movements across countries during crisis periods defined as extreme events (see, for example, Hartmann *et al.*, 2003, 2006). The idea is that market co-movements may look fairly different when measured far out in the tails, what is known as asymptotic dependence, and such crisis behavior may not have the same parametric form in different markets. These studies argue also that focusing on such events is justified since they are severe enough to be always a concern for policy.

Contagion, as defined above, would generally imply an increase in intercountry linkages, which may lead to especially high correlations, at least if we focus on linear dependence. Suppose that a world factor model governs returns. If the volatility of a particular world factor increases, then the returns with the highest exposures to this factor will be more correlated. Furthermore, it is possible that the exposures themselves are dynamic. As exposure increases, so will correlation. Hence, giving such a model, one defines contagion in terms of correlation over and above what one would expect from the factor model. In defining contagion this way, Bekaert *et al.* (2005) find substantial evidence of contagion during the Asian crisis but no evidence of contagion during the Mexican crisis.

As highlighted by several authors, a simple analysis of changes over time in correlation coefficients is fundamentally flawed because it may reflect not just contagion but also the influence of heteroscedasticity (higher volatility raising the co-movement of asset prices), or changes in omitted variables (such as a global shift in the attitude towards risk).[2] Forbes and Rigobon (2002) propose adjusting the test of correlation coefficients for possible changing variance in the crisis country. This typically leads to accepting fewer cases as genuine instances of contagion, since an increase in correlation can now sometimes be attributed to an increase in the variance of the crisis country, while the linear relationship between returns across countries remains stable. Indeed, recent empirical studies on contagion that have estimated changing correlations controlling for the possibility of these other influences (see, for example, Caporale et al., 2005) typically find it more difficult to detect contagion in the data.

The test proposed by Forbes and Rigobon (2002) has been criticized by Corsetti *et al.* (2005), who argue that one should think about linear relationships between returns across countries in the context of a factor model, which implies that linear coefficients become factor loadings. This also implies that variance in a crisis country can go up either because the idiosyncratic variance of the crisis country has increased, or because the factor variance as increased. If the variance of the factor increases, this has an effect on correlation. By contrast, if the variance of idiosyncratic shocks increases, this has no effect on correlation. Corsetti *et al.* (2005) argue that Forbes and Rigobon (2002) implicitly assume that all of the increase in variance of the asset returns in the crisis country is due to the increase in factor variance. If this is not the case, then they over adjust the test, meaning that they are too likely to accept the hypothesis of no contagion.

Bruche *et al.* (2007) examine the power of the Forbes and Rigobon (2002) and the Corsetti *et al.* (2005) tests and find that they have relatively low power in small sample sizes. For example, for a crisis of duration of one month, a test with daily data needs an increase in correlation well in excess of 35 percent for the test to find contagion. A test of contagion in a crisis where the increase in correlation is less than 35 percent might lead to the erroneous conclusion of interdependence and not contagion.

A different version of this kind of test has been proposed by Dungey *et al.* (2005), who let idiosyncratic shocks in the crisis country affect the return in other countries in times of crisis, instead of allowing for structural breaks in factor loadings.

---

[2] King and Wadhwani (1990) discuss the role of heteroskedasticity but do not correct for it.

3. Identifying Crises

The literature has identified several causes for currency crises, such as factors related to domestic macro fundamentals, financial markets, political factors or factors that are unknown. Crises can take a number of different forms: They can arise in a country and remain confined there, or can spread to countries in the same region, or to countries with similar characteristics. They could also spread to seemingly unrelated countries. A crisis might not appear at first in the behavior of the spot rate if, for example, monetary authorities temporarily manage to counter market pressures. A further type of event of interest is that of *near crises.*

One recent example that received much attention among policy markets and market commentary was the attack on the Icelandic krona in February 2006 following the decision of a rating agency to downgrade the outlook for Iceland's sovereign debt. Within a few hours, the Icelandic currency lost some 10 percent of its value, and pressure spread quickly to currencies of countries, such as Hungary, Brazil and New Zealand, that had no apparent significant trade or financial linkages with Iceland. Market commentary attributed these spillovers among other things to the way currency trading is set up at major international players, with, for example, one desk covering many countries and doing continuous 24-hour trading or rolling the trading portfolio between desks in different countries.

A key element of our study is the identification of crisis episodes. Our focus is not on identifying shocks that drive financial markets but rather on crisis episodes as periods of high volatility/turbulence/illiquidity in financial markets.

Ideally one would want to endogenously identify crisis episodes within the model. This could be done, for example, using Markov switching models (see, for example, Fratzscher, 2003), but such tests generally lack robustness. An alternative approach, commonly used in the literature, relies on changes in the statistical characteristics of key variables, such as exchange rate volatility, to identify crisis periods. Such an approach carries with it the danger of circularity, the potential lack of reliability of prices as a crisis indicator, and the risk of data mining. Finally, one can consider macroeconomic variables, news accounts, official reports, and the like to identify crisis episodes. The downside of such an approach is that it can only provide a very coarse identification of crisis episodes.

Bruche *et al.* (2007) attempt to avoid these issues by employing a three-level approach which combines anecdotal evidence and press reports,

Table 1. Crisis episodes

Crisis episode	Dates	Currencies expected to be affected
Attack on the Colombian peso	16.4–25.8.1999	BR, MX, CL
Stock market turmoil	21.7–5.10.1998	All emerging markets
Russian default	17.8–27.9.1998	All emerging markets
Collapse of LTCM	2–23.9.1998	All emerging markets
Attack on the Brazilian real	12.1–29.1.1999	Mainly MX, CL, CO, less so other EMEs
Crisis in Turkey	22.7–5.10.1998	TR, ZA
Financial crisis in Turkey	29.1–19.10.2001	TR, ZA
Argentinean default	3.1–25.6.2002 (or, 3–16.1.2002)	BR, MX, CL, CO
Turbulence in Brazil	12.9–22.10.2002	CL, MX, CO
Attack on the Icelandic krona	20.2–20.4.2006 20–22.2.2006	All EMEs

Source: Bruche *et al.* (2006).

existing event studies, and information from commonly used financial indicators. In practice, this involved taking crisis episodes from a recent analysis by Calvo *et al.* (2006) and supplementing their analysis with information from other sources such as the International Monetary Fund's World *Economic Outlook* or the Bank for International Settlement's (BIS) *Annual Report*.[3] Since these sources in some cases did not provide an identification of crisis dates at the daily frequency, Bruche *et al.* (2007) also examine the Emerging Markets Bond Index spreads for individual countries to pinpoint the exact timing. The start of a crisis would then be identified with the timing of a sudden widening of spreads, whereas the end of a crisis would coincide with the inception of a narrowing trend.

A sample of results from Bruche *et al.* (2007) is presented in Table 1.

4. Models

Bruche *et al.* (2007) propose a two equation factor model at the daily frequency to analyze linkages, where the factors are chosen to take into account specific features of currency markets. For example, the reference

[3] An example of an account of crises is given by http://www.bis.org/publ/ar99e3.pdf, p.32.

currency for all currencies in their study is the US dollar, and hence a shock that decreases the dollar's value across the board will affect all the currencies in the sample simultaneously giving the appearance of linkages. This is especially relevant for countries with relatively stable exchange rates and consequently low exchange rate volatility against the US dollar. Bruche *et al.* (2007) address this issue by using the euro/dollar exchange rate as a main exogenous factor. Secondly, global interest rates also affect currency markets and consequently changes in US interest rates are introduced as an additional factor.

Bruche *et al.* (2007) estimate the model pairwise, with a target country (T) and a source country (S), with two equations estimated simultaneously. The first equation obtains returns for the source country, adjusted for factor impacts. The second equation has the target country exchange rate returns dependent on three components: the same factors, lagged source country adjusted exchange rate returns, and possibly volumes for both countries. These models are estimated for both the full sample and crisis periods.

5. Data

Bruche *et al.* (2007) employ three categories of data, exchange rates, interest rates, and volume. The data set covers daily observations starting at the beginning of the year 1998 and ending in the middle of 2006.

Data on spot rates are taken from Datastream and collected at 4pm London time. The US interest rate used is the federal funds rate.

Finally, they use a unique set of daily data on turnover of domestic currencies vis-à-vis the US dollar in local markets, or volume in short, which was provided to the BIS. The data set captures spot turnover, with the exception of data for the Mexican peso and the shekel, which also include trading in forwards and swaps. Data from the Triennial Foreign Exchange and Derivatives Markets Survey suggest that offshore trading in these currencies is limited (BIS, 2005). Hence, the volumes used here can be taken as being fairly representative of total trading.

With only one exception (Galati, 2001), this is the first time an empirical cross-country study has been carried out using comprehensive data on foreign exchange market turnover at the daily frequency, where employing a shorter data set he focuses on the relationship between volumes and volatility in individual markets.

The individual markets are characterized by very different levels of average activity. The most active markets were those for the Mexican peso, the Brazilian real and the South African rand. To get an idea of the size of these markets, trading of dollars against one of these currencies on average was slightly less than interbank trading in Tokyo, and about one third of local trading of Canadian or Australian dollars against the US dollar in April 1998.

In order to compare the results with foreign exchange markets in industrial countries, and in order to allow a comparison with other studies on trading volumes (Wei, 1994; and Hartmann, 1999), we also used data from the Tokyo interbank market. This data is much less comprehensive. Trading in the Tokyo interbank market accounts for roughly 5 percent of total yen/dollar trading.

6. Summary of Results

Bruche *et al.* (2007) obtain several interesting results, some of which are discussed below. They find that their factor model is more robust in identifying contagious episodes than models employing correlations to identify contagion. One reason is that the factor structure is more robust than the more correlation-based techniques.

They further find significant improvement in estimates when incorporating volume, where volume induced contagion is as likely to spread from the country in crisis, as volume of other countries affecting the country in crisis.

As an illustration, consider the specific example of the contagious episodes in Iceland in February 2006 which shows exchange rates, daily trading volume, and 20 days moving average trading volume for Iceland from the middle of 2005 to the middle of 2006 (see Figure 1).

While in the second part of the 2005 there appears to have been a relatively weak link between trading volume and the exchange rates, at the beginning of 2006 trading volume increases sharply along with exchange rates. Volume peaks on April 21 which also corresponds to the day where the krona was weakest. After that, volume retreats towards its longer-term trend while the exchange rate remains weak. Similar patterns exist in other crisis episodes. During the crisis in Iceland, the Icelandic volume is partially able to predict exchange rates, both in Iceland and in other countries.

Bruche *et al.* (2007) generally find that trading volume plays a significant role in currency markets, especially during financial crisis, where the impact of volume is succinctly captured by their factor model. Generally,

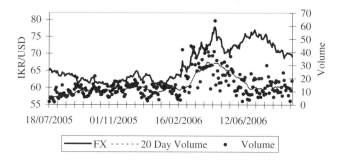

Figure 1. Trading volume and exchange rates in Iceland

they find that it is necessary to employ a formal model of the impact of volume to accurately account for its role in currency markets.

7. Conclusion

As this paper has illustrated, the results of Bruche *et al.* (2007) suggest that by employing a carefully crafted factor model it is possible to adapt existing contagion models to the specific problem of contagion in currency markets and currency crisis. By further incorporating trading volume, it is possible to clearly identify inter-linkages between countries and thus channels for the transmission of contagious episodes.

Foreign exchange market turnover can help policymakers to identify linkages between markets and understanding the potential of contagious crises. Within the framework discussed in this paper, trading volume appears to be very useful for the daily monitoring of currency markets and the potential contagion of crises.

One interpretation of this role of trading volume is that it captures phenomena such as international investors' strategies that span financial assets of a number of emerging markets. One recent example of such a strategy is carry trades involving several emerging market currencies.

References

Ang, A. and G. Bekaert (2002). Regime switches in interest rates. *Journal of Business & Economic Statistics*, 20(2), 163–182.

AuYong, H.H., C. Gan and S. Treepongkaruna (2004). Cointegration and causality in the Asian and emerging foreign exchange markets: Evidence from the 1990s financial crises. *International Review of Financial Analysis*, 13, 479–515

Bank for International Settlements (2005). *Triennial Survey of Foreign Exchange and Derivatives Market Activity.*

Bae, K.-H., G.A. Karolyi and R.M. Stulz (2003). A new approach to measuring financial contagion. *Review of Financial Studies*, 16, 717–763.

Baig, T. and I. Goldfajn (1999). Financial market contagion in the Asian Crisis. IMF Staff Papers, 46, 167–195.

Bekaert, G., C.R. Harvey and A. Ng (2005). Market integration and contagion. *Journal of Business*, 78, 39–70.

Bruche, M., J. Danielsson and G. Galati (2007). Contagion in FX markets. Mimeo, www.RiskResearch.org.

Calvo, G.A. and E. Mendoza (2000). Rational contagion and the globalization of securities markets. *Journal of International Economics*, 51, 79–113.

Caporale, G.M., A. Cipollini and N. Spagnolo (2005). Testing for contagion: A conditional correlation analysis. *Journal of Empirical Finance*, 12, 476–489.

Claessens, S., R. Dornbusch and Y.-C. Park (2001). Contagion: Why crises spread and how this can be stopped. In *International Financial Contagion*, S. Claessens and K. Forbes (eds.), pp. 19–41. Boston: Kluwer Academic Publishers.

Claessens, S. and K. Forbes, eds. (2001). *International Financial Contagion.* Kluwer Academic Publishers.

Corsetti, G., M. Pericoli and M. Sbracia (2005). Some contagion, some interdependence: More pitfalls in tests of financial contagion. *Journal of International Money and Finance*, 24, 1177–1199.

De Gregorio, J. and R.O. Valdes (2001). Crisis transmission: Evidence from the debt, tequila and Asian flu crises. World Bank Research Report.

Dungey, M., R. Fry, B. Gonzalez-Hermosillo and V.L. Martin (2005). Empirical modeling of contagion: A review of methodologies. *Quantitative Finance*, 5, 9–24.

Dungey, M. and D. Tambakis (2003). International financial contagion: What do we know?. Cambridge University Working Paper, No. 9.

Edwards, S. and R. Susmel (2001). Volatility dependence and contagion in emerging equity markets. NBER Working Papers 8506.

Eichengreen, B., A.K. Rose and C. Wyplosz (1996). Contagious currency crises. NBER Working Paper 5681.

Forbes, K.J. and R. Rigobon (2002). No contagion, only interdependence. *Journal of Finance*, 57, 2223–2261.

Forbes, K. and R. Rigobon (2001). Measuring contagion: Conceptual and empirical issues. In *International Financial Contagion*, S. Claessens and K. Forbes (eds.), pp. 43–66. Boston: Kluwer Academic Publishers.

Fratzscher, M. (2003). On currency crises and contagion. *International Journal of Finance and Economics*, 8(2), 109–130.

Glick, R. and A. Rose (1999). Contagion and trade: Why are currency crises regional?. *Journal of International Money and Finance*, 18, 603–617.

Goldfajn, I. and R. Valdes (1997). Capital flows and twin crises: The role of liquidity. IMF Working Paper No. 97/87.

Hartmann, P. (1999). Trading volumes and transaction costs in the foreign exchange market. *Journal of Banking and Finance*, 23, 801–824.

Hartmann, P., S. Straetmans and C.G. de Vries (2003). A global perspective on extreme currency linkages. In *Asset Price Bubbles: The Implications for Monetary, Regulatory and International Policies*, W. Hunter, G. Kaufman and M. Pomerleano (eds.), pp. 361–382. Cambridge: MIT Press.

Hartmann, P., S. Straetmans and C. de Vries (2006). Banking system stability: A cross-atlantic perspective. In *Risks of Financial Institutions*, M. Carey and R. Stulz (eds.). National Bureau of Economic Research and Chicago University Press.

Van Horen, N., H. Jager and F. Klaassen (2006). Foreign exchange market contagion in the Asian crisis: A regression-based approach. *Review of World Economics*, 142, 374–401.

Kaminsky G. and C. Reinhart (1999). The twin crisis: The causes of banking and balance-of-payments problems. *American Economic Review*, 89(3), 473–500.

Kaminsky, G. and S. Schmukler (1999). What triggers market jitters? A chronicle of the Asian crisis. *Journal of International Money and Finance*, 18, 537–560.

King, M.A. and S. Wadhwani (1990). Transmission of volatility between stock markets. *Review of Financial Studies*, 3, 5–33.

Lyons, R. (2002). *The Microstructure Approach to Exchange Rates*. MIT Press.

Masson, Paul (1998). Contagion: Monsoonal effects, spillovers, and jumps between multiple equilibria. IMF Working Paper No. 98/142.

Moser, T. (2003). What is international financial contagion?. *International Finance*, 6(2), 157–178.

Sander, H. and S. Kleimeier (2003). Contagion and causality: An empirical investigation of four Asian crisis episodes. *Journal of International Financial Markets, Institutions and Money*, 13, 171–186.

Wei, S.-J. (1994). Anticipations of foreign exchange volatility and bid-ask spreads. NBER Working Paper No. 4737.

What Do We Know about the Performance and Risk of Hedge Funds?

Triphon Phumiwasana*
Milken Institute

Tong Li
Milken Institute

James R. Barth
Auburn University and Milken Institute

Glenn Yago
Milken Institute

1. Introduction

A front-page story in September 2006 was the unraveling of the hedge fund Amarath Advisors. Its assets fell by a reported 65 percent in a month and 55 percent, or $6 billion, for the year. The back-page story was that financial markets barely reacted to this shocking development. This was in sharp contrast to the near-collapse of Long-Term Capital Management (LTCM) in 1998. Despite the lack of a broader market reaction, the rapid and huge losses suffered by Amarath raise serious issues about the performance and risk of hedge funds more generally.

The purpose of our paper is to use a comprehensive data source on hedge funds to examine the performance and risk of these funds. Mutual funds, unlike hedge funds, are widely available to the public and therefore must be registered with the Securities and Exchange Commission. They are, moreover, limited in the strategies they can employ. Hedge funds, on the

*Triphon Phumiwasana (ephumiwasana@milkeninstitute.org) and Tong Li (cli@milken institute.org) are economists at the Milken Institute; James R. Barth (jbarth@milkeninstitute.org) is a Lowder Eminent Scholar in Finance at Auburn University and Senior Fellow at the Milken Institute; Glenn Yago (gyago@milkeninstitute.org) is Director of Capital Studies at the Milken Institute. This is a shorter version of a longer paper that is available upon request from the authors.

other hand, are set up as limited partnerships and generally are not constrained by regulatory limitations on their investment strategies. Furthermore, although the word "hedge" typically refers to the hedging of the value of assets through the use of derivative instruments or the simultaneous use of long positions and short sales, most hedge funds employ strategies that do not involve hedging as more commonly understood. Indeed, many funds do just the opposite, which explains the collapse of Amarath and LTCM. The paper will therefore examine some of the different strategies employed by hedge funds, assess whether there are any differences among them in terms of performance and risk, and examine some of the factors that help explain why some funds remain in the industry and others exit.

So as not to raise expectations of the reader unduly, it is best at the outset to state what our paper does not do. It does not provide any particularly new or startling results regarding the implications of hedge funds for global financial stability or the need for greater regulation of them. These clearly are timely and important issues that need to be addressed. Indeed, others have already tried to address them. But the results of these efforts thus far have been less successful than one might hope. For instance, in a recent study that attempts to quantify the potential impact of hedge funds on systemic risk, Chan *et al.* (2005, p. 97) state that "we cannot determine the magnitude of current systemic risk with any degree of accuracy." Similarly, Garbaravicius and Dierick (2005, p. 55) conclude that "It is very difficult to provide any conclusive evidence on the impact of hedge funds on financial market." Moreover, as regards regulation, Timothy Geithner (2006, p. 8), President of the Federal Reserve Bank of New York, states that "Clearly, capital supervision and market discipline remain the key tools for limiting systemic risk. The emergence of new market participants such as leverage institutions does not change that." In addition, Danielsson *et al.* (2005, pp. 26–27) while arguing that there is a "need for a credible resolution mechanism to deal with the default of systemically important hedge funds ... the procedural issues and related incentive effects (to do so) are complex ... (and) ... require further consideration in order to provide the correct incentives for the various parties." Given the conclusions of these impressive efforts of well-recognized experts, we have decided not to try to expand and improve upon this line of enquiry in the present paper.

What we do instead in this paper is provide a comprehensive and detailed examination of many important aspects of the hedge fund industry. This examination is based on a dataset assembled by HedgeFund.net As Table 1 shows, there are several sources of hedge fund data with

Table 1. Comparison of selected commercial hedge fund databases

	Active Funds	Graveyard Funds	Assets of Active Funds ($ Billions)	Time Coverage (Years)
Hedgefund.net	6,500	3,350	1,032	26
Hedgefund Research.com (HFR)	5,900	3,500	500–600 (excluding FOF)	15
Morningstar (Altvest)	6,000	n/a	700	15
Barclay Alternative Asset Center	5,500	3,000	701	28
TASS — Hedgeworld	4,000	2,600	544	16
Hedgeco.net	4,000	n/a	n/a	n/a

differing coverage features. HedgeFund.net provides information in the most funds and the most assets. It starts with eight hedge funds with $57 million in assets in 1981 and grows to 6,445 funds with $969 billion in assets as of June 2006. We are able to use this dataset to examine differences in important characteristics of hedge funds both over time and by the type of strategy that funds choose to employ. We pay particular attention to the changes in the performance and risk of funds over time as well as assess whether there are differences in these dimensions based upon the strategies they employ. Also, we use regression analyses to examine the association between various characteristics of a fund and its performance and risk, and to examine the association between various characteristics and the likelihood that a fund will remain alive or enter the graveyard. Our hope is that readers of our paper will be motivated by the substantial amount of descriptive material provided to identify problems or issues that merit further consideration by us and others.

2. An Overview of the Hedge Fund Industry

2.1 *Growth and size*

The recent flurry of news stories about hedge funds might lead some to think that such funds are a relatively new development. However, Fung and Hsieh (1999) report that the first hedge fund was actually formed in

1949. It employed a long/short equity strategy and operated on the basis of leverage, which describes the strategies of many hedge funds today. They point out that the fund was relatively unknown until a magazine article in 1966 drew attention to its high return compared to the returns of mutual funds. The number of hedge funds subsequently grew fairly rapidly for a few years before suffering losses due to the poor performance in the equity market. According to Fung and Hsieh (1999), the industry rebounded once again when another magazine article in 1986 reported that a newly established hedge fund earned an extraordinary return in the first few months of its existence. The publicizing of high returns thus appears to have been a significant contribution to accelerated growth in the industry during its more formative years.

Table 2 documents the growth in the industry over the past quarter of a century. Both in terms of numbers and assets, the industry has experienced continuous and rapid growth until the decline in the number of funds during the first six months of 2006. From 1981 to June 2006 the number of funds grew at a 30 percent average annual rate, while total assets grew at a 47 percent average annual rate. Not all funds, of course, that entered the industry during this time period remained alive until the ending date. Indeed, the two tables show that by June 2006 there were 3,100 funds with $257 billion in assets that had exited the industry. Despite these exits, there were still 6,445 funds remaining with $969 in total assets.

2.2 *Differences in size, domicile, asset location, and age of funds*

Although there has been growth in both the number and assets of hedge funds, asset growth has exceeded number growth. As a result, the average size of hedge funds has increased by more than 2,000 percent from 1981 to June 2006, to $150 million from $7 million. This occurred despite the fact that the average size of exiting funds is greater than the average size of entering funds. This latter difference reflects the fact that the age of exiting funds is greater than that of the newly entering funds.

As regards the distribution in sizes of funds in terms of number and assets, the funds with $1 billion or more in assets account for only 3 percent of the total number of funds but 35 percent of total assets. Conversely, those with $100 million or less in assets account for nearly 70 percent of the total number of all funds, but they account for only 12 percent of the total assets.

Table 2. Total number and assets of hedge funds

| | Total | | Changes in | | Of which | | | | Graveyard (Accumulation of Exiting Funds) | |
| | | | | | Entering | | Exiting | | | |
	Number	Assets ($Mn)	Number	Assets ($Mn)	Number	Assets ($Mn)	Number	Assets ($Mn)	Number	Assets ($Mn)
1981	8	57	na	na	na	na	na	na	na	na
1982	12	78	4	21	4	8	na	na	na	na
1983	18	228	6	151	6	157	na	na	na	na
1984	27	531	9	302	9	8	na	na	na	na
1985	33	944	6	413	6	37	na	na	na	na
1986	46	1,177	13	232	13	35	na	na	na	na
1987	58	1,486	12	310	12	68	na	na	na	na
1988	76	2,328	18	842	18	104	na	na	na	na
1989	98	3,254	22	926	22	259	na	na	na	na
1990	139	5,006	41	1,752	41	726	na	na	na	na
1991	209	7,569	70	2,563	70	976	na	na	na	na
1992	300	9,553	91	1,984	91	1,248	na	na	na	na
1993	424	17,182	124	7,629	124	1,596	na	na	na	na
1994	563	19,697	139	2,515	139	894	na	na	na	na
1995	815	25,497	252	5,801	252	2,008	na	na	na	na
1996	1,117	35,535	302	10,038	302	2,952	na	na	na	na

(*Continued*)

Table 2. (*Continued*)

	Total		Changes in		Of which				Graveyard (Accumulation of Exiting Funds)	
					Entering		Exiting			
	Number	Assets ($Mn)	Number	Assets ($Mn)	Number	Assets ($Mn)	Number	Assets ($Mn)	Number	Assets ($Mn)
1997	1,522	58,261	405	22,726	405	4,793	na	na	na	na
1998	2,041	76,906	519	18,645	525	5,565	6	125	6	125
1999	2,733	140,265	692	63,359	740	15,506	48	2,022	54	2,147
2000	3,250	170,494	517	30,229	740	21,406	223	12,436	277	14,584
2001	3,825	237,871	575	67,377	915	18,601	340	10,115	617	24,698
2002	4,596	281,837	771	43,966	1,117	25,849	346	25,490	963	50,188
2003	5,333	508,811	737	226,974	1,176	59,503	439	15,552	1,402	65,740
2004	6,235	698,593	902	189,783	1,372	50,824	470	74,791	1,872	140,531
2005	6,526	839,069	291	140,476	1,057	45,262	766	67,725	2,638	208,256
June 2006	6,445	968,690	-81	129,621	381	16,467	462	48,582	3,100	256,838

Note: Data on exiting funds only became available since 1997.

Source: Hedgefund.net.

A different perspective of the hedge fund industry is provided by the domicile (or headquarter location) of hedge funds and the location of the assets of hedge funds. Of the 6,445 funds as of June 2006, slightly more than 50 percent — 3,354 — are domiciled in the United States, and of these about half have their assets located in the United States, with nearly all the remaining assets allocated globally. Europe is second to the United States in terms of number of domiciled funds, accounting for approximately 33 percent — 2,153 — of the total number of funds, and of these only about 20 percent have their assets located in Europe. The majority of the funds, 64 percent, have allocated their assets globally.

The funds domiciled in the United States account for the largest amount of assets, $503 billion, with those in Europe second with $371 billion. Together these regions account for slightly more than 90 percent of the $969 billion in total fund assets. For funds domiciled in the United States, 52 percent and 43 percent are allocated to the United States and globally, respectively, In contrast, for funds dominated in Europe 22 and 63 percent are allocated to Europe and globally, respectively. The European domiciled funds, moreover, allocate more assets to Asia in terms of both absolute amount and as a share of their total assets compared to funds domiciled in the United States.

As regards the degree of concentration of assets within the hedge fund industry, the top 1 percent of funds control 19 percent of all fund assets, the top 5 percent control 47 percent, and the top 10 percent control 63 percent. However, there is wide variation in concentration ratios with respect to the location of fund assets. The top 1 percent of funds with assets located in South America, for example, account for 58 percent of all assets located in South America and the top 1 percent of funds with assets located in Africa account for 46 percent of all assets located in Africa.

Similarly, there are substantial differences in the concentration ratios with respect to where the funds are domiciled. The top 1 percent of funds domiciled in Africa and the Middle East account for 72 percent of all assets of funds domiciled in the region. In Europe and the United States, however, the concentration ratios are relatively low at 18 percent in both cases because so many funds are domiciled in these places.

The last comment to be made in this section concerns the average age of hedge funds. Not surprisingly, the average age of a fund has increased since 1981. As of June 2006, the typical fund had been in existence 5.3 years.

2.3 *Hedge fund strategies*

Hedge funds not only come in a variety of sizes, asset locations and domiciles, but also in a variety of strategies. Our dataset lists 42 different strategies for the hedge funds being examined, including other and unknown. These 42 strategies, in turn, are collapsed into 12 strategies, including other and unknown. It is these strategies, after combining other and unknown into a single strategy, we examine next. The different strategies are defined in Table 3.

Table 4 contains information on the relative importance of the different strategies in terms of each strategy's share of the total number and assets of hedge funds. The two most important strategies employed are the fund-of-funds-multi-strategy and the long/short-equity-strategy, with 25 and 20 percent of all funds employing these two strategies, respectively. The funds employing these two strategies also account for 30 and 17 percent of the total assets of funds respectively.

It is also interesting to note the changing relative importance in strategies employed by hedge funds over time. The commodity trading advisor and directional funds accounted for the larger shares of number and assets in the 1980s, but those shares declined sharply thereafter. At the same time, they were replaced in relative importance by the fund-of-funds-multi-strategy and long/short equity-strategy funds.

Table 5 slows that the top 10 percent of the total number of funds for each of the 12 different strategies account for between 50 and 71 percent of the total assets of each of the strategies. The strategy with the lowest degree of concentration is the sector strategy (50 percent), while the one with the highest degree of concentration is the macro strategy (71 percent).

Overall, there is little variation in the average ages of funds employing different strategies, with the exception of the funds choosing the commodity trading advisor strategy.

2.3 *Management fees*

The management fees of hedge funds attract a lot of attention from not only potential investors but also the financial press. Managers of such funds rely on these fees and performance incentives for their income, above and beyond the returns they receive on their own investments in the

Table 3. Description of strategies of hedge funds

Strategy	Description
Fund of Funds — Multi-Strategies	A strategy that invest in many strategies of hedge funds and mutual funds. They are intended to benefit from diversification across strategies and across funds.
Long/Short Equity	A strategy that involves buying certain stocks long and selling others short. Thus the net positions are based on relative value rather than absolute value of stock. These types of funds usually invest in countries that allow short sales.
Fund of Funds	A strategy that invests in a strategy of hedge funds and mutual funds.
Event-Driven	A strategy that takes significant positions in a certain number of companies with special situations, including distressed stocks, mergers and takeovers.
Market-Neutral	A strategy that seeks to exploit differences in stock prices by being long and short in stocks within the same sector, industry, market capitalization, country, etc. This strategy creates a hedge against market factors. Fixed income, equity and futures arbitrage strategies fall into this category.
Commodity Trading Advisor	A strategy that engage in buying or selling commodity futures or option contracts
Multi-Strategy	A strategy that use many strategies to produce returns.
Global	A strategy that bases its investment on overall economic and political views of various countries, regions, or groups including emerging markets, Asian countries, and eastern European countries.
Macro	A strategy that bases its investment on macroeconomic principles, including relative performance of country interest rate trends, movements in the general flow of funds, political changes, government policies, inter-government relations, and other broad systemic factors.
Sector	A strategy that bases its investment on specific sector such as bio-tech, technology, auto industry and defense industry for example.
Directional	A strategy that bases its investment on long or short position only.

Source: Hedgefund.net.

Table 4. Total number and assets of hedge funds by strategy

| | Total | | Share of Total Number (%) | | | | | | | | | | |
| | | | Fund of Funds — Multi-Strategies | | Long/Short Equity | | Fund of Funds | | Event-Driven | | Market-Neutral | | Commodity Trading Advisor | |
	Number	Assets ($Mn)	Number	Assets ($Mn)	Number	Assets ($Mn)	Number	Assets ($Mn)	Number	Assets ($Mn)	Number	Assets ($Mn)	Number	Assets ($Mn)
1981	8	57	0	0	0	0	13	0	25	0	0	0	50	100
1985	33	944	12	3	12	4	3	22	15	2	6	0	27	9
1990	139	5,006	15	7	14	11	6	3	22	9	4	1	18	29
1995	815	25,497	16	16	16	15	9	9	14	8	10	9	12	18
2000	3250	170,494	16	14	20	21	9	8	15	13	11	14	9	6
2001	3825	237,871	18	17	21	21	9	8	13	13	11	14	8	5
2002	4596	281,837	20	22	20	19	10	8	12	10	12	14	8	6
2003	5333	508,811	23	29	20	14	9	8	10	10	11	12	8	9
2004	6235	698,593	24	27	20	16	9	8	10	10	10	12	8	6
2005	6526	839,069	25	30	20	17	9	8	9	10	9	9	7	5
June 2006	6445	968,690	25	30	20	17	10	9	9	10	9	8	7	5

(Continued)

Table 4. (*Continued*)

					Share of Total Number (%)						
	Multi-Strategy		Global		Macro		Sector		Directional		Other
	Number	Assets ($Mn)	Number	Assets ($Mn)	Number	Assets ($Mn)	Number	Assets ($Mn)	Number	Assets ($Mn)	Number	Assets ($Mn)
1981	0	0	0	0	0	0	0	0	0	0	13	0
1985	3	1	0	0	0	0	0	0	18	58	3	0
1990	3	1	1	0	5	6	0	0	7	31	5	1
1995	3	2	3	1	3	3	3	3	4	12	5	4
2000	3	4	4	2	3	2	4	3	3	3	5	12
2001	3	5	3	2	3	2	4	2	2	2	4	8
2002	4	7	3	2	3	2	3	2	2	2	3	4
2003	4	6	3	2	4	4	3	1	2	1	3	4
2004	4	6	3	3	4	4	3	2	2	1	3	4
2005	5	6	4	4	3	3	3	2	2	1	3	5
June 2006	5	7	4	5	3	3	3	2	2	1	4	5

Table 5. Asset concentration ratios of firms owning hedge funds by strategy (percent)

Strategy	Top 1%	Top 5%	Top 10%
Fund of Funds — Multi-Strategies	16%	43%	57%
Long/Short	13%	38%	54%
Directional	21%	41%	55%
Fund of Funds	13%	36%	52%
Event-Driven	18%	45%	61%
Market-Neutral	21%	46%	59%
CTA	19%	47%	64%
Multi-Strategy	23%	47%	64%
Global	19%	42%	56%
Macro	32%	58%	71%
Sector	8%	31%	50%
Other	32%	48%	64%
All Strategies	19%	47%	63%

Source: Hedgefund.net.

funds. The funds with only 5 percent of total assets set management fees at 0.75 percent or less. The funds accounting for 55 percent of total assets, however, set fees at 1.25 percent or higher. The funds with just 2 percent of the assets, which are those at the low and high extremes, set fees at less than 0.25 percent and greater than 2.25 percent, respectively. Over time, the shares of total assets reflecting different management fees have shifted into the higher categories but with substantial variation across the different ranges of fees.

The performance incentives of hedge funds clearly attract the most attention. As of June 2006, 60 percent of all hedge funds charged incentives of 15 percent or higher. The hedge funds charging these fees, moreover, accounted for 56 percent of total assets. There appears to be a bimodal distribution of incentive fees in the following sense. Most funds with the most assets either charge less than 10 percent or between 15 and 20 percent. There is roughly a 30 to 50 percent split, in terms of both number and assets, for the funds charging 10 percent or less and those charging between 15 and 20 percent respectively. The performance incentives, moreover, have tended to drift upwards since the early 1980s despite the tremendous increase in the number and assets of hedge funds.

2.4 *Lock-up periods*

In addition to fees, attention is frequently focused on the lock-up periods of hedge funds. When investors initially put their money into such funds, they cannot freely cash out at any time thereafter. Instead, investors are required to remain in the fund over a specified period of time before any withdrawals can take place. The required minimum time period is called the initial lock-up period. Nearly 50 percent of funds have a lock-up period of up to 30 days, with the vast majority of the remaining funds having a lock-up period of up to a year.

The distribution of the assets of funds by lock-up period closely parallels that for the number of funds. The data indicate that 49 percent of the assets of all funds are linked to lock-up periods of up to 30 days. Only 2 percent of assets are linked to lock-up periods exceeding a year. Over time, there has been a shift toward longer lock-up periods employed by more funds with more assets.

We also examine the lock-up periods employed by funds of different sizes and strategies. There is not much of a difference in lock-up periods employed by funds of varying sizes. However, for funds with different strategies, the lock-up period is shortest for the commodity trading adviser funds and longest for the sector funds. In the case of the former, 91 percent of the assets are in the funds with a lock-up period of 30 days or less, whereas in the latter case 61 percent of the assets are in the funds with a lock-up period of more than 90 days but less than a year.

Since hedge funds require the services of both accounting and brokerage firms, it is informative to examine which firms are most frequently used. Three accounting firms, PriceWaterhouse Coopers, Ernst & Young and KPMG, are the firms of choice for 54 percent of all hedge funds reporting such information, and those funds account for 65 percent of total assets. Nearly 40 percent of the funds with 41 percent of assets do not report information about which brokerage firms are used. Of those that do report this information, Morgan Stanley, Goldman Sachs and Bear Stearns are the top three firms, jointly servicing about one-quarter of all funds with about the same percentage of total assets.

3. Performance and Risk of Hedge Funds

The performance and risk of hedge funds understandably attracts the most attention. Table 6 shows the average monthly (annualized) return of hedge funds from 1981 to June 2006 range from a low of 0.4 (4.8 percent) in 1994 to a high of 2.7 (32.4 percent) in 1985. There is substantial variation in returns depending upon the strategy that a fund employs. As the table shows, the highest average monthly return was reported by those funds employing a global strategy (11 percent), while the lowest return was reported by those also employing a global strategy (−2.2 percent).

The volatility of average monthly returns, as measured by the standard deviation of returns, shows that volatility for all funds has decreased over time, but that it differs widely among funds depending upon the strategy being employed. The most volatile return was reported by those funds employing a macro strategy in 1987 while the lowest volatility was reported by the fund of funds employing multiple strategies in 1982.

It is also useful to examine the persistence of both positive and negative returns reported by funds. In Tables 7 and 8, the number and assets of funds with persistent positive returns over selected time periods are reported. The tables indicate that 1,559 funds with $442 billion in assets, as of June 2006, reported positive returns over the previous consecutive five-year period. In contrast, Tables 9 and 10 show similar information for funds reporting negative returns. Only two funds reported consecutive negative returns for any year from 1981 to June 2006. This happened in 1999 and the two funds had only $16 million in assets. However, as of June 2006, there were 1,128 funds with $104 billion in assets that reported negative returns in the previous year.

As regards the risk-return trade-offs for hedge funds grouped on the basis of strategy, there is a significantly positive relationship on average between return and risk. Still, as Figure 1 shows, some of the strategies employed by funds have underperformed compared to others in terms of generating a return that compensates for the associated risk. This is the case for several strategies when examining the trade-offs both for the most recent five-year period and the past year, but especially so in the latter case.

We also compare the annualized return on hedge funds to the rate on one-year US Treasury securities. The spread between the two returns has tended to narrow over the past 25 years, though the spread differs widely

Table 6. Average monthly (annualized) returns of hedge funds (percent)

					Strategy								All Strategies
	Fund of Funds — Multi-Strategies	Long/Short Equity	Directional	Fund of Funds	Event-Driven	Market-Neutral	Commodity Trading Advisor	Multi-Strategy	Global	Macro	Sector	Other	
1981	na	na	na	1.6	1.6	na	2.4	na	na	na	na	0.2	2.2
1982	1.5	na	na	2.6	2.5	1.9	2.1	4.2	na	na	na	3	2.4
1983	1.2	1	1.3	1.8	1.7	0.5	2	1.7	na	na	na	0.2	1.5
1984	0.7	1	1	-0.2	0.7	1.9	2.8	0	na	na	na	1.2	1.5
1985	2.8	2.6	3	2.4	2.5	1.9	3.1	1.5	na	na	na	2.4	2.7
1986	1.7	0.6	3	1.2	1.1	0.7	1.8	1.4	na	na	na	1.4	1.6
1987	2.5	0.5	1.1	0.7	1	1.7	3.6	1.1	na	1.9	na	-0.2	1.8
1988	1.4	1.4	1.5	1	2.2	1.6	1.9	0	na	0.9	na	1	1.6
1989	1.4	2.1	2.3	0.4	1.9	1.1	1.6	1.8	na	2.5	na	0.4	1.6
1990	1.7	0.4	-0.4	1	0.5	0.6	2.6	-0.2	2.2	5.2	na	-0.2	1.2
1991	1	3.1	2	1.3	2.1	2.1	2.4	1.6	1.5	3	1.9	2.7	2.1
1992	1.1	1.8	1.2	1.1	1.5	1	1.3	1.2	0.3	1.9	1.8	1.8	1.4
1993	2	2.1	1.5	2.1	1.9	1.4	2.4	1.7	11	4	3.1	2.1	2.3
1994	0	0.5	1.6	-0.1	0.2	0.9	0.6	0.3	2.8	-0.7	0.4	-0.1	0.4
1995	1.1	2.4	1.3	1.2	2	1.6	2.4	1.5	0.7	2.1	3.1	1.4	1.8
1996	1.4	2.2	1.4	1.5	1.9	1.4	2.2	1.7	2.9	2	3.3	1.3	1.8

(Continued)

Table 6. (*Continued*)

					Strategy								All Strategies
	Fund of Funds — Multi-Strategies	Long/ Short Equity	Directional	Fund of Funds	Event-Driven	Market-Neutral	Commodity Trading Advisor	Multi-Strategy	Global	Macro	Sector	Other	
1997	1.3	1.8	1.2	1.2	2	1.3	1.8	1.7	1.7	1.6	2	1	1.6
1998	0.3	1.6	0.9	0.4	1.1	0.9	1.6	0.7	-2.2	1.3	1.5	0.7	0.9
1999	2	4.1	1.7	2.2	3.1	1.4	0.9	2.6	4.5	2.1	5.4	1.4	2.6
2000	0.9	1.5	0.9	0.7	1.1	0.9	1.3	1.1	0.1	0.7	1.6	1.1	1.1
2001	0.5	0.6	0.5	0.3	0.8	0.6	0.8	0.7	2.2	0.9	0	1	0.7
2002	0.2	0	0.3	0.1	0.2	0.6	1.5	0.6	0.9	0.8	-0.6	0.6	0.3
2003	0.9	1.7	1.1	0.8	1.9	0.7	1.2	1.3	2.9	1.7	2	1.2	1.3
2004	0.6	0.8	0.6	0.6	1.2	0.4	0.5	0.9	1.5	0.4	1.1	0.7	0.7
2005	0.6	1	1.2	0.6	0.7	0.4	0.5	0.8	2.2	0.6	0.7	0.6	0.7
June 2006	0.6	0.7	0.7	0.5	1.1	0.7	0.6	1	1.1	0.7	0.9	0.6	0.7

Source: Hedgefund.net.

Table 7. Number of hedge funds with persistent positive returns

	Number of funds with consecutive positive returns for				
	1st year	last 2 years	last 3 years	last 4 years	last 5 years
1981	9				
1982	14	9			
1983	19	13	9		
1984	23	14	10	7	
1985	33	22	14	10	7
1986	42	30	20	13	9
1987	43	28	21	14	11
1988	72	39	24	20	13
1989	89	68	37	23	20
1990	108	67	50	29	17
1991	192	96	57	43	25
1992	270	174	85	50	37
1993	407	262	168	84	50
1994	347	244	157	94	45
1995	748	322	230	151	93
1996	1,061	729	315	226	147
1997	1,390	999	689	301	215
1998	1,480	993	709	491	237
1999	2,459	1,325	868	618	426
2000	2,698	1,863	1,004	659	471
2001	3,137	2,040	1,398	751	505
2002	3,218	2,072	1,386	952	496
2003	5,161	2,746	1,766	1,174	840
2004	5,728	4,316	2,293	1,494	992
2005	6,177	4,743	3,549	1,867	1,222
June 2006	5,573	4,862	3,814	2,861	1,559

Source: Hedgefund.net.

in some years. Moreover, the 60-month rolling annualized return correlations between the CSFB Tremont Hedge Fund Index and three other indices (namely equity, bond and commodity indices) have tended to increase significantly in recent years, with the exception of the commodity index. This means that rather than being a good hedge to stock returns, hedge fund returns have recently tended to move more closely in line with them.

Table 8. Assets of hedge funds with persistent positive returns ($ millions)

	Assets of funds with consecutive positive returns for				
	1st year	last 2 years	last 3 years	last 4 years	last 5 years
1981	18				
1982	78	18			
1983	190	33	18		
1984	362	315	34	18	
1985	922	694	599	57	27
1986	1,101	1,063	787	750	83
1987	1,425	1,210	1,112	845	829
1988	2,319	2,070	1,639	1,379	1,200
1989	2,933	2,667	2,335	2,097	1,783
1990	2,693	1,939	1,513	1,223	961
1991	7,391	3,668	2,609	2,138	1,496
1992	8,296	7,045	3,302	2,174	1,466
1993	16,763	13,344	9,707	5,275	3,817
1994	8,178	7,459	5,781	4,017	2,994
1995	24,354	11,742	10,227	8,103	5,275
1996	34,944	30,999	15,364	12,674	9,367
1997	56,458	51,317	42,752	21,300	16,771
1998	59,586	53,728	45,983	39,481	20,294
1999	130,467	83,767	71,135	54,725	46,580
2000	136,988	121,890	84,063	68,306	56,781
2001	204,820	166,155	137,658	88,413	71,677
2002	219,303	186,291	151,760	125,441	74,378
2003	490,756	356,276	276,249	223,287	184,287
2004	635,840	580,046	432,469	337,864	269,086
2005	788,039	713,267	610,264	424,411	333,090
June 2006	864,344	819,711	741,505	623,579	442,443

Source: Hedgefund.net.

Hedge funds have performed comparatively well over various time periods when compared to the performance of major benchmark indices, both using the aggregate return of the funds and the returns for funds employing different strategies. There is, however, a substantial difference in performance depending on the strategies that the funds employ. Furthermore, no single strategy dominates all other strategies over all the time periods examined.

Table 9. Number of hedge funds with persistent negative returns

	Number of funds with consecutive negative returns for				
	1st year	last 2 years	last 3 years	last 4 years	last 5 years
1981	1				
1982	0	0			
1983	1	0	0		
1984	5	0	0	0	
1985	2	0	0	0	0
1986	5	0	0	0	0
1987	16	1	0	0	0
1988	3	0	0	0	0
1989	6	0	0	0	0
1990	29	1	0	0	0
1991	16	2	0	0	0
1992	29	7	1	0	0
1993	17	7	4	1	0
1994	214	6	1	0	0
1995	63	17	0	0	0
1996	55	12	0	0	0
1997	124	9	5	0	0
1998	550	53	2	2	0
1999	289	60	6	2	2
2000	675	41	8	1	0
2001	817	221	7	0	0
2002	1,511	405	131	2	0
2003	395	67	11	1	0
2004	767	127	13	5	0
2005	736	149	35	0	0
June 2006	1,128	175	53	15	0

Source: Hedgefund.net.

4. Some Statistical Analyses

A. Relationship between the Return and Selected Characteristics of a Hedge Fund

There are a number of rigorous studies of the performance and risk of hedge funds in recent years (see the selected references). We do not

Table 10. Assets of hedge funds with persistent negative returns ($ millions)

	With consecutive negative returns for				
	1st year	last 2 years	last 3 years	last 4 years	last 5 years
1981	39				
1982	0	0			
1983	39	0	0		
1984	169	0	0	0	
1985	22	0	0	0	0
1986	50	0	0	0	0
1987	61	13	0	0	0
1988	9	0	0	0	0
1989	322	0	0	0	0
1990	2,313	0	0	0	0
1991	178	2	0	0	0
1992	1,257	55	0	0	0
1993	419	25	1	0	0
1994	11,519	240	4	0	0
1995	1,143	924	0	0	0
1996	591	28	0	0	0
1997	1,738	16	14	0	0
1998	17,314	499	2	2	0
1999	9,790	989	38	16	16
2000	33,506	1,825	21	2	0
2001	33,044	8,032	280	0	0
2002	62,521	14,895	4,740	228	0
2003	17,918	1,259	304	1	0
2004	62,313	8,164	416	50	0
2005	50,650	9,118	1,154	0	0
June 2006	103,798	10,485	3,201	838	0

Source: Hedgefund.net

attempt to provide a comparable study here. Instead, our goal is a much more modest one — to examine the relationship between returns and selected characteristics of hedge funds.

We examine the relationship between the risk-adjusted return, non-risk-adjusted return, standard deviation of non-risk-adjusted returns and selected characteristics of hedge funds. The return regressions show that there is a significantly positive relationship between the risk-adjusted

Figure 1. Five-year risk vs. return of hedge funds, by strategy (January 2001–December 2005)
Source: Milken Institute and Hedgefund.net.

return and the asset size of funds. Management fee, performance incentive, length of lock-up period and age of a fund are not related to risk-adjusted return. Furthermore, the positive relationship between risk-adjusted return and asset size appears to be solely due to the negative relationship between the standard deviation of returns and asset size, not the non-risk-adjusted return and size.

B. Relationship between the Likelihood of a Fund Being Alive and Its Characteristics

Our dataset allows us to examine the relationship between selected characteristics of a fund and its likelihood of being alive. To a very limited degree, this analysis provides information about the risk of individual funds. It does not, however, provide information about the more important issue of the likelihood of the collapse of several large or many medium size hedge funds and the costs such a collapse would impose directly and indirectly on economies. Yet, this is an important issue for as Schinasi (2006, p. 191) points out: "…the turbulence surrounding the near-collapse of LTCM in the autumn of 1998 posed the risk of systemic consequence for the international financial system, and seemed to have created consequences for real economic activity." To the extent that a similar or worse situation could occur again, this topic clearly merits further study.

The results of our logit regressions for the relationship between the likelihood of a fund being alive and selected fund characteristics are reported in Table 11. They indicate the following:

- The more volatile the return the greater the likelihood of the fund not being alive.
- The greater the average monthly returns over the period 1997 to 2005, the higher probability of a fund being alive.
- The likelihood of a fund being alive is greater the bigger the fund and the longer it has been in existence.
- Management fees and performance incentives are positively associated with the likelihood of a fund being alive.
- The longer the initial lock-up period the greater the likelihood of a fund being alive.
- Funds domiciled outside of the United States and funds with assets located outside of the United States are associated with a higher probability of being alive, even after controlling for different strategies that fund employ.

5. Conclusions

The hedge fund industry has grown rapidly in recent years in terms of both number and assets. Such funds represent an alternative and important investment vehicle for wealthier and more financially sophisticated investors. They also help better allocate resources by seeking out exploitable inefficiencies in firms and markets located throughout the world. The returns of hedge funds have generally been relatively high over the years, but so too have the risks. Indeed, the returns for some funds over the selected time periods examined have not compensated for their risk as compared to other funds employing different strategies. This means investors face different risk-return tradeoffs when investing in funds employing different strategies. This, of course, should not a cause for alarm, given the type of investors and lenders putting money into hedge funds.

The fundamental cause for concern about hedge funds is the degree to which they pose a systemic risk to the stability of financial markets and

Table 11. The relationship between the likelihood of a fund being alive and selected fund characteristics

	(1)	(2)	(3)	(4)	(5)	(6)
C	-1.0436***	-1.4829***	-2.0763***	-1.8219***	-2.1217***	-2.6305***
	-0.1012	-0.1083	-0.1203	-0.129	-0.1334	-0.1451
STDEV9705	-0.2277***	-0.2170***	-0.2018***	-0.2151***	-0.2049***	-0.1912***
	-0.0113	-0.0114	-0.0121	-0.0116	-0.0117	-0.0124
RTN9705	0.3602***	0.3502***	0.3396***	0.3678***	0.3595***	0.3443***
	-0.029	-0.0293	-0.031	-0.0296	-0.0298	-0.0314
LOG(ASSET9705)	0.1875***	0.1591***	0.1295***	0.1774***	0.1536***	0.1276***
	-0.0158	-0.0162	-0.0172	-0.0161	-0.0165	-0.0174
LIFE9705	0.0114***	0.0138***	0.0184***	0.0118***	0.0139***	0.0184***
	-0.0009	-0.001	-0.0011	-0.0009	-0.001	-0.0011
MANFEE	0.6997***	0.5957***	0.4100***	0.6635***	0.5790***	0.4276***
	-0.0488	-0.0498	-0.0525	-0.05	-0.0509	-0.0534
INFEE	0.0028	0.0111***	0.0199***	0.0336***	0.0379***	0.0409***
	-0.0038	-0.004	-0.0042	-0.005	-0.0051	-0.0053
INILOCK	0.0006***	0.0012***	0.0013***	0.0005***	0.0011***	0.0012***
	-0.0001	-0.0002	-0.0002	-0.0002	-0.0002	-0.0002
D_ROFF		0.4218***			0.3208***	
		-0.106			-0.1085	
D_RASA		1.3095***			1.1980***	
		-0.2406			-0.2438	
D_REUR		1.0528***			0.9431***	
		-0.0753			-0.0767	

(Continued)

Table 11. (*Continued*)

	(1)	(2)	(3)	(4)	(5)	(6)
D_ROTH		1.1737***			1.0610***	
		-0.1991			-0.2042	
D_LGLO			1.8986***			1.8602***
			-0.0713			-0.0742
D_LEUR			1.8832***			1.8435***
			-0.1394			-0.1419
D_LASA			2.5745***			2.5180***
			-0.1898			-0.1928
D_LOTH			0.6988***			0.8347***
			-0.1399			-0.1468
D_SLS				0.3695***	0.2802***	0.2996***
				-0.0736	-0.0752	-0.0806
D_SFOF				0.9567***	0.8428***	0.6591***
				-0.0881	-0.0898	-0.0942
D_SEVD				-0.3791***	-0.3333***	-0.2096**
				-0.0868	-0.0877	-0.0921
D_SGLOB				0.6003***	0.3735**	-0.0437
				-0.1658	-0.1715	-0.1908
D_SMAC				0.3141**	0.2499	-0.4013**
				-0.1498	-0.152	-0.1637

(*Continued*)

Table 11. (*Continued*)

	(1)	(2)	(3)	(4)	(5)	(6)
McFadden R-squared	0.14	0.16	0.24	0.16	0.18	0.25
Probability (LR stat)	0	0	0	0	0	0
Number of Observations	7,649	7,649	7,649	7,649	7,649	7,649
Number of Live Funds	4,967	4,967	4,967	4,967	4,967	4,967

***, **, and * denote significance level at 1, 5, and 10 percent, respectively. The numbers in parentheses are standard errors.

Note: STDEV9705 is the standard deviation of monthly returns from 1997 to 2005, RTN9705 is average monthly return from 1997 to 2005, LOG(ASSET9705) is log of average assets from 1997 to 2005, LIFE9705 is the age of funds by months from 1997 to 2005, INFEE is incentive fees, INILOCK is the longer of minimum initial lockup period, period between capital withdrawals, or number of days require to give notice before withdrawals, MANFEE is management fees based on assets under management, D_LASA is the dummy for location of assets in Asia, D_LEUR is the dummy for location of assets in Europe, D_LGLO is the dummy for location of assets in global, D_LOTH is the dummy for location of assets in other regions, D_RASA is the dummy for region of domicile in Asia, D_REUR is the dummy for region of domicile in Europe, D_ROFF is the dummy for region of domicile in off-shore centers, D_ROTH is the dummy for region of domicile in other regions, D_SEVD is the dummy for event driven strategy, D_SFOF is the dummy for fund of funds strategy, D_SGLOB is the dummy for global strategy, D_SMAC is the dummy for macro strategy, and D_SMN is the dummy for market neutral strategy.

economic activity. The current state of knowledge appears to be that no one knows for sure the exact magnitude of this risk. Unfortunately, this paper provides no information to help resolve this uncertainty. Yet, to the degree the industry has thus far operated without causing any serious disruptions in markets and economies, there would appear to be no need for introducing new governmental regulation at this time. After all, wealthier and more sophisticated investors can always take action that attracts its displeasure by simply withdrawing their funds. And the banks lending to such funds as well as the brokers and accounting firms servicing them can also take appropriate action to impose greater market discipline on those funds they view as taking on too much risk.

References

Agarwal, V. and N.Y. Naik (2000). Multi-period performance persistence analysis of hedge funds. *Journal of Financial and Quantitative Analysis*, 35, 327–342.

Agarwal, V. and N.Y. Naik (2004). Risks and portfolio decisions involving hedge funds. *Review of Financial Studies*, 17, 63–98.

Brown, S.J., W.N. Goetzmann and J.M. Park (1998). Hedge funds and the Asian currency crisis of 1997. Yale School of Management Working Paper No. F-58, May. http://ssrn.com/abstract=58650

Brown, S.J., W.N. Goetzmann and R.G. Ibbotson (1999). Offshore hedge funds: Survival and performance. *Journal of Business*, 72, 91–117.

Chan, N., M. Getmansky, S. Haas and A.W. Lo (2005) Systemic risk and hedge funds. National Bureau of Economic Research Working Paper No. 11200, March.

Danielson, J., A. Taylor and J.-P. Zigrand (2005). Highwaymen or heroes: Should hedge funds be regulated?. *Journal of Financial Stability*, 1, 522–543.

Edwards, F.R. and M.O. Caglayan (2000). Hedge funds and commodity fund investment styles in bull and bear markets. *Journal of Portfolio Management*, 27, 97–108.

Fung, W. and D.A. Hsieh (1999). A primer on hedge funds. *Journal of Empirical Finance*, 6, 309–331.

Fung, W. and D.A. Hsieh (2000). Measuring the market impact of hedge funds. *Journal of Empirical Finance*, 7, 1–36.

Garbaravicius, T. and F. Dierick (2005). Hedge funds and their implications for financial stability. European Central Bank, Occasional Paper Series, No. 34, August.

Geithner, Timothy F. (2006). Hedge funds and derivatives and their implications for the financial system. Speech, Federal Reserve Bank of New York,

September 15, 2006. http://www.ny.frb.org/newsevents/speeches/2006/gei060914.html

Getmansky, M. (2005). The life cycle of hedge funds: Fund flows, size and performance. Working Paper, January. http://ssrn.com/abstract=676742.

Lhabitant, F.L. (2004). Hedge funds investing: A quantitative look inside the black box. EDHEC Risk and Asset Management Research Center, EDHEC Business School, working paper, April.

Liang, B. (2000). Hedge funds: The living and the dead. *Journal of Financial and Quantitative Analysis*, 35, 309–326.

Lo, A. (2001). Risk management for hedge funds: Introduction and overview. *Financial Analysts Journal*, 57, 16–33.

Lumpkin, S. and H.J. Blommestein (1999). Hedge funds, highly leveraged investment strategies and financial markets. *Financial Market Trends*, 73, 27–50.

Schinasi, G.J. (2005). *Safeguarding Financial Stability: Theory and Practice*. Washington, DC: International Monetary Fund.

Remarks on Causes and Conditions of Financial Instability Panel

Garry Schinasi*
International Monetary Fund

1. Introduction

Let me say something about what I will and will not discuss. There are many causes of, or triggers for, banking problems and financial imbalances more generally. They range from homegrown macroeconomic imbalances and unanticipated macro-economic disturbances to micro-economic and micro-financial decisions. The latter include unpredictable behavior, such as fraudulent activities. The morning session dealt with many of these causes and their consequences, so I will not address them.

My presentation will focus mainly on two areas: 1) the potential channels through which financial imbalances can be transmitted across borders — cross-border banking groups, hedge funds and global markets, and 2) challenges in managing the potential systemic risks in cross-border finance. The discussion will focus to a large extent on hedge funds, because large banking groups are closely regulated and supervised and global markets are subject to surveillance. However, many important challenges remain to be addressed for these closely supervised and watched parts of the international financial system, which I will touch on as well.

2. Context and Background

The three papers in this session examine different but related aspects of these challenges. Bent Vale's paper discusses — within the context of the

*Garry Schinasi, an Advisor in the International Monetary Fund's Finance Department, thanks the organizers of the conference and the Federal Reserve Bank of Chicago for continuing to host this important, global, annual conference. The author is expressing his personal views, not the views of the International Monetary Fund (IMF) or IMF policy, or the views of the IMF's management, staff or board.

Nordic experience — the benefits and challenges of cross-border banking groups, for home and host countries in which various parts of the entity operate and for the various members of the group. The paper by Jim Barth and his coauthors examines the growth and transformation of the hedge fund industry. Jon Danielson's and Gabriel Galati's paper studies a familiar channel and problem but in a different way.

The channels through which financial problems can be transmitted from one country to another can usefully be classified into three broad categories: institutions, markets and infrastructures. This triad, together with legal and monetary arrangements, and business practices and codes of conduct, are a reasonable way of defining what is normally meant by the term "financial system". Cross-border linkages of components of this triad can be seen as constituting the main channels through which problems in one national financial system get transmitted to another one. It should not be forgotten, however, that the global economy is probably the most basic and prevalent cross-border transmitter of economic or financial weaknesses, but this is the purview of macroeconomists and monetary and fiscal policymakers.

The subject of Bent Vale's paper falls into the first category, that of Danielson's and Galati's into the second, and that of the Milken team's in between the first and second. The papers say little, if anything, about infrastructure, so I will say next to nothing. This can be justified on the grounds that much of what can be said about the pubic policy challenges surrounding financial institutions and markets applies to infrastructures.

To provide some further context for these papers, the rows of Table 1 summarize the main public policy issues and concerns that can arise for the institutions and markets examined collectively in the papers. There are three broad areas where policy issues arise to varying degrees from cross-border banks, foreign exchange (FX) and other global markets, and hedge funds: protecting investors and markets, dealing with safety net issues and moral hazard, and assessing and mitigating cross-border and systemic risk. All three issues are very important for banks generally and cross-border banks in particular and for global markets. Investor protection and safety net issues are seen widely as not being relevant for hedge funds, while many, though not all, believe that hedge funds can pose systemic risk. The potential systemic risk associated with the collapse of the hedge fund Long-Term Capital Management (LTCM) is a case in point.

Taking this classification as given, how are these risks and public policy concerns addressed through financial policies? That is, to what extent are the tools of financial policies used to address these concerns? Table 2 is one, perhaps exaggerated, way of answering this question.

Table 1. Public policy issues and concerns

Issues and Concerns	Cross-Border Institutions	International Markets	Hedge Funds
Protection/ Integrity?	Investor protection	Market integrity	No; Possibly for retail investors (of funds of funds)
Moral Hazard from Safety Net?	Yes; and home/ host burden sharing issues	Possibly from G-3 Central Bank liquidity	No
Cross-Border and Systemic Risks?	Maybe, depends on size, complexity, etc.	Yes, via OTC markets and infrastructure linkages	Yes, via opacity, complexity, and with institutions and markets

Table 2. Oversight regimes

Oversight	Cross-Border Institutions	International Markets	Hedge Funds
Regulation	National with cooperation	Not really; over-the-counter transactions	No
Supervision	National and home/host issues	N.A.	No
Surveillance	Indirect, as participant	Direct, national and international	Indirect, as participant
Market Discipline	Partially	Primarily	Exclusively

As indicated in the first column of Table 2, large cross-border banking groups — including the large internationally active banks — are probably the most closely regulated and supervised organizations on the planet, and for good reasons.

- These institutions pose financial risks for depositors, investors, markets, and even unrelated financial stakeholders because of their size, scope, complexity, and of course their risk taking.
- Some of them are intermediaries, investors, brokers, dealers, insurers, reinsurers, infrastructure owners and participants, and so on all rolled up into a single complex institution.

- They are systemically important: all of them nationally, many of them regionally, and about 20 or so of them globally.
- Protection, safety net, and systemic risks issues are key pubic policy challenges.
- Oversight occurs at the national level, through both market discipline and official involvement, and at the international level through committees, groups.

As a result, banks generally, and cross-border and global banks are probably the most closely watched financial institutions in the world.

At the other extreme of regulation and supervision are hedge funds, as can be seen in the right-most column of Table 2.

- They are neither regulated nor supervised. Many of the financial instruments hedge funds use strategically and tactically are not subject to securities regulation and the markets in which they transact are by-and-large the least regulated and supervised. This is part of their investment strategy and it defines the scope of profit making.
- Hedge funds are forbidden in some national jurisdictions. In jurisdictions where they are partially regulated, this is tantamount to being forbidden — given the global nature and fungibility of the hedge-fund business model.
- Their market activities are subject to market surveillance just like other institutions, but this does not make transparent who is doing what, how they are doing it, and with whom.
- Investor protection is not an issue for most individual hedge funds, as they restrict their investor base to wealthy individuals and institutions willing to invest in relatively high minimum amounts.
- Investor protection is becoming an issue with the advent of funds-of-hedge-funds that allow minimum investments of relatively small amounts less than $100,000 or even less than $50,000.
- Probably beginning with the Asian crisis and then LTCM, and intensifying with their tremendous growth over the past several years, hedge funds are increasingly being seen as potentially giving rise to systemic risk concerns, a theme I will return to later.

Global markets fall in between being and not being regulated and supervised. What is meant by global markets? Examples are the FX markets and their associated derivatives markets (both exchange-traded and over-the-counter) and the G-3 fixed-income markets as well as others associated with international financial centers (pound, Swiss franc, etc) as well as their associated derivatives markets. Dollar, euro, and yen government bonds are traded more-or-less in a continuous global market, and the associated derivatives activities are also global.

Global markets are only indirectly regulated. They are subject to surveillance through private international networks and business-cooperation agreements, through information sharing by central banks and supervisory and regulatory authorities, and through official channels, committees, and working groups. Parts of these markets are linked to national clearance, settlement and payments infrastructures, so they are also subject to surveillance through these channels. The risks they potentially pose are less of a concern to the extent that the major players in them — the large internationally active banks — are well supervised and well market-disciplined by financial stakeholders. And both investor protection and systemic risk are challenging public-policy issues.

Regarding infrastructure, the financial activities discussed in all three papers pass through the third transmission channel, at least their balance sheet transactions involving securities trading. Large internationally active banks typically are major participants in domestic and international clearance, settlement and payments infrastructures — both public and private — as well as the major trading exchanges. Many of them co-own parts of the national and international infrastructures and have a natural interest in their performance and viability. Incentives are to some extent aligned to achieve both private and collective net benefits.[1] Increasingly, however, internationally active banks are becoming more heavily involved in over-the-counter transactions, which do not pass through these infrastructures. This poses systemic risk challenges.

---

[1] The phrase "to some extent" needs to be emphasized. Consider, for example, that the G-10 central banks decide to get out of the business altogether of providing clearance, settlement and payment services on foreign-exchange transactions — as might have been considered years ago when they challenged private institutions to solve the Herstatt problem. If this decision was taken, then the major international banks would have the incentive to organize fully the clearance, settlement, and payment on FX transactions. But if this were to happen, then this organization would clearly be too big to fail or even to liquidate in a timely manner without enormous global systemic consequences.

3. The Papers: Cross-Border Banking Groups

Let me now turn to more specific aspects of the papers. As far as regulation and supervision are concerned, the domain covered in Bent Vale's paper — large cross-border banking groups — is extensively regulated and supervised, because they incur the full gamut of public-policy issues. Bent examines these groups as transmitters of both financial stability (FS) and instability (FI), depending on whether you take the host countries perspective, the home countries perspective, the perspective of other members of the banking group or a global perspective.

Vale finds that while in normal times banks in a group receive diversification benefits, when problems arise — such as large loan losses — the problem bank might continue to receive benefits, but other members of the group might be subject to adverse consequences related to contagion. For example, to the extent that the parent of the group provides liquidity and perhaps even additional capital to bolster the problem banks balance sheet, the host country of the troubled bank receives FS benefits, whereas the other host countries might not, and may even experience FI costs as the other banks in group might be seen as also subject to the same weaknesses of the problem bank within the group.

Vale examines the Nordic experience and finds support for these hypotheses. Moreover, if the foreign banks are branches rather than subsidiaries the costs and benefits play out differently just as one might expect.

There are other important issues not taken up in Vale's paper.

- Many banking groups are complex organizations at the group level and lack transparency (at least to financial stakeholders, if not also regulators/supervisors). This can diminish the effectiveness of both market discipline and official oversight in mitigating the build up of weaknesses and imbalances within members of the group and the group.
- Large cross-border groups often are large conglomerations of different business lines from different regulatory regimes (insurance, banking, investment banking, etc.).
- There are counterparty relationships between the group and its members within both home and host countries not necessarily reflected in their balance sheet accounts and transactions.
- Cross-border banks and groups have increasingly become more involved in financial markets activities, including in the global OTC

derivatives markets, which as noted lack transparency and where official oversight and surveillance are important public-policy issues.

4. FX and Other Global Markets

Jon Danielson and Gabriele Galati's paper tries to improve on models of currency crises, which usually take place to some, if not a large, extent through the intermediary activities of the large institutions transacting in the global markets, including derivatives markets. The FX markets are some of the deepest and most liquid markets in the world, at least when they are functioning normally. The paper is innovative in terms of techniques and it introduces a key quantity variable in determining price, namely volume. It is hard to believe this has not been done before, but data constrains the possibilities.

The paper reaches intuitive results, namely that volume matters. The set of models could be a helpful addition to the tool kits for both monetary and financial stability analysis, but further development and refinement would be needed.

While the models examined by D and G might in the end help in calibrating risk, a key issue for the global FX market, as well as other global, international and regional markets, is systemic risk: how to monitor and assess it, and how to prevent it without creating moral hazard. Here counterparty risk is key, because much of the positioning and trading in these markets involves OTC derivatives markets — for currencies as well as fixed-income instruments.

5. Hedge Funds

James Barth and his coauthors engage in an impressive and fruitful exercise of data mining. The paper is encyclopedic in scope given the paucity of information on this industry. It provides a good narrative of the key points to be gleaned from an extensive set of tables and charts, including in the appendix. Readers will be well served by taking the time to review the data provided.

Barth and his coauthors acknowledge up front that systemic risk is an important issue. But they shy away from it, noting that the literature has so far been unable to calibrate the extent of it. Fair enough, but the possibility of hedge-fund related systemic risk is too important not to be discussed here in this conference. Moreover, if it was not an important unknown in the complex world of global finance, why would central bankers and regulators be openly discussing the risks associated with hedge funds in their speeches and in op-ed pieces in the *Financial Times*? The fact that these discussions are taking place is probably a reasonable indicator of the potential for some concern including the possibility of systemic risk.

There are several policy-related questions worth considering.

First and foremost, do hedge funds pose systemic risk? Ed and his coauthors are correct in observing that hedge-fund related systemic risk is difficult to identify. This is probably especially so in the early stages of imbalances. But this is also true of other potentially costly systemic events — or "tail" events — in other fields of study, such as health (heart attacks), geology (earthquakes), and weather patterns (tsunami's and hurricanes). Each of these fields has ways of monitoring and assessing the possibility of unlikely events because the cost of not knowing when they might occur are potentially very high. Expenditure of effort should be balanced against the potential cost of not being aware of the event. Long-Term Capital Management suggests there is the risk of systemic consequences. As a result, it might be worthwhile devoting resources to calibrating the risk and even preventing its occurrence. I don't know how to do this, but maybe the disciplines mentioned above have some techniques that might be useful.

Second, most jurisdictions rely on market discipline to 'regulate' hedge funds and their activities. This usually includes relying on the large financial institutions to manage their counterparty risks with hedge funds. From a systemic-risk management perspective, is it optimal to rely on systemically important private financial institutions to "regulate" hedge funds?

Third, hedge funds are required to disclose, and actually disclose, very little, including to their investors. Moreover, their strategies, tactics, market activities, and counterparty risks lack transparency. While many of their counterparties are regulated and supervised, and while this provides a window on hedge fund activities, it is not clear that authorities have sufficient information and knowledge about how to aggregate it into an assessment of the systemic risk potential. The question is: Has public policy yet achieved the appropriate balance of transparency and disclosure on the one hand and protecting proprietary information for risk taking on the other?

A fourth question: Are private incentives consistent with the public good; that is do they create the possibility of systemic risk? Let's consider Amaranth, which does not seem to have posed systemic issues. Why did Amaranth encounter the fast-breaking problems it faced. Once a hedge fund becomes successful — say 20 to 30 percent returns over a period of years — money pours into them like a flood. Hedge funds managers don't like to turn money away, so they invest more in the area in which they are successful and open new desks with new exposures. This creates several tendencies for increasing risk:

* their original positions get larger relative the market;
* returns on investments go lower, so they apply more leverage; and
* the new people they hire to open new desks lack the experience to invest the sums of money they are given to invest.

If all of the risks were incurred privately, then there would be no need for regulation. But if there is the possibility of systemic risk, then some form of oversight is justifiable and probably desirable. Does this mean hedge funds should be regulated?

Several other questions are worth considering.

First, what constitutes a "good" solution for better containing the risk of a systemic problem relating to hedge funds? An important part of answering this question is better understanding the benefits and costs. Hedge funds provide liquidity, they pool and share risks that many are not willing to take, and tend to stabilize price movements during normal times. But, they also take great risks — including through highly leveraged strategies and positions. This means when things go wrong, they really go wrong. How should these potential benefits and costs be balanced?

Second, what is the actual scope for achieving a solution? That is, what can actually be done in today's environment of national orientations for regulation and supervision? The hedge fund industry is global. If one jurisdiction outlaws them or, what is the same thing, tightly regulates them, they will spring up somewhere else. The solution must be global. The current set of policymakers seem to be moving in a constructive direction, but until something is institutionalized, it is difficult to be confident that their solution will endure beyond their tenures in service.

Third, why is it difficult to reach a consensus for regulating hedge funds as closely as other financial institutions? It comes down to costs and benefits. We more or less know the benefits. What have been the social costs of hedge fund disasters?

- It is difficult to gauge the "dead weight" losses to societies from the meltdowns, perhaps with the exceptions of what happened in some emerging markets during the Asian crises in 1997–2000. Even then, it is not certain that hedge funds were the important players, though they clearly have been portrayed as such.
- Usually what has happened is that a hedge fund goes out of business, assets and liabilities get re-priced and sold in the market, and gains and losses get redistributed. To the extent that there has been collateral damage, it seems to have been small, or at least hidden.
- Consider LTCM. On the one hand, the private sector was incapable of reaching a solution: there was a private coordination failure. The Federal Reserve Bank of New York stepped in and facilitated a private rescue, in part because of concerns over systemic problems. How potentially systemic was it? This is difficult to measure.
- One way of thinking about the cost of LTCM's collapse is to consider what it took to avoid further problems. That is we can ask the following question: If a reduction of 50–75 basis points on the Federal Funds rate for several weeks was sufficient to quell the systemic consequences and collateral damage, was the event systemic?
- This is difficult to answer. There probably was not a high probability of a systemic threat. But there was the possibility of one with potentially very costly and widespread consequences.
- Should policy opt for the "better to be safe than sorry" solution? If so, policy needs to ensure that financial stakeholders bear the full cost of their mistakes — to minimize the moral hazard of such a solution.

Finally, what is actually being done? There seems to be a growing consensus that there is scope for improving transparency through disclosure, and improving the exercise and effect of market discipline. This is essentially what is meant by improving counterparty risk management — advocated publicly recently by Ben Bernanke, Tim Geithner and Gerry Corrigan.

This was advocated in 1999, in the aftermath of LTCM, and not much progress has been made. Beyond this, there does not seem to be much consensus.

In summary, there are three main areas where challenges remain, each requiring continuing innovation, enhancement, and updating.

- The ability to *assess systemic risk* is in a formative stage of development and is likely to remain so for some time to come. There are formidable jurisdictional, informational and analytical challenges in assessing systemic risk. Moreover, the nature of systemic risk is continually changing as a result of financial innovation, globalization and integration.
- The *effectiveness of market discipline* as a line of defense against both private and systemic risk needs to be enhanced. There are three areas where it is obvious that transparency and disclosure are insufficient for the exercise of effective market discipline: large complex financial institutions; global over-the-counter derivatives markets; and hedge funds and other financial institutions or hybrids that fall outside the scope of existing radar screens.
- The third area is *official oversight*. Because finance is inherently beset with market imperfections (information asymmetries, externalities, imperfect competition), relying exclusively on market discipline would tend to fall short of safeguarding financial systems against the potential costs of systemic risk and financial crises. Thus, there clearly is a role for official involvement in the form of financial regulation, supervision, and surveillance. But excessive involvement tends to inhibit financial and economic efficiency and the ability of economies to allocate resources, to grow and ultimately to prosper. A key challenge is to strike an economically and socially acceptable balance between relying on market discipline and official oversight and intervention.

Many of the papers in this conference strongly suggest that there is a lot of work before us in dealing with these issues as they pertain to cross-border banking, and cross-border finance more generally.

Thank you.

IV. PRUDENTIAL SUPERVISION

Home Country Versus Cross-Border Negative Externalities in Large Banking Organization Failures and How to Avoid them

Robert A. Eisenbeis*

Federal Reserve Bank of Atlanta

1. Introduction

A recent trend around the world beginning in the early 2000s has been the production of financial stability reports designed to communicate and evaluate the health of individual country financial systems. Virtually every major central bank, except the Federal Reserve and Bank of Italy, are now publishing stability reports on a regular basis. These reports evaluate developments in financial markets and across various types of financial institutions that may affect the health of financial systems.[1] However, these reports have had little to say about the risks that are beginning to evolve related to changes in the banking structures themselves, such as the expansion of banking organization across country borders.

To date, the risks associated with multinational banking have been the focus of banking supervisors whose primary concern is that the failure of a large multinational banking organization might result in systemic risks that threaten the solvency of other banking organizations or the health of financial markets. This chapter attempts to do two things. First, it drills down to consider exactly what these systemic risks are. Second, it attempts to examine whether there is anything special about cross-border banking

* Robert A. Eisenbeis is Executive Vice President and Director of Research at the Federal Reserve Bank of Atlanta. The author is indebted to George G. Kaufman and William Roberds for helpful comments and suggestions.

[1] See International Monetary Fund (2006), Norges Bank (2006), Reserve Bank of New Zealand (2006), Banco de Espana (2006), Bank of England (2006) for examples. For a review of these reports, see Oosterloo *et al.* (2006).

and how problems in a large banking organization may be resolved should it experience financial difficulties that might either exacerbate or moderate systemic risk concerns.

2. Sources and Nature of Systemic Risks

While central banks and regulators are concerned with limiting systemic risks, the exact nature of those risks and how they can adversely affect financial markets or the real economy are not always spelled out in sufficient detail to be amenable to analysis. Without a specific enumeration of the problems, it is difficult to evaluate alternative policies and regulatory efforts to control them.

In the theoretical literature systemic risk concerns have typically focused on Great Depression-style bank runs.[2] Diamond–Dybvig's model describes when participating in a run and suspension of convertibility of deposits represent optimal depositor and bank behavior. But it does not explain what triggers that run, which simply emerges exogenously. Furthermore, since there is only one bank in the Diamond–Dybvig world, a run on a bank is in fact a run on the banking system. How a run on one bank in a multiple-bank banking system gets propagated into a run on many banks is not examined.

The supervisory concern about a flight to currency from deposits resulting from uncertainty about the health of one bank is that it could spill over to healthy banks. In this sense, a currency run on a single bank could quickly become contagious. The result would be a cumulative collapse in the deposit money supply as deposits are exchanged for currency and withdrawn from the banking system. The sudden and unanticipated withdrawal of funds could bring down even a solvent bank if it didn't have sufficient funds on hand to meet the demand, thereby creating a liquidity problem.

Theoretical work extending this liquidity component as a propagator of a banking crisis relies upon a shock to aggregate output that lowers expected returns on assets. This creates a systemwide liquidity crisis and collapse of asset values.[3] Because early liquidation of banking assets is

---

[2] See Diamond and Dybvig (1983), Kaufman (1988), Chari and Jagannanthan (1988), Chari (1989), Jacklin (1987), Jacklin and Bhattacharya (1988) and Wallace (1988, 1990).
[3] See Gorton (1988).

costly, intervention by the central bank though its lender of last resort function and/or through open market operations has been justified.[4] Importantly, intervention in such a case is not designed to stem the runs but rather to prevent the decline in asset values (Allen and Gale, 1998).

Despite the large volume of theoretical work, the basic causes of runs and liquidity crises in banking and sources of the shocks to information about bank soundness or to asset values remain largely unexplained. Researchers who have attempted to do so have argued 1) that banks were unstable (see Minsky, 1975; or Chari, 1989), 2) that depositors are irrational, or 3) that information about bank asset values is asymmetric and not uniformly available to all market participants, making it both difficult to distinguish among good and bad firms and rational for depositors to withdraw their funds.[5] However, none of these explanations are particularly satisfying. Lastly, another body of work has evolved from the Real Business Cycle literature suggests that such shocks are simply a natural byproduct of the business cycle and thus, what remains is to limit the damage.

More recently, those that have taken a market (or macro) view of crises look to liquidity problems in particular financial or product markets rather than to problems in individual institutions.[6] Theoretical work in this area has focused on episodes like the US stock market decline in 1987 or the Asian, Mexican and Latin American crises which were crises in international foreign exchange and currency markets. [7–9]

---

[4] See Allen and Gale (1998) whose model generates a run without a first come first served assumption. See also Schoenmaker and Oosterloo (2005) who specifically examine the potential contagion concerns within the EU. Boot (2006) provides a discussion of some of this literature.

[5] See Rochet (2004)

[6] Allen and Gale (2000) have provided a modeling framework that attempts to explain how a shock to one sector of an economy or financial market may become contagious and spread to other sectors.

[7] Schwartz (1998) argues that it is questionable whether there is evidence of country contagion similar to that feared in the bank contagion literature. Indeed, she argues that imprudent fiscal policies and inattention to reform of insolvent banking systems were the cause of financial problems. Meltzer (1998) argues that Asian crises in 1997 reflected moral hazard behavior that had it roots in IMF and governmental bailout responses to the 1995 crisis in Mexico.

[8] See Chang and Velasco (2000, 2001), Champ *et al.* (1996) for examples.

[9] Contrary to what some have asserted, the Federal Reserve did not provide central bank funds but simply provided a meeting place for counterparties and creditors of LTCM to meet and work out an acceptable restructuring.

While we have still not gained a good understanding of the causes of either financial crises or contagion for banks or in financial markets more generally, two conclusions do flow from this work. First, studies of individual crises suggest that problems in the real side tend to lead rather than result from financial crises. Second, once a financial crisis does occur, it can sometimes amplify or feed back to the real side, making problems there worse. However, neither the theoretical work nor empirical work helps to understand why some market may implode while others may not.

Despite these short comings, however, history is filled with various examples of financial crises and governments and central banks have typically stepped in to limit supposed negative externalities they may involve. It is important, at least in the case of banking, to understand exactly what these negative externalities are before one can evaluate proposals to deal with them or assess whether certain regulatory arrangements may dampen or perhaps exacerbate these externalities when a crisis emerges.

3. Negative Externalities and Banking Failures[10]

Understanding the negative externalities associated with banking crises requires identification of who the affected parties are and how they are impacted.[11] When a bank also cannot pay out all its debts, including deposits in full and on time, it goes into default, losses will be incurred, and the resolution process to allocate those losses and dispose of the failed bank must begin. Insured depositors will be paid, and uninsured depositors and other creditors will share in the losses according to their legal priority with equity holders receiving any residual values, if any remain.

During the resolution process, claimants may experience both credit and liquidity losses. The size and duration of those losses depend critically on the nature of the resolution processes and legal arrangements in place. Credit losses to debt holders and depositors may occur when the recovery value of the bank, as a whole, or in parts falls short of the par value of its debts on their respective due dates. In the case of uninsured depositors, for

---

[10] This section draws heavily on and may repeat material from Eisenbeis and Kaufman (2005, 2006), and Wall and Eisenbeis (1999).

[11] In the US, for example, the banking supervisor determines that a bank is insolvent and should be closed, but the triggering event is when the Federal Reserve presents a cash letter to the bank that can't be paid. In other countries, the triggering event is typically when a payment to a private customer can't be made.

example, losses are a function of not only the size of the claim, but also whether depositors are allowed to offset any deposit claims against any loans they may owe to the bank before sharing in any pro-rata claims. In the case of collateralized deposits, the ability to avoid losses depends upon the legal status of the collateral claims and where the collateral is held. Of course, collateralization of deposits, like discount window borrowing, creates a preferred liability in that payment is tied to the value of high quality assets — usually the highest quality assets that the bank has, such as Treasury obligations. This also means that the pledged assets would not be available to meet the claims of other depositors who then have to rely on recovering from the liquidation of lower quality assets, thereby increasing the probability that they will incur losses.

Liquidity losses may occur for four reasons. First, depositors may not have immediate (next business day or so) and full access to the par value of their insured claims or to the estimated recovery value of their *de jure* uninsured claims. Delays in access to funds could force depositors to liquidate other assets or cause them to default on loans to other creditors, including suppliers if they don't have other assets to sell. Second, qualified borrowers may not be able to utilize their existing credit lines immediately. Those with no established substitutes could experience business disruption, loss of access to working capital, or be forced to default on obligations. Third, there may be both liquidity problems and ultimately credit losses associated with payment and settlement system failures when a problem in one institution is transmitted via the payments system to others who are awaiting payments but that can't be settled because of the failure of the bank counterparty.[12] Fourth, with the growth of derivative and swap markets, the failure of a major player in those markets would disrupt hedges and force counterparties to re-establish their positions. Some may not be able to do so, and the priority of contingent claims in bankruptcy is not always clear. Thus the failure of a bank that was also a major counterparty in derivatives markets might have negative spillovers to other market participants, increasing their risk exposures and the cost of both credit to borrowers and liability issuance to financial institutions.[13]

The potential for disruption to derivatives markets was the concern in the case of Long-Term Capital Management (LTCM). Now, it is debatable whether and what type of government or central bank intervention would

---

[12] See Schoenmaker and Oosterloo (2005).

[13] Mengle (2006) argues that actions have been taken in an attempt to provide private sector solutions to this problem.

be appropriate in such cases, and whether that intervention would be justified if the troubled institution was a bank as opposed to some other type of financial firm. In the LTCM case, the Federal Reserve only brought LTCM together with its creditors who resolved LTCM without use of government or central bank funds. It was also the case that prompt resolution by its major creditors did avoid serious disruptions to the markets in which LTCM was a major player. Furfine (2006) has demonstrated through exploration of Fedwire data that there is no evidence that counterparties to LTCM experience liquidity problems during the episode. Whether central bank funds would have been involved or whether, had the same factual circumstances existed for a large bank, it would have been permitted to borrow at the discount window is an interesting question to be explored.[14]

The extent of these liquidity and credit costs to depositors and borrowers, and the secondary spillovers to their creditors and customers, determine the negative externalities and social costs of the failure. Clearly, the larger the institution, the greater and more complex are the linkages to other institutions and markets. These linkages increase the chance that negative externalities associated with their failure might have undesirability spillover effects to other markets and institutions.

Experience suggests that that both the legal and regulatory structure may generate both conflicts of interest and agency costs resulting in forbearance or delay in resolving troubled institutions causing credit and liquidity problems. Moreover, these negative externalities may be exacerbated when cross-border banking organizations experience financial difficulties.

4. Conflicts of Interest, Agency Costs, and Bankruptcy Laws: Their Role in Affecting the Negative Externalities of Banking Failures

The responsible agencies often are subject to agency costs or conflicts of interest that can incent them to engage in forbearance by delaying the closure of insolvent institutions or to delay resolving institutions once they

---

[14] Both markets and regulators do learn from dealing with large troubled institutions, and may be less prone to intervene after the first major case has occurred. Recently, for example, the reported loss by the large hedge fund Amaranth Advisors of over $6 billion, or nearly 65 percent of its assets, from taking positions in energy derivatives caused scarcely a ripple in financial markets, and there was no call for intervention. See Sender (2006).

have been legally closed, and this can increase credit losses.[15] Liquidity problems can be increased if there are legal or other impediments to prompt resolution, closure, recapitalization, and return to operations of large banking organizations that have failed.

Credit losses are most likely to arise when conflicts adversely affect the incentives of regulators to act promptly to deal with problems as they arise. Self interest and incentive problems of the classical principle/agent type exist between and among banking supervisors and taxpayers usually result in delay. The reason is that regulators have incentives to pursue policies that preserve their agencies and protect their turf and self interest. These incentives lead to a "not-on-my-watch" mentality and lead to regulatory gambling that the agency can "work out the problem or aid in restoring troubled institutions to solvency." It is perceived to be better not to have major institutions fail if you are the regulator and responsible at the time the failure occurs. Agency preservation provides incentives to ensure that problems are "worked out" rather than result in the closer of a major institution. Institution failure, given that the supervisor is charged with surveillance and intervention when problems arise, can quickly be interpreted by outside parties as an agency failure or, in the case of the person in charge, a leadership failure. Either or both reinforce incentives of regulators to pursue their own private self-interest and to maintain their agency's reputation in order to protect their own jobs and future marketability and employment in the banking industry.[16] These conflicts may lead to more accommodating policies in the form of lower than appropriate capital requirements and to regulatory forbearance when institutions get in trouble, thereby shifting risk and any associated costs to taxpayers and/or the deposit insurance fund as regulators attempt to ingratiate themselves with constituent banks.

An example of such delay, despite the Federal Deposit Insurance Corporation Improvement Act's (FDICIA) early intervention and prompt

---

[15] Horvitz (1983) discussed the problems that overlapping regulatory structure may involve specifically in the context of financial regulation of US banking. He suggested that policies may be interpreted, applied and implemented differently and jurisdictional conflicts might arise between the regulatory agencies over the form, substance, and implementation of regulations. The range of policy areas with possible goals that may be subject to possible conflicts for bank regulators includes: consumer protection (for both retail and wholesale customers), monetary policy, community development, investor protection, market transparency, safety and soundness, ensuring the safety net, reducing systemic risk and antitrust. See also Kane (2000).

[16] See Kane (1991, 1989, 2006), Schüler (2003) and Lewis (1997).

corrective action mandate, was seen recently in the problems surrounding the handling of the failure of Superior Bank whose failure cost its insurance fund an estimated $763 million or about 40 percent of the institution's assets.[17] A recent Government Accountability Office (GAO) report found several problems with the supervision and handling of this institution by Office of Thrift Supervision (OTS) including: failure to recognize warning signs that the institution was engaged in risky behavior many years before its failure; lack of cooperation and coordination with the FDIC who sought to exercise its right to examine the institution when its analysis suggested that the institution was engaging in excessively risky strategies, problems with the accounting which interfered with proper functioning of prompt corrective action (PCA), questionable findings by the institution's external auditors concerning accounting practices, undue reliance by OTS on the belief that the owners who where both prominent and wealthy individuals would not let the institution fail, and delays on the part of the FDIC to promptly resolve the failure in the hopes that principals would provide additional capital.[18]

While there were numerous breakdowns in the supervisory process, two key features of US law and banking regulation prevented the failure from having negative externalities on customers, depositors or financial markets. The first was the existence of special bankruptcy laws that enabled the institution to be closed by the regulators. The second was resolution policies that permitted the FDIC to transfer assets and liabilities immediately to a newly chartered Federal Savings Bank and to serve as conservator until it was subsequently re-privatized through sale to another banking organization.[19] This enabled insured depositors to have continuous and immediate access to their funds and causing little disruption to borrowers.[20] It is these two features — a special bankruptcy law and authority of the regulator to close a trouble institution — if exercised so

---

[17] See Office of Inspector General (2002).

[18] GAO (2002) and Johnson (2005).

[19] In a bank failure, the FDIC was given authority in 1987 under the Competitive Equity and Banking Act to create a bridge (or temporary) bank to facilitate the resolution of the failed entity while enabling depositors to have access to their funds. Functionally, this process is similar to that used in the Superior, FSB case where the FDIC lacked authority to create a bridge federal savings bank. For a detailed discussion and comparison of bankruptcy processes for banks as compared to non-banks, see Bliss and Kaufman (2006).

[20] To be sure there were law suits filed against the auditors, but the case was dismissed and uninsured depositors lost funds.

as to provide depositors and borrows' immediate access to their funds and borrowers' access to credit that are key to minimizing negative externalities associated with banking failures. Borrowers and creditors know with certainty that they will have immediate access to their resources and thus the incentive to engage in a run, for example, is minimized and failures become isolated events. Agency problems and goal conflicts, to the extent that they provide incentives for regulators to engage in forbearance, increase the losses that the taxpayer and deposit insurance funds may have to bear, but do not in all circumstances increase the negative externalities to bank customers of a failure.

Cross-border banking arrangements raise additional issues and considerations which suggest that the risks of negative externalities may be greater should a large, cross-border institution fail.[21] Likely externalities depend on not only the relative importance of the activities in the home country relative to the host country, but also on whether cross-border banking takes place through branches or though separately chartered subsidiaries. For example, if a large banking organization has a very large share of the banking business in the host country, but not in the home country, and it fails, there could be substantial disruptions to both banking and commerce in the host country if customers don't have ready access to their funds, but there might be little impact on customers of markets in the home country.[22]

Deciding when to close the institution, for example, may not only affect the availability of funds, but also may determine the incident of loss. For example, in the failure of Herstatt Bank, the home country German authorities decided to close the bank during the middle of the banking day, such that certain foreign exchange transactions hadn't totally settled.[23] While the closure policy did not affect the fact that losses had

---

[21] See Schüler and Heinemann (2005).

[22] The relative shares of banking organizations in Europe, for example, suggest just this kind of concern. In Estonia, foreign banking organizations control 98 percent of the banking assets and in at least 8 of the 25 EU countries, out of country banks control 50 percent or more of the banking assets. See Eisenbeis and Kaufman (2006), and Schoenmaker and Laecke (2006). Lindgren (2006) suggests that the failure of Meridien Bank BIAO in Africa in 1995 was an example of negative cross-border externalities associated with the failure of that institution.

[23] In particular, for certain mark-dollar settlements, the mark side of the transaction had settled, but the dollar payments were not due to settle until later in the day after the institution had closed. This meant that dollar claimants were put into a potential loss position.

occurred, it did affect which parties bore the loss. This case illustrates the dilemma the regulators may face in weighing the consequences for the customers and economies of different countries of alternative regulatory and supervisory policies and especially decisions when to close troubled institutions and when to invoke lender-of-last resort or emergency lending to provide additional liquidity to markets and institutors.[24]

Divided loyalties and conflicts may lead banking supervisors and regulators of troubled banking organizations to prefer resolutions that favor their own citizens and to operate in what they consider is the best interest of their country, however defined or perceived (see Herring, 2007; and Bollard, 2005).[25] Logically, the incentives of the regulators, deposit insurance provider and/or failure resolution entity are typically aligned with the residents of the regulators' home rather than with the interests of all customers in the whole market or geographic area within which the institution operates. Thus, it seems inevitable that negative externalities that may result from a large cross-border banking failure will be shifted to host countries rather than imposed upon home countries.

As foreign banking organizations' market share of host country assets increases through merger or acquisition host country regulators face two problems, both of which deal with problems of access to information. When expansion takes place through branching and acquisitions, host country regulators face not only a loss of constituents to supervise and regulate, but also, if the host country is responsible for lender of last resort functions, then lending to the branch of a troubled bank that they don't supervise faces the central bank (or lender of last resort) with the prospect of having to rely upon the home country for information on the solvency

---

[24] Provisions of FDICIA changed the rules in an attempt to eliminate Herstatt problems for US banks. It essentially gave priority in bankruptcy to netting arrangements among banks over all other claimants.

[25] This problem has arisen in France with the country's attempt to preserve Credit Lyonnais with injections of governmental funds in more than three separate instances in the past several years. More recently, an editorial in the *Wall Street Journal Europe* (2005) entitled "Spaghetti Banking" pointed out that the governor of the Bank of Italy had refused to approve the acquisition of a single Italian bank by a foreign institution for the last 12 years. The governor indicated his desire to "preserve the banks' Italianness also in the future". This protectionism was challenged by the European Union's Internal Market Commission in connection with the proposed acquisitions of two Italian banks by ABN Amro and Banco Bilbao Vizcaya Argentina, and the governor of the central bank was ultimately forced out amid criminal investigations associated with the blockage of the proposed transactions.

of the bank. In the European Union (EU), agreements have been struck that vest primary supervisory and regulatory responsibility for a banking organization with the country in which an institution is chartered. Branches come under the responsibility of the home country as does umbrella supervisory authority for banking organizations with multiple independently chartered subsidiaries.

In contrast, when expansion takes place through separately chartered subsidiaries, the information problem is a bit different. Supervision and regulation responsibility for the subsidiaries lie with the countries in which they are chartered, but the information gleaned about the subsidiary may not adequately reflect its true risk position if the parent, for example, is experiencing financial difficulties or the subsidiary is operationally dependant for management or operational support from the parent or its other subsidiaries. Again, the true financial risks can only be determined with adequate sharing of information between the home and host countries of the parent and the subsidiaries (Committee on the Global Financial System, 2004).[26] Without adequate and timely information, the host country may be in a poor position to assess the potential risks or externalities its citizens and economy may be exposed to from its foreign branches. These incentive conflicts may be especially acute in host countries with a large foreign banking presence.

The logistics and costs to host country regulators of quickly accessing information on these arrangements, or even finding it, can be daunting, even when the foreign banking organization enters by way of a bank subsidiary rather than a branch. Should a foreign-owned institution become insolvent and be legally closed, it may not be possible to keep those portions of the institution's operations in the host country physically open and operating seamlessly during the resolution process in an attempt to limit any adverse consequences that may accrue to deposit and loan customers. The necessary senior management, operating records, and computer facilities may be physically located in the home rather than in the host countries or in separately owned and operated affiliates and subsidiaries in third countries. For these reasons, regulatory oversight and discipline is likely to be more difficult and less effective in host countries with a substantial foreign bank presence than in countries without this presence. The resolution process is also less effective.

[26] Differences in quality can exist simply because countries fund their banking regulators differently or because they have had only limited experience in supervising market entities. Schüler (2003) argues that this problem of information access issue constitutes a form of agency problem between the home and host country regulator.

Perception of these problems is likely to heighten incentives on the part of host country regulators to seek to protect their own citizens through ring-fencing of assets, even at the expense of host country citizens.[27] However, attempts to engage in ring fencing may be of little value. With so many assets now being in electronic form or booked in other locations, it may be impossible to actually get hold of the assets. At best, the main benefit of ring fencing may to be to establish legal claim to certain assets that would have to be settled in international courts, a process that could prove difficult and time consuming and adding to the negative externalities that may result.

Adding to potential depositor confusion and information asymmetries is the fact that two banking organizations headquartered in different host countries may be subject to different bankruptcy procedures; to different policies concerning the timely availability of funds in the event of a bankruptcy; and even different policies as to whether deposits in foreign branches are or are not insured. The US, for example, doesn't insure the foreign deposits in offshore branches of US banks, but may insure the deposits in the branches of foreign institutions operating in the US.

With respect to the international dimension to the agency problem, home country regulators may take insufficient account of how the externalities that a failure, and the way that it is resolved, may affect the host country. That is, because all the regulators in countries in which a banking organization operates may have different objective functions and incentives, they may not all be pulling in the same direction at the same time with respect to prudential supervision and regulation. And these conflicts may be important, even when there exist coordinating bodies or agreements and understandings as to principles.[28] Even when there is a

---

[27] New Zealand has addressed this issue by requiring that subsidiaries be structured in such a way that if the parent becomes insolvent, solvent subsidiaries can be operated effectively without interruption in terms of capabilities and management. This doesn't seem to be a practical solution for large multi-national banking organizations on a broad scale since this may deny these institutions the economies of scale and scope and risk management.

[28] Schüler (2003) indicates that in Europe, for example, that there were over 90 memoranda of understanding (MoUs) in Europe as of 1999 governing the exchange of information and commitments for handling troubled institutions. With the addition of the accession countries, 300 bilateral arrangements need to be put in place for handling troubled institutions, and this may not cover the needed information sharing when a bank operates in more than two EU countries. The two main problems with these MoUs are that they are secret, so the depositors have no information as to how they might be treated, and that these MoUs rely upon "soft law" for enforcement and can be disavowed at any time. See also Boot (2006).

statutory mandate for regulators with overlapping responsibilities to cooperate, agency problems sometimes prevent this from happening. When cooperation breaks down, as it is most likely to do when a crisis arises and real money is at stake, agency self interest often trumps even the law. This is more likely to happen when agreements lack even the force of law, and there is no way to enforce agreements that may have been made *ex ante*. Regulators may take conflicting actions to benefit their own country's residents or institutions, say, with respect to the nature and timing of any sanctions imposed on a bank for poor performance, the timing of any official declaration of insolvency and the associated legal closing of the bank, the resolution of the insolvency, or the timing and amount of payment to insured and uninsured depositors.[29,30]

From the home country perspective, the incentives are not only to pay less attention to the externalities that failure may impose on host countries, but also to protect home country residents from possible costs of failure. These incentives may be especially significant with respect to the provision of deposit insurance, which is one of the main tools designed to assure and protect depositors in the event that a bank gets into financial difficulty. However, the structure of the deposit insurance system, deposit insurance coverage, and how the guarantee system is funded can significantly affect incentives and may introduce potential conflicts between regulators, who may or may not have the authority to close banks, the legal system governing the declaration of bankruptcy and the resolution of failed institutions, and distribution, size and sharing of loss burden.

Consider first the issue of the declaration of bankruptcy and how that affects losses. The longer an insolvent institution is kept open, the greater the losses are that both uninsured creditors and the deposit insurance scheme must absorb. If a regulator has the closure responsibility, and engages in forbearance, then the regulator is one of the main sources of loss (risk) to uninsured creditors and the deposit insurance fund. On the other hand, if an economically insolvent institution legally must keep operating until it can no longer meet a payment obligation, then the bankruptcy law, and not the regulator, affects the amount of the losses that exist. Ironically, in the US, while the closure decision is the responsibility of the regulator (the chartering agent), the losses are born by depository institutions who

---

[29] A classic case of just such a decision occurred in the Herstatt Bank failure.

[30] In the US, such conflicts have existed among state regulators and among federal banking regulators despite a national mandate to coordinate regulatory and supervisory policies and the existence of the Federal Financial Institutions Examination Council.

must *ex post* recapitalize their fund. But the institutions at risk have no oversight responsibilities for evaluating regulatory performance. That is, the regulator is not accountable to the institutions that must bear the risk of lack of performance. If the deposit insurance scheme is publicly funded, as it has been in the past in the US and is in many other countries, then deficiencies in the fund must be born by the taxpayer. And here, it is not always clear that the taxpayer will step up, even if there is an implicit, let alone explicit responsibility to do so. There are many instances, such as the State of Ohio, where taxpayers reneged on their implicit guarantees and their deposit insurance system failed.[31] The likelihood of taxpayers not living up to their guarantees is directly linked to the size of the losses. It is hard to imagine countries like Luxembourg or the Netherlands incurring large fiscal debts to honor claims of a significant number of depositors located in other EU countries. Of course, if deposit insurance guarantees are not honored, then not only may losses be incurred by both insured and uninsured creditors, but they may also experience significant liquidity problems as well.

Finally, the nature of deposit insurance coverage may also impose negative externalities in cross-border situations. For example, not only does the US deposit insurance system not cover deposits in foreign branches of US banks, the deposit insurance fund also stands ahead of uninsured creditors in terms of priority of claims to recovered assets. Hence, the failure of a large and significant US institution with branches in another country that may have a large share of the market would put the depositors of that branch into limbo until the failure is resolved.[32] Similarly, uninsured depositors would also suffer liquidity and credit losses. For US banks, these externality risks are not large, because the failure of a large bank is intended be resolved promptly, and both insured and uninsured creditors should have prompt access to most of their funds.[33] In Europe, and many other countries, it is much less certain as to how depositors may fair if a large cross border banking organization were to fail. First, there are no special bankruptcy provisions in most EU countries for bank failures, so resolution depends upon the courts.[34] Second, most laws

---

[31] See Eisenbeis and Kaufman (2006).

[32] Again, when the branch in the host country is significant in size, there would be a strong temptation to engage in ring fencing of assets, which is what the US did in the failure of BCCI.

[33] See Kaufman (2004) for a detailed discussion of how US bank failures typically are resolved now.

[34] For a discussion, see Lastra (2006).

do not require immediate access to funds. Third, while deposits in branches of other EU countries are covered, they typically are not in branches in non-EU countries.

Probably the least explored set of issues in the literature are the negative externalities associated with market disruptions that involve liquidity or other problems in international debt or equity markets. The sudden breakdown of financial markets, for example, might have both domestic and international consequences, and it is not at all clear who or under what circumstances governmental intervention might either be justified or occur. Clearly, central bank intervention can incur through either use of the discount window, as was done following the September 11th terrorist attack in the US, or through broad based open market operations. Similarly, a rescue package was also put together to deal with the problem that occurred in Mexico. International organizations, such as the World Bank or IMF, have also stepped in to deal with problems in individual countries. But with the internationalization and cross border ownership of exchanges and spread of derivatives markets, the potential for financial disruptions seem to have become greater and potentially more significant.[35]

A related issue concerns recent developments in world payments systems and the finality rules in real time gross settlement systems (RTGS) in which settlement payments are made in central bank funds and once accepted into the system are final. Under Fedwire, for example, payments initiated into the system are guaranteed by the Fed as final, which interposes a central bank between counterparties. New arrangements in the clearing and settlement of foreign exchange transactions involve a private sector solution to the Herstatt problem through a consortium of banks that created CLS bank. Work has just begun exploring the implications that these arrangements may have for systemic risk issues. A concern is that because CLS settles using central bank funds, the effect is to link payments systems together in ways that failures may require liquidity to be provided by central banks in ways that are both difficult to predict.[36] Moreover, to the extent that central banks de facto must provide such credit to avoid meltdowns, disincentives may be created for counterparties to monitor their risk exposure, giving risk to moral hazard.[37]

---

[35] Lindgren (2006) found little evidence of cross-border contagion in his examination of recent financial crises.

[36] For discussions, see Kahn and Roberds (2000), Kahn and Roberds (2006), and the references therein.

[37] See Fujiki *et al.* (2006).

5. Summary and Conclusions

This chapter has attempted to examine the issues surrounding the negative externalities that may occur when a large bank fails, to describe the nature of those externalities and to determine whether they are greater in a case involving a large cross-border banking organization. The analysis suggests that the chief negative externalities are associated with credit risk and losses of liquidity and these losses are critically affected by how promptly an insolvent institution is closed, how quickly depositors gain access to their funds, and how long it takes borrowers to re-establish credit relationships. While regulatory delay and forbearance may affect the size and distribution of losses, the likely incident of systemic risk and the negative externalities are more associated with the structure of the applicable bankruptcy laws and methods available to resolve a failed institution and quickly get it operating again. The assumption here is that a large organization will not be liquidated but instead must be promptly reorganized, recapitalized and re-privatized in order to limit the externalities that the failure may bring with it. The analysis also suggests that, while agency conflicts and goal conflicts among the responsible regulators, deposit insurance funds and taxpayers may increase the size of potential losses, as was the case for a large domestic-only institution, the incident of negative externalities are more determined by the bankruptcy and resolution policies that are in place. This implies that regulatory concerns about systemic risk should be directed first at closing institutions promptly, at reforming bankruptcy statues to admit special procedures for handling banking failures and to provide mechanisms to give creditors and borrowers prompt and immediate access to their funds and lines of credit.

References

Allen, F. and D. Gale (1998). Optimal financial crises. *Journal of Finance*, 53, 1245–1284.

Allen, F. and D. Gale (2000). Financial contagion. *Journal of Political Economy*, 108, 1–33.

Banco de Espana (2006). Financial Stability Report. May.

Bank of England (2006). Financial Stability Report. Issue 20, July 12.

Bliss, R.R. and G.G. Kaufman (2006). A comparison of US corporate and bank insolvency resolution. *Economic Perspectives*. Federal Reserve Bank of Chicago, 2nd Quarter.

Boot, A.W.A. (2006). Supervisory arrangements, LOR and crisis management in a single European banking market. Conference on International Financial Instability: Cross-Border Banking and National Regulation, Federal Reserve Bank of Chicago, October.

Champ, B., B. Smith and S. Williamson (1996) Currency elasticity and banking panics: Theory and evidence. *Canadian Journal of Economics*, 29, 828–864.

Chang, R. and A. Velasco (2000). Financial fragility and the exchange rate regime. *Journal of Economic Theory*, 92, 1–34.

Chang, R. and A. Velasco (2001). A model of financial crises in emerging markets. *Quarterly Journal of Economics*, 116, 489–517.

Chari, V. and E. Jagannanthan (1988). Banking panics, information, and rational expectations. *Journal of Finance*, 43, 749–760.

Chari, V. (1989). Banking without deposit insurance or bank panics: Lessons from a model of the US national banking system. Federal Reserve Bank of Minneapolis Quarterly Review, 13, Summer.

Committee on the Global Financial System (2004). *Foreign Direct Investment in the Financial Sector of Emerging Market Economies*. Basel, Switzerland: Bank for International Settlements, March.

Diamond, D.W. and P.H. Dybvig (1983). Bank runs, deposit insurance, and liquidity. *Journal of Political Economy*, 91, 401–419.

Eisenbeis, R.A. and G.G. Kaufman (2005). Challenges for deposit insurance and financial stability in cross-boarder banking environments with emphasis on the European Union. In *Systemic Financial Crises: Resolving Large Bank Insolvencies*. D.D. Evanoff and G.G. Kaufman (eds.), Singapore: World Scientific Publishing.

Eisenbeis, R.A. and G.G. Kaufman (2006). Cross-border banking: Challenges for deposit insurance and financial stability in the European Union. Presented at the Third Annual DG ECFIN Research Conference: Adjustments Under Monetary Unions: Financial Markets Issues, European Commission, September 7.

Fujiki, H., E.J. Green and A. Yamazaki (2006). Incentive efficient risk sharing in settlement mechanisms. Manuscript, March.

Furfine, C.H. (2006). The costs and benefits of moral suasion: Evidence from the rescue of long-term capital management. *Journal of Business*, 79, 593–622.

Government Accountability Office (2002). Analysis of the failure of superior bank, FSB, Hinsdale, Illinois. Statement of T.J. McCool, before the Committee on Banking, Housing and Urban Affairs, US Senate, Thursday, February 7.

Gorton, G. (1988). Banking panics and business cycles. *Oxford Economic Papers*, 40, 751–781.

Herring, R.J. (2007). Home-host country conflicts. In *International Financial Instability: Cross-Border Banking and National Regulation*, D. Evanoff,

G. Kaufman and J.R. LaBrosse (eds.). Singapore: World Scientific Publishing.

Horvitz, P.M. (1983). Reorganization of the financial regulatory agencies. *Journal of Bank Research*, Winter, 245–263.

Ingves, S. (2007). Cross-border banking regulation — A way forward: The European case. In *International Financial Instability: Cross-Border Banking and National Regulation*, D. Evanoff, G. Kaufman and J.R. LaBrosse (eds.). Singapore: World Scientific Publishing.

International Monetary Fund (2006). Global financial stability report: Market developments and issues. April.

Jacklin, C. (1987). Demand deposits, trading restrictions, and risk-sharing. In *Contractual Arrangements for Intertemporal Trade*, E. Prescott and N. Wallace (eds.). Minneapolis, MN: University of Minnesota Press.

Jacklin, C. and S. Bhattacharya (1988). Distinguishing panics and information-based bank runs: Welfare and policy implications. *Journal of Political Economy*, 96, 568–592.

Johnson, C.A. (2005). Justice and the administrative state: The FDIC and the superior bank failure. *Loyola University Chicago Law Journal*, 36, 483.

Kahn, C.M. and W. Roberds (2000). The CLS bank: A solution to the risks of international payments settlement? Paper prepared for the Carnegie-Rochester Series on Public Policy, April.

Kahn, C.M. and W. Roberds (2006). An introduction to payments economics. Federal Reserve Bank of Atlanta, September.

Kane, E.J. (1991). Incentive conflict in the international regulatory agreement on risk based capital. In *Pacific Basin Capital Markets Research*, Vol. II, R.P. Chang and S. Ghon Rhee (eds.), pp. 3–21. Amsterdam: Elsevier.

Kane, E.J. (2006). Confronting divergent interests in cross-country regulatory arrangements. *Bulletin of the Reserve Bank of New Zealand*, 69, 5–17.

Kane, E.J. (2000) The dialectical role of information and disinformation in banking crises. *Pacific Basin Finance Journal*, 8(July), 285–308.

Kane, E.J. (1989). Changing incentives facing financial-services regulators. *Journal of Financial Services Research*, 2(3), 265–274.

Kaufman, G.G. (1988). Bank runs: Causes, benefits, and costs. *Cato Journal*, 7(3), 559–587.

Kaufman, G.G. (2006). Depositor liquidity and loss sharing in bank failure resolutions. *Contemporary Economic Policy*, 22(2), 237–249.

Norges Bank. Financial Stability. June.

Lastra, R.M. (2007). Cross-border resolution of banking crises. In *International Financial Instability: Cross-Border Banking and National Regulation*, D. Evanoff, G. Kaufman and J.R. LaBrosse (eds.). Singapore: World Scientific Publishing.

Lindgren, C.-J. (2007). Actual and near-miss cross-border crises. In *International Financial Instability: Cross-Border Banking and National Regulation*, D. Evanoff, G. Kaufman and J.R. LaBrosse (eds.). Singapore: World Scientific Publishing.

Meltzer, A. (1998). Asian problems and the IMF. *Cato Journal*, 17(3), 267–274.

Mengle, D. (2006). Derivatives governance and financial stability. In *International Financial Instability: Cross-Border Banking and National Regulation*, D. Evanoff, G. Kaufman and J.R. LaBrosse (eds.). Singapore World Scientific Publishing.

Minsky, H.P. (1977). A theory of systematic financial fragility. In *Financial Crises: Institutions and Markets in a Fragile Environment*, E.J. Altman and A.W. Sametz (eds.), pp. 138–152. New York: Wiley.

Office of Inspector General (2002). Marketing and resolution of superior federal. FSB, FDIC, Audit Report No. 02-024, July 24.

Oosterloo, S., J. de Haan and R.A.P. Johng (2007). Financial stability reviews: A first empirical analysis. In *International Financial Instability: Cross-Border Banking and National Regulation*, D. Evanoff, G. Kaufman and J.R. LaBrosse (eds.). Singapore: World Scientific Publishing.

Reserve Bank of New Zealand (2006). Financial stability report. May.

Rochet, J.C. (2004). Bank runs and financial crises: A discussion. In *Credit Intermediation and the Macro Economy*, S. Bhattacharya, A.W.A. Boot and A.V. Thakor (eds.). Oxford, UK: Oxford University Press.

Schoenmaker, D. and S. Oosterloo (2005). Financial supervision in an integrating Europe: Measuring cross-border externalities. *International Finance*, 8(1), 1–27.

Schoenmaker, D. and C. van Laecke (2007). Current state of cross-border banking. In *International Financial Instability: Cross-Border Banking and National Regulation*, D. Evanoff, G. Kaufman and J.R. LaBrosse (eds.). Singapore: World Scientific Publishing.

Schüler, M. (2003). How do banking supervisors deal with Europe-wide systemic risk?. Center for European Economic Research, Discussion Paper No. 03-03.

Schüler, M. and F. Heinemann (2005). The costs of supervisory fragmentation in Europe. Center for European Economic Research, Discussion Paper No. 05-01.

Schwartz, A. (1998). International financial crises: Myths and realities. *Cato Journal*, 17(3).

Sender, H. (2006). Being ready in case of crisis. *Wall Street Journal*, September 23.

Wall, L. and R.A. Eisenbeis (1999). Financial regulatory structure and the resolution of conflicting goals. *Journal of Financial Services Research*, 16(2/3), 223–245.

Wall Street Journal Europe (2005). Spaghetti banking. Friday/Saturday, April, p. A8.

Wallace, N. (1988) Another attempt to explain an illiquid banking system: The diamond and dybvig model with sequential service taken seriously. *Federal Reserve Bank of Minneapolis Quarterly Review*, 12(Fall), 3–16.

Conflicts Between Home and Host Country Prudential Supervisors

Richard J. Herring*

University of Pennsylvania

Potential conflicts between home and host supervisors are legion and may impose heavy compliance costs on internationally active banks, create competitive distortions and jeopardize financial stability. Nonetheless, in comparison to efforts to achieve international cooperation in other economic spheres such as trade, exchange rates and macroeconomic policy, efforts to achieve international cooperation among bank supervisors are relatively recent. They sprang from the unanticipated consequences of applying traditional domestic closure practices to a bank that had substantial cross-border activities.[1] When the West German authorities closed Bankhaus Herstatt at 4:00 pm CET on June 26, 1974, they followed normal domestic procedures and waited until the end of the business day. But this was mid-morning in New York, where the dollar leg of $625 million of Herstatt's foreign exchange contracts remained to be settled. The closure of Herstatt thus resulted in abrogation of these foreign exchange contracts in New York and caused a prolonged disruption in foreign exchange trading and dislocations in the broader Eurodollar market as well.[2]

*Richard J. Herring is the Jacob Safra Professor International Banking and co-director of the Wharton Financial Institutions Center at the Wharton School, University of Pennsylvania. The author is grateful to George Kaufman, Eric Rosengren, and the other participants at the Chicago Fed conference on "Cross-Border Banking and National Regulation" for comments on an earlier version of this paper and to Tim Ng, Adrian Orr and Ian Woolford of the Reserve Bank of New Zealand for stimulating discussions on these topics.

[1] For simplicity, this brief review will focus on banks and mainly on the efforts of the Basel Committee, largely ignoring the parallel initiatives of the European Union and other regional organizations. A consideration of the financial conglomerates would increase the complexity of the analysis by creating scope for more conflicts among specialized functional regulators within and across countries. For an overview of some of these issues, see Herring (2003).

[2] For additional information regarding the Herstatt crisis see Herring and Litan (1995) and the references cited there.

In reaction to the Herstatt crisis, the central bank governors of the Group of Ten formed what later became known as the Basel Committee on Banking Supervision ("Basel Committee") in the hope that better cooperation among banking supervisors could prevent such disruptions in the future. Although the Basel Committee was formed in 1975, almost 30 years passed before "Herstatt risk" in foreign exchange markets was virtually eliminated.[3] Other, broader conflicts in bank closure and resolution policies, however, have received relatively little attention in the public pronouncements of the Basel Committee.[4] This paper argues that these issues deserve a much higher place on the international supervisory agenda.

1. Home/Host Cooperation in Historical Perspective: The Concordat

The first official document of the Basel Committee (1975), known as the Concordat, set out guidelines for allocating supervisory responsibilities between home and host governments. The original Concordat delineated three main principles that have informed all subsequent cooperative efforts: (1) No foreign banking establishment should escape supervision; (2) Supervision is the joint responsibility of the host and parent authority, with the host assuming primary responsibility for supervision of liquidity and the parent assuming primary responsibility for the supervision of solvency; and (3) Transfers of information between host and parent authorities should be facilitated including both direct inspections by the home country authorities of foreign establishments and indirect inspections by the home country through the agency of host country authorities.

In several jurisdictions, significant legal barriers, often with criminal sanctions, impeded the sharing of banking information across borders and so new legislation was necessary to enable cross-border cooperation in banking supervision. Even though these at-the-border prohibitions have been removed, the reluctance to share bad news about weak institutions remains a significant barrier to effective cooperation.

The Concordat was silent with regard to international lender of last resort responsibilities and deposit insurance. The central bank governors

---

[3] This required the extension of central clearing hours at central banks in the major centers and the launch of the Continuously Linked Settlement Bank.

[4] The chief exception is the report of the task force on dealing with weak banks (Basel Committee, 2002).

preferred to pursue a policy of "constructive ambiguity", with regard to lender of last resort arrangements (if such arrangements actually were in place).[5] Moreover, during 1975, most of the members of the Basel Committee lacked formal deposit insurance although most have adopted some form of deposit insurance since then. Nonetheless, the interests of both the lender of last resort and the deposit insurer must be coordinated with those of the prudential supervisors and may cause conflicts if they are not. All three functions rely on timely and accurate information regarding the safety and soundness of banks.

The first real test of the Concordat occurred with the collapse of Banco Ambrosiano in 1982.[6] Unfortunately, the incident revealed a failure in the application of the first principle of the Concordat — that no internationally active bank should escape supervision. The Italian authorities (along with a consortium of Italian banks) bailed out creditors of the parent bank, but declined to bail out the creditors of the bank's Luxembourg subsidiary, Banco Ambrosiano Holdings. This entity was regarded as a nonbank holding company by the authorities in Luxembourg and therefore not subject to banking supervision even though it raised more than half a billion dollars in the interbank market and owned two banks — Banco Ambrosiano Overseas Ltd, the fourth largest bank in Nassau, and Banco Ambrosiano Andino in Lima, Peru. Moreover, Luxembourg corporate secrecy laws protected it from scrutiny by the Italian authorities. The Basel Committee responded to the incident with a revision to the Concordat (Basel Committee, 1983) that recommended measures that should be taken to prevent another internationally active bank from evading effective official oversight.

This revision also strengthened the allocation of responsibilities between home and host countries by giving the home country authority explicit oversight of the entire consolidated balance sheet of the parent bank including foreign branches and controlled subsidiaries.[7] Although this was intended to enhance the rigor and efficiency of official oversight, it was not sufficient to relieve the host authorities from concerns regarding the solvency of the local offices of foreign banks. If all creditors of all

---

[5] See Guttentag and Herring (1983) for a critique of the policy of constructive ambiguity.

[6] For additional details regarding the collapse of Banco Ambrosiano see Herring and Litan (1995) and the references cited there.

[7] The principle of consolidated supervision was intended to be part of the original Concordat, but the West Germans needed to enact new legislation in order to be able to implement the principle. It was officially announced in March 1979 (Basel Committee, 1979).

bank affiliates had an equal claim on consolidated assets of the banking group, the location of a banking group's capital would not matter. However, the reality of depositor preference laws and national bankruptcy procedures that often favor domestic creditors means that the location of capital does matter, and the supervisory authorities cannot rely on surpluses in one location to offset losses in another.[8] Solvency must be monitored on both a standalone and a consolidated basis. Thus, solvency supervision is likely to be duplicative to some extent and internationally active banks will find it very difficult to exploit the full gains from diversification that might be achieved by managing an integrated, worldwide network of banking offices without the constraint that each foreign office must satisfy stand-alone capital requirements. Differences among national bankruptcy regimes undermine the effectiveness of consolidated solvency supervision as a mechanism for enhancing the efficiency of international bank supervision.

The allocation of primary responsibility to the host country for oversight of liquidity is also less straightforward than it appears at first glance. Leaving aside the practical difficulties that sometimes arise in disentangling liquidity problems from solvency problems,[9] the allocation of supervisory responsibility to the host country seems most sensible when the foreign banking establishment is heavily engaged in local currency activity. But in many cases, foreign banking establishments deal largely in foreign currencies, and the local currency competence of the host country is largely irrelevant.

The next crisis involving an internationally active bank was the collapse of Bank of Credit and Commerce International (BCCI) in 1991.

---

[8] This has particular force if the foreign affiliate is a subsidiary. The local supervisory authority must assume that under some extreme circumstances the parent bank may choose to exercise the option of limited liability and walk away from a troubled affiliate. Thus, in the absence of legally enforceable guarantees from the parent bank, host country authorities can take only limited comfort in the assurance that a deficiency in the net worth of the local office could be offset by a capital surplus in another office in another country.

[9] There are, to be sure, a number of occasions, in which the distinction is clear cut. The liquidity problems faced by a number of banks in the aftermath of 9/11 provide an example. These banks were illiquid because their operational systems were down, but their solvency was never in doubt. If a bank's inability to borrow to meet liquidity needs stems from doubts about its solvency, the local authority may lack the appropriate information to make an evaluation. Moreover, as Altman (2006, p. 115) has argued, for members of the European Monetary Union "where currency considerations are no longer a concern, the shift of responsibility for liquidity from host to home supervisors is already long overdue".

It revealed that the Basel Committee had still not fully succeeded in implementing the first principle of the Concordat, even within the original member countries of the Basel Committee. Like Banco Ambrosiano Holdings almost a decade earlier, BCCI had taken root in the gaps in the international supervisory network. Not only did BCCI manage to evade consolidated supervision by the home country authority, it also managed to evade consolidated external oversight altogether for most of its existence by hiring different external auditors for each of its two main subsidiaries.[10] The Basel Committee responded to the BCCI affair with a restatement of the Concordat as a set of minimum standards for the supervision international banks (Basel Committee, 1992). The new revision also placed responsibility on the host authority to take action if not satisfied that a foreign bank is properly supervised on a consolidated basis by a competent home country authority. These actions could include the imposition of restrictive measures or the prohibition of operations.

The BCCI case highlighted the challenge of making consolidated supervision a reality when neither the home nor host authority was willing to take the lead. The "supervisory college" that was improvised as a substitute proved entirely inadequate. But, most importantly, it revealed fundamental differences across countries in processes and procedures for resolving an insolvent bank.

2. Harmonization Attempts: The Core Principles and Basel II

In addition to the Concordat, the Basel Committee has made substantial efforts to reduce conflicts between home and host country supervisors by harmonizing supervisory frameworks and regulations. Progress in this regard has been remarkable. When the Basel Committee was formed in 1975, not only did most supervisors not know their counterparts, even in neighboring countries, but also they approached their work with fundamentally different conceptual frameworks and remarkably different views on even the most basic concepts of supervision such as how to define capital and the appropriateness of onsite examination of banks. In a series of papers on supervisory concepts and best practices, the Basel Committee has made progress in reducing, if not eliminating many of these differences.

---

[10] For a broader discussion of the rise and fall of BCCI and its implications for international supervision see Herring (1993 and 2005a).

The two most important notable achievements are: (1) The Core Principles of Effective Banking Supervision (Basel Committee, 1997), and (2) The Accord(s) on Capital Adequacy (1987 and 2006).

The Basel Committee (1997, 2006) identified 25 core principles for effective banking supervision, organized under seven broad categories that included the preconditions for effective supervision, prudential regulations and requirements, methods of ongoing banking supervision, information requirements, and the formal powers of supervisors. These principles reflected a consensus among the members of the Basel Committee regarding good (if not best) practices in banking supervision and were intended to facilitate convergence in supervisory frameworks between home and host countries not only within the Basel Committee, but in all other countries as well. Although the principles were not intended to be enforceable, the Financial Sector Assessment Program conducted by the International Monetary Fund and the World Bank has used the Core Principles as a benchmark against which the supervisory frameworks of individual countries are evaluated. This has had the practical consequence of obliging countries to justify instances in which their approach to banking supervision diverges from the Core Principles and has probably accelerated international convergence in supervisory approaches.

The second harmonization initiative has been even more ambitious. It has moved beyond a mere convergence of supervisory concepts and frameworks to achieve convergence in rules for the minimum acceptable capital standards for internationally active banks. This required the Basel Committee to reach a consensus on how to measure regulatory capital and how various exposures should be risk weighted to form a risk-adjusted capital ratio that would be subject to a common minimum.[11] The first version of the Accord on capital adequacy (Basel I) (Basel Committee, 1988) defined two kinds of regulatory capital, set out fairly broad guidelines for assigning risk weights to exposures based on gross distinctions across borrowers or counterparties, and established minimum, risk-adjusted capital ratios that internationally active banks should meet. The Basel I approach offered relatively few options and thus little scope for conflict between home and host supervisory authorities.

---

[11] Since no attempt was made to harmonize accounting standards or enforcement procedures, the consistency the application of rules was uneven.

Since 1997, however, the Basel Committee has been working on a new version of the Accord (Basel II) that is intended to be much more sensitive to market measures of risk and is also much more prescriptive than Basel 1 (Basel Committee, 2006b). Even so, it leaves open several hundred implementation choices over which home and host supervisors may differ. Under Pillar 1, banks may choose a standardized approach or either of two internal-ratings-based approaches for computing capital charges for credit risk. If unconstrained by the preferences of home or host country supervisory authorities, a bank could choose a different methodology for each of six kinds of credit risk exposure. The choices for computing capital charges for operational risk exposure include another three approaches with the possibility of making a different choice over eight different lines of business. Some supervisory authorities have chosen to constrain choice severely. Others have not. This can lead to conflicts between the home and host country with regard to the appropriate way to evaluate the capital adequacy of a foreign bank subsidiary. In the worst case, a bank that has foreign offices in several different countries may find that each country prefers a different methodology.

Pillar 2 of Basel II is intended to improve the harmonization of the monitoring and enforcement of rules, but requires much greater intensity of supervision than has been customary in many countries. Even though it should bring about a measure of convergence in supervisory approaches, it is also likely to lead to disagreements among supervisors regarding the validation of models, how to design stress tests and, indeed, the appropriate level of stress that a bank should be able to withstand. Moreover, the need for, and the size of negotiated additional capital requirements for concentrations of risk, liquidity risk, and interest rate risk may be viewed quite differently by the parent and host supervisor. Preferences for Pillar 3 disclosures may also vary with regard to supervisory emphasis on market discipline and transparency versus direct supervisory intervention.

The Basel Committee is aware that this ambitious, new initiative requires closer cooperation between home and host country supervisors. In order to reduce potential sources of conflict, it has formed an Accord Implementation Group and guidelines for home-host information sharing for effective Basel II implementation (Basel Committee, 2006). There has also been a proliferation of bi-lateral information sharing agreements and even attempts to form supervisory colleges for some of the largest, most complex internationally-active banks. These efforts may help reduce what might otherwise be enormous compliance costs.[12]

While these conflicts between home and host country supervisory authorities jeopardize the efficiency of the international banking system, they do not pose a serious threat to financial stability. Most of the efforts of the Basel Committee — from the Concordat to the Core Principles to the Accord — have focused on how to supervise internationally active banks that are in sound condition. While many of these initiatives have sought to ensure that banks remain in sound condition, surprisingly little has been done to harmonize supervisory practice and procedures with regard to troubled or insolvent banks. Yet these banks pose the most serious threats to financial stability and may cause some of the most intractable conflicts between home and host supervisory authorities.

3. Conflicts That May Arise with Regard to Weak or Insolvent Banks

Experience has shown that in times of stress, information-sharing agreements are likely to fray. Bad news tends to be guarded as long as possible.[13] An example is the reluctance of the Japanese supervisory authorities to share with the US authorities the news of trading losses in Daiwa's New York branch. A trader in the New York Daiwa office had lost $1.2 billion in a series of unauthorized trades over an eleven-year period from 1985 to 1996. When the trader finally confessed and the Japanese (home country) authorities were informed, a two-month lag occurred before the information was shared with the US (host country) authorities, the Concordat notwithstanding.

Bank managers are often reluctant to share bad news with their regulators because they fear they will lose discretion for dealing with the problem (and, indeed, may lose their jobs). Similarly, the primary supervisor is likely to be reluctant to share bad news with other supervisory authorities

---

[12] The Basel Committee has set out essential elements of a Memorandum of Understand to be used a model for establishing bilateral relationships between banking supervisory authorities in different countries (Basel Committee, 2001). See Herring (2005) for broad discussion of the potential implementation costs.

[13] As Baxter *et al.* (2004, p. 79) note, "Once the bank's condition degrades, supervisors think less about monitoring and more about protecting their creditors. This creates a conflict among supervisors".

out of concern that the leakage of bad news could precipitate a liquidity crisis or that the other supervisory authority might take action — or threaten to take action — that would constrain the primary supervisor's discretion for dealing with the problem or cause it to take action rather than forbear.

Generally, the primary supervisor will use its discretion to forbear so long as there is a possibility that a bank's condition may be self-correcting, particularly if the alternative is closure.[14] A closure decision is sure to be challenged, and so supervisors will tend to forbear until losses are so large that there can be no reasonable doubt that the institution is insolvent. Losses that spill across national borders, however, will intensify conflicts between home and host authorities and make it difficult to achieve a cooperative resolution of an insolvent bank.[15]

Currently, approaches to bank resolution differ substantially across countries. For example, countries differ with regard to the point at which a weak bank requires resolution. In many countries, intervention is required when a bank's net worth (which may be defined in a number of different ways) declines to zero, but in the United States, which has adopted a Structure Early Intervention and Resolution policy, action must be taken before net worth reaches zero, when the ratio of tangible equity to total assets is equal to or less than 2 percent. In Switzerland, the authorities may intervene even earlier if they perceive a threat to depositors' interests. Countries also differ with regard to what entity initiates the resolution process. The supervisory authorities? The courts? Or the bank itself? Clearly cross-border differences in regard to how and when the resolution process is initiated can cause delays that may be costly in a crisis.

In the event that a bank is declared insolvent, which jurisdiction will be the insolvency jurisdiction? The place where the bank was chartered? Where the management resides? The principal place of business? The domain of the largest concentration of assets? Or where the largest concentration of creditors resides? The collapse of BCCI revealed that each of these questions may have a different answer. Baxter, Hansen, and

---

[14] Supervisors are more likely to be criticized for bank failures than for letting an insolvent institution continue operations and so this reinforces the tendency to forbear.

[15] Freixas (2003) has argued that disagreements regarding the causes of losses and metrics for allocating losses across countries would lead to the underprovision of recapitalizations of international banks even when the social benefits of recapitalization exceed the cost. Goodhart and Schoenmaker (2006) share his pessimism about *ex post* burden sharing and consider two *ex ante* burden sharing mechanisms for the European Union.

Sommer (2004, p. 61) observe that it is difficult to devise a good jurisdictional rule that "would be both *ex ante* predictable (to defeat forum shopping or subsequent jurisdictional squabbling) and sensible in application (to discourage name-plate incorporations or prevent unseemly jurisdictional choices)".

The choice of jurisdiction, however, may have important implications for the outcome of the insolvency proceedings. Most countries have adopted a universal approach to insolvency in which one jurisdiction conducts the main insolvency proceedings and makes the distribution of assets, while other jurisdictions collect assets to be distributed in the main proceedings. But the United States follows a more territorial approach with regard to US branches of foreign banks. It will conduct its own insolvency proceedings based on local assets and liabilities. Assets are transferred to the home country only after (and if) all local claims are satisfied.[16]

The choice of jurisdiction will also determine a creditor's right to set-off claims on the insolvent bank against amounts that it owes the bank.[17] The BCCI case revealed striking differences across members of the Basel Committee (Basel Committee, 1992). In the United States, the right of set off can be exercised only with regard to claims denominated in the same currency on the same branch. Claims denominated in different currencies or on different branches may not be set off. In contrast, in the United Kingdom, the right to set off may be exercised even when the claims are not denominated in the same currency, on the same branch or even on branches in the same country. And in Luxembourg, the right to set off may not be exercised after a liquidation order and may be exercised before a liquidation order only when the claims "are fixed in amount, liquid, and mature".

Similarly the ability to exercise close-out netting provisions under International Swap Dealer Association (ISDA) Master Contracts may vary from jurisdiction to jurisdiction. In principle, in the event of a default, the non-defaulting counterparty can close-out all existing transactions under the Master Agreement, which may include many different

---

[16] Baxter, Hansen and Sommer (2004, p. 61) note that in the US, although the nationality of creditors is irrelevant, "only creditors of the local branch of the insolvent firm may participate. ... On the asset side, the insolvency official asserts jurisdiction over all local assets and assets outside the jurisdiction that are 'booked' to the jurisdiction".

[17] The Basel Committee (1992, p. 3) defines set off as "a nonjudicial process whereby mutual claims between parties such as a loan and a deposit, are extinguished".

kinds of derivative contracts with many different affiliates of the defaulting bank, making them immediately due and payable. The non-defaulting counterparty can then offset the amount it owes the defaulting bank against the amount it is owed to arrive at a net amount. In effect, close-out netting permits the non-defaulting counterparty to jump the bankruptcy queue for all but the net value of its claims. But the ability to apply close-out netting and the extent to which it may be applied may depend on whether the country in which the insolvency proceeding is conducted has enacted legislation to ensure that all outstanding transactions under a master netting agreement can be terminated upon the occurrence of an insolvency and that close-out netting will be respected by the bankruptcy trustee.

The outcome of insolvency proceedings will also depend on the powers and obligations of the resolution authority, which may differ from country to country. For example, does the resolution authority have the authority to impose haircuts on the claims of creditors without a lengthy judicial proceeding? Does the resolution authority have the power (and access to the necessary resources) to provide a capital injection? Is the resolution authority constrained to choose the resolution method that is least costly to the deposit insurance fund as in the United States?[18] Or is the resolution authority obliged to give preference to domestic depositors as the law requires in Australia and the United States?

More fundamentally, what is the objective of the supervisory intervention and the resolution process? Is it to protect the domestic banking industry? Or to safeguard the domestic financial system? Or to protect domestic employment? Or to protect the deposit insurance fund? Or to minimize the fiscal costs of the insolvency to domestic taxpayers? Or to minimize the spillover costs in all countries in which the insolvent bank conducts business? Only the last of these alternatives is implausible. The priority that supervisors will inevitably place on domestic objectives in the event of an insolvency is the main source of conflict between home and host authorities.

---

[18] The US resolution authority can choose a more costly resolution method only if the systemic risk exception is invoked which requires concurrence by two-thirds of the Federal Reserve Board, two-thirds of the Federal Deposit Insurance Corporation board, and the Secretary of the Treasury in consultation with the President that implementation of least-cost resolution would "have serious adverse effects on economic conditions or financial activity".

4. Asymmetries between Home and Host Supervisory Authorities

Three asymmetries between the home and host country may create additional conflicts. First is asymmetry of resources. Although international agreements among sovereigns are, necessarily, based on the polite fiction that all sovereigns are equal, this is demonstrably not the case. Supervisory authorities may differ greatly in terms of human capital — the number and quality of employees — and financial resources. This means that even if the fundamental conflicts of interest could be set aside, the home supervisory authority may not be able to rely on the host supervisory authority (or vice versa) simply because it may lack the capacity to conduct effective oversight.

Second, asymmetries of financial infrastructure may give rise to discrepancies in the quality of supervision across countries. Weaknesses in accounting standards and the quality of external audits may impede the efforts of supervisors just as informed, institutional creditors and an aggressive and responsible financial press may aid them. The legal infrastructure matters as well. Inefficient or corrupt judicial procedures may undermine even the highest quality supervisory efforts.

But, perhaps the most important conflict arises from asymmetries of exposures: what are the consequences if the bank should fail? Perspectives may differ with regard to whether a specific bank jeopardizes financial stability. The key issues are whether the bank is systemically important in either or both countries and whether the foreign office is economically significant within the parent banking group. The various possibilities are arrayed in Table 1 where the columns indicate whether the foreign office is of significance to the solvency of the parent bank and whether the parent bank is considered to be of systemic importance in the home country. The rows indicate whether the parent bank is considered to be of systemic significance to the host country.

In general, if the host country entity is a branch, the host supervisory authority has a less active role to play and is much more dependent on decisions taken in the home country. But this vulnerability is offset to some extent by the greater likelihood that in the event of trouble, the branch is more likely to benefit from financial support from the parent or, if necessary from the parent country.

In cases (f), (g) and (h), conflicts of interest are not likely to be a problem. In all three cases the local office is not of systemic importance in the host country and so, apart from issues that might raise concerns

Table 1. Alternative patterns of vulnerability

Host Country Entity	Home Country/Parent Bank			
	Systemic		Non-Systemic	
	Significant	Insignificant	Significant	Insignificant
Systemic	(a) High Priority Both	(b) High Priority Host Country	(c) High Priority Host Country	(d) High Priority Host Country
Non-Systemic	(e) High Priority Home Country	(f) Low Priority Both	(g) Low Priority Both	(h) Low Priority Both

about the reputation of the host country financial system, the host country supervisors will lack incentive to take an active role in supervision. In cases (f) and (h), the foreign office is assumed to account for an insignificant amount of the parent bank's profits and exposures, and so the parent supervisory authority is likely to be content to exercise oversight with a very light touch. Similarly, with regard to (g), even though the foreign office does account for a significant share of the parent group's profits and exposures, the institution is not sufficiently large to be systemically important in either the home or host country. And thus, both the home and host supervisors are likely to be willing to exercise relatively light oversight. Given the assumption the foreign entity does not pose a systemic risk in either the home or host country, these situations are not likely to pose serious problems.[19]

[19] Two recent events involving rogue traders illustrate these cases. The first involves the losses in foreign exchange trading at the Baltimore office of the Allied Irish Bank. This appears to have been an example of case (f). The office was not systemically important in the U.S. and was not a significant part of the Allied Irish Bank group, even though the Allied Irish Bank group might be argued to be systemically important in Ireland. The losses were painful to shareholders, but did not pose a systemic threat in either Ireland or the United States. The collapse of Barings is an example of case (g). The Singapore office of Barings was not systemically important in Singapore and Barings, the Bank of England concluded, was not of systemic importance in the United Kingdom, but the Singapore office had accounted for a very significant part of the profits of the Baring Group in the years preceding the collapse. [See Herring (2005a) for additional details regarding the collapse of Barings.]

The most difficult situations are likely to arise when supervisory responsibility, potential fiscal responsibility, and accountability to the electorate are misaligned. From the home country's perspective, the nightmare scenario is case (e) where the foreign office is not regarded as systemically important by the host country, but is a significant part of a systemically important bank in the home country. Whether the foreign entity is a branch or a subsidiary, the home country may feel that it needs to have primary supervisory oversight. The Concordat provides it with this right and responsibility to do so in the case of a branch. The situation is a bit more ambiguous with respect to a subsidiary because both the home and host country can claim to be the primary supervisor. In view of the asymmetry of vulnerability, however, the host country may be happy to defer to the home country even if the entity is organized as a subsidiary. Case (a) may also pose a conflict because the entity is assumed to be systemically important in the host country and of economic significance to a systemically important bank in the home country. Both the home and host country will have an incentive to supervise the entity intensively. This may result in conflicts, but it is unlikely to result in gaps in supervisory attention.[20]

Cases (b) and (d) represent the nightmare scenarios for host supervisory authorities. The foreign entity is assumed to have a large enough share of local markets to be systemically important, while at the same time, being so small relative to the parent group that it is not regarded as significant to the condition of the parent banking group. In this case, the home country lacks incentive to exercise strong consolidated supervision that could be relied upon to ensure systemic stability in the host country. These kinds of situations are increasingly prevalent in central Europe, Latin America, and Africa. The situation is only a little bit more tractable with regard to case (c) where the foreign office is systemically important to the host country and large enough to be economically significant to the parent banking group. Although the parent banking group is assumed not to be of systemic importance, the fact that the foreign office is a significant part of the banking group may elicit more attention from the home country supervisor.

---

[20] New Zealand provides a good example of case (a) because the big four subsidiaries of Australian banks that dominate the banking system in New Zealand are each economically significant to the parent banking group and each of the parents is arguably systemically important in Australia.

How can these asymmetries be addressed in a way the will provide adequate assurances to both home and host country supervisors without imposing excessive compliance costs on internationally active banks? One possibility is an über-supervisor model, where sovereign nations cede the necessary powers and resources to an international supervisory authority. Although there has been some discussion of this model in the context of the European Monetary Union, where countries have already ceded one important aspect of sovereignty, control of the money supply, to the European Central Bank, such proposals have encountered seemingly insuperable concerns about how to share fiscal costs should a capital injection become necessary.[21]

A similar concern, applies to the Lead Supervisor Model, where the home country takes responsibility for supervision, and host countries act as agents of the home country supervisor when necessary. Host countries, inevitably express misgivings about the misalignment of supervisory incentives with the political and economic costs of dealing with systemically important banking crises in the host country. Even a commitment by the home country to bear the fiscal costs of a capital injection should it become appropriate may not be sufficient to allay this concern, since the willingness to undertake a capital injection may depend on whether the losses are likely to fall most heavily on the home country if no action is taken. Moreover, some relatively small countries, such as the Netherlands and Switzerland, have such large, internationally-active banks, that they may not be able to make a credible commitment to absorb the fiscal costs of a recapitalization.

The Supervisory College Model has regained attention as a way of reducing the implementation costs of Basel II. However, the abject failure of a supervisory college to provide adequate oversight for BCCI raises a question about how accountability could be improved sufficiently to compensate for asymmetries in capabilities, resources, and objectives across countries.

Finally, the New Zealand supervisory authorities have introduced a Complete Autonomy Model.[22] More than 85 percent of the banking system

---

[21] See Altman (2006) for a proposal that the 12 members of the European Monetary Union (EMU) adopt a common, EMU supervisory authority and form a common deposit insurance scheme that would better align supervisory responsibilities and financial burdens for members of the EMU.

[22] See Woolford and Orr (1995) for an exposition of the New Zealand model. See Kane (2006) for a discussion of the contrasts in regulatory cultures between Australia and New Zealand.

is controlled by foreign-owned banks and the New Zealand authorities have been uncomfortable accepting the passive role assigned to the host country authorities with regard to resident foreign branches. They have insisted that systemically important foreign entities be organized as subsidiaries.[23] Moreover, they have buttressed this corporate separateness by additional measures that assure a subsidiary could continue operation without interruption (and without its previous owners) should it become necessary. This minimizes the extent to which the host supervisory authority must rely on the home country supervisory authority, but at some cost to banks that would prefer to manage their resources on a more integrated basis through a branch network.

5. Concluding Comment

Conflicts between home and host supervisory authorities have contributed to and exacerbated cross-border banking crises.[24] Baxter *et al.* (2006, p. 79) list 10 major banking problems that occurred from 1992 to 2002 in the overseas offices of internationally active banks. These problems included major losses and criminal wrongdoing, and were enabled by poor internal controls. Since the adequacy of internal controls is a major focal point of supervision, many of these events can be attributed, at least in part, to weaknesses in consolidated supervision and in host country supervision.

The Basel Committee has made remarkable progress since 1975 in establishing protocols for international cooperation between home and host supervisory authorities and in harmonizing regulatory frameworks, concepts, and even minimum capital standards. However, little has been accomplished with regard to how to deal with weak banks to ensure that they do not become a source of systemic instability.

Yet, supervisory cooperation is most likely to break down when weak banks become insolvent and create losses that must be allocated across national borders. Loss-sharing agreements are very difficult to

---

[23] This option is not available to host country supervisory authorities in the member states of the European Union. The single European passport concept gives banks chartered in any member state to open a branch in any other member state. See Mayes (2006) for a comparison between the system in New Zealand and the European Union.

[24] Baxter *et al.* (2004, p. 67) list 19 international bank insolvencies that have been adjudicated at least in part in the United States.

negotiate either *ex ante* or *ex post* and conflicts over the allocation of losses may undermine efforts to manage a crisis and achieve an appropriate resolution. International cooperation may breakdown precisely when it is most needed. International efforts should focus instead on intervening in weak banks to achieve prompt corrective action before they become insolvent.

In this regard, Pillar 2 was a significant, missed opportunity. It came very close to adopting a Prompt Corrective Action (PCA) standard. Pillar 2 (Basel Committee, 2006a, p. 166) exhorts supervisory authorities to "undertake prompt remedial action if a bank fails to meet the capital standards set forth in this Framework." Unfortunately, it did not reinforce this exhortation with policies and procedures that would remove concerns about usual tendency for supervisory authorities to exercise forbearance that can lead to large losses at resolution.

The next revision of the Concordat should correct this omission and emphasize meaningful prompt corrective action. This will certainly not eliminate conflicts among supervisors. Indeed, the reality of integrated international financial markets requires that supervisors execute such policies in a perfectly coordinated way and this will require changes in the laws in many countries governing the resolution of banks. However, the potential gains are substantial. Prompt corrective action, strengthened by structured early intervention[25] and resolution measures, will buttress supervisory discipline with market discipline, thus adding force to Pillar 3. When the losses that must be allocated are confined to shareholders, conflicts among supervisors should greatly diminish.

References

Altman, T. (2006). Cross-border banking in Central and Eastern Europe: Issues and implications for supervisory and regulatory organization on the European level. Working paper, Wharton Financial Institutions Center.

Basel Committee on Banking Supervision (1975). Report to the Governors on the supervision of banks' foreign establishments. *Bank for International Settlements*, September 26.

Basel Committee on Banking Supervision. (1979). Consolidated supervision of banks' international activities. March.

---

[25] See Kaufman (1995) for an analysis of the prompt corrective action, structured early intervention and resolution policy in the United States.

Basel Committee on Banking Supervision. (1983). Principles for the supervision of banks' foreign establishments. *Bank for International Settlements*, May.

Basel Committee on Banking Supervision. (1988). International convergence of capital measurement and capital standards. *Bank for International Settlements*, July.

Basel Committee on Banking Supervision (1996). The supervision of cross-border banking. *Bank for International Settlements*, October.

Basel Committee on Banking Supervision (1997). Core principles for effective banking supervision. *Bank for International Settlements*, September. A revised version was published in October, 2006.

Basel Committee on Banking Supervision (2001). Essential elements of a statement of cooperation between banking supervisors. May.

Basel Committee on Banking Supervision (2002). Supervisory guidance on dealing with weak banks, Report of the task force on dealing with weak banks. *Bank for International Settlements*, March.

Basel Committee on Banking Supervision (2006a). Home-host information sharing for effective Basel II implementation. *Bank for International Settlements*, June.

Basel Committee on Banking Supervision (2006b). Basel II: International convergence of capital measurement and capital standards: A revised framework — Comprehensive version. *Bank for International Settlements*, June.

Baxter, T.C. Jr., J. Hansen and J. Sommer (2004). Two cheers for territoriality: An essay on international bank insolvency law. *American Bankruptcy Law Journal*, 78, 57–91.

Freixas, X. (2003). Crisis management in Europe. In *Financial Supervision in Europe*, J. Kremers, D. Schoenmaker, and P. Wierts (eds.), pp. 102–119. Cheltenham: Edward Elgar.

Goodhart, C. and D. Schoenmaker (2006). Burden sharing in a banking crisis in Europe. Working paper available at SSRN, March.

Guttentag, J.M. and R.J. Herring (1983). The lender of last resort function in an international context. *Essays in International Finance*, 151, Princeton University, May.

Herring, R.J. and R.Z. Litan (1995). *Financial Regulation in the Global Economy*. Washington: Brookings Institution.

Herring, R.J. (1993). The collapse of BCCI: Implications for the supervision of international banks. In *Reforming Financial Institutions and Markets in the United States: A Progress Report*, G. Kaufman (ed.), pp. 121–140. Boston: Kluwer.

Herring, R.J. and F. Kübler (1995). The allocation of risk in cross-border deposit transactions, *Northwestern University Law Review*, 89(3), pp. 801–887.

Herring, R.J. (2003). International financial conglomerates: Implications for national insolvency regimes. In *Market Discipline and Banking: Theory and Evidence*, G. Kaufman (ed.), pp. 99–129. Amsterdam: Elsevier.

Herring, R.J. (2005a). BCCI and barings: Bank resolutions complicated by fraud and global corporate structure. In *Systemic Financial Crises: Resolving Large Bank Insolvencies*, D. Evanoff and G. Kaufman (eds.), pp. 321–345. Singapore: World Scientific Publishing.

Herring, R.J. (2005b). Implementing Basel II: Is the game worth the candle?. In *Basel II and the Future of Banking Regulation*, a special issue of *Financial Markets, Institutions, and Instruments*, 14(5), pp. 267–287, H. Benink, J. Danielsson, and C. Goodhart (eds.).

Kaufman, G. (1995) FDICIA and bank capital. *Journal of Banking and Finance*, 19, 721–722.

Kane, E. (2006). Confronting divergent interest in cross-country regulatory arrangements. *Reserve Bank of New Zealand Bulletin*, 69(2), 5–17.

Mayes, D. (2006). Responsibility without power: Nordic and antipodean solutions to the problem of foreign-owned systemic bank branches. Working Paper, Bank of Finland.

Woolford, I. and A. Orr (2005) The limits to hospitality. *The Financial Regulator*, 10(1), 41–46.

Cross-Border Nonbank Risks and Regulatory Cooperation

Paul Wright*
Financial Services Authority, United Kingdom

1. Introduction

This chapter examines the following questions:

- What types of prudential cross-border risks do nonbanks pose?
- What are the implications of this, together with the fact that regulation is nationally based?
- Is it possible to identify "optimal" patterns of cross-border regulatory cooperation?
- What are the constraints and realities governing what cross-border collaboration can achieve?

2. What Types of Prudential Cross-Border Risks Do Nonbanks Pose?

Nonbanks are clearly capable of creating cross-border risks. There is scope for disagreement about the extent to which these may be systemic but the scope for financial disturbance is clear. Three examples will serve to illustrate the point:

2.1 *Broker dealers*

Prior to the introduction of the Consolidated Supervised Entity (CSE) regime by the Securities and Exchange Commission (SEC), there was

*Paul Wright is head of international strategy and policy coordination at the Financial Services Authority, United Kingdom. The chapter is presented in a personal capacity. The views expressed in it do not necessarily reflect those of the FSA.

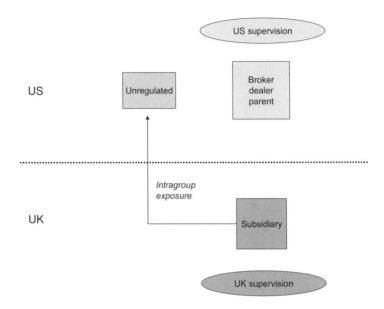

Figure 1. Intra-group transfers, U.S.

concern about the risks posed by the lack of consolidated oversight of broker dealer groups. The overseas operations of such groups are extensive with European operations of the major groups sometimes accounting for between a quarter and a third of global revenues. The SEC's remit did not extend to the non-US operations of such groups despite the fact that, in common with other major financial institutions, they are run and managed on a trans-national basis. Intra-group risk transfers, sometimes involving the backing out of substantial risk positions to unsupervised entities in the groups were common, while the SEC was not required or expected to undertake any group-wide oversight either of financial resources or systems and controls. Notwithstanding the high standards of management and extensive financial resources of such groups, the potential for cross-border disturbance was clear. The relationships involved can be illustrated in Figure 1.

No supervisory regime can — or should aim to — eliminate risks. But the introduction of the CSE regime, under which the SEC assesses capital adequacy on a group wide basis and engages in extensive dialogue with host regulators such as the Financial Services Authority (FSA) has gone a long way to mitigating them.

2.2 *Reinsurance*

The extent to which the reinsurance market is a potential source of systemic disturbance remains an extensively debated topic. A recent Group of 30 (G30) report on reinsurance[1] played down the possibility of systemic risks but helpfully articulated the channels through which disturbances in the reinsurance sector can be transmitted more broadly throughout the financial sector. The report pointed out that 150 active providers of reinsurance worldwide account for some $7 billion of premiums in 2004. The failure of a major reinsurer could have repercussions through at least three different (and not mutually exclusive) routes:

- A primary insurer which has sought cover from failed reinsurers may sustain losses;
- Banks which have provided credit to a failed reinsurers may suffer credit losses; and
- In seeking to meet their obligations, reinsurers may undertake forced liquidations in asset markets leading to price and liquidity distortions.

These sources of disturbance can be summarized in Figure 2.

The G30 report examined each of these sources of disturbance in some detail and concluded that all of them were manageable. It was

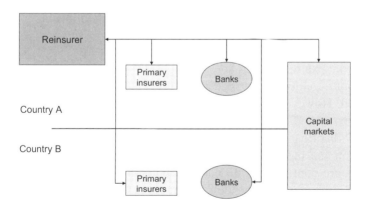

Figure 2. Sources of disturbances

---

[1] Group of Thirty, 2006, "Reinsurance and the International Financial Markets".

judged unlikely in other words that the failure of a major reinsurer would be a source of unmanageable systemic risk. Notwithstanding this, the strengthened regulatory oversight of reinsurers undertaken as a result of the Reinsurance and Solvency 2 Directives in Europe for example, provides significant mitigation of these risks.

2.3 *Hedge funds*

Hedge funds are not supervised in the UK; neither does the FSA wish to supervise them. Hedge fund managers are authorized and those based in the UK manage at least \$250 billion of hedge fund assets or around 20 percent of the global total. The FSA has set out a range of potential disturbances that may, in principle, arise from hedge funds.[2] These range from market abuse, operational and valuation risks through to the failures of one or more funds with concentrated positions in complex or opaque instruments in several markets and/or jurisdictions. Extensive reliance is placed on "indirect" means of identifying and addressing such risks. Supervisors undertake dialogues with investment managers for example as well as assessing counterparty risk management within the firms we do authorize, in particular the prime brokers.

3. What are the Implications of the Fact That Regulation is Nationally Based?

In all of the examples cited above, heightened supervisory oversight provides some comfort that risks are being identified and to some extent addressed. However, many nonbanks, like banks, run their businesses on a global basis and are therefore capable, in principle, of being a source of financial disturbance across borders. Supervisors, by contrast, typically operate on the basis of national statutes and their direct oversight and activities are confined within national boundaries. Whether dealing with banks or nonbanks, the question of how to deal with this paradoxical situation is an increasingly pressing one.

---

[2] Financial Services Authority, 2005, "Hedge Funds: A Discussion of Risk and Regulatory Engagement", June.

Not all of the activities above warrant regulation as such. As noted above for example, many regulators see no necessity at the moment to regulate hedge funds. Where regulation is appropriate, the solution to the paradox is a simple one — supervisors need to collaborate. There have recently been some conspicuously successful examples of cross-border supervisory collaboration in respect of specific market-wide issues. In 2005/06 the FSA, Federal Reserve Bank of New York and the SEC conducted a very effective operation to reduce the level of outstanding confirmations in the credit derivatives market. By October of this year the level of confirmations outstanding for more than thirty days had been reduced by around 85 percent compared to a few months previously.[3] It is possible to point to a number of reasons why such an exercise should have been particularly successful. There was a manifest market failure (giving rise to a high level of outstanding confirmations) and it was in no firm's interest for this to persist. No individual firm was able to deal with what was, by definition, a multilateral problem. All of these factors meant that regulatory intervention was appropriate and the fact that the issue manifested itself in cross-border markets meant that international collaboration proved particularly effective.

This was an example of successful cross-border collaboration in respect of a specific high profile issue. However, this chapter is mostly about lower profile issues of day-to-day prudential supervision of global firms. Effective collaboration is necessary to achieve effective supervision of such firms. This requires an oversight of the full range of a firm's activities, an assessment of financial adequacy at a group-wide level and the assessment of group wide controls and governance. Collaboration is also necessary if supervisors are to do their job efficiently — in a way which imposes minimum costs on the firms — as a result of duplication for example. But collaboration is not always easy to achieve in practice.

4. Is It Possible to Identify "Optimal" Patterns of Cross-Border Regulatory Cooperation?

Collaboration, even in respect of day-to-day prudential supervision can take a variety of forms. It is possible to imagine a spectrum ranging from no contact between supervisors (the reality for many global firms until not so long

---

[3] *Financial Times*, 2006, "A Safer Strategy for the Credit Products Explosion", September 28.

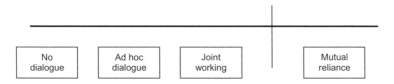

Figure 3. Types of dialogue among regulators

ago), moving through ad hoc discussions between regulators at one end, all the way to extensive mutual reliance at the other, as is shown in Figure 3.

It is apparent that moving beyond "joint working" to "mutual reliance" involves a step change in the nature of collaboration. At this point supervisors need to ask themselves some searching questions along the lines of mutual reliance in respect of what? Two possibilities immediately present themselves:

- Delegation of tasks — in which case supervisor A may rely on supervisor B to undertake certain supervisory activities even though responsibility remains with A.
- Delegation of responsibilities — in which supervisor A passes supervisory responsibility, for a firm or group of firms, fully or in part to supervisor B.

Delegation of responsibilities is a very tall order indeed and would be hard to countenance without profound legal changes in most regimes.[4] Delegation of tasks however is, in principle, much more manageable and the willingness of supervisors to do this depends to some degree on their appetite for risk. It is important to note that the supervisory regime within the European Union (EU) prescribes supervisors' activities in this regard. Under the relevant European directives responsibility for most of the prudential oversight of firms, including branches within the EU, falls to "home" supervisors. This means that there is less scope for home and host supervisors to agree on the allocation of tasks in respect of branches than is the case with supervisors outside of the EU. Home/host arrangements within Europe are being increasingly codified within measures such as the Capital Requirements and Markets in Financial Instruments Directives.

---

[4] See for example the discussion in the European Financial Services Round Table, 2005, "Towards a Lead Supervisor for Cross Border Financial Institutions in the EU", June.

Table 1. Criteria for discussions

Objectives	We work to the same ends (consumer protection, financial stability)
Scope	We focus on the same sources of risk (sectors, markets, firms, activities)
Powers	We have the same powers (including legal ones) to pursue our objectives
Risk preferences	We agree on the relative importance of issues. I am motivated equally by risks to your objectives as I am to risks to my own
Approach	We use the same supervisory tools in the same ways
Skills and access	Our staffs have the same skills which they apply in the same way to achieve common ends

Where they are free to do so, in what circumstances would a supervisor in jurisdiction A be willing unquestioningly to place reliance on his counterpart in jurisdiction B? Table 1 suggests a set of criteria that would need to be met.

If the discussion here was about banks, it would be necessary to supplement this list with some requirements regarding commonality of insolvency regimes and deposit protection and clarity about lender of last resort arrangements. Confining ourselves to the list above, however, it is apparent that these conditions for total reliance will seldom, if ever, be met. Strictly this would only happen if A and B, instead of being two national supervisors were actually two "branches" of a single trans-national supervisor. The creation of such a trans-national body is sometimes proposed as a *sine qua non* for achieving a true single market in financial services in Europe. If the above list is regarded as the basis for a "gap" analysis, this illustrates what a major step the creation of such an entity would be.

In reality therefore, we seldom find any precise match between supervisors. Table 2 sets out some of the disparities we identify in practice.

Inevitably differences exist among supervisors under each of these headings. In the light of this, it is possible to draw the following broad conclusions about the scope for collaboration.

- Clearly, all supervisors must meet their legal obligations at all times. This limits the scope for delegation of responsibilities (even if

Table 2. Potential disparities

Objectives	Objectives are set in national statutes and vary widely — for example, responsibility for financial stability
Scope	Scope differs widely — for example, responsibilities for hedge funds, listing, exchanges
Powers	Powers are based in national statute, together with insolvency and deposit/investor protection arrangements
Risk preferences	Domestically generated objectives will typically result in different approaches and appetites towards risk
Approach	Different emphasis on inspection, prudential vs. conduct of business, stances vis a vis firms, use of enforcement
Skills and access	Skill sets vary widely reflecting differences in national structures and all the differences outlined above

supervisors wished to do this) but it provides scope for delegation of tasks.

- Supervisors cannot rely unquestioningly on others in this (although, as noted above, EU directives circumscribe this within Europe to a large degree).
- It is therefore necessary to think in terms of "judicious mutual reliance".
- Willingness to undertake mutual reliance will reflect a number of trade offs between:
  - judgments regarding other supervisors' skills, powers, etc.,
  - the "impact" of the firm or issue (that is, how much it would really matter if something went wrong), and
  - the wish to minimize burdens on firms and/or markets.

- Supervisors' attitudes to these trade offs will often come down to the supervisor's risk appetite — in other words their willingness *ex post* to invoke judicious mutual reliance as a defensible approach in the event of risks crystallizing.

What this means in practice is that there is no single right answer to the question of how much supervisors can and should rely on one another. This will vary according to whether the counterpart supervisor is within or outside of the EU; how different its approach and priorities are; the nature of the supervised entity (for example, whether it is a deposit taking institution, a broker dealer or a general insurer); and the amount and type of risk it poses (for example, whether it is a predominantly wholesale firm dealing with professional counterparties, or whether it has large numbers of retail depositors, or is a systemically important provider of infrastructure). This has prompted the creation within the FSA of a "taxonomy" intended to draw out some of these complexities and provide a guide (it can be no more than that) for what type of collaboration might be appropriate in different circumstances.

In the event, two taxonomies were created. One reflecting the constraints placed on reliance with other supervisors within the EU and the other intended to address the issues arising in dealings with non-EU counterpart supervisors. In its full form, each took the form of a large matrix, setting out "preferred" forms of supervisory collaboration in the following scenarios

- In each case, the FSA is the "host" in the sense of being the supervisor of a branch or the supervisor of a UK incorporated subsidiary of a non-UK firm
- The matrix identifies firms according to the type of business they do and/or the types of risk they pose (for example, banks, life insurers, infrastructure providers, prudential, conduct of business etc)
- The matrix identifies whether the firm operates as a branch or subsidiary in the UK
- The matrix distinguishes operations that are "low" impact from those that are "high" impact in terms of their potential impact on the FSA's statutory objectives.

Sub-sections of these large matrices are reproduced in Tables 3 and 4.

Table 3. Prudential supervision (example of a bank or securities firm) within the EU

	High Impact in UK	Low Impact in UK
Branch in UK	Home state responsibility "Enhanced" host oversight in collaboration with home	Home responsibility Minimum host involvement
Subsidiary in UK	UK responsibility Maximum collaboration with home	UK responsibility Maximum reliance on home

The table deals with optimum collaboration in respect of prudential supervision within the EU. The interpretation of the table is as follows:

Branches are formally a home country responsibility.[5] There is emphatically no suggestion that this should be changed (this would require a change in European directives). But a different approach might be warranted according to whether the branch is high or low impact. In the case of a high impact branch there may be a case — while retaining home state responsibility — for the host to undertake some oversight of branch operations. This could be justified in terms of the effectiveness and efficiency of supervision, for example if the branch operation is one of a group of similar operations in the host market that represent a peer group. It would also serve to provide the host with some insight into the operations of a major potential source of risk. For a low impact branch however, the host has no reason to go beyond the strict constraints of the directives and should thus have no reason to have any oversight of the operation.

Subsidiaries are still formally a host country responsibility in the EU in the sense that prudential supervision is undertaken by the authority in which the subsidiary is incorporated (the UK in this case).[6] If the subsidiary is high impact however the host responsibility has every incentive to collaborate closely with the home authority which will take a consolidated view of the financial position of the group as well as group-wide systems and controls. There is certainly scope within the EU for a more systematic and rational pattern of collaboration and sharing of tasks on this basis. In the case of low impact subsidiaries on the other hand, the host, while carrying out its legal obligations, has every incentive to place the maximum judicious reliance on the home authority — for example in seeking and relying on assurances about group-wide controls, quality of management and other factors on which it will base its judgments.

It should be emphasized that the suggestions above are about more rational, risk based collaboration within existing European requirements. There is no implication that these should be changed (for example, by changing patterns of formal home and host state responsibilities for branches or subsidiaries).

---

[5] Host countries have responsibility, other things equal, for liquidity of branches.
[6] Though the trend is to shift some key decisions (especially regarding capital) towards the supervisor of the parent.

Table 4. Prudential oversight with counterpart supervisors outside the EU

	High Impact in UK	Low Impact in UK
Branch in UK	Home and host responsibility *Reliable home?* Yes: maximum feasible collaboration with home No: subsidiarize	Home and host responsibility *Reliable home?* Yes: maximum feasible reliance on home No: subsidiarize
Subsidiary in UK	UK responsibility Maximum collaboration with home	Host responsibility Maximum reliance on home

This table deals with the case in which the counterpart supervisor is from outside the EU. The nature and extent of collaboration in this case are much less circumscribed, leaving the supervisors to operate more freely in principle on the basis of their risk-based judgments.

Supervision of branches is a shared home and host responsibility. Regardless of the impact of the branch, if the home supervisor cannot be relied upon (for example to ensure that the group as a whole is properly capitalized) the host supervisor may wish to consider whether they should insist on subsidiarization within the host market. This will provide a degree of ring-fencing which will better enable the host supervisor to meet its obligations. Assuming that the home supervisor is broadly reliable, the pattern of collaboration may again depend on whether the branch is high or low impact. In the case of a high impact branch, the supervisors will wish to aim for the most efficient and effective pattern of collaboration — for example with the host taking some primacy in respect of activities that are specific to its market or where it has a comparative advantage. Where the branch is low impact however the host, in discharging its legal responsibilities, may wish to place the maximum amount of reliance it prudently can on the work of the home.

This pattern extends to the supervision of locally incorporated subsidiaries where the legal responsibility rests clearly with the host. Here too, the host of a high impact firm will wish to collaborate in the most rational and effective way with the home authority, while in respect of a low impact subsidiary the host may wish to assess the maximum amount of reliance that it can prudently place on the home.

5. Concluding Comments: What Are the Constraints And Realities Governing What Cross-Border Collaboration Can Achieve?

To some extent the ideas advanced above represent little more than common sense. The fact that they are by no means applied universally at the moment, however, suggests that they are nevertheless worth airing. Real progress has been made in supervisory collaboration in recent years. We have seen successful examples of this in respect of specific market-wide issues such as credit derivatives documentation. Day to day collaboration has become relatively common in the supervision of cross-border banking groups and increasingly a feature of the supervision of global securities firms. It still has some way to go however in insurance supervision. Even where collaboration is a feature, discussions and joint working are understandably much more the norm than extensive mutual reliance. There are also good reasons to hope that extensive collaboration will be a feature of future cross-border financial crises, though the factors governing behavior here are very different, resulting in more defensive and in some respects less rational behavior than might be expected in day-to-day supervision.

Ultimately, however, the extent to which supervisors are willing judiciously to place reliance on one another depends on their risk appetite. To what extent are they willing to take reputational and legal risks in pursuit of more effective and efficient supervision? Supervisors are, quite rightly, held accountable for what they do. This requires them to explain from time to time why they judged a particular choice of supervisory tools to have been the right one even though things subsequently went wrong. Judicious mutual reliance is a supervisory tool like all others and can be defended *ex post*. Supervisors currently reveal a diversity in their willingness to go down this route but the exigencies of supervising global groups suggests that all may need to think more carefully about it than they have done to date.

Challenges in Cross-Border Supervision and Regulation

Eric Rosengren*
Federal Reserve Bank of Boston

This set of three papers addressing the critical issue of whether our supervisory and regulatory structures are sufficiently developed to meet the challenges of truly global financial institutions. They all come to a similar conclusion that while financial institution regulation and supervision remain focused within domestic borders; the problems posed by global banks are increasingly likely to span national borders. While there are some differences in approach, all three papers argue for enhanced international coordination, the need to move to intervene in problem institutions earlier, and the advantages to further developing bankruptcy laws for global financial institutions.

This paper will first discuss why the issues addressed in these papers are so important and briefly discuss the findings in the papers. The next section will amplify on some of the home-host challenges for bank regulation, where arguably the most progress has been made. This will be followed by a discussion of the home-host challenges for bank supervision where more work needs to be done on international coordination. The last section will provide some conclusions

1. Trends in Global Banking

Over the past decade there have been waves of large intra-national bank mergers. This has created banks of unprecedented size, with several banks in Japan, America, and Europe now exceeding one trillion dollars. As markets in each of these regions get more concentrated, increasingly banks will be looking beyond their borders for future growth opportunities.

*Eric Rosengren is a vice president and economist at the Federal Reserve Bank of Boston.

The motivation for creating these huge financial institutions has varied. In Japan, the extensive credit quality problems created by the dramatic fall in real estate and the stock market in the early 1990s crippled domestic banks. One solution to the problem has been to encourage mergers of troubled Japanese banks with the hope of creating a more streamlined and competitive group of large banks.

In the United States, many of the mergers have been driven by the desire to create national bank franchises. Because of the highly fragmented banking market, only Bank of America has a franchise that covers most significant regions of the United States. Despite JP Morgan Chase and Citigroup being well over one trillion dollars in assets, they still remain absent from several major retail markets in the United States. With only one truly national bank in the United States, it is likely we will continue to see acquisitions to create truly national franchises.

In Europe, intra-market mergers have been the public policy in several nations with the hope of creating "national champions". However, because of the small size of many of the national markets, it is likely that over the next decade there will be mergers that create pan-European banks. In some countries in Europe, the market concentration within countries is forcing their largest banks to already look outside of national borders for future acquisitions.

While the past decade has established trillion-dollar banks, most remain heavily concentrated in their home country. Over the next decade, these large banks will be forced by competition laws to increasingly search for acquisitions outside of their home country borders. In addition to expanding across national borders, these banks are likely to search for opportunities that expand their scope of operation.

A good example is provided by Citigroup. They are geographically diversified with activities in over 100 countries. They have $1.6 trillion in assets, $115 billion in stockholders equity, $25 billion in net income, and 133 billion in total revenue. Despite their size, they still are not truly a national bank in the United States, and are likely to be searching for opportunities to grow domestically, either by *de novo* entry or by acquisitions, as they also continue to fill out their international franchise. Given their size, they have more significant financial capacity than many of the countries in which they operate. For example, note that with $133 billion in total revenue, it produces roughly three times the size of government revenue in Argentina.

The creation of these trillion-dollar financial institutions does pose potential public policy issues, as is discussed in all three of these papers.

As the authors note; deposit insurance is focused on domestic deposits, bankruptcy laws are national, access to funds and lines of credit in a failure situation could cause significant delays in retrieving funds, and the allocation of losses is unclear. I would add to the list provided in these three papers that accounting rules still varies by jurisdiction, lender of last resort rules is nationally focused and the legal standing of bank supervisors varies by jurisdiction.

The set of papers in this conference have suggested several remedies to avoid problems in the event of an insolvency of a large global bank. First, any resolution of a failed institution should be dealt with promptly. Second, bankruptcy laws and resolution procedures for global banks should be clarified. Third, actions should be taken to insure prompt access to funds in the event of insolvency. Most of these solutions will require significantly more international coordination. The problem becomes particularly acute when global banks become large relative to government spending and gross domestic product (GDP) of the home country. Global banks are becoming too large to save for many smaller countries, making national solutions particularly problematic.

2. Progress on Home-Host Issues

Over the past several years there has been significant progress on home-host coordination. However, the progress in coordinating is probably much further developed with bank regulation than with bank supervision. This is because much of the regulatory coordination is being done through activities such as Basel II, which provides a uniform regulatory framework. In contrast, many of the changes needed to promote home-host coordination with bank supervision require major changes in national laws.

Home host coordination places a premium on improved communication. The Basel II process has resulted in regular supervisory colleges coordinated by the home country supervisor. This process has also resulted in more visits between home and host supervisors and the management of the parent bank. In order to promote information transfers, many countries have adopted bilateral memoranda of understanding MoUs. This process has significantly increased formal and informal communication between supervisors.

The increased regulatory coordination has also had benefits for the parent bank. Both parent management and the home supervisor are better informed about deficiencies in risk management in the host country. In addition, Basel II has encouraged banks to adopt a common platform. This more uniform management information system, makes it easier for banks to make risk return trade-offs across the entire organization.

The coordination in bank supervision probably lags that of bank regulation. However, many supervisors are exchanging supervisors for some target exams, and results of exam work are being shared more broadly. Despite these initial steps, it is fortunate that coordination of supervision has not been tested recently.

With no recent insolvencies of large global players, it is difficult to be certain how well coordination would work. However, history would indicate some cause for concern. Bank of Credit and Commerce International illustrated that international coordination is a challenge when there are multiple legal entities spanning different countries. Daiwa bank's losses in the host country that were not revealed promptly indicate that there may still be more work to coordinate information between bank supervisors. Argentinian policies in a country with significant foreign bank penetration highlighted that home and host regulators may not have the same incentives in banking problems.

During a banking crisis, the host country supervisor is frequently focused on protection of domestic depositors. Not only is there deposit insurance in most countries, but failure to payoff depositors in a timely fashion can have a significant impact on how depositors vote in the subsequent election. Host supervisors are also concerned with maintaining loans to domestic borrowers to prevent banking problems from having significant macroeconomic consequences. A good example of this is the actions taken in Japan to avoid a credit crunch. However, these actions require banks to expand credit during difficult times, actions that may be inconsistent with the managers in the home country. In addition, the host supervisor will try to prevent problems at individual banks from causing contagion for the whole banking system.

The home country supervisor has different incentives. They are primarily concerned that problems in the host country minimally impact the capital and earnings of the parent. Actions taken by the parent may limit parent exposure to host country problems and limit the capital infusions into the host country. These actions would be taken to avoid importing a banking problem that could impact depositors and borrowers in the home country.

These incentive differences between home and host country may become magnified as the problems get worse. The host country may have broader macroeconomic concerns while the home country has microeconomic concerns. In addition, the incentives for communication which should become more important, actually may diminish. The host country supervisor will place a premium on addressing the crisis, not communication with the home supervisor. As a result, communication with the home supervisor is often done by increasing communication with the parent bank which is not an unbiased observer.

During a crisis, the host country often holds the trump cards. Banks operating in their border are bound by that nation's laws. The laws for banks may change during a crisis and foreign banks are likely to have little political leverage. In addition, bank employees in the host country may be subject to criminal penalties in their home country if their actions are viewed as circumventing domestic laws.

The incentive problems are much less severe when there is a troubled parent but a healthy subsidiary because a healthy subsidiary can be sold. The home supervisor benefits from having the capital infusion from the sale of the healthy subsidiary. The host supervisor often would prefer a healthy and well capitalized parent. A good example is the Japanese bank sales of assets in the United States during the 1990s. Japanese banks benefited from selling subsidiaries that could command a high price, and the increased capital and reduction in assets were beneficial to the parent.

When a global bank does encounter difficulties, it is likely to be problematic for the home country supervisor. There is likely to be international pressure to forbear in order to have an orderly resolution. In addition, there is likely to be pressure to back up the foreign liabilities. This raises questions of whether home countries will have the capacity to orchestrate an orderly resolution. Given the difficulty when dealing with legal entities in many countries and the ability to shift assets, it is questionable whether prompt action is likely to result with an insolvent global bank.

3. Conclusion

All three papers highlight the need for further work in home-host coordination. While much progress has occurred, particularly in regulatory coordination, supervisory coordination is a more difficult problem. As these three papers highlight, we have global banks but we do not have global legal systems, accounting systems, or tax systems. These national differences could potentially be a problem when truly global banks become troubled.

V. GOVERNMENT SAFETY NET

Bagehot and Coase Meet the Single European Market

Vítor Gaspar*

Banco de Portugal

1. Introduction

Europe's financial landscape has been changing gradually, but rapidly. The pace of change seems to have accelerated with the creation of the euro area. Clearly, the introduction of the single currency had very pronounced (and measurable) effects on cross-border trading, in particular in money markets and bond markets (see, for example, Gaspar *et al.*, 2003, Baele *et al.*, 2004, and Capiello *et al.*, 2006). Nevertheless, it is clear that the process of financial integration in Europe is broader than the single currency area. It is well known that the process of European financial integration was given a tremendous impetus by the Single European Act of 1987, providing the ground for the establishment of an internal market, allowing for the exercise of the four fundamental freedoms. That is the unrestricted freedom of movement of goods, services, persons and capital. More recently, in 1999, European policymakers, decided on a Financial Services Action Plan aiming at achieving, by 2005, (1) a single market for wholesale financial services; (2) open and secure retail markets; (3) state-of-the-art prudential rules and supervision. The progress in the last five years has been notable. And finally, the transformation of Europe's financial landscape also reflected driving forces relevant for developments in the world economy. Among these, the most important has likely been technology.

*Vitor Gaspar is Special Adviser at the Banco de Portugal. The views expressed in this paper are the author's own and do not necessarily reflect those of Banco de Portugal or the Eurosystem. The author is grateful to Marta Abreu, Thorsten Beck, Adelaide Cavaleiro, Vítor Constâncio, Charles Evans, Mauro Grande, George Kaufman, Manuel Sebastião and Joaquim Martinez da Silva for useful comments and corrections. The responsibility for remaining errors is his own.

As European financial integration progresses, the cross-border financial services and transactions expand. Such developments contribute to substantial improvements in market efficiency and liquidity, while, at the same time, disturbances become more likely to spread across borders. There is a coincidence of an integration process, leading to deeper interdependence with a financial stability set-up based on national responsibilities. Such coincidence has been the object of attention by academics and policy makers (see Padoa-Schioppa, 2004, for an overview and extensive references). The interest is increased by the fact that interdependencies are obviously also deepening at the global level. Issues to do with how to manage cross-border spillovers in banking are, therefore, of general relevance. Since the process of European financial integration is more advanced, a follow-up question is naturally: What can we learn from Europe for global financial stability?

In Europe, the regulatory and supervisory framework for financial stability is based on the following four elements: First is European Union (EU) wide regulation (called harmonized regulation or *harmonization* in European jargon). Second is *mutual recognition* of national rules. Third is national responsibility for supervision, that is, for the enforcement of the rules, based on *home-country control*. Fourth is *close cooperation* among the competent authorities at all levels.

In the area of banking the supervision framework is specified by community law in the first and second banking directives). The idea is that national responsibility for supervision allows monitoring to take place close to the supervised institutions. Such proximity allows for timely and detailed monitoring of banks' activities. According to the home-country control principle, all banks, by virtue of a single European license, have the right to provide services throughout the EU. Supervision is the responsibility of the member state where the bank is licensed. The decentralized approach is completed by the principle of cooperation to avoid the drawbacks of such an approach in the face of an increasingly integrated European financial system.

The combination of a process of integration with potentially systemic implications, with responsibilities and competencies still segmented at the national level, justifies questions about the stability and efficiency implications of such arrangements. Researchers and policymakers have focused especially on issues pertaining to banking, in general, and, specifically, to lender of last resort and emergence liquidity assistance. Goodhart and Schoenmaker (2006), Eisenbeis and Kaufman (2006), Schinasi and Teixeira (2006), and Schoenmaker and Osterloo (2005) have all contributed to a fast growing literature. In this paper, we will focus on lending of last resort in the European Union's Single Financial Market.

The literature on lender of last resort is very extensive and started more than two hundred years ago with Henry Thornton who, in 1802, elaborated on it in his *An Enquiry into the Nature and Effects of the Paper Credit of Great Britain*. However it was only more than a half-century later, that Bagehot (1848, 1873), elaborating on the contribution of Thornton, established the definite form of the classical lender of last resort doctrine. Such an approach was followed in the last third of the nineteenth century by the Bank of England. This coincided with a relatively long period of financial stability. Nevertheless, in the relevant literature, the concept of lender of last resort is not unique. Therefore, some of the differences between authors can be attributed to semantics.

The rest of this chapter is organized as follows. In the next section, I will present a short characterization of the classical approach to lending of last resort doctrine, associated with Thornton and Bagehot. Following the agenda initially proposed by Humphrey (1975) and then followed by many, including Humphrey and Keleher (1984), Goodfriend and King (1988), Humphrey (1989, 1992), Kaufman (1991) and Freixas *et al.* (2005), I ask, in the third section, whether the classical doctrine is still relevant and how best to interpret it today. I will argue that the classical doctrine is very illuminating and help us to frame the contemporary debate. I will further argue that it is particularly applicable to the framework relevant for the euro area. In the fourth section, I will make some remarks on the on-going transformation of the European financial landscape with a particular emphasis on banking. I will also briefly outline the European framework for dealing with financial regulation and supervision. I will briefly mention the arrangements in place to deal with financial crises. In the fifth section, I will comment on a number of questions, challenges and open issues, and conclude.

2. The Classical Lender of Last Resort Doctrine: Thornton and Bagehot

Despite the association of the classical lender of last resort doctrine with Thornton and Bagehot, the term seems to have originated with Sir Francis Baring. In 1797, he referred to the Bank of England as the Bank of "the dernier resort", which all banks had to rely on to obtain liquidity in stressful times.[1]

---

[1] As quoted in Humphrey (1989), p. 8.

Thornton and Bagehot both start by stressing the special position of the central bank (in their writings the Bank of England) as the holder of the ultimate reserve of the country. The special role of the Bank of England derived not only from its holding of substantial gold reserves but also, most importantly, from its monopoly of issuance of the non-gold component of the monetary base in the form Bank of England's notes. Thornton made the fundamental empirical assumption that, because of the Bank of England's unquestioned soundness and the universal acceptance of its notes, the Bank of England had a virtually unlimited ability to provide the final means of settlement. Bagehot (1848) made a similar point already in 1848, 25 years before writing *Lombard Street:*

> "The power of issuing notes ... should only be used also in rare and exceptional cases. But when the fact of a sudden demand is proved, we see no objection, but decided advantage, in introducing this new element into a metallic circulation. We see here only one other case of government intervention to ensure steadiness in the standard of value." (quotation I)

Coming back to Thornton, the ability to issue bank notes lies at the root of the feasibility of performing a lender of last resort function. Conceptually, this is a fundamental point. It is the central bank's ability to create virtually unlimited amounts of the ultimate means of settlement that, according to the classical approach, lies at the root of its responsibility as lender of last resort.

Interestingly, as early as 1802, Henry Thornton identified the fundamental moral hazard problem associated with it when he wrote:

> "It is by no means intended to imply, that it would become the Bank of England to relieve every distress which the rashness of county banks may bring upon them: the bank, by doing this, might encourage their improvidence ... The relief should neither be so prompt and general as to exempt those who misconduct their business from all the natural consequences of their fault, nor so scanty and slow as deeply to involve the general interests. These interests, nevertheless, are sure to be pleaded by every distressed person whose affairs are large, however indifferent or even ruinous may be their state."(II)

Two important additions from Bagehot's complete a summary characterization of the classical lender of last resort doctrine:

> "The Bank of England ... in time of panic ... must advance freely and vigorously to the public out of the reserve. ... For this purpose there are

two rules: First, that these loans should only be made at a very high rate of interest. ... Second, at this rate advances must be made on all good banking securities, and as largely as the public asks for them."(III)

He then observes "... an immense system of credit, founded on the Bank of England, as its pivot and its basis, now exists. The English people, and foreigners too, trust it implicitly. ... Those who live under a great and firm system of credit must consider that if they break up that one they will never see another, for it will take years upon years to make a successor to it."(IV)

In short, (following very closely Humphrey (1989, 1992), while, occasionally, departing slightly from his presentation) the classical lender of last resort doctrine may be characterized by the following principles:

1) The lender of last resort aims at protecting the integrity of the financial system rather than individual institutions. (I, II)
2) It supports the central bank's monetary policy objectives. (I)[2]
3) Insolvent institutions should be allowed to fail. (II, III)
4) Only institutions that are illiquid but solvent should receive lender of last resort assistance. (III)
5) Lending of last resort should be conducted at penalty rates. (III)
6) Lending of last resort should only be granted against good collateral. (III)
7) The conditions ruling lending of last resort should be announced and well-understood in advance of the event of a crisis. (IV)

At the end of each proposition, there is a bracketed reference to a quotation that supports it. The argument given is clearly insufficient. For a more detailed argument and further references see the various works by Humphrey.[3] The issue is difficult and subtle, as was made clear by Bagehot himself:

"The practical difficulties of life often cannot be met by very simple rules; those dangers being complex and many, the rules encountering them cannot well be single and simple. A uniform remedy for many diseases often ends by killing the patient."

---

[2] Humphrey (1992) refers specifically to the goals of gold convertibility and stable long run monetary growth.
[3] Specifically, the references are Humphrey (1975), Humphrey and Keleher (1984), Humphrey (1989) and Humphrey (1992).

Bagehot quotes approvingly the description by Mr. Harman, from the Bank of England, of the way through which the 1825 panic was stopped:

> "We lent it," said, Mr. Harman on behalf of the Bank of England, "by every possible means and in modes we had never adopted before; we took in stock on security, we purchase exchequer bills, we not only discounted outright, but we made advances on every possible means, consistent with the safety of the Bank and we were not on some occasions over nice. Seeing the dreadful state in which the public were, we rendered every assistance in our power. After a day or two of this treatment, the entire panic subsided, and the City was quite calm." (V)

Historically, the classical approach to lender of last resort was followed by the Bank of England in the last third of the 19th century. It seems that the doctrine worked well, as there were no financial crises on record from 1866 to the end of the century. As Humphrey says, in today's world, the classical position, is honored as much in the breach as in the observance. Thus, it is worthwhile revisiting it from today's perspective. I will do so in the next section.

3. The Classical Lender of Last Resort Doctrine and Monetary Policy Implementation Today

It is worthwhile revisiting the classical paradigm from the viewpoint of contemporary economic theory, financial systems and monetary policy regimes. Current literature provides basically two main rationales for a role as lender of last resort. The first is systemic stability (see de Bandt and Hartmann, 2000, for a survey of the literature on systemic risk). Widespread financial instability, associated with a crisis situation, may impair the ability of the financial system to perform its main functions. Those functions are to allocate available savings to investment opportunities, to produce and process information, to allocate risks and to provide payments' services. Widespread instability may also disrupt the monetary transmission mechanism. Such systemic problems may stem from disturbances to a large financial institution or a group of smaller ones. The second is asymmetric information concerning the balance-sheet position of financial intermediaries (the focus is typically on banks). Specifically, the difficulties in monitoring the quality of assets, in particular the loan portfolio, make solvent banks vulnerable to liquidity shocks. Such shocks may come either from its depositors or from the interbank market. Either way solvent banks may be vulnerable making liquidation inefficient (see Freixas *et al.* 2004 for a very clear presentation of this argument). In my discussion, in this chapter, I will focus on the first rationale and will disregard the second.

It is important to start by noting an important difference between the perspective of Bagehot and most positions held today. Bagehot[4] advocates that, in times of panic, the central bank should make advances (albeit at penalty rates and against good collateral) to the public at large. Bagehot is very clear that lending should be available "to merchants, to minor bankers, to 'this man and that man', whenever the security is good". The reason, according to him is that, "The problem of managing a panic must not be thought of as mainly a banking problem. It is primarily a mercantile one. All merchants are under liabilities; they have bills to meet soon, and they can only pay those bills by discounting bills on other merchants. In other words, all merchants are dependent on borrowing money, and large merchants are dependent on borrowing much money. At the slightest symptom of panic many merchants want to borrow more than usual; they think they will supply themselves with the means of meeting their bills while those means are still forthcoming. If the banks gratify the merchants, they must lend largely just when they like it least; if they do not gratify them, there is a panic." Clearly, Bagehot was of the view that mercantile activity lies at the root of the propagation mechanism of a panic.

Today most, if not all, authors would focus on the preservation of the liquidity and orderly functioning of the interbank money market. Therefore, the focus would be on banks. In my view, the clearest rationale for this position has been presented by Padoa-Schioppa (2004, chapters 2 and 8) relying on the theoretical framework of Kashyap *et al.* (1999). The key ideas are that the financial system can be best understood as based on a pyramid structure and that banks are special because it is part of their core business to provide liquidity on demand. On the liabilities side of the balance sheet, banks stand clearly ready to convert deposits into currency. On the asset side, banks provide the same service through credit lines.

Thus, Padoa-Schioppa argues, the central bank stands at the top of the pyramid as the provider of the ultimate means of settlement: central bank

---

[4] In quote III, op. cit.

money. Below the central bank we have licensed banks that act as lenders of next to last resort. And, finally, at the bottom we have nonbank financial institutions that need support from banks in the management of their liquidity needs. For my purposes, Padoa-Schioppa makes a key remark. He states that the general need for liquidity is not affected by technological and financial innovation, as long as the pyramid structure of the financial system is kept.

Padoa-Schioppa's conclusion concerning the need to involve central banks in financial stability is fully in line with the starting point of Thornton and Bagehot, described at the beginning of section 2. Specifically, Padoa-Schioppa writes:[5]

> "The provision of final liquidity remains the most powerful rationale for the role of central banks in promoting and providing financial stability. Indeed, central bank money has proven to be the most valuable settlement medium in times of crisis, when confidence in the ability of commercial banks to meet their liabilities has faded away. Central banks are the only public institutions that can provide large amounts of liquidity and act fast as needed."

Rephrasing what I have said before, the role of central banks derives from its monopoly power in the provision of the final means of settlement. The credibility and universal acceptance of central bank money lies at the root of the central bank's ability to act.

A second important point concerns the relation between lender of last resort and monetary policy implementation. According to Humphrey (1992), Thornton was the first to look at lender of last resort as primarily a monetary function and not as a banking or credit function. Goodfriend and King (1988) explore the implications for modern central banking. They state (p. 17):

> "... [L]ender of last resort policy and the routine provision of an elastic currency are functionally equivalent. Both are directed at insulating the nominal interest rate from disturbances to the demand for currency. Both can be executed by using open market operations to create and destroy high-powered money. Since both are monetary policy ... banking and financial regulations are neither necessary nor sufficient for a central bank to pursue effective last resort lending."

---

[5] See Padoa-Schioppa (2004), Chapter 8, p. 97.

The argument is particularly useful to understand why it is consensual that central banks are responsible for the provision of liquidity to financial markets as a whole, with a view to maintain orderly market conditions. Actions and announcements by the Fed and the European Central Bank (ECB) on September 11, 2001, illustrate the point. Observers are unanimous in agreeing that central banks' interventions, following September 11, were justified and successful.

For Goodfriend and King, lender of last resort is just a part of interest rate smoothing. It comes naturally as a by-product of conducting monetary policy through the control of a money market interest rate. From this viewpoint, Goodfriend and King (p. 15) characterize Bagehot's lender of last resort doctrine as occasional interest rate smoothing policy. It is worthwhile to follow the line of argument in Goodfriend and King (1988) from the perspective of a central bank implementing monetary policy through a "corridor system".

In recent years, the practice of central banks concerning the way to implement monetary policy has been evolving. It may be argued that the corridor system or "channel system" is becoming standard. In a corridor system, overnight market interest rates are bound by the existence of two standing facilities provided by the central bank, with predetermined interest rates. One is a deposit facility where banks can deposit their excess clearance balances, earning a given return. The other is a marginal lending facility which provides access to liquidity, at a given interest rate, against the pledging of eligible collateral. Inside the corridor interest rates are steered through regular or occasional open market operations. Outside the US, the corridor system has been adopted by a series of countries during the last decade, namely Australia, Canada, Denmark, the euro area, New Zealand, Sweden and the UK (see, for example, Bindseil, 2004, for an overview). Since the start of the ECB's single monetary policy in 1999, a significant amount of research has been devoted to identifying the relevant empirical facts characterizing the euro market for overnight funds.[6] Woodford (2003) advocates the channel system as particularly simple and effective to implement interest rate policy. The empirical evidence vindicates this view. The corridor system allows for tight control over interest rates in the market for daily funds, while, at the same time, limiting their volatility. The system is designed so that disturbances in the demand for

---

[6] See chapter 4, of ECB (2004) for a brief description of the operational framework of the Eurosystem, and Gaspar *et al.* (2004) for a recent review of the empirical evidence.

liquidity are automatically buffered. Hence, the system is compatible with limited volatility of interest rates. By implementing monetary policy in this way, the Eurosystem provides an elastic currency, meeting economic agents' demand for currency and, thereby, contributing to well-functioning transaction mechanisms.

Coming back to the classical lender of last resort doctrine, it is striking to notice that the marginal lending facility, a fundamental element in a corridor system, fulfills, by design, the function of guaranteeing access to liquidity, against sound collateral, to all credit institutions. The marginal lending facility can be accessed in unlimited amounts by individual credit institutions at their own initiative. The only constraint is the availability of eligible collateral. Given that the interest rate applicable to marginal lending operations is significantly higher than daily market rates (by about 100 basis points) credit institutions only use it in the absence of viable market alternatives. Thus, as far as credit institutions are concerned, the Eurosystem's marginal lending facility is in line with Bagehot's prescriptions. The same applies to all central banks providing a marginal lending facility. Specifically, such facility: (1) is accessible at a penalty rate, (2) requires pledging of eligible collateral (defined *ex ante*), and (3) is permanently available, according to publicized and well-understood rules, but it is used only occasionally.

Moreover, it contributes to the smooth implementation of monetary policy. In the context of a corridor system, where, as a rule, all monetary policy operations are performed against adequate collateral, Thornton and Bagehot's concerns with creditworthiness are explicitly dealt with *ex ante*.[7] In the euro area, the fact that the marginal lending facility may always be used by commercial banks provides permanent insurance against idiosyncratic liquidity shocks. It is important to stress that collateral does not seem scarce in the euro area. Bindseil and Papadia (2006) report that eligible collateral was, in 2005, about € 8.2 trillion. The amount deposited, on average, during 2005, for possible use in monetary policy operations was only about 10 percent of this total (€ 853 billion). The Eurosystem's collateral framework is evolving and will be expanding to include some bank loans as eligible collateral.

---

[7] The same point was made by Friedman (1960) and Goodfriend and King (1988) when they stress that liquidity provision through open market operations automatically deals with the problem of protecting the central bank's balance sheet against bad loans.

It is useful to recapitulate the argument thus far. A corridor system for monetary policy implementation provides a very effective framework to ensure a central bank's control over daily interest rates. It does so while providing an elastic currency, in other words by accommodating economic agents' demands for payments media in a way compatible with the smooth functioning of transactions mechanisms in the economy. A corridor system includes a marginal lending facility that fulfills the principles of the classical lender of last resort doctrine. Therefore, the corridor system for monetary policy implementation subsumes the classical lender of last resort function.[8] It ensures it either through open market operations or through the automatic functioning of the marginal lending facility (or both). Hence, such framework contributes to financial stability, in accordance with the general principle of an open market economy, with free competition.

To conclude this section, I will make just one remark on Emergency Liquidity Assistance. For our purposes it is useful to define Emergency Liquidity Assistance (ELA) as the discretionary provision of liquidity, in exceptional circumstances, to individual credit institutions and markets, on the part of the central bank.

Padoa-Schioppa (2004) argues that, in today's world, "bank runs occur mainly in textbooks". The reason is mainly the almost universal adoption of deposit insurance schemes in industrialized countries. And so, he concludes, "The textbook case for emergency liquidity assistance to individual solvent institutions, as a matter of fact, has been a most rare event in industrial countries over the past decades." An effective operational framework for monetary policy implementation, subsuming the lender of last resort function, makes the presumption stronger. The experience of the Eurosystem, with its own emergency liquidity assistance, is completely in line with such position.

4. Integration and Stability in the Single European Financial Market

In this chapter, I have argued that, up to now, the creation of the euro area has likely contributed to improved financial stability. As stated in the introduction, financial markets and institutions have undergone and will continue

---

[8] I am grateful to Charles Evans for suggesting this formulation.

to undergo gradual but rapid change. The main drivers of change have been the European single financial market process — spearheaded in the last years by the Financial Services Action Plan (1999–2005) — the single currency and the single monetary policy (from 1999), technological change and worldwide globalization. In the euro area, unsecured money markets are fully integrated and government bond markets almost perfectly so. Market infrastructure is consolidating in Europe. Integration, however, is far from uniform. Equity markets seem less integrated than bond markets but, more importantly, cross-border provision of financial services at the retail level remains quite limited. In any case, it seems undeniable that financial markets have become deeper and more liquid, providing opportunities for improved risk sharing. The creation of the euro area has also contributed to increased overall macroeconomic stability (Gaspar and Kashyap, 2006), thereby also favoring financial stability. It is also worth noting that Dermine (2003) has found that cross-border banking activity in Europe is done predominantly through subsidiaries (and not through branches) creating lesser challenges for national responsibilities.

There have not been, in the literature, many attempts to measure systemic risk empirically. An exception is Hartmann *et al.* (2005), who focus on the banking system. They use a data sample covering the larger 50 banks in the US and in the euro area, in the period 1992–2004. They find that the risk of multivariate extreme spillovers involving US banks is larger than risk spillovers for euro area banks. They also find that the explanation of lower spillovers in Europe is related mainly to relatively weak cross-border spillovers. The analysis in their paper is motivated by the remark that the banking system, both in the US and in the euro area, has undergone important structural changes. One of the marking characteristics of this evolution has been consolidation in banking and the emergence of large and complex institutions. Such developments make the evaluation of systemic risk in banking increasingly difficult. In order to assess the evolution of risk over time, they perform statistical stability tests for their risk indicators. They find that both aggregate risk and the risk of interbank spillovers have increased both in Europe and in the US Specifically, they are able to identify structural break points in the second half of the nineties. Importantly, they find that the introduction of the euro was either associated with no-effect on risk or even with a reduction in risk. They interpret this finding as possibly related with the fact that deeper and more integrated markets have two contradictory effects on systemic risk. On the one hand, in line with the argument earlier of Schinasi and Teixeira (2006), they increase cross-border linkages. On the other hand, as mentioned above, deeper and more efficient markets afford additional opportunities to absorb and diversify risk. Moreover, I have argued, in section 3, that the characteristics of the Eurosystem's operational framework are such that the marginal lending facility constitutes a very effective line of defense against liquidity shocks. The current situation will gradually change. As European financial integration progresses, the cross-border financial services and transactions expand. The coincidence of a process leading to deeper interdependencies with a financial stability architecture based on the exercise of national responsibilities has been the object of attention by academics and policymakers (see, for example, Padoa-Schioppa, 2004; and Schinasi and Teixeira, 2006).

Intense efforts at coordination and cooperation have been taking place using the EU committee structures, leading to an overall strengthening of the framework for supervision and crisis management. These efforts have already given rise to Memoranda of Understanding (MoU). These include the 2003 MoU between supervisors and central banks and the 2005 MoU between Ministries of Finance, supervisors and central banks. It has been widely reported that, in April and May 2006, responsible authorities have been performing simulated crisis scenarios in order to test communication and coordination procedures. Naturally progress can be expected.

In 1960, Ronald Coase stated a tautology with far-reaching implications, which became known as the Coase Theorem. The idea is that in an environment with perfect information and costless bargaining a mutually beneficial agreement will be reached whenever there is one.[9] Coase's theorem was supposed to apply to bargaining among private sector agents in an environment characterized by externalities or spillovers. The coordination of a multiplicity of government agencies, brought together in committees, to agree on how to deal with important cross-border spillover in crisis situations, raises interesting questions. The one that I am most curious about is: Will the Coase Theorem be a good approximation for coordination among government officials operating in an environment where bargaining is far from costless and information far from perfect? In my view, experts in this area, gathered in various committee composition (that together form a complex maze known, in Europe, as European commitology), are very well trained and informed, have very long horizons, and are well-aware of all the challenges listed in the literature (and more). I am optimistic that progress will be forthcoming.

---

[9] Coase (1960) is the original reference. See Bowles (2004, pp. 221–232) and Shavell (2004, p. 84).

5. Conclusion

The classical lender of last resort doctrine was developed by Henry Thornton and, especially by Walter Bagehot in the 19th century. Historically, it was followed successfully by the Bank of England in the last third of the nineteenth century. Following Humphrey, and in particular, Goodfriend and King (1988), I have argued that the lender of last resort should be, first and foremost, understood as a monetary policy function. Thus, I have found a classical lender of last resort function is subsumed in the Eurosystem's operational framework for monetary policy, based on the corridor system. I have further argued that the use of emergency liquidity assistance will likely be a most rare event. This has been the case in industrial countries in recent decades. The permanent availability of the marginal lending facility makes significant use of emergency liquidity even more unlikely in the Eurosystem.

Nevertheless, European financial integration raises other interesting challenges. The deepening of cross-border banking linkages (for example, through the interbank money market, cross-border branching, etc.), increased integration of bond and equity markets, the consolidation of market infrastructure, the emergence of large pan-European banking groups and the attenuation of home bias in portfolios mean that the European architecture will likely be reviewed and debated intensely in the next few years. A particularly difficult question relates to the issue of burden sharing in case of a financial crisis with significant cross-border spillovers. There is good reason to think that the overall architecture of the financial system will depend on institutions, practices and perceptions. *Ex ante* clarity may be required in order to ensure not only transparency but also an adequate incentive structure. In this context, an interesting question is: can we rely on Coase's Theorem to provide a good approximation, to the outcome of negotiations, among government, officials in an environment of costly bargaining and imperfect information? In other words: will bargaining involving European commitology deliver efficient outcomes?

References

Baele, L., A. Ferrando, P. Hördahl, E. Krylova and C. Monnet (2004). Measuring financial integration in the Euro area. ECB Occasional Paper 14, May.

Bagehot, W. (1848). The currency monopoly, the prospective review. In *The Collected Works of Walter Bagehot*, Volume 9, N. St. John-Stevas (ed.). London: The Economist.

Bagehot, W. (1873). Lombard street, London: H.S. King. In *The Collected Works of Walter Bagehot,* Volume 9, N. St. John-Stevas (ed.). London: The Economist.

Bindseil, U. (2004). *Monetary Policy Implementation: Theory, Past and Present.* Oxford: Oxford University Press.

Bindseil, U. and F. Papadia (2006). Credit risk mitigation in Central Bank operations and its effects on financial markets: The case of the eurosystem. ECB Occasional Paper Series 49, August.

Bowles, S. (2004). *Microeconomics: Behavior, Institutions and Evolution.* Princeton: Russell Sage Foundation, Princeton University Press.

Capiello, L., P. Hordahl, A. Kadareja and S. Manganelli (2006). The Impact of the Euro on financial markets. ECB Working Paper 598, March.

Coase, R. (1960). The problem of social cost. *Journal of Law and Economics,* 2, 1–40.

De Bandt, O. and P. Hartmann (2000). Systemic risk: A survey. In *Financial Crises, Contagion and Lender of Last Resort: A Book of Readings,* C. Goodhart, and G. Illing (eds.). Oxford: Oxford University Press.

Dermine, J. (2003). Banking in Europe: Past, present and future. In *The Transformation of the European Financial System,* Gaspar *et al.* (eds.). Frankfurt: European Central Bank.

European Central Bank (2004). *The Monetary Policy of the ECB.* Frankfurt: European Central Bank.

Eisenbeis, R.A. and G.G. Kaufman (2006). Cross border banking: Challenges for deposit insurance and financial stability in the European Union. Paper presented at the Third Annual DG ECFIN Research Conference, 7–8 September 2006.

Freixas, X., J.-C. Rochet and B. Parigi (2004). The lender of last resort: A twentieth century approach. *Journal of the European Economic Association,* 2(6), 1085–1115.

Friedman, M. (1960). *A Program for Monetary Stability.* New York: Fordham University Press.

Gaspar, V., P. Hartmann and O. Sleijpen (eds.) (2003). *The Transformation of the European Financial System.* Frankfurt: European Central Bank.

Gaspar, V., G. Perez-Quirós and H.R. Mendizábal (2004). Interest rate determination in the interbank market. European Central Bank Working Paper Series 351, April.

Gaspar, V. and A. Kashyap (2006). Stability first: Reflections inspired by Otmar Issing's success as the ECB's chief economist. NBER Working Paper 12277.

Goodfriend, M. and R. King (1988). Financial deregulation, monetary policy and central banking. *Federal Reserve of Richmond, Economic Review,* May/June, 3–22.

Goodhart, C. and D. Shoenmaker (2006). Burden sharing in a banking crisis in Europe. Mimeo, March.

Hartmann, P., S. Staetmans and C. de Vries (2005). Banking system stability: A cross-atlantic perspective. ECB Working Paper 527, September.

Humphrey, T. (1975). The classical concept of the lender of last resort. *Federal Reserve of Richmond Economic Review*, 61, 2–9.

Humphrey, T. (1989). Lender of last resort: The concept in history. *Federal Reserve of Richmond Economic Review*, 75, 8–16.

Humphrey, T. (1992). Lender of last resort. In *The New Palgrave Dictionary of Money & Finance*, P. Newman, M. Milgate and J. Eatwell (eds.). London: Macmillan.

Humphrey, T. and R. Keleher (1984). The lender of last resort: A historical perspective. *Cato Journal*, 4(1), 275–318.

Kashyap, A., R. Rajan and J. Stein (1999). Banks as liquidity providers: An explanation for the co-existence of lending and deposit-taking. *Journal of Finance*, 57(1), 33–73.

Kaufman, G. (1991) Lender of last resort: A contemporary perspective. *Journal of Financial Services Research*, 5(2), 95–110.

Padoa-Schioppa, T. (2004). *Regulating Finance: Balancing Freedom and Risk.* Oxford: Oxford University Press.

Shavell, S. (2004). *Foundations of the Economic Analysis of Law.* Cambridge: Harvard University Press.

Schinasi, G. and P. Teixeira (2006). The lender of last resort in the European single financial market. In *Cross-Border Banking: Regulatory Challenges*, D. Evanoff, G. Kaufman and G. Di Caprio (cds.). Singapore: World Scientific Publishing.

Schoenkmaker D. and S. Oosterloo (2005). Financial supervision in an integrating Europe: Measuring cross-border externalities. *International Finance*, 8(1), 1–27.

Thorton, H. (1802). *An Enquiry into the Nature and Effects of the Paper Credit of Great Britain,* F. von Hayek, (ed.). London: George Allen & Unwin, 1939.

Woodford, M. (2003). *Interest and Prices: Foundations of a Theory of Monetary Policy.* Princeton: Princeton University Press.

Banking in a Changing World: Issues and Questions in the Resolution of Cross-Border Banks

Michael Krimminger*

Federal Deposit Insurance Corporation

The globalization of finance has led to the development of more integrated global exchange networks among countries and deeper interrelationships between their economies. Many financial institutions and activities that once were local are now international. While business and finance are global, most regulatory systems and laws are not. Many of the regulatory and legal norms that govern these networks and interrelationships have not kept pace with these innovations. There are few international rules and norms to govern the linkages between financial institutions, payments systems and markets. National laws almost exclusively define the relationships between internationally active banks and other financial institutions. The real task of the future is to develop regulatory and legal norms that allow the benefits of increased global interaction to blossom while mitigating the more troubling consequences of global finance.

This chapter focuses on the challenges faced by national authorities in responding to financial instability in a cross-border bank. In the absence of a common international insolvency system for cross-border banks, national authorities must improve their understanding of the options available and improve coordination with other regulators if they are to be successful in limiting the consequences of a potential cross-border failure. This chapter seeks to describe some of the key difficulties and to identify some of those practical steps.

*Michael Krimminger is Senior Policy Advisor to the director of the Federal Deposit Insurance Corporation's Division of Resolutions and Receiverships. The views expressed in this chapter are solely those of the author and do not necessarily represent the policies or views of the FDIC.

1. Background — Insolvency Principles

The ultimate insolvency of any individual or company is not an event but a process of continuing efforts over a longer or shorter period of time to stem the slide into the financial abyss of bankruptcy. For highly regulated banks, and many other financial companies, this process will entail extensive efforts by bankers and supervisors to restructure, revitalize and recapitalize the bank. If the crisis intervention efforts are unsuccessful, then the supervisors face the question of whether the bank must be placed into a formal insolvency legal process or whether some form of supervisory forbearance should be exercised.

If banks truly are "different" from other companies, then a flexible insolvency system triggered by clear, mandatory standards that require action before the bank's capital is exhausted should be applied. At this point, the bank has demonstrated that it is unlikely to survive, delay will only increase losses, and intervention is necessary to ensure protection of the public interest. A well-developed insolvency system must balance the need to avoid increasing moral hazard in the financial system by imposing losses on those creditors, obviously starting with equity holders who could have averted the failure, while allowing a prompt protection of smaller depositors and facilitating the continued availability of credit in the economy. Once clear and mandatory criteria for intervention have been triggered, the insolvency authorities must have the power to implement a flexible resolution of the failed bank to strike this balance.

Some common components of effective insolvency systems for banks have been identified.[1] First, the laws should have clear criteria for initiating insolvency proceedings to avoid allowing unsalvageable institutions to operate indefinitely by raising funds from depositors and acting as a drag on or diversion of economic capital. Next, this process should be designed to reimburse depositors up to the insured maximum as soon as possible, while minimizing the cost to the deposit insurance fund. While depositor confidence in the guarantee is based on the certainty of repayment, it is equally based on the speed of repayment. A more limited deposit guarantee, combined with explicit requirements to minimize losses in the resolution, promotes a well-funded insurance system as well

---

[1] See Group of Ten, 2002, "Insolvency Arrangements and Contract Enforceability", September; Financial Stability Forum, 2001, "Guidance for Developing Effective Deposit Insurance Systems", September, pp. 8–11; IMF Legal Dept., 1999, "Orderly & Effective Insolvency Procedures".

as limiting the moral hazard that can be engendered by deposit insurance. A third component is that the insolvency laws should give the resolution authority the immediate power to control, manage, marshal and dispose of the bank's assets and liabilities once it is appointed. Many difficulties in resolving individual insolvencies, and in addressing broader instability, have been exacerbated by the inability of trustees or receivers to take prompt action. Finally, the insolvency laws should confer adequate legal powers on the resolution authority that are sufficient to permit flexible and decisive action to maximize recoveries on assets and minimize delays in providing money back to depositors.

2. International Complications

The difficulties in balancing the competing interests in bank insolvencies are made even more complex when the supervisory and insolvency laws of two or more nations are involved. The few international rules that exist tend to address insolvency rules within defined geographical or economic relationships, such as the European Union's winding up directives.[2] Even these few rules address primarily judicial and regulatory cooperation and not the substance of the law governing an insolvency.

The absence of a common international approach affects both the home country of the cross-border bank and the host country of the bank's branches or subsidiaries. Some home countries must supervise large global banks with their principal operations located outside the home country. Switzerland is the home to two banks — United Bank of Switzerland and Credit Suisse — whose domestic Swiss operations are only a small part of their total business. Their global operations, however, could spread turbulence to Switzerland through their many market, interbank and settlement linkages with financial institutions around the globe.[3]

---

[2] See Group of Ten, 2002, "Insolvency Arrangements & Contract Enforceability", Appendix A, A16–17, September; Michael Krimminger, 2004, "Deposit Insurance and Bank Insolvency in a Changing World: Synergies & Challenges", *Current Developments in Monetary and Financial Law*, IMF, pp. 10–16; Nierop, Erwin and Mikael, Stenstrom, 2002, "Cross-Border Aspects of Insolvency Proceedings for Credit Institutions — A Legal Perspective", Paper delivered at the International Seminar on Legal & Regulatory Aspects of Financial Stability, Basel, Switzerland, January, p. 11.

[3] For further information see Hupkes, Eva, 2004, "Bank Insolvency Resolution in Switzerland", in David Mayes and Aarno Liuksila (eds.), *Who Pays for Bank Insolvency?* Helsinki: Bank of Finland, pp. 262–264.

Other countries are the hosts of foreign banks which hold a large, or even predominant, share of the host banking market. In some cases, those foreign banks are far less systemically significant in their home country. For example, in New Zealand, approximately 85 percent of the banking assets are Australian-owned.[4] Some European countries have even higher levels of foreign-owned banking assets — in Luxembourg 95 percent of the banking assets are foreign-owned, while in Estonia three foreign banks control over 97 percent of the banking assets.[5]

These host jurisdictions can face a daunting task. Where a foreign bank occupies a dominant position in the host banking market, the host country may find itself without the information or tools to act effectively.

3. The Division of Labor between Home and Host Countries

When a bank has operations in more than one country fundamental choices must be made about which jurisdiction will have primary responsibility for supervision, crisis intervention and any insolvency, and what will be the role of other affected supervisors. The commonly used principle to determine primary supervisory responsibility is "home-country control".[6] Under this principle, the home supervisor is the consolidated supervisor for the world wide activities of international banks chartered in that country, including its branches, subsidiaries and other operations. The host supervisor is responsible for ensuring that foreign subsidiaries operating within its borders are effectively supervised.

While the principle of home country control could logically extend to determine primary responsibility for crisis intervention and insolvency, it has not commonly been extended to those issues. Today, most countries will seek to exercise authority for the resolution of a failing bank subsidiary

---

[4] See Bollard, Alan, Governor of Reserve Bank of New Zealand, speech to Trans-Tasman Business Circle in Sydney, Australia on August. 11, 2004, *RBNZ Bulletin* 67(3).
[5] See European Central Bank, 2005, "Banking Structures in the New EU Member States", Table 4, p. 17; de Haas, Ralph and Iman van Lelyveld, 2002, "Foreign Bank Penetration and Private Sector Credit in Central and Eastern Europe", DNB Staff Reports No. 91, July.
[6] See Basel Committee on Banking Supervision, 1997, "Core Principles for Effective Banking Supervision", Section VI: Cross-Border Banking; Basel Committee on Banking Supervision, 1992, "Minimum Standards for the Supervision of International Banking Groups and Their Cross-border Establishments", both available at http://www.bis.org/publ/index.htm.

or branch operating within their borders under their national insolvency law. For subsidiaries, the host country is the "home" country since the entity was incorporated under its laws. For branches, most nations permit coopcration with foreign insolvency authorities within constraints imposed by the national insolvency policies, while reserving the right to conduct wholly separate insolvency proceedings to protect creditors of the branches' local operations.[7]

To the extent that national insolvency laws directly address how to deal with debtors, creditors, assets and liabilities outside the national boundaries, these laws adopt one of two basic positions: territorialism or universalism. Under a territorial approach each country adjudicates claims against the assets within its borders for the benefit of creditors of the insolvent local firm. This approach focuses on the primacy of national law within the territory of the country, although courts or administrators may cooperate with foreign proceedings. In general, the law where the assets are found thus controls their distribution. A universal approach, on the other hand, allows a single jurisdiction to adjudicate the worldwide claims against the debtor and its worldwide assets with the cooperation of courts or other authorities in each affected country. This approach effectively applies national law to all worldwide assets and claims. Most nations currently apply a territorial approach to cross-border insolvencies. Ultimately, cooperation between different national authorities remains based on principles of comity.

The European Union (EU) has taken significant steps to break down the barriers to cross-border banking. In October 2004, the EU adopted the "European Company Statute" that allows cross-border companies, including banks, to operate more easily through a European-wide branch structure under a unified set of rules and reporting systems.[8] The EU also has

---

[7] See Hüpkes, Eva, 2000, "The Legal Aspects of Bank Insolvency: A Comparative Analysis of Western Europe, the United States, and Canada", The Hague: Kluwer Law International, pp. 141–142; Baxter, Thomas C., Jr., *et al.*, 2004, "Two Cheers for Territoriality: An Essay on International Bank Insolvency Law", *Am. Bankr. L. J.* 57, pp. 73–76.

[8] EU Council Regulation (EC) No 2157/2001 of 8 October 2001 on the Statute for a European company; see Schoenmaker, Dirk and Sander, Oosterloo, 2004, "Cross-Border Issues in European Financial Supervision", prepared for Bank of Finland conference "The Structure of Financial Regulation," Helsinki, Finland, September, 2–3, 2004. As of October 2004, only Belgium, Austria, Denmark, Sweden, Finland and Iceland had taken the necessary measures to allow European Companies to be founded on their territory. EU Press Release, Oct. 8, 2004.

adopted a common approach to cross-border crisis management and crisis resolution for EU banks. The home-country's authorities will have primary responsibility for crisis management as the home-country supervisor and, if appropriate, as provider of liquidity to the bank.[9] Even within the EU, many issues remain to be resolved and the actual roles of home and host supervisors and insolvency authorities in a crisis have yet to be tested.

Within these complexities, a useful way of identifying the key questions for home and host countries is to look at the issues in two phases: pre-failure crisis management and post-collapse crisis resolution.

4. Pre-Failure Crisis Management

Effective crisis management is an extension of effective supervision, but also may involve other tools such as central bank liquidity lending or public recapitalization. In defining the respective responsibilities of the home and host countries during crisis management the key questions include:

- Does the home or host country have primary responsibility for supervision?
- What role is assigned to the supervisor without primary responsibility?
- What is the availability of information to home and host supervisors and crisis managers?
- What is the effect of different regulatory and supervisory infrastructures?
- Is the bank systemically significant in the home or host country? If so, what will be the response of the supervisors or of the central bank as the lender of last resort?
- How will different corporate structures for cross-border banking — such as branches or subsidiaries — affect crisis management?

The answers to these questions raise additional issues that will have a significant effect upon the effectiveness of crisis management.

---

[9] See EU Winding Up Directive for credit institutions 2001/24/EC of April 4, 2001, Articles 2, 3, and 9; Brouwer, Henk, *et al.*, 2004, "A European Approach to Banking Crises", in David Mayes and Aarno Liuksila (eds.), *Who Pays for Bank Insolvency?*, Helsinki: Bank of Finland, p. 211.

4.1 *Primary supervisory responsibility*

Crisis management may include both supervisory and non-supervisory steps. The home-country supervisor can be expected to take the lead on corrective actions for branches, while the host country can take appropriate action for subsidiaries. Within the European Union, it is anticipated that the home-country supervisor will be coordinating policymaker for a distressed international bank with branches, while the host-country supervisor will coordinate responses to a subsidiary in crisis. It is fair to say that the US supervisors take a more direct role in crisis management as host supervisors both for branches and subsidiaries.[10]

One way for the host country to address its secondary role for cross-border branches is to require that all cross-border operations be conducted through subsidiaries. For example, New Zealand has opted to require all foreign banks operating in the country — which dominate the New Zealand banking market — to be locally incorporated as subsidiaries able to operate independently of the parent bank. In this way, the Reserve Bank of New Zealand strengthens its ability to respond to the slide toward insolvency of a cross-border bank with a potentially systemically important New Zealand subsidiary. For example, the Reserve Bank conditioned its approval of the acquisition of the National Bank of New Zealand by Australian-owned ANZ Banking Group (New Zealand) Ltd. in 2003 on capital adequacy for the New Zealand subsidiary and on the subsidiary maintaining local systems to enable it to operate independently.[11]

4.2 *Availability of information*

A critical element in successful crisis management is access to timely and complete information about the troubled bank. With branch operations, the home country of the parent can directly access information, while the host nation must gain this information through cooperation with the

---

[10] See Baxter, Thomas C., Jr., *et al.*, 2004, "Two Cheers for Territoriality: An Essay on International Bank Insolvency Law", *Am. Bankr. L. J.* 57, pp. 70–77.

[11] See RBNZ Consent to ANZ Purchase of National Bank (Oct. 24, 2003), available at www.rbnz.govt.nz/news/2003/0141629.html; see also Bollard, Alan, 2004, Governor, Reserve Bank of New Zealand, in address to Trans-Tasman Business Circle in Sydney, Australia, *RBNZ Bulletin*, 67(3), p. 33.

home-country authorities. Even with cross-border subsidiary operations, the host supervisor needs access to information about the overall risk characteristics of the home bank as well as developments that may affect its stability whether in the home country, other host countries, or the specific host country, from the home supervisor of the larger bank. The host supervisor can contribute a view of the trends and risks in its national market that may not be otherwise evident to the home country supervisors. It is crucial that the home country supervisors have the ability to assess the aggregate effect upon the cross-border bank.[12]

Supervisory information exchanges are normally arranged through bilateral memoranda of understanding (MoU). Under the memoranda of understanding, the banking regulators of each country typically would agree to share information about developments or supervisory concerns, administrative penalties and other information. The agreements usually recognize that concerns about sovereignty, security or other public policy questions are grounds to refuse to exchange information. However, these supervisory memoranda of understanding usually do not address the special information needs in a crisis.[13] Some steps are now being taken to address crisis management. In May 2005, the EU member states entered into a memorandum of understanding on cooperation during financial and banking crises. While the MoU is not public, it has been described as a set of principles and procedures for sharing information, analyses and views during crises along with calls for the development of contingency plans for the management of cross-border crises. Similarly, in June 2003, the Nordic countries (Finland, Denmark, Iceland, Norway and Sweden) agreed to crisis management procedures, which included setting up a crisis contact group, the sharing of key information and steps to address liquidity funding.[14]

---

[12] See Mayes, David and Jukka Vesala, 1998, "On the Problems of Home Country Control", *Bank of Finland, Studies in Economics and Finance* 20/98, 12; see also Basel Concordat (1983); The Supervision of Cross-Border Banking (1996); and Supervision of Financial Conglomerates (1999).

[13] See Brouwer, Henk *et al.*, 2004, "A European Approach to Banking Crises", in David Mayes and Aarno Liuksila (eds.), *Who Pays for Bank Insolvency?*, Helsinki: Bank of Finland, p. 211. It is important to note, as well, that coordination issues are discussed internationally within the Basel Committee structure and within a variety of other coordinating bodies. See Gulde, Anne-Marie and Holger C. Wolf, 2004, "Financial Stability Arrangements in Europe: A Review", Proceedings of Oestereichische Nationalbank conference, November, pp. 56–57.

[14] See Text of Memorandum of Understanding available at www.norges-bank.no; Borchgrevink, Henrik and Thorvald Moe, 2004, "Management of Financial Crises in Cross-Border Banks", *Norges Bank Economic Bulletin* Quarter 4, p. 161.

In a crisis, national supervisors may perceive a benefit from delaying or avoiding the sharing of confidential information if the information may cause regulatory action in another jurisdiction. In addition, if either the home or host supervisor has no financial stake in the losses that may be caused by delays in governmental intervention, that supervisor is more likely to delay intervention.

In fact, the incentives inherent in a universal resolution process focused on home-country supervisory authority — such as that in the EU — may create additional challenges. Since the host supervisor has little ability to protect the branch creditors by initiating formal intervention, the host supervisor may be less likely to take any available supervisory steps. The home supervisor may delay intervention for reasons other than the solvency of the bank.[15] In such a system, some constraints on the home-country supervisor's ability to delay needed supervisory action or intervention may be needed to better balance the home–host relationship.

The host country of a large cross-border bank operating through a branch structure is faced with a difficult dilemma — it lacks the means to independently gain key information and take direct supervisory control over the larger bank, but it must remain responsible for and bear the burden of the potential effect on its national economy. As a cross-border bank deteriorates, the gaps between available information and legal power to act will become increasingly crucial. The host country will likely demand detailed information about host-country operations and reviews of the larger bank and on-site examinations. In addition, the host country can be expected to require the branch to confirm independent functionality of key banking services. The host country also may require maintenance of additional assets and collateral for obligations within the host country. While the home country may accede to the information requests of the host country, it is unlikely to respond positively to the efforts to separate functions, capital and assets for the host country. At this stage of the crisis, the home country can be expected to pursue supervisory action to ensure the survival of the cross-border bank without expenditure of public money — including disposing of certain operations, strengthening the bank's internal controls and perhaps, withdrawal from some host countries.

---

[15] See Baxter, Thomas C. Jr., *et al.*, 2004, "Two Cheers for Territoriality: An Essay on International Bank Insolvency Law", *Am. Bankr. L. J.* 57, pp. 78–79.

4.3 *Regulatory and supervisory infrastructure*

Cross-border coordination in supervision and in crisis management can be affected as well by differences in national regulatory and supervisory infrastructures. For example, the United States has four primary federal regulators of banks and thrifts, 50 state banking regulators and a national deposit insurer with direct responsibility for administrative proceedings to resolve failing insured depository banks and thrifts. European banks are supervised by national banks or by separate supervisory entities, or by a combination of both.

National differences in who regulates different activities and how this regulation is implemented will give rise to divergent policy choices, incentives and mandates.[16] The array of possible policy alternatives raises a number of questions. The questions include whether the laws in the home country provide for a system such as "prompt corrective action" or whether action is at the discretion of the supervisor? What has been the home supervisor's historical pattern — strong action or inaction? Are there contextual incentives that will affect the home supervisor's response — such as past successes or failures with intervention, political considerations, inadequate staffing or training and policy perspectives? Are coordination problems created by supervisory jurisdictional issues arising from a multiplicity of regulators either in the home or host country or as a result of the complexity of the bank's internal organization and business lines? Are the home or host authorities sufficiently creative, or legally empowered, to foster a privately organized recapitalization or rescue?[17]

4.4 *Systemically significant banks*

If the bank is systemically significant, the normal division of labor between the home and host countries may be called into question. Under

---

[16] See Gulde and Wolf, 2004, "Financial Stability Arrangements in Europe: A Review", pp. 54–55 and Table 1; Eisenbeis, Robert A., 2004, "Agency Problems in Banking Supervision: The Case of the EMU", paper presented at a conference on The Structure of Regulation, September, Helsinki, Finland; Bliss, Robert, 2003, "Resolving Large Complex Financial Organizations", Federal Reserve Bank of Chicago Working Papers 2003-07.

[17] See Mayes, David, "The Role of the Safety Net in Resolving Large Financial Institutions", pp. 14–16; Robert Bliss, "Resolving Large Complex Financial Organizations", pp. 28–29.

the principle of home-country responsibility, the home country of the international bank would have primary responsibility to provide liquidity lending to support its operations, including branches in other countries. If the bank is not systemically significant in the home country, but its branches are systemically significant in the host country, the dilemma becomes whether the home country will continue to provide liquidity resources or other support. While other considerations, such as political concerns, international relationships and governmental desires to prevent cross-border contagion from the home country, may lead to liquidity funding by the home country, it is apparent that the initial incentives militate against such funding.

Conversely, while the host country may have more at stake, it may be reluctant to lend to a foreign bank. Differing structures and protections for depositors also may become a key issue for the home and host countries. If the home-country's deposit insurance system covers the host-country's branch depositors — as it must under the applicable EU directive — the home country may be reluctant to take action that could lead to a payoff of those foreign depositors. These incentive questions will loom ever larger if the bank continues its slide to insolvency.

If the cross-border bank is systemically significant in the host, but not the home country, it is unlikely that the home country will take broader steps to prop up the institution to reduce the impact on host country creditors or its economy. Both with subsidiaries and branches, the host country may have to take responsibility for protecting its creditors and economy through supervisory efforts or, if unsuccessful, through a territorial or "ring fencing" approach. The difficulty is that the host country likely will not have complete supervisory information if the home country is the primary supervisor under a branch structure. A ring-fencing approach may allow the host country to control its exposures and localize the resolution process, but its prospect will complicate the efforts to resolve the crisis short of liquidation.

These issues are increasingly significant. Finland and other Nordic countries are hosts for Nordea Bank, which holds a predominant position in Finland but not in Sweden, its home country. While the Nordic crisis management MOU seeks to address some of these difficult issues, the actual response to a crisis remains untested. As a home country to two very large global banks, Switzerland faces the dilemma of supervising banks whose resolution could swamp the available Swiss resources. Switzerland has responded to this reality by placing a cap on the outstanding expenditures from the Swiss deposit insurance system for bank failures.[18] Naturally, the cap itself raises a number of questions.

4.5 *Crisis management by the bank*

Crisis management planning must take into consideration the reaction of bank management to the crisis and to supervisory initiatives. A key issue in countries in which foreign banks occupy a predominant market position is that foreign banks are likely to respond to financial crises differently than host-country domestic institutions. While a large foreign bank can be a stabilizing influence through its diversified business operations and greater capital resources, it may be less likely to support flagging operations in the host country in a crisis and may reallocate liquidity and capital to other operations. Even in the absence of a crisis, such cross-border banks will reallocate capital to more promising investments if host country operations lag behind.[19]

4.6 *Corporate structures*

Clearly, these difficulties are at their most extreme for systemically significant banks operating through foreign branches. However, the issues do not go away entirely for banks operating through the more common subsidiary structure. The host's greater access to information about the subsidiary bank will not provide a full understanding of the overall risks unless there is active sharing of information and analyses with the home country supervisor about the home bank and, perhaps, other third country operations of that bank.[20] In effect, the host country does not fully control crisis management of the larger bank — whether it operates through branches or subsidiaries — while the home country will naturally be

---

[18] See Hüpkes, Eva H.G., 2004, "Bank Insolvency Resolution in Switzerland", in David Mayes and Aarno Liuksila (eds.), *Who Pays for Bank Insolvency?*, pp. 262–264.

[19] See European Central Bank, 2005, "Banking Structures in the New EU Member States", 26; Cárdenas, Juan, *et al.*, 2005, "Foreign Banks Entry in Emerging Market Economies: A Host Country Perspective", Bank for International Settlements.

[20] See Calzolari, Giacomo, and Gyongyi Loranth, 2004, "Regulation of Multinational Banks: A Theoretical Inquiry", ECB Occasional Papers, July.

focused on its domestic concerns and will be less concerned about the effects upon host countries.

To be sure, if the bank operates through subsidiaries, the host country can take decisive action on the subsidiary itself.[21] Nonetheless, the host country will continue to suffer from an information deficit that may impede its ability to act in a timely manner unless coordination remains effective with the home country authorities throughout the crisis. If the crisis requires formal intervention or resolution proceedings, a "ring-fencing" response — both with branches (for banks outside the EU) and subsidiaries — is the likely result in any event because it allows the host country to initiate the process and define the terms of the resolution.

Today, most international banks conduct their foreign operations through subsidiaries in each country. Indeed, while the EU goal has been to encourage European-wide integration of credit and financial markets through a single charter recognized throughout the EU with free branching into all EU countries, European banks have continued to rely on subsidiary banking. Over time, however, and particularly in long-integrated regional financial markets, it could well make business sense for even a systemically significant bank to operate in other countries through branches. For example, the largest Nordic bank, Nordea Bank, currently conducts its foreign business through subsidiaries, but is restructuring into a European company operating through branches.[22] While there may be practical difficulties that inhibit the changes, such as variable taxation regimes for cross-border transactions and the differences in deposit insurance between countries, the EU rules may make it difficult for small host countries to object. Smaller countries will then be faced with the necessity of protecting their economy from the systemic consequences of foreign bank failure while, under the principle of home country supervision, lacking the full panoply of tools to control the risks.

5. Crisis Resolution

Once events pass from crisis management to the need for formal crisis resolution, the difficulties in dealing with cross-border banks continue and

[21] See Sigurdsson, Jon, 2002, "Small Countries, Large Multi-Country Banks: A Challenge to Supervisors — the Example of the Nordic-Baltic Area", in David Mayes and Aarno Liuksila (eds.), *Who Pays for Bank Insolvency?*, pp. 151–154.

[22] See Nordea Press Release, dated June 19, 2003, available at www.nordea.com

intensify on a number of questions. Among the key questions are the following:

- What laws govern the initiation of government intervention or insolvency proceedings?
- Under the applicable laws, what are the "triggers" for regulatory or judicial intervention, such as prompt corrective action?
- What law applies — both to determine what law governs initiation and conduct of insolvency proceedings and to govern key banking issues, such as collateral, payment finality and financial markets transactions?
- What deposit insurance laws apply and how do they affect different claimants?
- Which governmental entities, if any, will provide funding for any resolution?
- How will the applicable insolvency laws interact with the regulatory, legal, and financial systems of other affected countries?
- Do responsible authorities have the legal powers, incentives and resources to facilitate a prompt resolution and availability of depositor funds and credit to the public?

The resolution of a cross-border bank should proceed under laws and policies consistent with recognized components of an effective insolvency system. As discussed earlier in this chapter, among the key components of an effective insolvency system are (1) clear criteria for initiating insolvency proceedings, (2) prompt reimbursement of depositors within controls to minimize costs, (3) immediate authority to control and sell assets and liabilities, and (4) adequate legal powers to permit flexible and decisive action to mitigate the effects of the failure. Measured against these criteria, it is apparent that the current processes for dealing with the resolution of cross-border banks falls short.

5.1 *The law governing initiation of proceedings*

While the principle of home-country control will often provide the home country of an international bank operating through a branch structure with the first opportunity to initiate formal intervention or insolvency proceedings, nothing prevents a host country of a branch from starting such proceedings under local law.[23] The uncertainty about what law applies and which nation's authorities will take action is increased by the absence of any common international standard for when a banking institution should be subject to formal intervention or insolvency proceedings.

While the European Union has defined what law and which nation's authorities will control reorganization or insolvency proceedings, it has not created a common substantive standard. Under the EU's Winding Up Directive for credit institutions, the home country's authorities have exclusive jurisdiction to decide to open "reorganization measures" and "winding-up proceedings". The home country's substantive law also governs critical legal issues, such as determination of claims, assets covered by the proceedings, conditions for set-off, and effects of the proceedings on current contracts. The decisions of the "home member state" on these and other issues are recognized and fully effective in other EU states.[24] Under the EU directive, if the bank operates through foreign subsidiaries — as is currently the norm — then the host country will have plenary power to initiate formal intervention or insolvency proceedings against that separately chartered subsidiary.[25] The rules are unresolved for international banks outside the EU and even for those non-EU banks operating within the EU. Since the home country's substantive law governs these issues, the variations between different EU countries on the standards for intervention as well as the substantive rights after intervention can give rise to significant differences for cross-border banks operating in the same host country.

5.2 *Grounds for intervention*

To be effective, the triggers for intervention and resolution should be clear and mandatory. The prompt corrective action process codified in the United States provides a calibrated system of increasingly stringent supervisory

---

[23] See Baxter, Thomas C. Jr., *et al.*, 2004, "Two Cheers for Territoriality: An Essay on International Bank Insolvency Law", *Am. Bankr. L. J.*, 57, pp. 78–79; US law explicitly allows the US as a host country to institute insolvency proceedings for branches. 12 U.S.C. § 3100-3102.

[24] EU Directive 2001/24/EC of April 4, 2001, Articles 3, 9, 10 and 21.

[25] See Mayes, David and Jukka, Vesala, 1998, "On the Problems of Home Country Control", Bank of Finland, Studies in Economics and Finance 20/98, p. 20; see also Gulde and Wolf, 2004,"Financial Stability Arrangements in Europe: A Review", proceedings of Oestereichische Nationalbank conference, November, pp. 58–59.

controls and, once capital reaches a defined threshold, mandatory appointment of a receiver within a brief timeframe.[26] The benefit of a system of required action in response to specified trigger points is to provide clear notice of the consequences of declining capital to banks and to mitigate the pressures on the supervisor which, in some countries, have contributed to delayed intervention and higher resolution costs. Since prompt corrective action begins before the bank must be closed it provides an effective array of supervisory powers to rehabilitate institutions that can be salvaged, while providing the prod necessary to spur the bank's management to seek a privately developed solution. In fact, in the US, most banks which receive a "critically undercapitalized" notice do achieve a private solution through a merger or new capital even at that late date.

A well-designed system of mandatory triggers for action also provides an opportunity for insolvency authorities to get the information necessary to plan and implement a closing strategy. In the US, the FDIC's resolution staff typically gains direct access to a failing bank's asset, liability, and operational information once a notice of "critically undercapitalized" is sent to the bank. At this point, the supervisory efforts continue to salvage the institution, but the resolution staff must begin to focus on how to resolve this bank if cannot be salvaged.

Unfortunately, the law in many countries does not include a clear trigger for intervention or insolvency proceedings. While differing trigger points are subject to debate, a definite trigger mechanism allows intervention before capital is completely exhausted and limits opportunities for unproductive forbearance. If properly designed, such a triggering mechanism provides resolution authorities with a better opportunity to fashion a resolution transaction that will allow the continuation of critical banking functions.[27]

5.3 *Deposit insurance*

A limited deposit guarantee, combined with explicit requirements to minimize losses in the resolution, promotes a well-funded insurance system

---

[26] 12 U.S.C. § 1831o.

[27] See Mayes, David, "An Overview of the Issues"; Hüpkes, Eva, "Bank Insolvency in Switzerland"; and Hadjiemmanuil, Christos, "Bank Resolution Policy and the Organization of Bank Insolvency Proceedings: Critical Dilemmas", in David Mayes and Aarno Liuksila (eds.), *Who Pays for Bank Insolvency?*, Helsinki: Bank of Finland, pp. 33–35, 251–252, and 279.

as well as limiting the moral hazard that can be engendered by deposit insurance. The goal of prompt reimbursement of depositors may be achieved under applicable national laws, but even here the inconsistencies between national deposit insurance rules may create disincentives for effective action by the home or host country and differential coverage for depositors in the same country. The rules for deposit insurance vary widely from country to country. Differences often exist on the types of accounts covered, the maximum limits to coverage, the funding mechanisms for the deposit insurance system, the extent of government backing for coverage, the speed of payment to insured depositors, the availability of other supplementary insurance and how the insolvency process is administered.[28]

The differences between different national deposit insurance systems introduce additional complications. Under EU directives, the principle of home country control extends to the protection of branch depositors in the host country. Alternatively, the branches of the cross-border bank can opt to seek coverage under the host country's laws. If a cross-border bank's branches have opted for such host country coverage, it could balance some incentive issues for the home and host supervisors.[29]

In the EU scenario, the host country will be able to take comfort in protection of its depositors, while the home country will be required to consider the potential liability for those foreign depositors in making decisions about the resolution. Within the European Union, the home country authorities will have to judge the costs and chances of success of supervisory forbearance through injections of public money or central bank liquidity funding against the costs of insolvency proceedings and outlays for deposit insurance payments. The host country will lack the authority to impose a solution. Even if the host country desired to threaten or impose a ring fencing solution, the EU's Winding up Directive denies it this option.

The situation, however, is quite different if the failing bank is American. Under US law, depositors in foreign branches of a US bank are

---

[28] See Eisenbeis, Robert A. and George G. Kaufman, 2005, "Bank Crisis Resolution and Foreign-Owned Banks", Presentation at Norges Bank Conference on Banking Crisis Resolution — Theory and Policy, June.

[29] See Directive 94/19/EC of the European Parliament and of the Council of 30 May 1994 on deposit guarantee schemes, OJ 1994 L 135/5, Article 4; Gulde and Wolf, 2004, "Financial Stability Arrangements in Europe: A Review", proceedings of Oestereichische Nationalbank conference, November, pp. 54–55 and Table 1.

not insured under the FDIC's deposit insurance and are subordinated to uninsured depositors of the US branches in the distribution of the proceeds from the sale of the bank's assets. Depositors in foreign branches of US banks are covered by FDIC deposit insurance only if the deposit is payable in the US in addition to the foreign branch.[30] If the cross-border bank is American, the host country will have to rely on its deposit insurance coverage system to protect depositors (if foreign branch depositors are covered under the host country's laws) and bear those costs or aggressively seek collateral or other protection from the American bank or its regulators. Certainly the absence of coverage for the host country's depositors under US law makes a ring fencing response by the host country more likely.

5.4 *Legal powers of controlling authorities*

An effective resolution process also must give the insolvency authority clear legal power to take flexible and decisive action to maximize recoveries on assets and minimize delays in providing money back to depositors. These legal powers should include independence from undue interference by other governmental bodies, the ability to terminate contracts, the power to enforce contracts, the authority to sell assets, the right to avoid fraudulent or unauthorized transfers, and broad flexibility to design resolution and asset sales structures to achieve the goals of the resolution. Many difficulties in resolving individual insolvencies and in addressing broader instability have been exacerbated by the inability of trustees or liquidators to take prompt action.

The ability to take prompt and decisive action is critical if the bank is systemically significant. One solution is simply to prop up the bank through government funding or guarantees. However, this response — particularly if undertaken without a stringent restructuring of operations, management, and ownership — can create a drag on the economy, distort banking competition and dramatically increase the costs to the public. The use of a bridge bank or other temporary institution to continue critical banking functions through an insolvency process allows termination of shareholder and management control as well as the restructuring of operations to focus on profitable businesses and impose losses on appropriate

---

[30] 12 U.S.C. § 1813(l) and (m).

parties. While an open bank solution may make continuation of operations easier, it does not eliminate the need for restructuring, close oversight, valuation of assets to support write downs of shareholder and other claims, and determination of appropriate capital or other mechanisms to require repayment of any governmental funding.

Under US law, the FDIC as deposit insurer is delegated broad authority to operate or liquidate the business, sell the assets and resolve the liabilities of a failed insured bank immediately after its appointment as receiver or conservator. This authority enables the FDIC to immediately sell many of the assets of a failing institution to an open bank or to an FDIC-created bridge bank — and, in effect, maintain critical banking functions. A crucial component of the ability to immediately transfer banking operations is the availability of detailed information about the failing institution, its operations, assets and liabilities. If the ultimate resolution authority gains access to this information only after intervention proceedings begin, a prompt sale and transfer of functioning banking operations is very unlikely.

Will this authority to act quickly and decisively be available in a cross-border resolution? This appears unlikely. First, as discussed above, the relevant countries may lack clear, mandatory triggers to start the insolvency process. Without such triggers, there is a strong likelihood that necessary action will be delayed until it is more costly and ineffective. Second, many countries do not provide a strong and immediate power to an insolvency administrator to control and sell assets and resolve liabilities. Among the impediments are legal structures that require court approval for sales of assets and provide for extensive rights of appeal by shareholders and other interested parties before sales can be completed. In addition, some laws simply do not include authorization for flexible transactions, such as a bridge bank or a similar temporary "bank".[31] If a bank is systemically significant, the traditional bankruptcy stay that halts or, at least, calls into question the validity of new claims is not a viable option. Third, even if the home or host country's administrators possess such authority, the potential for ring-fencing and the uncertainties about the applicable law for different issues will impede a prompt and effective resolution. The alternatives of government recapitalization or other bail-outs serve only to increase

---

[31] See Hüpkes, Eva, 2004, "Protect Functions, Not Institutions", *The Financial Regulator* 9(3), pp. 46–49.

moral hazard and to impair the efficient functioning of the banking market.[32]

Under US and some other national laws, the power to act decisively is provided directly to the central bank or to deposit insurer. Under other systems, the resolution power is provided to the judiciary. The locus of power may not be crucial, but the ability to act promptly and decisively to stem the effects of the failure is. While there are clear advantages to creating a wholly administrative process by conferring this power on a single actor, such as the deposit insurer, other considerations may militate towards a more judicially based approach.[33] Irrespective of the ultimate decision-maker, the opportunities for delay and challenges to asset and function transfers must be limited and clearly defined.

6. Future Directions?

Where a deteriorating bank operates in multiple countries the affected parties' divergent interests and incentives may be difficult to discern or resolve. The parties' interests and incentives are complicated by the interaction and conflict between different national supervisory, deposit insurance, central bank, and insolvency rules and cultures. As our discussion has illustrated, the home and host country authorities may face a mismatch between supervisory control, access to information, and responsibility for protecting the local economy. The law in one or more countries may preclude effective cooperation, as where there are legal limitations on sharing of confidential information, or the law may mandate certain crisis management tools or require particular resolution strategies, such as ring fencing.

While this mismatch most often affects the host country, the home country of the cross-border bank faces uncertainty about how the host country's laws and authorities will respond. These uncertainties, and the

---

[32] See Mayes, David, 2005, "The Role of the Safety Net in Resolving Large Financial Institutions", in Douglas Evanoff and George Kaufman (eds.), *Systemic Financial Crises: Resolving Large Bank Insolvencies*, Singapore: World Scientific Publishing.

[33] See Hadjiemmanuil, Christos, 2004, "Bank Resolution Policy and the Organization of Bank Insolvency Proceedings: Critical Dilemmas" in David Mayes and Aarno Liuksila (eds.), *Who Pays for Bank Insolvency?*, Helsinki: Bank of Finland, pp. 291–300; Hüpkes, Eva, 2000, *The Legal Aspects of Bank Insolvency: A Comparative Analysis of Western Europe, the United States, and Canada.*

potential for ring fencing by the host country, make successful crisis management and crisis resolution much more difficult for the home country as well. The uncertainties increase the likelihood that affected parties — the bank, customers and other private sector participants as well as national authorities — will take steps to define their exposures in a way that may destroy any opportunity for continued banking operations. The understandable desire to avoid continued uncertainty and "limit" exposures may lead to a collapse of communication and coordination.

How can the national authorities respond to these risks? As a first step, the key participants in the management and resolution of a crisis need to recognize and understand the considerations that will affect their and other parties' responses to a potential crisis. More specific and practical contingency planning by affected participants — including national regulators, insolvency authorities and bankers — is a crucial step.

In recognition of the different interests and incentives, contingency planning should focus on the critical goals of crisis management and resolution. If the bank is not systemically significant, then the focus should be on an orderly private restructuring of the bank or a timely closing. Where the failing cross-border bank is systemically significant either to the home country or the host country the management and, if necessary, the formal resolution of the crisis should focus on maintaining the critical functions performed by that bank. This does not necessarily require a bailout of the bank or even the overall bank's continued operation. It does require a skeptical appraisal of precisely which operations of the bank are truly systemically significant. Once such operations are identified, then pre-resolution planning and resolution implementation should focus on maintaining those functions.

The use of a bridge bank or even a privately developed entity to maintain these functions are workable solutions that do not necessarily require continuation of the complete banking enterprise. The practical details for implementation of these approaches are many and complex, but these approaches may offer significant advantages to propping up the entire failed bank.

If a resolution is necessary, it is imperative that the responsible authorities continue to share key information about the failing bank. While the incentive issues described in this chapter will undoubtedly complicate cooperation, pre-crisis agreements and cross-border contingency planning will help create the environment for better coordination. As we have discussed, much of the difficulty lies in the diversity of national laws, standards, and cultures affecting crisis management and resolution. Memoranda of understanding should reflect realistic cooperation protocols and be expanded to include crisis management. An agreement, however, is insufficient unless adherence to it can be stress tested by realistic appraisals of the conflicting incentives, legal requirements and the limits of cooperation in an actual crisis.

A helpful precursor to such agreements may be legal changes to ensure some degree of harmonization in key elements of the crisis management and crisis resolution processes. A common legal infrastructure for the resolution of insolvencies is very unlikely and is not required. However, greater harmonization of key elements of effective resolutions would be an important step forward. For example, greater harmonization and clarity about the triggers for action, the tools to return insured funds quickly to depositors, the authority to implement a quick resolution, and the legal powers to restructure and continue key banking functions would allow more effective crisis planning.

If those legal changes prove impossible, a more modest goal for legal changes could focus on insuring the continuation of systemically significant banking functions, such as payments linkages and the capital markets. An important way to prevent instability from spreading is to harmonize the cross-border or national insolvency rules governing the key linkages between systemically significant cross-border banks. Over the past 20 years, vast improvements have been made toward standardized laws that protect the settlement of transactions and the reduction of interbank and cross-border credit risk in the capital markets and payments processing.

Further improvements can be achieved through national legal reforms and international protocols that allow authorities to take prompt and decisive action to continue systemically significant functions. As Eva Hüpkes has pointed out, preservation of the systemically significant functions does not require preservation of the entire failing bank. Combined with practical contingency planning, harmonization of these national standards may serve to reduce moral hazard by providing more realistic alternatives to a broad government bail-out.

International Banks, Cross-Border Guarantees and Regulation

Andrew Powell*
Inter-American Development Bank

Giovanni Majnoni
World Bank

1. Introduction

While banking has gone global, deposit insurance and lender of last resort remain predominantly national concerns. Banking supervision is also essentially a national responsibility although the 1974 creation of the Basel Committee on Banking Supervision (BCBS) reflected the importance placed on cross border issues. A consensus has developed over time that has stressed the importance of consolidated supervision by the home (or consolidator) regulator. Consolidated supervision by the lead regulator is seen to be particularly important as banks have become more international and more complex. This view was strengthened with bank failures and associated regulatory coordination failures including the 1974 Herstatt and the 1993 Bank of Credit and Commerce International (BCCI) crises.

The lead regulator model considers the risk of the entire entity and an attractive assumption is that an international bank is one entity that would survive or fail as one unit. However, as international banks have moved increasingly into emerging economies this view might be questioned. In many cases the subsidiaries of foreign banks in emerging countries are

*Andrew Powell is lead research economist at the Inter-American Development Bank. Giovanni Majnoni is executive director, Italy at the World Bank. The views expressed in this paper are strictly the views of the authors and do not necessarily represent the views of the IDB, the World Bank, the boards of either institution or the countries they represent or any other institution. They thank Juan Francisco Martinez Sepulveda for research assistance. They wish to thank Thorsten Beck, Rafael Repullo and Roberto Rigobon for comments. Naturally, any mistakes remain their own.

among the largest and most systemic institutions for the local regulators and yet they may be only a small part of the global bank. To give an idea, the total foreign claims of international banks on developing countries amounts to around US$2.3 trillion, but this is only about 10 percent of those banks' total cross-border portfolio and would be a much smaller percentage of their total — including domestic — assets.

Another view of an international bank is that of a core of large central units and a periphery of subsidiaries that may be smaller and less integral to the bank. There may then be states of the world in which the bank would indeed walk away from these units. While this may have been considered only a remote technical possibility, the recent Argentine crisis suggests that the issue does require serious consideration.[1]

Rating agencies appear to agree that guarantees to subsidiaries in emerging economies may be partial. In Figure 1, we plot the ratings of international bank groups and their branches and subsidiaries in emerging economies. A regression of the rating of the subsidiary/branch on the rating of the international bank and the rating of the host country reveals that in general both are significant.

In Table 1, we give the results from such an experiment on a cross section of 79 subsidiaries/branches across different countries and on a subset of 44 subsidiaries/branches where the subsidiaries are all in developing countries using ratings from Standard and Poors. If international banks extended full guarantees then we would expect only the rating of the parent to matter and with a coefficient close to unity whereas if there was no guarantee then the coefficient on the host should be significant and the rating of the bank not significant. As we find that in general both the host country rating and the rating of the parent are significant, we conclude that perceived guarantees are partial.[2]

The regression and our analysis make little attempt to distinguish between subsidiaries and branches. If we were considering banks expanding within U.S. territory then we would agree that the model of a bank as

---

[1] In fact all of the larger major international bank subsidiaries stayed in Argentina. Scotia Bank, Credit Agricole (that had three subsidiaries) and Italy's Intesa withdrew — the latter maintaining a minority shareholding in the subsidiary. Moreover, while the Argentine case did have its peculiarities and might be considered as somewhat special, these banks did not appear to suffer any negative reputation effects on other parts of their businesses; a common argument suggesting that banks would not walk away from a subsidiary.

[2] It might be thought that ratings are limited to sovereign ratings. However, the three major rating agencies, including Standard and Poor's, all now allow ratings to exceed those of the sovereign, especially where there is an outside guarantor.

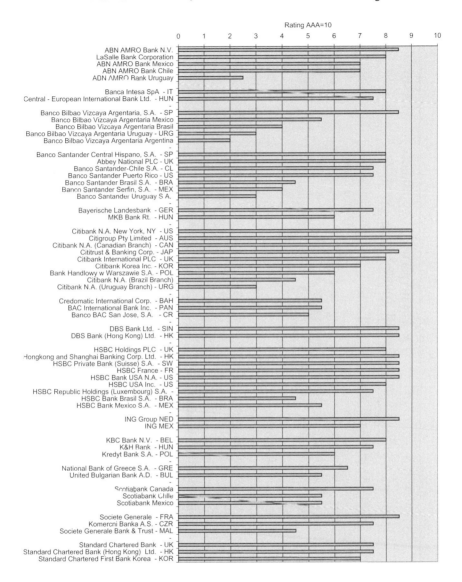

Figure 1. Ratings of subsidiaries and parents

a unified unit could be identified as a set of branches, while that of a core and a periphery might be thought of more as a subsidiary structure. However, the legal position of a branch of a US bank in Bangkok or Buenos Aires may be quite different to that of one in Boston or Boise. On the other hand, a subsidiary may imply greater responsibility than only the

Table 1.

Papa Name	P_Counterparty_LT_Number	PA_Country_sovereign	SUBSID_Country
ABN AMRO Bank N.V.	**ABN AMRO Bank N.V.**		
LaSalle Bank Corporation	LaSalle Bank Corporation	8.5	Netherlands	NED
ABN AMRO Bank Mexico	ABN AMRO Bank Mexico	8	United States	US
ABN AMRO Bank Argentina	ABN AMRO Bank Chile	7		MEX
ABN AMRO Bank Uruguay	ABN AMRO Bank Uruguay	7		ARG
		2.5	Uruguay	URY
Banca Intesa SpA	**Banca Intesa SpA — IT**	8	Italy	IT
Central — European International Bank Ltd.	Central — European International Bank Ltd. — HUN	7.5	Hungary	HUN
	—			
Banco Bilbao Vizcaya Argentaria, S.A.	**Banco Bilbao Vizcaya Argentaria, S.A. — SP**	8.5	Spain	SP
Banco Bilbao Vizcaya Argentaria Mexico	Banco Bilbao Vizcaya Argentaria Mexico	5.5	Mexico	
Banco Bilbao Vizcaya Argentaria Brasil	Banco Bilbao Vizcaya Argentaria Brasil	4	Brazil	
Banco Bilbao Vizcaya Argentaria Uruguay	Banco Bilbao Vizcaya Argentaria Uruguay — URG	3	Uruguay	URG

(*Continued*)

Table 1. (*Continued*)

Papa Name	P_Counterparty_LT_Number	PA_Country_sovereign	SUBSID_Coutry
Banco Bilbao Vizcaya Argentaria Argentina Banco Bilbao Vizcaya Argentaria Argentina —	2	Argentina	
Banco Santander Central Hispano, S.A. **Banco Santander Central Hispano, S.A. — SP**	8	Spain	SP
Abbey National PLC Abbey National PLC — UK	8	United Kingdom	UK
Banco Santander-Chile S.A. Banco Santander-Chile S.A. — CL	7.5	Chile	CL
Banco Santander Puerto Rico Banco Santander Puerto Rico — US	7.5	United States	US
Banco Santander Brasil S.A. Banco Santander Brasil S.A. — BRA	4.5	Brazil	BRA
Banco Santander Serfin, S.A. Banco Santander Serfin, S.A. — MEX	4	Mexico	MEX
Banco Santander Uruguay S.A. Banco Santander Uruguay S.A. —	3	Uruguay	
Bayerische Landesbank **Bayerische Landesbank — GER**	7.5	Germany	GER
MKB Bank Rt. MKB Bank Rt. — HUN	6	Hungary	HUN

(*Continued*)

Table 1. (*Continued*)

Papa Name	P_Counterparty_LT_Number	PA_Country_sovereign	SUBSID_Country
Citibank N.A. New York, NY **Citibank N.A. New York, NY — US**	9	United States	US
Citigroup Pty Limited Citigroup Pty Limited — AUS	9	Australia	AUS
Citibank N.A. (Canadian Branch) Citibank N.A. (Canadian Branch) — CAN	9	Canada	CAN
Cititrust & Banking Corp. Cititrust & Banking Corp. — JAP	8.5	Japan	JAP
Citibank International PLC Citibank International PLC — UK	8	United Kingdom	UK
Citibank Korea Inc. Citibank Korea Inc. — KOR	7	Korea	KOR
Bank Handlowy w Warszawie S.A. Bank Handlowy w Warszawie S.A. — POL	6	Poland	POL
Citibank N.A. (Brazil Branch) Citibank N.A. (Brazil Branch)	4.5	Brazil	
Citibank N.A. (Uruguay Branch) Citibank N.A. (Uruguay Branch) — URG	3	Uruguay	URG
Credomatic International Corp. **Credomatic International Corp. — BAH**	5.5	Bahamas	BAH

(*Continued*)

Table 1. (*Continued*)

Papa Name	P_Counterparty_LT_Number	PA_Country_sovereign	SUBSID_Coutry
BAC International Bank Inc.	BAC International Bank Inc. — PAN	5.5	Panama	PAN
Banco BAC San Jose, S.A.	Banco BAC San Jose, S.A. — CR	5	Costa Rica	CR
DBS Bank Ltd.	**DBS Bank Ltd. — SIN**	8.5	Singapore	SIN
DBS Bank (Hong Kong) Ltd.	DBS Bank (Hong Kong) Ltd. — HK	8.5	Hong Kong	HK
HSBC Holdings PLC	**HSBC Holdings PLC — UK**	8	United Kingdom	UK
Hongkong and Shanghai Banking Corp. Ltd.	Hongkong and Shanghai Banking Corp. Ltd. — HK	8.5	Hong Kong	HK
HSBC Private Bank (Suisse) S.A.	HSBC Private Bank (Suisse) S.A. — SW	8.5	Switzerland	SW
HSBC France	HSBC France — FR	8.5	France	FR
HSBC Bank USA N.A.	HSBC Bank USA N.A. — US	8.5	United States	US
HSBC USA Inc.	HSBC USA Inc. — US	8	United States	US

(*Continued*)

Table 1. (*Continued*)

Papa Name		P_Counterparty_LT_Number	PA_Country_sovereign	SUBSID_Coutry
HSBC Republic Holdings (Luxembourg) S.A.	HSBC Republic Holdings (Luxembourg) S.A. — LUX	7.5	Luxembourg	LUX
HSBC Bank Brasil S.A.	HSBC Bank Brasil S.A. — BRA	4.5	Brazil	BRA
HSBC Bank Mexico S.A.	HSBC Bank Mexico S.A. — MEX	5.5		MEX
	—			
ING	ING Group NED	8.5	Netherlands	
	ING MEX	7	Mexico	
KBC Bank N.V.	**KBC Bank N.V. — BEL**	8	Belgium	BEL
K&H Bank	K&H Bank — HUN	7.5	Hungary	HUN
Kredyt Bank S.A.	Kredyt Bank S.A. — POL	6	Poland	POL
	—			
National Bank of Greece S.A.	**National Bank of Greece S.A. — GRE**	6.5	Greece	GRE
United Bulgarian Bank A.D.	United Bulgarian Bank A.D. — BUL	5.5	Bulgaria	BUL
	—			

(*Continued*)

Table 1. (*Continued*)

Papa Name	P_Counterparty_LT_Number	PA_Country_sovereign	SUBSID_Coutry
Scotiabank Canada			
Scotiabank Chile	7.5	Canada	
Scotiabank Mexico	5.5	Chile	
	5.5	Mexico	
Societe Generale — FRA			
Komercni Banka A.S. — CZR	8.5	France	FRA
	7.5	Czech Republic	CZR
Societe Generale Bank & Trust — MAL	4.5	Malaysia	MAL
Standard Chartered Bank — UK			
Standard Chartered Bank (Hong Kong) Ltd. — HK	7.5	United Kingdom	UK
	7.5	Hong Kong	HK
Standard Chartered First Bank Korea — KOR	7	Korea	KOR

capital invested depending on the internal structure of the bank and concepts such as the "veil of ownership". In general, the legal consequences of expanding abroad through a network of branches versus subsidiaries appear to be subtle and not necessarily clear-cut.[3] In view of this, we prefer to discuss subsidiaries with different levels of guarantees.

To our knowledge, despite the intense diplomacy between international regulators, there has been very little previous academic work that examines when banks may wish to extend full guarantees to a subsidiary and when it would prefer to limit its liability, and hence the implications for regulation and supervision.[4] In the next section, we first describe the bank's joint decision in terms of (1) deciding on its structure and (2) deciding on the allocation of capital across the different units. In Section 3, we then consider the issues that the theoretical results raise for host regulators. In Section 4, we analyze the tensions that may then arise between home and host regulators. Section 5 concludes.

2. Bank Structure and Capital Allocation with Lead Supervision and Local Deposit Insurance

In this section, we report on some more theoretical ideas regarding bank structure and capital allocation. Our idea is to consider an imaginary bank that must decide whether to extend a full guarantee to a subsidiary or to limit its liability only to the capital invested. We are the first to admit that this is a fairly stark characterization, however, we believe it may be a useful way to contrast two extreme alternatives of structural form. As discussed above, it is tempting to characterize the former as a branch network and the latter as a set of autonomous subsidiaries and this might be one interpretation but we do not necessarily share this view. We believe the distinction is murkier when it comes to international structural forms and so for these reasons, we will refer to all the sub-units as subsidiaries.

We will assume that the bank has one unit in each country where it operates and extends a certain amount of loans funded by deposits raised in that country and by capital maintained in that country. This capital also represents an asset on the balance sheet of the core unit of the international bank but we do not consider here more subtle issues regarding

---

[3] See Del Negro and Kay (2002) for an interesting discussion regarding these issues motivated by the Argentine crisis.

[4] See Cerutti *et al.* (2005) for an empirical examination of this issue.

consolidation. The bank faces many sources of risk, but let us suppose that its main risk stems from the asset returns in the countries where it operates. Suppose first of all, that the structure of the bank is given and the bank considers itself as a fully guaranteed core and a set of limited liability subsidiaries. The solvency of the bank may then be expressed as follows.

$$S = \sum_{m \in Core} (L_m a_m - D_m r) + \sum_{m \in Periphery} Max[L_m a_m - r_m D_m, 0],$$

where L_m are the assets of the mth subsidiary, D_m the deposits of the mth subsidiary, a_m is the uncertain gross return on the assets in the mth subsidiary, r is the gross interest rate that must be paid on liabilities in the core, and r_m is the interest rate that is paid on liabilities in each of the subsidiaries in the periphery. The first term in this equation represents the solvency of all of the core units of the bank, which may be positive or negative, and the second term is a summation across the units in the periphery. Note that this latter sum includes a Max term. This implies that this second term cannot be negative. If the solvency of a subsidiary in the periphery is negative, then it is assumed that the bank walks away. The equation may also be written as:

$$S = \sum_{m \in Core} L_m(a_m - r(1 - k)) + \sum_{m \in Periphery} Max[L_m(a_m - r_m(1 - k_m)), 0],$$

where k is the capital to assets ratio of the core $k = \sum_{m \in I} K_m/L_m$ and where k_m is the capital to asset ratio of the mth subsidiary in the periphery. One way of thinking about the future solvency of the bank is as a portfolio of forwards representing the bank's core F_m, where the "delivery price" is of each forward is $r(1 - k)$ plus a portfolio of call options representing the bank's periphery C_m with exercise prices $r_m(1 - k_m)$. Note that the exercise price of each call is endogenous; each is a function of the capital invested in that subsidiary, which we treat as a variable under the bank's control. Hence, the solvency of the bank might be expressed as:

$$S = \sum_{m \in Core} F_m + \sum_{m \in J} C_m,$$

where against the first term may be positive or negative reflecting the success of the bank's core activities. The second term (reflecting the value of a portfolio of call options) is always non-negative. This reflects the fact that the loss that the bank may suffer on its activities in the periphery is limited to the capital invested. If the solvency of a subsidiary falls below zero, then we assume that the subsidiary is abandoned without further cost but also without any future potential profits for the bank.

We assume that the interest rates paid on liabilities in the core and in the periphery are exogenous. To make things simple, suppose the shareholders will always recapitalize the core of the bank so the funding cost of the core is then equal to the riskless rate of interest. Remember that in the equation above, r is then the gross riskless rate or one plus the net riskless rate. Regarding the periphery, we assume that there is a local deposit insurance scheme. Hence, as depositors are insured locally, the funding cost of the subsidiary is exogenous to the bank. This local exogenous interest rate may be higher than the riskless rate of interest reflecting the country risk of the host or the possibility that the deposit insurance fund itself may fail — but we assume that this is exogenous in relation to the decisions of an individual bank. A further extension might consider an endogenous interest rate for non-insured liabilities in the periphery.[5]

Now, suppose that the bank has an overall capital requirement, KR, but that capital may be allocated to any part of the bank but such that the overall level of capital meets the overall requirement:

$$K = \sum_{m \in I} L_m k + \sum_{m \in J} L_m k_m \geq KR.$$

We assume that the cost of capital for the bank is $r_k > r$. We further assume that if actual capital falls below the regulatory minimum, then the shareholders must recapitalize at a higher cost than the original cost of capital. This is justified as the regulator may impose additional penalties on the bank, or shareholders may demand higher returns given a forced recapitalization. More precisely, the shareholders must inject capital to ensure that the regulatory minimum is met. The penalty that shareholders must pay if the solvency of the bank falls below the regulatory minimum may then be expressed as follows:

$$P = \pi Max[KR - S, 0],$$

where $\pi > r_k$. The penalty is akin to a short position in a put option where the exercise price of the put is the regulatory minimum capital. The bank

---

[5] Interestingly, if the interest rate r_j is made endogenous and applies to all liabilities (there is no local deposit insurance), then, for constant capital, the expected value of the subsidiary in the periphery is a constant with respect to the volatility of asset returns. As the volatility rises, so too does the funding costs and these two exactly cancel each other out.

will calculate its expected future solvency and maintain a current level of capital such that it trades off the probability that future capital may fall under the regulatory minimum versus the cost of keeping excess capital on its balance sheets.

2.1 *The capital allocation decision with structure given*

We presume that the bank will maximize its expected value choosing the level of capital in each unit. This then assumes that the bank can shift capital around the group. In other words, the bank solves the following maximization problem.

$$Max_{k,k_m} V = E\left\{ \sum_{m \in I} F_m + \sum_{m \in J} C_m - P \right\}$$

$$s.t. K = \sum_{m \in I} L_m k + \sum_{m \in J} L_m k_m, \quad k \geq 0, \quad k_m \geq 0$$

$$K \geq KR.$$

It can be shown that there is likely to be **no internal maximum** to this problem. More specifically there is an internal maximum for the overall level of capital but not the capital in a subsidiary in the periphery. Considering the overall level of capital, there is a trade-off in that capital is expensive (the cost is assumed to be more than that of raising deposits in the core, which is the riskless rate), but having capital decreases the probability of having to recapitalize the bank (which is even more expensive due to the penalty) if solvency falls below the overall regulatory minimum. However, consider putting capital in the core versus in the subsidiary. The gain to placing capital in the core is that is that this lowers the probability that the bank will be subject to the penalty if overall capital falls below the regulatory requirement. Putting capital in the subsidiary has the same effect, but only if the subsidiary is solvent. If the subsidiary's solvency is negative (assets are worth less than liabilities) then by assumption the bank walks away. Hence, there is a gain to placing capital in the subsidiary, but in this model, that gain must be only a fraction of the gain in putting the capital in the core, the fraction given by the probability that the subsidiary remains solvent and the capital is not lost.

Another way to think about this is to note that the value of a call option rises if the exercise price is lowered — it is then more likely that the call is in the money. But for each dollar that the exercise price is lowered the value of the call goes up by less than a dollar. Placing one dollar of capital in the core is then worth one dollar of capital but putting it in the subsidiary, it is worth less than a dollar — again the fraction being equal to the probability that the subsidiary survives. If the bank is free to distribute capital around the group it would then prefer to keep it in the core.

2.2 *The structure decision assuming capital is given*

Now let us consider the decision regarding structure assuming that capital allocation is fixed. Suppose the bank must decide whether to place a particular subsidiary in the periphery or in the core. It follows that the expected solvency of the bank would be greater with the mth subsidiary in the periphery rather than in the core if[6]:

$$E[Max[L_m(a_m(1 - r_m(1 - k_m)),0] > E[L_m(a_m(1 - r(1 - k))].$$

The trade-off is that if the subsidiary is placed in the periphery, then there is a benefit as if the subsidiary fails the bank may walk away and not recapitalize. Hence, the left hand side of the expression contains the Max[.]. However, the cost of placing the subsidiary in the periphery is that the bank's overall cost of funding is higher as it is assumed that $r_m > r$. If the subsidiary is placed in the core, the funding cost drops to the riskless rate of interest but the bank will have to bail out the subsidiary if it is insolvent. It is well-known that the value of a call option increases with the volatility of the underlying asset. As the volatility of the asset returns in the subsidiary rises, it becomes more attractive to place the subsidiary in the periphery. Indeed, it can be shown that there is a critical volatility σ_m^c, such that for $\sigma_m > \sigma_m^c$ the bank would prefer to place the subsidiary in the periphery, and for $\sigma_m \leq \sigma_m^c$, the bank would prefer to place the unit in the core.

Note that there is also an interaction with the capital in the subsidiary. One way to think about this is to remember that the value of an option that is well "in the money" increases more slowly than the value of an option that is closer to being "at the money". In our case, this translates into the argument that if the capital in the subsidiary is high (the call is more in the money), then for a particular level of volatility it is best to place the subsidiary in the core whereas if capital in the subsidiary is low then for

[6] This condition is derived simply with independent asset returns. It is also approximately true given correlated asset returns depending on the relation between the truncated and the non truncated covariance of a_m with rest of the bank's portfolio.

the same volatility it is best to maintain the subsidiary in the periphery. The critical volatility is then a function of the capital placed in the subsidiary. We come back to this point below in discussing the role of host capital regulation.

2.3 *The capital allocation and structure decision combined*

Now let us combine the arguments considered above. On the one hand, a subsidiary with greater asset return volatility should be placed in the periphery rather than in the core. On the other hand, there is in general no internal solution for capital in the periphery, and indeed, the incentive for the bank is likely to be to reduce the capital in a subsidiary in the periphery to zero. To maximize its expected value, the bank must then compare various possibilities. First, it should compute its expected value with the subsidiaries in the core. There will be an internal solution for its capital structure here that trades off the cost of capital against the possibility of shareholders having to pay a penalty if future solvency falls below the regulatory minimum. Second, the bank should consider placing its riskiest subsidiaries in the periphery and calculate the expected value of the bank with zero capital in the periphery and the new optimum level of capital in the core. In complex cases where there are many subsidiaries and correlated asset returns, the bank faces a somewhat complex programming problem, but the principals regarding structure and capital allocation discussed here should imply that an optimum can be found.

3. Concerns for Host Regulators and the Role of Host Capital Supervision

These more theoretical results suggest some concerns for host regulators in countries considered of high risk. If the decision of the bank is to place a subsidiary in the periphery and its incentives are then to minimize the level of capital, then there will be a relatively high probability that the bank might walk away. Naturally, host regulators will not wish this to be the case. The model then provides a strong motivation for host capital regulation. Host regulators would wish capital in a subsidiary in the periphery to be such that the probability that the subsidiary is insolvent is rather low. Basel II suggests a 0.1 percent failure rate for example. Such a failure rate would imply a minimum capital level in the subsidiary.

However, this raises an interesting possibility. Suppose host regulators insist on a particular level of capital, the bank must now compare the expected value of the bank with that subsidiary in the core versus in the periphery with the host-stipulated level of capital. As a bank is forced to hold more capital in a subsidiary, it becomes relatively more attractive to place that subsidiary in the core. Indeed, it follows that there is a critical level of capital that the host regulator may insist on, such that it would be best for the bank to place the subsidiary in the core. In general this critical level of capital will be an increasing function of the volatility of the asset return. In other words, if asset returns are more volatile, the host supervisor will have to set a higher capital requirement to ensure that the bank has the incentive to place the subsidiary in the core.

4. Tensions between Home and Host Regulator Suggested by the Model

Recently and especially with the proposed introduction of Basel II, there has been some tension regarding the role of home versus host regulators.[7] The roots of these tensions may stem from the underlying incentives of the different agents. If it is not apparent that international banks are one unit, that would fail or survive as one, then the model does indicate that incentives will diverge. This can be illustrated by various results.

First, the home regulator may wish, in common with the bank, for the entire capital of the bank to be kept in the core and the amount of capital in the periphery to be minimized. This reduces the downside risk of the entire bank as in certain states of the world, the bank would walk away from subsidiaries in the periphery protecting the solvency of the core. A host regulator would prefer more capital in a subsidiary in the periphery to reduce the risk the parent would walk away and may strive for a level of capital such that the bank would consider the subsidiary in the core.

Second, it can be shown that if the home regulator gets tougher in terms of increasing the overall capital requirement, or increasing the penalty for non-compliance, then the more likely is the bank to place subsidiaries in the periphery and not in the core. The intuition is fairly clear, if the penalty for non compliance with the overall capital requirement rises, then the bank will wish to decrease the probability of this occurring and that implies lowering

---

[7] See Bernanke (2004).

the downside risk and placing more subsidiaries in the periphery. Again, the home regulator may prefer this result, as with more subsidiaries in the periphery the downside risk of the whole bank certainly is more limited. But the host regulator would certainly not appreciate this outcome.

Another way to state the same result is that as the home regulator gets tougher, then the international bank will wish to place subsidiaries in the periphery at lower volatilities for asset returns than otherwise. As the home regulator gets tougher, then the host regulator would also have to get tougher in terms of increasing the host capital requirement to ensure that the bank maintains the incentive to keep the subsidiary in the core.

There is also a graver tension not truly captured in the way the model is set up currently. The capital requirement for the home regulator is assumed to be a constant, and hence is not related to whether the bank decides to walk away from any of its subsidiaries or not. It might be the case that if the bank walked away from a subsidiary in the periphery, then its consolidated capital requirement would fall. The bank might argue that its legal responsibility did not extend to a subsidiary beyond the capital invested, and the home regulator's incentives may well be to agree with that interpretation precisely to protect the solvency of the core of the bank.

5. Conclusions: Implications for Cross-Border Supervision

International diplomacy between international bank regulators has tended to stress consolidated bank supervision such that a lead regulator can gain an overall picture of a global institution's risks. We wish to stress that we are not against consolidated supervision in any way. Moreover, the focus on consolidated supervision is perfectly understandable as international banks have become more complex and as a response to a set of international bank failures, where the primary responsibility for regulation and supervision of the entire entity was unclear. However, as banking has become globalized, there are some uncomfortable questions that must be addressed regarding the nature of an international bank, and in particular, whether it would, if push comes to shove, survive or fail as one unit or whether there would be incentives to limit guarantees to certain subsidiaries.

Indeed, banks have in many instances used the option to enter overseas markets through subsidiary legal structures that may limit the liability of the international bank. At the same time, however, deposit insurance and lender of last resort remain a national responsibility. In this paper, we have developed some theoretical ideas that suggest that with local deposit insurance, in a risky environment it will be in the interest of the bank to consider its liability limited to the capital invested and to maintain a very low level of capital in the relevant subsidiary. On the other hand, subsidiaries in low risk environments may attract full guarantees to form the core of the bank. Within the core, consolidated supervision is fully appropriate as the bank would survive or fail as one but where it comes to the periphery consolidated supervision, while necessary, may not be sufficient.

Indeed, the analysis may present a problem for a host regulator in an emerging economy of higher perceived risk and no doubt the host regulator will wish to impose and supervise local regulations to ensure that an acceptable failure probability of the subsidiary is attained. Moreover, we suggest that if home supervisors get tougher in imposing tighter minimum capital standards or harsher penalties on a bank that faces a capital deficiency, then the incentives to place a subsidiary in the periphery and limit liability increase. In turn, this might provoke "tensions" between the host regulator and the bank, and possibly even with the home regulator, that may favor a consolidated approach in the name of greater regulatory homogeneity and efficiency.

In our view, multiple supervision is a price that most likely will have to be paid and both consolidated and local capital regulation, have important legitimate roles. However, we also believe that there are many further questions that should be addressed in this area. For example, in our work we have not considered the case where the interest rate paid on liabilities in the host country is endogenous to the capital invested. Also, we have not considered the case where the consolidated capital requirement is endogenous to the decision of the bank to exit a particular country. Finally, we have not considered issues regarding reputation or other interactions between the units of an international bank that may imply higher costs to exit. These and other considerations raise many further issues regarding cross border supervision making this a rich area for future research.

References

Basel Committee for Banking Supervision (1988). The Basel Capital Accord. July, available on www.bis.org

Basel Committee for Banking Supervision (2004). The New Basel Capital Accord. Available on www.bis.org

Basel Committee for Banking Supervision (2003). High-level principles for the cross-border implementation of the new Accord. Available on www.bis.org

Bernanke, B. (2004). Remarks of Governor Ben Bernanke at the International Bankers' Annual Breakfast Dialogue.

Calomiris, C. and A. Powell (2002). Can emerging economy bank regulators establish effective discipline. In *Prudential Supervision: Why Is It Important and What Are the Issues*, F.S. Mishkin (ed.). Chicago: University of Chicago Press and NBER.

Cerutti, E., G. Dell'Ariccia and M.S.M. Pería (2005). How banks go abroad: Branches or subsidiaries? World Bank Working Paper, WPS3753, October.

Del Negro, M. and S. Kay (2002). Global banks, local crises: Bad news from Argentina. *Economic Review, Federal Reserve Bank of Atlanta*, Q3, 89–106.

Financial Stability Institute (2004). Implementation of the new capital adequacy framework in non-basel committee member countries. FSI Occasional Paper No 4, July, http://www.bis.org/fsi/fsipapers04.htm

Majnoni, G. and A. Powell (2004). Bank capital and loan loss reserves under Basel II: Implications for emerging countries. World Bank Policy research Working Paper No 3437.

Miller, M., ed. (2003). *Credit Reporting Systems and the International Economy*. MIT Press, Boston, MA.

Standard & Poors (2002). Sovereign rating history since 1975. Available on www.standardandpoors.com

Standard & Poors (2000). Ratings performance 2000: Default, transition, recovery, and spreads. Available on www.standardandpoors.com

Weder, B. and M. Wedow (2002). Will Basel II affect international capital flows to emerging markets?. Mimeo, University of Mainz.

World Bank (2002). Implementation of the Basel core principles for effective banking supervision, experiences, influences and perspectives. Mimeo.

Deposit Insurance, Bank Resolution, and Lender of Last Resort — Putting the Pieces Together

Thorsten Beck*
World Bank

1. Introduction

Academics and policymakers alike often discuss individual components of the financial safety net while ignoring their interaction. As this comment will discuss, the consistent interplay of the different components is as important as the incentive compatible design of the individual components. While the safety net can be interpreted in a wider sense, including entry requirements and regular monitoring and disciplining of banks before entering distress, I will focus on deposit insurance, bank failure resolution and lender of last resort, as these are the relevant components of the safety net for problem banks and were discussed in the three papers in this session. I will first discuss the trade-off inherent to financial safety and its components and also analyze the interests of the different stakeholders of the safety net. I will then show the importance of the consistent design of the different components and their interaction, exemplifying it for the case of bank failure resolution and deposit insurance. Finally, I will turn to complications in cross-border banking.

2. Moral Hazard versus Bank Runs — Different Components of the Financial Safety Net

Deposit insurance, bank failure resolution and lender of last resort have opposing objectives. On the one hand, they are designed to minimize

*Thorsten Beck is a senior financial economist at the World Bank, 1818 H Street NW, Washington DC, 20433, TBeck@worldbank.org. This presentation has benefited from comments by Luc Laeven and discussions at the International Financial Instability Conference in Chicago in October 2006. This paper's findings, interpretations, and conclusions are entirely those of the author and do not necessarily represent the views of the World Bank, its executive directors, or the countries they represent.

disruptions in the financial system stemming from problem banks; on the other hand, they have to be designed to reduce *ex ante* moral hazard risk that can result in the same fragility the safety net is supposed to minimize. The importance of this second aspect has often been underestimated. Bank owners and managers face incentives to take more aggressive risk than is optimal for depositors and other debt claimants as with limited liability they only participate in the upside part of this risk. While market discipline alone might not be sufficient to keep these incentives in check, due to free rider problems and asymmetric information, and reliance on supervisors might thus be a necessary complement, the financial safety net has to be designed to enhance market discipline as much as possible and reduce imprudent risk taking incentives of bankers.

To better understand the functioning of the financial safety net and the trade-off discussed above, it is best to consider its main players and their interests, thus assessing the safety net as a nexus of a multi-party contract (Kane, 2000). As discussed above, bank managers and owners have strong incentives to take aggressive and imprudent risk.[1] Depositors care mostly about the safety of their deposits. In the presence of a generous safety net, they are tempted to rely on this net even if they have the means to monitor banks and exercise market discipline. The owners of the financial safety net, ultimately the taxpayers, want to minimize the costs while at the same time fostering financial intermediation. The managers of the safety net, finally, might have different interests than the owners and might be subject to political and regulatory capture.

Using this framework, let me discuss this trade-off between protection and moral hazard risk for each of the three components.[2] On the one hand, lender of last resort facilities aim to help overcome short-term liquidity problems of illiquid but solvent banks. However, given the intrinsic lack of transparency of banking, authorities in charge of the lender of last resort facilities might not be able to distinguish between illiquid solvent and illiquid insolvent banks. To reduce the risk that illiquid and insolvent banks bet their way out of insolvency with resources from the lender of last resort, resources are provided not only at high interest rates but also

---

[1] I am not distinguishing in this context between owners and managers of banks, whose relationship might be subject to agency problems.

[2] See Santos (2006) for an overview on the literature on lender of last resort and deposit insurance.

against collateral, as discussed by Vitor Gaspar. The objective of helping overcome short-term liquidity problems of solvent banks thus has to be appropriately balanced with the objective of not delaying the day of reckoning for insolvent banks. While bankers are interested in easy access to lender of last resort resources, the safety net owners, that is, taxpayers, will be mostly worried about the final cost. Further, depositor behavior might depend on the existence and behavior of a lender of last resort. On the one hand, easy access to lender of last resort resources might reduce the likelihood of costly bank runs; on the other hand, it might reduce market discipline if depositors perceive that access to lender of last resort facilities is granted independent of the solvency of the bank. The behavior of the manager of the lender of last resort facility, in most cases the central bank, very much depends on its institutional mandate and structure, as we will discuss further below.

The trade-off in the case of deposit insurance has been extensively discussed in the theoretical and empirical literature (see Demirgüç-Kunt and Kane, 2002, for an overview). On the one hand, deposit insurance schemes have been introduced to prevent bank runs from uninformed depositors and to protect small depositors from losing their lifetime savings. On the other hand, deposit insurance can reduce market discipline as even large depositors and creditors might rely on deposit insurance to bail them out in the case of failure. This reduced market discipline can result in increased risk-taking by banks, especially in the absence of a sound and effective supervisory regime.

The trade-off in the case of bank failure resolution — the intervention and resolution of failing banks — consists in reducing spillover damage from one failing bank to the rest of the system, on the one hand, and reducing banks' incentives to take aggressive and imprudent risk on the other hand, as discussed by Michael Krimminger. The first objective calls for a rapid resolution that ensures depositors' uninterrupted access to their savings, the conservation of lender–borrower relationships by keeping good assets within the financial system and the protection of the payment system. In order to minimize aggressive and imprudent risk-taking, an incentive compatible distribution of losses has to be announced *ex ante* and complied with *ex post*. This implies an ordering of claims that puts shareholders last and might involve creating a specific class of debt holders required to take the first hit, such as subordinated debt holders.

3. Putting the Pieces Together — From Components to the Safety Net

As has become clear from the previous discussion, lender of last resort facilities, deposit insurance and bank failure resolution face similar trade-offs and similar design challenges. To minimize adverse selection, all banks should be treated equally and be subject to the same rules. Access to lender of last resort facilities should be given to all banks at the same terms, membership in deposit insurance schemes should be mandatory, but pricing should ideally be risk-adjusted, and intervention and resolution rules should apply to all banks equally thus avoiding too-big-to-close banks. Second, all components have to be structured in a way that the interests of depositors, bankers, and owners and managers of the safety net are aligned. These similar challenges also imply that the structure of the different components have to be consistent with each other, as will become clear from the following examples.

Unlimited access to lender of last resort facilities without appropriate collateral can provide perverse incentives to the authorities in charge of bank failure resolution. In order to avoid realization of the losses to the lender of last resort, the bank resolution authority might be unwilling to intervene into the failing bank, effectively allowing it (and the lender of last resort) to bet the bank. Similarly, unlimited access to lender of last resort resources (even against sound collateral) can increase losses to the deposit insurer if the lender of last resort takes a privileged position due to her collateral. Finally, there is an important interaction between deposit insurance and bank failure resolution (Beck, 2004). Bank failure resolution that effectively bails out large creditors and even bank owners can undermine an explicit deposit insurance that was designed to give all but small depositors incentives to exercise market discipline. Bangladesh is a good example. In spite of systemic distress in all government — and several privately owned banks — the explicit deposit insurance has never been used because Bangladesh Bank regularly bails out banks (and thus all creditors and even owners) with regulatory forbearance (Beck and Rahman, 2006). On the positive side, an efficient bank failure resolution scheme can maintain a deposit insurance scheme financially viable through minimization of losses and speedy recovery of assets.

The interactions between the different components of the financial safety net raise the question of institutional links and relationships. While the three components of the safety net face similar trade-offs, they have different objective functions that might conflict with each other and might call for institutional separation. Repullo (2000) shows that lender of last resort and deposit insurance functions should be separated, with the central bank providing lender of last resort facilities in the case of small liquidity shocks, while the deposit insurer providing assistance in the case of large shocks.[3] Kahn and Santos (2005) also argue that it is best to separate lender of last resort and deposit insurance mandates, as the deposit insurer might face perverse incentives of regulatory forbearance if she also assumes lender of last resort responsibilities.

Institutional division of labor, however, requires frictionless sharing of information, which might not be possible in every institutional setting. Memorandums of understanding (MoU) or specific regulations might be necessary to facilitate such information sharing. Complementary regulatory frameworks that force institutions to take specific actions, such as a prompt corrective action framework, might be helpful in reducing conflicts of interest between different regulatory entities. The underlying institutional framework has to be the same for the different institutions, specifically operational and financial independence to thus minimize the risk of both political and regulatory capture.

As an example of the interaction of different parts of the financial safety net, Beck and Laeven (2007) focus on the interaction between deposit insurance and bank failure resolution. They observe a large variation in the institutional link between these two components of the financial safety net. While in the US, the Federal Deposit Insurance Corporation has supervisory powers over its member banks and is in charge of resolving problems banks, deposit insurance in Brazil is a pure paybox with no institutional mandate beyond paying out to depositors of failed banks. This raises the question whether some institutional set-ups are better than others. Deposit insurers might have stronger incentives to monitor their member banks and intervene into failing banks to thus minimize costs to their funds. On the other hand, deposit insurers worrying about the costs to their funds might be too tough on problem banks, not taking into account external effects of the resolution on the financial system at large (Repullo, 2000). Further, deposit insurance schemes managed by the member banks might face a conflict of interest when giving the responsibility to resolve failing banks. Finally, similar to managers of other components of the safety net, deposit insurers might face incentives to postpone

---

[3] A similar argument can be made for failure resolution. The deposit insurer might intervene too early to protect her funds, while the central bank (or another regulatory entity) takes into account interests of the financial intermediation.

interventions into failing banks ("not on my watch"). Using bank-level data for 57 countries with explicit deposit insurance scheme, Beck and Laeven explore the institutional interaction between bank failure resolution and deposit insurance. They find that banks are more stable, that is, further away from insolvency, in countries where deposit insurers have the right to intervene into failing banks and where they have the right to revoke membership of a bank. This finding is robust to controlling for other bank- and country-level characteristics. These empirical results and the theoretical insights discussed above (Repullo, 2000; Kahn and Santos, 2005) suggest that the functions of deposit insurance and bank failure resolution benefit from a close institutional link, while the lender of last resort facility should rather be institutionally separated.

4. Complications in Cross-Border Banking

While the design of domestic financial safety nets already faces trade-offs, expanding across borders complicates the picture. There are different legislative, regulatory and institutional frameworks, but most importantly, "home and host country authorities may face a mismatch between supervisory control, access to information, and responsibility for protecting the local economy" (Krimminger). It is helpful to apply the same framework of the different players to understand their incentives and the interaction. Such an analysis shows that the different stakeholders might be based in different jurisdictions and thus subject to different regulatory and supervisory arrangements and also to diverse and not-overlapping interest groups. Further, a bank and its clients might be subject to several safety nets, with different managers and owners. This not only can induce regulatory arbitrage in the reporting of certain assets, but also an intensification of the not-on-my-watch problem, if there is no clear coordination between different supervisory agencies across countries. Further, and as I discuss below, home and host supervisors will not necessarily pursue the same interests. Krimminger discusses the current situation in Europe where cross-border banking has increased in importance over the past years, while the safety nets are still mostly national, with some cooperation and coordination, but untested as of yet in times of crisis. While the European Union (EU) has moved forward in creating an enabling regulatory framework for EU-wide banking, the financial safety net has not been adapted to this new reality beyond MoUs and committees. Further, and as discussed by Krimminger, small home countries' deposit insurance schemes might be overwhelmed with claims stemming from operations outside the home country.

The potential for conflict of interest between home and host country in the case of North–South cross-border banking is shown by Giovanni Majnoni and Andrew Powell. Their analysis makes a compelling case that consolidated supervision is not a sufficient answer to the risk behavior and resource allocation of international banks across different subsidiaries. The bank's decision to put a subsidiary in the core or periphery (thus take full responsibility for all losses or only up to paid-in capital) will cause reactions by the host supervisor, which in turn might cause conflicts between home and host country supervisor. Let me discuss the implication of North–South cross-border banking in more detail, specifically the case of an international bank incorporated as subsidiary in the host country. While the relevant authorities for deposit insurance and bank failure resolution are located in the host country, it is not clear *a priori* whether the subsidiary would prefer to rely on liquidity support from the local lender of last resort, that is, the central bank in most cases, or on the parent bank in the home country (Majnoni and Powell). Further, the host supervisor might not have all the necessary information to properly monitor the bank and decide the appropriate moment to intervene, and the host country authority in charge of failure resolution might not have access to all the assets and information in the case of a failure. Finally, the objectives might again differ between home and host supervisors, with both worried primarily about financial system stability in their respective countries. While the northern home country is most likely characterized by a vibrant competitive financial system where the closure of the bank in question would not make a difference, the southern host country's financial system structure might turn toward monopolistic structures in case this bank is closed or sold to another northern bank that is very prominent in the host country.[4] The interests of host and home supervisors clearly differ in such a case. The asymmetry of information, responsibility and accountability is even more unbalanced in the case of branches, where depending on the legal situation, host country depositors might be subject to host or home country deposit insurance if they exist (or neither of the two) and supervisory authority lies clearly with the home country.

---

[4] Mozambique offers a good example where the largest two banks — both subsidiaries of Portuguese banks — merged because their parent banks in Portugal merged (though outside any crisis situation). It is doubtful that Portuguese regulators took into account the implications of this merger for the banking market in Mozambique.

Is the Coase theorem a good approximation for potential coordination between authorities to help resolve contractual problems between home and host country managers and owners of financial safety nets, as Vitor Gaspar seems to suggest? Given the asymmetric importance that parent and subsidiary or branch might have in home and host country, given the different institutional and legal frameworks and given the unequal balance of political and economic powers, this might be difficult to achieve in Europe and close to impossible when trying to resolve problems across continents.

5. Conclusions

This short comment has been trying to make three main points. First, all components of the financial safety net face a trade-off between the objectives of protection and moral hazard risks. While the protection of illiquid but solvent banks, small depositors and the financial system is often quoted as the prime objective of financial safety net, moral hazard risks loom prominently. The financial safety net has to be designed to minimize incentives for banks to take imprudent risks that can undermine the safety net itself. Second, the consistency and interaction of different components is important, as we have shown for the case of bank failure resolution and deposit insurance. Third, the analysis of cross-border complications of the financial safety net can benefit from taking into account the interests and incentives of the different stakeholders, such as bankers, depositors, managers and owners of the safety net. Compared to purely domestic safety net, the different geographic (and thus socioeconomic and political) location of different stakeholders complicates the analysis. The three papers of this session have a made start, but more rigorous analysis — theoretical, empirical and country — and case studies are needed in this area.

References

Beck, T. (2004). The incentive-compatible design of deposit insurance and bank failure resolution — Concepts and country studies. In *Who Pays for Bank Insolvency?*, D.G. Mayes and A. Luiksila (eds.), Basingstoke: Palgrave-McMillan.

Beck, T. and L. Laeven (2007). Resolution of failed banks by deposit insurers: Cross-country evidence. In *Deposit Insurance*, A. Demirguc-Kunt, E. Kane and L. Laeven (eds.). Cambridge, MA: MIT Press.

Beck, T. and M.H. Rahman (2006). Creating a more efficient financial system: Challenges for Bangladesh. World Bank, Research Policy Working Paper, No. 3938

Demirgüç-Kunt, A. and E. Kane (2002). Deposit insurance around the world: Where does it work? *Journal of Economic Perspectives*, 16, 175–195.

Kahn, C.M. and J. Santos (2005). Allocating bank regulatory powers: Lender of last resort, deposit insurance, and supervision. *European Economic Review*, 49, 2107–2136.

Kane, E. (2000). Designing financial safety nets to fit country circumstances. World Bank, Policy Research Working Paper, No. 2453.

Repullo, R. (2000). Who should act as lender of last resort? An incomplete contracts model. *Journal of Money, Credit, and Banking*, 32, 580–605.

Santos, J. (2006). Insuring banks against liquidity shocks: The role of deposit insurance and lending of last resort. *Journal of Economic Surveys*, 20, 459–482.

VI. INSOLVENCY RESOLUTION

Cross-Border Resolution of Banking Crises

Rosa María Lastra*

Queen Mary, University of London

1. Introduction

Since the banking industry is inherently unstable, the authorities always need to be prepared to confront the possibility of crises or problems. Crisis management in banking involves an array of instruments that extend beyond the insolvency proceedings that are the only tool typically available to deal with corporate bankruptcy in other industries. Such array of instruments includes the lender of last resort role of the central bank, deposit insurance schemes and government policies of implicit protection of depositors, banks (the "too-big-to-fail doctrine") or the payment system.

The growth in cross-border banking activities presents a number of challenges for regulators around the World. These challenges become particularly evident in the field of cross-border insolvency. Though the markets have grown international, regulation remains nationally based, constrained by the domain of domestic jurisdictions. In the absence of an international insolvency legal regime, the solution to the liquidation of a bank with branches and subsidiaries in several countries needs to be based on national legal regimes and on the voluntary cooperation between different national authorities. This cooperation is often uneasy and the

*Rosa María Lastra is a senior lecturer in international financial and monetary law, Center for Commercial Law Studies, Queen Mary, University of London (r.lastra@qmul.ac.uk). This paper draws on Chapters 4 and 14 of Lastra, 2006, *Legal Foundations of International Monetary Stability*, Oxford University Press, http://www.oup.com/uk/catalogue/?ci= 9780199269341 and on Lastra, 2003, "Cross-Border Bank Insolvency: Legal Implications in the Case of Banks Operating in Different Jurisdictions in Latin America", *Journal of International Economic Law*, 6(1), pp. 79–110. The author is grateful to Iwa Akinrinsola-Salami for research assistance.

division of responsibilities between home and host country authorities remains a matter of controversy.[1]

The challenge is further compounded by the fact that insolvency laws differ greatly from country to country. They differ in various ways. Given the intimate link between insolvency law and other areas of commercial law, different legal traditions (civil law, common law) have given rise to different insolvency rules. Some laws are more favorable to creditors, while others are more pro-debtor. The choice between *lex generalis* and *lex specialis* leads to different approaches to bank insolvency.

- *Lex generalis.* In some jurisdictions banks are treated like other corporations, that is, subject to the general insolvency law. This is the case in England, where ordinary insolvency principles are applied to banks (with some modifications for financial contracts, netting and setoff). Typically, they are judicial proceedings or court-administered proceedings (approach prevalent in many European countries).
- *Lex specialis.* In other jurisdictions, banks are subject to a special insolvency regime, administered by the bank supervisor or the depositor protection agency (for example, Canada, Italy and the US).

2. The Case for *Lex Specialis*

The case for a *lex specialis* with regard to bank insolvency can be supported by the existence of specific goals.[2] According to Schiffman,[3] corporate insolvency laws should seek to fulfil two principal objectives: fair and predictable treatment of creditors and maximisation of assets of the debtor in the interests of creditors. However, the main goals in a bank insolvency proceeding are the safety and soundness of the financial system at large and the integrity of the payment systems. Furthermore, the prompt payment to depositors as well as minimising the costs to the

---

[1] For instance, the issue of foreign ownership of banks makes some host jurisdictions (where foreign ownership is high) reluctant to rely upon home country control. Benston and Eisenbeis (2006) have studied this issue, which has relevant implications in many eastern European countries (such as Poland).

[2] See Hüpkes (2003).

[3] See Schiffman (1999), "Legal Measures to Manage Bank Insolvency", in R. Lastra and H. Schiffman (eds.), *Bank Failures and Bank Insolvency Law in Economies in Transition*, The Hague: Kluwer Law International, pp. 89–90.

insurance funds, are also mentioned as important considerations (certainly in the US).[4]

In addition to the specificity of the goals, there are other differences between the insolvency of a corporation and the insolvency of a bank. Some of these differences are rooted in the specialty of banks (given their role as credit providers, deposit takers and payments intermediaries), the risk of contagion in the case of bank failures (special vulnerability; under a fractional reserve system a bank will be unable at any time to honour the convertibility guarantee) and the public interest associated with sound banking and the smooth functioning of the payment systems.

The role of creditors is more active in general insolvency (Hüpkes, 2003). They can initiate the insolvency proceeding and can act individually (right to be heard) or collectively (creditor committees). Bank supervisors typically have the powers to commence the insolvency proceedings.

In banking, the definition of insolvency (the trigger point for an insolvency proceeding) is sometimes a matter or controversy. As acknowledged, there are two traditional definitions of insolvency in commercial bankruptcy laws: failure to pay obligations as they fall due (equitable insolvency) and the condition when liabilities exceed assets (balance sheet insolvency).[5] In banking the line of demarcation between illiquidity (lack of liquid funds) and insolvency is not always clear. An economically insolvent bank is not always declared legally insolvent by the responsible authorities and may be offered instead financial assistance. The test of insolvency as the inability to meet payments as they fall due, is not applicable to banking, since the inability to honour the convertibility guarantee of deposits is not a proof of insolvency, but rather evidence of illiquidity (Hüpkes, 2003).

A bank is considered to have failed when the competent authorities order the cessation in its operations and activities. However, the authorities are often wary of liquidating a bank (in part because an "orderly liquidation of assets" is not always easy, due to the possible contagion effect on other institutions) and therefore choose instead to rehabilitate the bank. As a matter of "good policy", the bank should be closed as soon as the market value of its net worth reaches zero, because at this moment, direct losses are only suffered by shareholders. If the bank is declared legally insolvent when the market value of its net worth is already negative, losses will accrue not only to shareholders, but also to uninsured creditors and/or to the insurance fund/the government.

---

[4] See Krimminger (2005).
[5] See Schiffmann (1999), pp. 96–97.

In banking, the pre-insolvency phase is fundamental and, in recent years PCA (prompt corrective action) rules, including SEIR (structured early intervention and resolution) have been advocated. In the USA, these rules are now legally binding since the enactment of FDICIA (Federal Deposit Insurance Corporation Improvement Act) in 1991. PCA rules are only effective if they are enshrined in the law, in particular the mandate to initiate early closure when the bank still has capital (even if it is critically undercapitalized). As Goodhart (2004) points out, "the window of opportunity between closing a bank so early that the owners may sue and so late that the depositors may sue may have become vanishingly small".

Insolvency proceedings typically imply liquidation or reorganization (sometimes, they are carried sequentially, that is liquidation proceedings will only run their course if reorganization is unlikely to be successful or if reorganization efforts have failed). Since the failure of a bank is often a matter of public interest and can cause a disruption in the payment system if not properly handled, and since the bank supervisor has the power to initiate insolvency, bank insolvency proceedings exhibit idiosyncratic features.

Though liquidation is the simplest resolution procedure, it is not necessarily the least costly, as a valuable depositor base gets dissipated, vital banking services in a community may be disrupted, and confidence in the banking system may be seriously damaged. In banking, liquidation typically entails a system of depositor preference, that is, depositors' claims are typically paid before those of general creditors. If the country has a deposit guarantee scheme, the insured depositors are paid off up to the insurance limit; uninsured depositors and other creditors are likely to suffer losses in their claims.

In the case of bank rehabilitation, reorganization or restructuring, the laws vary widely from country to country. A take over or merger (also called purchase and assumption, that is purchase of assets and assumption of liabilities) generally preserves the going-concern value of an institution, as the acquirer succeeds both to a deposit base and to a base of loan customers. As opposed to a straight liquidation, it eliminates the danger that vital banking services in a community will be disrupted. A merger can be "unassisted" when the acquirer assumes all assets and liabilities (also called "whole bank's acquisition"), and "assisted", when all the liabilities but only the good assets go to the acquirer (also referred to as "clean bank's acquisition"). In an assisted transaction, the bad assets are subject to special administration. Sometimes, failed banks may be placed under special administration, in the form of bridge banks, new banks, special funds or other arrangements. This is often meant to be a temporary solution in order to take over the operations of a failed bank and preserve its going-concern value while the government fiduciary seeks a more permanent solution to the problems or until an acquirer is found.

In some cases, an implicit or explicit "too big to fail" policy is applied. That was the case in Continental Illinois in the USA and in Credit Lyonnais in France. Government-led rescue packages may not only induce moral hazard behavior, but may also pose questions of fair competition, particularly when the too-big-to-fail doctrine is applied, as other smaller or less troubled institutions may have to navigate through crises or problems on their own. In the US, FDICIA (1991) requires the resolution of bank failures on a "least cost basis" to the insurance fund, unless it threatens to trigger a payment system breakdown, in which case FDIC and Fed may recommend a more costly solution (FDICIA, 12 USC 1823 (c)(4)).

The Basel Committee on Banking Supervision acknowledges that in a market economy, failures are part of risk-taking and that a prompt and orderly liquidation of institutions that are no longer able to meet supervisory requirements is a necessary part of an efficient financial system, as forbearance normally leads to worsening problems and higher resolution costs. However, the Committee explicitly states that "in some cases the best interests of depositors may be served by some form of restructuring, possibly takeover by a stronger institution or injection of new capital or shareholder. Supervisors may be able to facilitate such outcomes. It is essential that the end result fully meets all supervisory requirements, that it is realistically achievable in a short and determinate timeframe and, that, in the interim, depositors are protected."[6]

3. International Law Principles Governing Insolvency

"Most nations currently apply a territorial approach to cross-border insolvencies. This simply is a consequence of the domestic focus of most insolvency laws." (Krimminger, 2005) Sovereignty as a supreme power is typically exerted over the territory of the state: principle of territoriality. Sovereignty has a territorial dimension. The demise of national frontiers in today's global financial markets shows the limitations and inadequacies of this principle (territoriality — sovereignty) to deal with financial conglomerates, international holding structures and cross-border banking

---

[6] Basel Committee on Banking Supervision. Core Principles for Effective Banking Supervision (Basel Core Principles), http://www.bis.org/publ/bcbsc102.pdf.

and finance.[7] These inadequacies are particularly evident in the case of insolvency (though this paper does not address specifically the challenges involved in the liquidation of a financial conglomerate).

The principle of **plurality of bankruptcy** — which typically goes hand-in-hand with the "separate entity" approach to liquidation — means that bankruptcy proceedings are only effective in the country in which they are initiated and that therefore there is a plurality of proceedings, as they need to be initiated in every country in which the insolvent bank holds realizable assets or branches. Thus, this principle assigns territorial effect to the adjudication of bankruptcy. Under a separate entity approach, a domestic branch of a foreign bank receives a liquidation preference, as local assets are segregated for the benefit of local creditors (practice of "ring fencing").[8] Ring fencing is contrary to the *pari passu* principle, since some creditors receive more favourable treatment than others.[9] Under the separate entity approach, local branches of the foreign bank are treated as separate entities. This is the approach the US applies to the liquidation of US branches of a foreign bank. US bank insolvency law is territorial for US branches of a foreign bank.

The principle of the **unity and universality of bankruptcy** — which typically goes hand-in hand with the unitary or "single entity" approach to liquidation — means that there is only one competent court to decide on the bankruptcy of the bank (unity), and that the bankruptcy law of the country in which the insolvency has been initiated is effective in all other countries in which the bank (parent entity) has assets or branches (universality). All assets and liabilities of the parent bank and its foreign branches are wound up as one legal entity. Thus, this principle assigns extraterritorial effect to the adjudication of bankruptcy. All assets and liabilities of the parent bank and its foreign branches are wound up as one legal entity (single entity approach). Under this unitary system, it is impossible to start separate insolvency proceedings against a domestic branch of a bank which has its head office in another country. US law applies this unitary principle to the liquidation of a US bank with foreign branches.

---

[7] See Lastra (2006), Chapter 1.

[8] According to Curtis, "This manner of segregating local assets to pay local claims is known as the 'separate entity' approach to multinational bank liquidation. 'Balkanization' might be a more appropriate term." See Curtis (2000), "The Status of Foreign Deposits under the Federal Deposit Preference Law", *University of Pennsylvania Journal of International Economic Law*, 2, p. 254. See Campbell (2003).

[9] See Campbell (2003). Article 13.1 of UNCITRAL's model law on cross-border insolvency does not permit "ring-fencing".

The Federal Deposit Insurance Corporation as receiver of a failed bank collects and realizes all assets, and responds to all claims of the institution regardless of their situs. US bank insolvency law is universal with respect to US banks. (However, US law applies a different regime to the liquidation of US branches of a foreign bank, as I explained above).

The inconsistency of the US legal approach to the liquidation of multinational banks,[10] depending on whether it is dealing with foreign branches in the US or with US branches of a foreign bank, illustrates the difficulties of reaching a common international platform with regard to the liquidation of multinational banks.

4. Cross-Border Bank Insolvency

Bank insolvency laws vary widely across jurisdictions. Cross-border insolvency adds a layer of complexity to the resolution of a failed bank. Since complexity frustrates accountability, it is important to reach a clear *ex ante* understanding of what the applicable rules are if things turn sour. Institutions with global operations and aspirations may wish to explore the opportunities presented by "legal arbitrage". Conflicts or inconsistencies may arise. And, in some cases, the temptation to exploit legal inconsistencies (or possible legal vacuums) with fraudulent intentions cannot be ignored (example of BCCI). In addition, some jurisdictions present important deficiencies or gaps in their legal systems (for example, offshore centers and some emerging economies).[11]

There are three possible approaches to deal with the problems of cross border insolvency.

1. Creation of an international authority. However, the idea of an international bankruptcy court appears farfetched and, even at the EC level, the idea of a single authority appears distant (if not impossible).
2. Establishment of common rules. Rule harmonization appears to be the solution. Some rules are procedural and some others are substantive. In the field of insolvency, some conflict of laws/private international law/division of labor type of rules have been harmonized, but so far

---

[10] Baxter *et al.* (2004) consider, however, that this difference in approach is a good policy choice, which takes account of the fact that financial services are different and that they are highly regulated and supervised.

[11] Group of Ten Contact Group on The Legal and Institutional Underpinnings of the International Financial System, "Insolvency Arrangements and Contract Enforceability", 2002.

there is no international substantive bank standard applicable to cross-border insolvency.[12]

3. Co-operation and information sharing, through memoranda of understanding (bilateral and multi-lateral MoUs) and other mechanisms. However, resolution procedures (in particular if they imply burden sharing) cannot be expected to rely upon "*ex post* cooperation". They need *ex ante* rules.

Adoption of Common Rules Though there is no international treaty on insolvency law, there have however been some attempts at reaching some commonly agreed international rules (mostly "soft law"). The Basel Committee has addressed throughout its 31 years of existence various issues concerning the allocation of supervisory responsibilities (home-host), capital regulation and other principles for the effective supervision of international banks. However, the Basel Committee provides little guidance concerning bank exit policies and the problems involved in the resolution of cross-border banking crises.[13]

5. International Rules

5.1 *International rules on insolvency*

UNCITRAL (the United Nations Commission on International Trade Law) adopted the Model Law on Cross-Border Insolvency in Vienna in May 1997. However, this model law contains an optional clause whereby special insolvency regimes applicable to banks may be excluded from its scope.[14] The Model law deals with the recognition of foreign insolvency proceedings, the cooperation between judicial authorities and administrators and other issues concerning the coordination of concurrent insolvency proceedings in multiple jurisdictions.

Another example of international soft law rule that is often mentioned is the International Bar Association's (IBA) Cross-Border Insolvency

---

[12] See Krimminger (2005).

[13] In December 1992, the Basel Committee published a document on The Insolvency Liquidation of a Multinational Bank. This document is included in the Compendium of Documents produced by the Basel Committee on Banking Supervision (February 2000), Volume III, International Supervisory Issues, Chapter III, Other Supervisory Issues, is available at http://www.bis.org/publ/bcbsc333.pdf.

[14] Article 1(2) of the Uncitral Model Law.

Concordat, approved by the Council of the Section on Business Law of the IBA in September 1995, which set out some essential principles that can assist insolvency practitioners faced with concurrent proceedings in relation to the same debtor in two or more jurisdictions.[15]

In 1999, UNCITRAL commenced work on the Legislative Guide on Insolvency Law, considering corporate insolvency. Work proceeded through a joint colloquium with INSOL (a world-wide federation of national associations for accountants and lawyers who specialize in insolvency) and the IBA. The Legislative Guide was completed in 2004 and adopted by the United National General Assembly on 2 December 2004.[16]

The World Bank has coordinated the effort of the UNCITRAL Legislative Guide with its own Global Bank Insolvency Initiative to articulate a set of standards on insolvency and creditor rights for the purposes of the Bank/Fund initiative on Standards and Codes. Accordingly, the World Bank, in collaboration with staff of the Fund and UNCITRAL (United Nations Commission on International Trade Law) and other experts, has prepared a document, setting out a unified Insolvency and Creditor Rights Standard (the "ICR Standard"), which integrates the World Bank Principles for Effective Creditor Rights and Insolvency Systems (one of the twelve areas under the joint World Bank and International Monetary Fund initiative on standards and codes)[17] and the UNCITRAL Recommendations (included in the UNCITRAL Legislative Guide on Insolvency). This document was published on 21 December 2005.[18]

This ICR standard (one of the 12 areas identified by the Bank and the Fund in their joint initiative)[19] will be used for the purposes of assessing

---

[15] There has been a revision to the IBA Cross Border Insolvency Concordat in the form of the UNCITRAL Legislative Guide on Insolvency Law which can be found at http://www.uncitral.org/pdf/english/texts/insolven/05-80722_Ebook.pdf. The history of this revision can be found in: http://www.ibanet.org/images/downloads/uncitral%20memorandum%20for%20website.pdf

[16] The text of UNCITRAL Legislative Guide on Insolvency Law is available at http://www.uncitral.org/uncitral/en/uncitral_texts/insolvency/2004Guide.html.

[17] The text of the Principles is available at http://worldbank.org.gild.

[18] The ICR ROSC Standard has been posted for public review and comment since December 2005. See http://siteresources.worldbank.org/GILD/ConferenceMaterial/20774191/ICR_Standard_21_Dec_2005_Eng.pdf.

[19] The other eleven areas are: accounting, auditing, anti-money laundering and countering the financing of terrorism (AML/CFT), banking supervision, corporate governance, data dissemination, fiscal transparency, insurance supervision, monetary and financial policy transparency, payment systems, and securities regulation. See Lastra (2006), Chapter 14.

member countries observance in the ROSCs, Reports on the Observance of Standards and Codes.

The ICR standard recognizes that banks may require special insolvency laws, when it talks about exclusions (in point 3):

> Exclusions from the application of the [general] insolvency law should be limited and clearly identified in the insolvency law.

And then, the explanatory footnote concerning these exclusions further states:

> *Highly regulated organizations such as banks and insurance companies may require specialized treatment that can appropriately be provided in a separate insolvency regime or though special provisions in the general insolvency law.*

The ICR standard only briefly refers to "international considerations" (point 15), stating — as a World Bank Principle — that,

> Insolvency proceedings may have international aspects, and a country's legal system should establish clear rules pertaining to jurisdiction, recognition of foreign judgments, cooperation among courts in different countries and choice of law. Key factors to effective handling of cross-border matters typically include:

(1) A clear and speedy process for obtaining recognition of foreign insolvency proceedings.
(2) Relief to be granted upon recognition of foreign insolvency proceedings.
(3) Foreign insolvency representatives to have access to courts and other relevant authorities.
(4) Courts and insolvency representatives to cooperate in international insolvency proceedings.
(5) Non-discrimination between foreign and domestic creditors.

The ICR standard supports the "single entity" approach and the "unity and universality" principle in its recommendation 31, which states:

> The law applicable to the validity and effectiveness of rights and claims existing at the time of the commencement of insolvency proceedings should be determined by the private international law rules of the State in which insolvency proceedings are commenced.

However recommendation 32 brings back territoriality in the following exception, relevant in the case of bank insolvency:

> Notwithstanding recommendation 31, the effects of insolvency proceedings on the rights and obligations of the participants in a payment or settlement system or in a regulated market should be governed solely by the law applicable to that system or market.

5.2 *International rules concerning the regulation of branches and subsidiaries*

A number of principles developed by the Basel Committee throughout the years to deal with the cross-border supervision of branches and subsidiaries can be applied when dealing with cases of insolvency of a bank operating in different jurisdictions. In particular, the principle of parental responsibility (home country control) in the supervision of branches — as legally dependent units — and the consideration that subsidiaries become independent legal entities under the laws of the country of incorporation (under the laws of the host country) are principles observed generally and often included in Memoranda of Understanding between supervisory authorities in different countries.

Principles for the supervision of branches and subsidiaries were first developed in 1975 and refined in 1983. Following the collapse in 1974 of the German bank, Bankhaus I.D. Herstatt, and of the US bank, Franklin National Bank, the Committee issued in September 1975 a paper (subsequently know as the Basle Concordat) outlining some principles — in the form of recommended guidelines of best practice — regarding the supervision of banks operating internationally through branches, subsidiaries and joint ventures.[20] The Concordat was revised in 1983 following the collapse of the Luxembourg-based Banco Ambrosiano Holdings in 1982, under the title of "Principles for the Supervision of Banks' Foreign Establishments".[21]

---

[20] The 1975 "Condordat" was reproduced as an Annex ("Supervision of Banks' Foreign Establishments") to Williams and Johnson's paper (1981), "International Capital Markets: Recent Developments and Short-Terms Prospects", IMF Occasional Paper No. 7. See R. Lastra, 1996, Central Banking and Banking Regulation, Financial Markets Group, London School of Economics and Political Science, London, p. 175.

[21] Principles for the supervision of banks' foreign establishments (the "Concordat") (May 1983) at http://www.bis.org/publ/bcbsc312.pdf

According to the Basel Committee, there are two basic principles, which are fundamental to the supervision of banks' foreign establishments: that no foreign banking establishment should escape supervision; and that the supervision should be adequate.[22] An adequate supervision is one in which the host authorities are responsible for the foreign bank establishments (subsidiaries) operating in their territories as individual institutions, while the parent authorities are responsible for them as parts of larger banking groups.

The solvency of branches is the responsibility of the parent authorities, though the host authorities can demand endowment capital for foreign branches. The solvency of subsidiaries is the joint responsibility of both host and home authorities. The supervision of liquidity remains the primary responsibility of the host country, though in the case of branches, liquidity will also be a concern for the home authorities. The 1983 Concordat explicitly stated that "references to the supervision of liquidity did not relate to the lender of last resort role of the central bank, but to the control systems and procedures established by banks."

Parent authorities should be informed immediately by the host authorities of any serious problems which arise in a parent bank's foreign establishment and similarly, parent authorities should inform host authorities when problems arise in a parent bank which are likely to affect the parent bank's foreign establishment.

Thus, the principles related to the management of crisis and bank insolvency of foreign establishments should be analysed within this context of mutual cooperation between supervisory authorities. In some jurisdictions also, supervisory authorities have responsibility for managing pre-insolvency situations and when insolvency occurs there is another authority which is in charge of the actual liquidation of the institution.

---

[22] The Committee has published other documents and standards regarding the supervision of cross border banking. In April 1990, it published a supplement to the 1983 Concordat on "Information flows between banking supervisory authorities". Following the collapse of BCCI in July 1992, the Committee published the "Minimum standards for the supervision of international banking groups and their cross-border establishments". In October 1996, the Committee published a document entitled "The Supervision of Cross-Border Banking". In September 1997 the Committee published the "Core Principles for Effective Banking Supervision", that I refer to below. See also the Compendium of documents produced by the Basel Committee on Banking Supervision (February 2000), Volume III International Supervisory Issues, Chapter I: The Basel Concordat and Minimum Standards at http://www.bis.org/publ/bcbsc004.htm

In 1997, the Basel Committee published the "Core Principles for Effective Banking Supervision"[23] which have important implication for the supervision of international banks. The following principles are particularly relevant for the subject I elaborate in this paper:

(1) An effective system of banking supervision will have clear responsibilities and objectives for each agency involved in the supervision of banking institutions.[24]
(2) A prompt and early exit of banks that are no longer able to meet supervisory requirements is a necessary part of an efficient financial system and supervisors should be responsible for and assist in such an orderly exit.[25]
(3) Bank supervisors must practice global consolidated supervision adequately monitoring and applying appropriate prudential norms to all aspects of the business conducted by these banking organizations world wide, primarily at their foreign branches, joint ventures and subsidiaries.[26]

The principle of consolidated supervision,[27] means that parent banks and parent supervisory authorities monitor the risk exposure of the banks or banking groups for which they are responsible, as well as the adequacy of their capital on the basis of the totality of their business wherever conducted.

Consolidated supervision is based on the assumption that financial groups form a single economic entity. However, when one comes to the question of the resolution of a failed multinational bank, or of a complex financial group with activities and business units with different legal entities incorporated in various jurisdictions, the assumption that financial

[23] Basel Committee on Banking Supervision. Core Principles for Effective Banking Supervision (Basel Core Principles), http://www.bis.org/publ/bcbsc102.pdf. The Basel Core Principles for Effective Banking Supervision are intended to serve as a basic reference for supervisory and other public authorities worldwide to apply in the supervision of all banks within their jurisdictions.
[24] Basel Core Principles, pp. 4 and 11–12. Principle 1 determines the preconditions for effective banking supervision.
[25] See explanatory note accompanying Principle 22 of the Basel Core Principles of Effective Banking Supervision of September 2007. See also Hüpkes (2003) and Hadjiemmanuil (2004).
[26] Basel Core Principles, Principle 23, pp. 6–7 and 41.
[27] Consolidated supervision was first emphasized in the revised 1993 Concordat.

groups form a single economic entity appears to be not always valid in a bankruptcy scenario where the group is split up into its many legal entities and where foreign branches are sometimes liquidated as separate units.[28]

(4) The Basel Committee recommends that the supervisory authority be responsible for or assist in the orderly exit of problem banks in order to ensure that depositors are repaid to the fullest extend possible from the resources of the bank (supplemented by any applicable deposit insurance) and ahead of shareholders, subordinated debt holders and other connected parties.[29]

(5) Close cooperation with other supervisors is essential and particularly so where the operations of banks cross national boundaries.

6. Regional Rules

6.1 *The Montevideo Treaties of 1889 and 1940 and the Bustamante Code of 1928*

In Latin America, two multilateral treaties, the Montevideo Treaties of 1889 and 1940, and the Bustamante Code sanctioned by the sixth Panamerican Conference (Havana Conference) of 1928 establish private international law rules concerning bankruptcy. These treaties provide for the recognition and enforcement of foreign bankruptcies, and generally rely upon the principles of unity and universality of bankruptcy.

6.2 *The EU insolvency regime*

The EU insolvency regime consists of one regulation on insolvency pro-ceedings (Council Regulation (EC) No. 1346/2000 of 29 Mary 2000) and

---

[28] Zuberbuhler, Daniel (2000). "The Financial Industry in the 21st Century. Introduction, Director of the Secretariat, Swiss Federal Banking Commission. Document at http://www.bis.org/review/rr000921c.pdf, p. 2.

[29] See Basel Core Principles for Effective Banking Supervision, Section II, "Preconditions for Effective Bank Supervision," at p. 12. According to the Basel Committee, banking supervision is only part of wider arrangements that are needed to promote stability in the financial markets. One of these arrangements should include precisely procedures for effi-cient resolution of problems in banks. When problems are not remediable, the prompt and orderly exit of institutions that are no longer able to meet supervisory requirements is a necessary part of an efficient financial system.

of two directives: a directive on the reorganisation and winding up of credit institutions (Directive 2001/24/EC of 4 April 2001), and a directive concerning the reorganisation and winding-up of insurance undertakings (Directive 2001/17/EC of 19 March 2001).

The EU insolvency regime is binding for all EU Member States. As such, the EU regime is the most clear example of binding supranational/regional rules in the field of insolvency law in general and of bank insolvency law in particular. However, the EU rules are mainly of a private international law character. They introduce the principles of unity and universality of bankruptcy, conferring exclusive jurisdiction to the home Member State, but they do not seek to harmonize in a substantive way national legislation concerning insolvency proceedings, which remain different across the Member States of the EU.

The difficulty to reach some common standards in this area of law is illustrated by the hurdles and delays that the EU has faced over the years in trying to agree on some common principles on bank insolvency. Indeed, only in 2001 has the Directive on the Winding Up and Liquidation of Credit Institutions been adopted (Directive 2001/24/EC), though the proposed directive was published in 1988. This Directive does not seek to harmonize national legislation concerning reorganization measures and winding-up proceedings, rather it ensures mutual recognition and coordination of these procedures by the Member States of the EU, based upon the principle of home-country control.[30] It embraces the principles of unity and universality, single entity approach to liquidation, and the equal treatment of creditors.

Given the differences in bankruptcy laws in the Members States of the EU, I propose that large banking institutions and financial conglomerates should be incorporated as *Societas Europeae* (as Nordea proposed) and that a specific insolvency regime should apply to them.[31]

---

[30] For an analysis of the Directive, see Campbell (2003), Hadjiemmanuil (2005) and Nierop and Stenström (2002).

[31] A "Societas Europeae" (SE) or European Company is a public-limited company set up in the territory of the EU under the European Company Statute, which consists a Regulation (Council Regulation 2001/2157/EC of 8.10.2001 on the Statute for a European Company) and a Directive (Directive 2001/86/EC of 8.10.2001 supplementing the Statute for a European company with regard to the involvement of employees. See http://ec.europa.eu/internal_market/company/se/index_en.htm#legislation.

7. Bilateral Rules

In the absence of a formal international insolvency legal regime, countries resort to bilateral agreement, often in the form of a Memorandum of Understanding, to establish some principles of cooperation in the regulation of cross-border establishments.

7.1 *The need for a European Standing Committee for Crisis Management*

Multilateral memoranda of understanding were agreed in 2003 and 2005 (the first between central banks and supervisory authorities and the second also including finance ministries) to address the issue of cooperation in the case of a pan-European banking crisis. It is regrettable that they have not been published. In both cases, only a press release was made publicly available, but not the actual rules and procedures that would be applicable in the case of a crisis. These two MoUs should be published in the same way as the MoU that established the UK tripartite Standing Committee was published in 1997. Ambiguity and uncertainty as to the procedures and loci of power are not constructive. In the event of a crisis, the procedures to follow should be crystal clear *ex ante* for the institution affected, other market participants and the public at large.

The parties to the 2005 MoU comprise a total of 66 different authorities: national central banks, national banking supervisory authorities and national finance ministries of the 25 EU Member States and the European Central Bank.

Laudable as the setting of principles and procedures for sharing information in crisis situations is (the objective of both MoUs), it is not enough to deal with a crisis, particularly when so many parties are involved. I argue that an institutional solution is needed and that the current structure for crisis management in the EU is inadequate to deal with the possibility of a pan-European banking crisis.[32]

I propose the setting up of a standing committee or high-level group with adequate representation of the interested parties: the European Central

---

[32] See Chapter 10 of *Legal Foundations of International Monetary Stability* (Oxford University Press, 2006). My approach has been adopted as a recommendation by the European Shadow Financial Regulatory Committee, ESFRC (of which I am a member) in its Statement 23, available at http://www.aei.org

Bank (ECB) and NCBs, supervisory authorities, Ministers of Finance (MoF), the European Commission's (EC) Commissioner for Competition Policy and the EC Commissioner for the Internal Market. This Standing Committee could meet at very short notice. Though the meeting would typically take place over the phone (or video conference), the physical location of the Committee could be in Frankfurt, the headquarters of the ECB. The composition of this Committee could vary depending on the number of countries affected by the crisis. The rule for the composition of the Committee could be based on 3n + 3 members, with n being the number of countries affected by the crisis. Hence, there would be a tripartite representation from the national central bank, supervisory authority and Ministry of Finance for each Member State affected, and the other three members would be the EC Commissioner for Competition Policy, the EC Commissioner for the Internal Market and a representative of the ECB.

Since time and an expedient course of action are of the essence in any support operation and since it difficult to calculate *ex ante* the extent of the crisis, the rules of this Committee should be characterized by speed, efficiency and flexibility. So how would it work in practice? Suppose that a bank or group or banks in a Member State get into trouble. The supervisory authority in that country, together with the national central bank (if supervision is separated from the central bank) would take the lead in the procedure, keeping the Treasury/MoF informed. The NCB would immediately inform the European Central Bank, which, in turn, would communicate with the Commissioner in Charge of Competition Policy and the Commissioner for the Internal Market and with the authorities in the country/countries where spill-over effects are expected.

The rules and procedures of the European Standing Committee for Bank Crisis Management ought to be publicized and known *ex ante*, even though the actual details of the institution or institutions that receive support as well as the information about the level of such assistance ought to remain confidential.

A European Standing Committee for Bank Crisis Management, such as the one I propose, would not be exempt from problems.[33] Tom Baxter

---

[33] For instance the issue of burden sharing, the *ex post* allocation of the fiscal burden of the costs of recapitalization, is fundamental, as Goodhart and Schoenmaker have pointed out. But that would be the subject for another paper. 'He who pays the piper calls the tune' could be the motto for the allocation of costs. On the important issue of 'who pays for banking failures?' see generally David Mayes and Aarno Liuksila, eds. (2004). *Who Pays for Bank Insolvency?*, Hampshire and New York: Palgrave, MacMillan.

lucidly points out that there is always a potential for conflict amongst supervisors from different countries, and this potential becomes ominous when a bank weakens, since conflict rather than cooperation often characterizes the resolution process for troubled banks.[34] However, these problems are not insurmountable, since compromise is in the nature of EU politics.

8. Concluding Observations

This paper has presented some of the various issues at stake in the cross-border resolution of banking crises.

The need for a coordinated liquidation of multinational banks would be best served by the adoption of an international convention or regime on cross-border bank insolvency, based upon the principles of *lex specialis,* single entity approach to liquidation and unity and universality. However, these last two principles can only be accepted in an environment of mutual trust. Mutual recognition assumes a degree of mutual trust, and requires the prior minimum harmonization of essential rules. In the EU, mutual recognition presupposes the equivalence of the objectives national legislations and the existence of similar public interest goals. At the international level, the rules to be agreed upon by the national regulators should be preceded by an agreement as regards the objectives to be pursued, which in turn will generate mutual trust. Some rules and objectives must be harmonised to foster mutual trust. In this respect, the following substantive elements ought to be considered in a bank insolvency regime: clear definition of the triggers for the commencement of insolvency proceedings including PCA rules, provisions concerning the role of supervisors, courts and other authorities,[35] rules on minimum rights and obligations of debtors and creditors, clear rules on set-off, netting and

---

[34] See Thomas Baxter (2004). "Cross-Border Challenges in Resolving Financial Groups", in *Systemic Financial Crises: Resolving Large Bank Insolvencies*, Singapore: World Scientific Publishing.

[35] Eva Hüpkes (2003) notices that "given the realities of the bankruptcy law, it can be observed that bank supervisors supervise branches of foreign banks differently, according to the way such branches would be treated in a bankruptcy proceeding in the supervisor's country. Whereas a host supervisor in a single entity jurisdiction tends to act in the interests of the bank as a whole, a host country supervisor in a separate entity jurisdiction is likely to place greater emphasis on the protection of creditors transacting business with the host branches. Thus, bank insolvency resolution is very much a matter of international supervisory concern and, therefore, should not be left to bankruptcy courts".

treatment of financial contracts, rules concerning burden sharing, protection of the payment systems and prompt resolution.

References

Baxter, T. (2005). Cross-border challenges in resolving financial groups. In *Systemic Financial Crises: Resolving Large Bank Insolvencies*, D. Evanoff and G. Kaufman (eds.). Singapore: World Scientific Publishing.

Baxter, T., J.M Hansen and J.H. Summer (2004). Two cheers for territoriality: An essay on international bank insolvency law. *American Bankruptcy Law Journal*, 57, 57–91.

Campbell, A. (2003). Issues in cross-border bank insolvency: The European community directive on the reorganization and winding up of credit institutions. In *Current Developments in Monetary and Financial Law*, Vol. 3. Washington DC: International Monetary Fund.

Curtis, C.T. (2000). The status of foreign deposits under the federal deposit preference law. *University of Pennsylvania Journal of International Economic Law*, 2.

Eisenbeis, R. and G. Kaufman (2006). Cross-border banking: Challenges for deposit insurance and financial stability in the European Union. Mimeo, August.

Goodhart, C. (ed.) (2000). *Which Lender of Last Resort for Europe*. London: Central Banking Publications.

Goodhart, C. (2004). Multiple regulators and resolutions. In *Systemic Financial Crises: Resolving Large Bank Insolvencies*, D. Evanoff and G. Kaufman (eds.). Singapore: World Scientific Publishing.

Group of Ten (G-10) Contact Group on The Legal and Institutional Underpinnings of the International Financial System (2002). Insolvency arrangements and contract enforceability.

Krimminger, M. (2005). Deposit insurance and bank insolvency in a changing world: Synergies and challenges. In *Current Developments in Monetary and Financial Law*, Vol. 4. Washington, DC: International Monetary Fund.

Hadjiemmanuil, C. (2005) Europe's universalist approach to cross-border bank resolution issues. In *Systemic Financial Crises: Resolving Large Bank Insolvencies*, D. Evanoff and G. Kaufman. Singapore: World Scientific Publishing.

Hüpkes, E. (2003). Insolvency — Why a special regime for banks. In *Current Developments in Monetary and Financial Law*, Vol. 3. Washington, DC: International Monetary Fund.

Lastra, R. (2006). *Legal Foundations of International Monetary Stability*. Oxford University Press.

Lastra, R. (2003). Cross-border bank insolvency: Legal implications in the case of banks operating in different jurisdictions in Latin America. *Journal of International Economic Law*, 79, 79–110.

Lastra, R. (1996). *Central Banking and Banking Regulation*. London: Financial Markets Group, London School of Economics and Political Science.

Lastra, R. and H. Schiffman (eds.) (1999). *Bank Failures and Bank Insolvency Law in Economies in Transition*. The Hague: Kluwer Law International.

Mayes, D. and A. Liuksila (eds.) (2004). *Who Pays for Bank Insolvency?* Hampshire and New York: Palgrave, MacMillan.

Nierop, E. and M. Stenström (2002). Cross-border aspects of insolvency proceedings for credit institutions: A Legal perspective. Paper presented at the International Seminar on Legal and Regulatory Aspects of Financial Stability, Basel, January.

Padoa-Schioppa, T. (2004). *Regulating Finance*. Oxford University Press.

Zuberbuhler, D. (2000). The financial industry in the 21st century. Swiss Federal Banking Commission, http://www.bis.org/review/rr000921c.pdf

Bridge Banks and Too Big to Fail: Systemic Risk Exemption

David G. Mayes*

University of Auckland and Bank of Finland

In the United States (US), Canada, and a number of other countries (LaBrosse and Mayes, 2007) it is the duty of the deposit insurer to minimize the losses to itself from a bank failure. This entails not simply that the insurer should apply a technique that results in the lowest cost in the event of failure but that it should manage its risk exposure all the time and ensure that the system of regulation, supervision, corrective action prior to failure and the procedures set up for handling failure all contribute to ensuring that the losses are minimized.

If the deposit insurer is in effect a junior claimant on the bankruptcy estate, by virtue of succeeding to the insured claims of depositors, then, in minimizing its own losses, it will be working in line with the rest of the creditors and ensure that the return they get is maximized. It is normally the duty of the receiver to maximize the value of an insolvency estate, which should be equivalent to minimizing the loss provided the value of the estate is measured after the various charges including those from the receiver. If the deposit insurer is higher up the hierarchy of claims, then it has an incentive to make sure that the more junior claimants bear all the loss after the shareholders have been wiped out. However, this presupposes that all those encountering losses from the failure can join in the claims on the estate. Many concomitant losses will not be covered — borrowers may have to pay more for new loans, if assets are concentrated then their sale may reduce their price to the detriment of other asset holders and so on.

*David G. Mayes was a visiting professor at the University of Auckland and Advisor to the Board at the Bank of Finland. Although this chapter was prepared while the author was at the University of Auckland, which he thanks for providing the facilities, the usual disclaimer applies. He is grateful to Michael Krimminger of the FDIC for updating him on their views and experience on this topic, and to Peter Brierley and Robert Eisenbeis for comments.

There is therefore a case for considering minimizing some wider concept of loss when dealing with the framework for bank failure and the event of failure itself. In the case of the United States, this is only spelt out if the external loss is considerable,[1] then the Federal Deposit Insurance Corporation (FDIC) is entitled to request that the "systemic risk exemption" be invoked. In this case, it could then take into account the wider impact on society.[2] In practice, this has not been exercised but other countries, for example Finland, Norway and Sweden in their crises about 15 years ago, did take steps to limit the contagion to other parts of the economy, by, inter alia, issuing blanket guarantees, or allowing a public agency to become the "owner of last resort" (Moe, 2004).[3] This fear of contagion is one of the fundamental explanations for having deposit insurance in the first place (Diamond and Dybvig, 1986).[4] If depositors know they will be safe then they will not start a run on the bank, thereby rapidly sparking a crisis and — more importantly — they will not start runs on other solvent banks in the pursuit of rumors that they too may be under threat.

This wider concern for contagion forms part of what has been formalized more thoroughly as the desire for financial stability (Schinasi, 2005). There is an industry growing up in defining what this concern for stability is (Allen and Wood, 2006) but their definition is a good description: "financial stability is a state of affairs in which an episode of financial instability is unlikely to occur, so that fear of financial instability is not a material factor in economic decisions taken by households or businesses. ... Episodes of financial instability are episodes in which a large number of parties, whether they are households, companies or (individual) governments, experience financial crises which are not warranted by their previous behavior, and where these crises collectively have seriously adverse macroeconomic effects." (pp. 8–9).

---

[1] The Act uses the words "serious adverse effects on economic conditions and financial stability" (12 USC 1823(c)(4)(G)).

[2] FDICIA makes a further important proviso in this regard, namely, that the systemic risk exemption can only be used if not only is there a risk of serious harm but that the FDIC can mitigate the effect by using techniques not available to it under the ordinary working of the Act.

[3] The techniques the three countries used differed, as set out in Moe *et al.* (2005), which explains in some detail why in the Norwegian case a blanket guarantee was not thought the best way to go. In Norway, the government ended up owning 60 percent of the banking system in 1993.

[4] The other main reason normally advanced is to protect the interests of ordinary depositors, who are not in a position to be adequately informed about the risks they face or avoid them readily.

A narrow interpretation would suggest that, even for the claimants themselves, taking the spillovers into account would reduce their losses, as it would reduce the fall in market values that would otherwise occur without the intervention. Both they and the rest of society will benefit from the greater stability. Since stability is a rather soft concept and highly nonlinear in the way it operates it will be difficult to judge how extensive the public sector response should be. Here, I therefore suggest approaches that are clearly defined and hence strictly limited in any cost that might be imposed on the insurance fund or the taxpayer.

The discussion is easiest to delimit if the circumstances are simply the failure of a single institution for "idiosyncratic" reasons. However, it is often difficult to determine whether the failing institution is simply the most exposed of several institutions and hence any discussion of the resolution method employed must effectively allow for the possibility of a stream of actual or feared insolvencies in other financial institutions. It is therefore not possible to organize this on a highly discretionary basis or the result will be both misleading and inequitable. In the same way, "constructive ambiguity" will not be helpful as banks and their creditors will expect, in the absence of explicit history or a plan, that they will be favorably treated on the basis that the problem will be too difficult or too complex to allow them to fail.

This chapter deals with how the problems of failure can be dealt with in a predictable manner to handle the wider worries about financial system stability without exposing the taxpayer or those not directly exposed to extensive cost and giving strong incentives to those owning and managing banks to run them prudentially.

1. The Issue

If a financial institution that is small compared to the markets it operates in fails, the ripples that spread out to the rest of the financial sector and the economy at large are also likely to be small, largely irrespective of the methods used for resolving the problem. Only "largely irrespective", because methods which revealed that insolvency procedures were inefficient or inequitable would lead people to reappraise the risks they were taking. Such spillovers need not be negative as methods could reveal a better set of outcomes than expected. The spillovers can also be large if the economy is in a period of weakness when many institutions are under threat. However, it is not correct to consider these effects on a case by case basis as the expectation of what will happen under insolvency will be built up by the sequence of cases.

If an institution that is large in its markets fails then the methods used in resolution can have very different effects on the size of the ripples. This chapter explores methods that can be used to minimize the size of the external consequences, particularly the use of what are known as bridge banks in the United States, and builds on the ideas in Mayes *et al.* (2001) and Mayes and Liuksila (2003). The concern is to have methods of resolution that enable functions of the bank that are crucial to the maintenance of financial stability to remain in operation without a break (Hüpkes, 2004; Harrison, 2005) while nevertheless allowing the authorities to effectively take over the running of the bank from its previous owners. Thus the business continues even if, as in the US case, the bank is failed as a legal entity and reborn again as a new institution under FDIC control.[5] Approaches to this problem have been developed in both Switzerland and New Zealand and the necessary structures and rules exist in the US but have fortunately not been called into use since the passing of FDICIA.

It is not at all clear in many countries round the world whether they have such a coherent and prima facie effective system for keeping systemically essential functions of the banking system running in the event of a failure, without following some strategy of open bank assistance. Even in the US, the FDIC has made it clear that it requires regulatory changes if it is to be able to handle the failure of a large bank satisfactorily, whether or not it is subject to the systemic exemption (FDIC, 2006). Given the choice between the financial crisis and support most governments are likely to opt for support. Banks know that and hence this opens the system up to moral hazard. However, with some large cross-border banks, particularly in Europe, it is not clear whether the authorities would be able to keep such a bank open if it is large relative to the economy or if a large number of countries would be involved in deciding what to do in a case of difficulty.

Here, we begin by setting out some principles that might govern any effective resolution method before going to consider the problems of the particular methods and finally what can be done in the cross border case. For such a resolution system to work it needs to have the following five characteristics.

---

[5] Murton (2005) spells out how the FDIC would propose to act in the event of the failure of a large bank including how a bridge bank would be set up.

1.1 *Key characteristics of an effective framework for handling systemic banks*

1) A rapid implementation so that the systemically essential functions can be maintained without a material break.
2) A predetermined means of deciding what losses are to be taken into account and how they are to be assessed.
3) A means of allocating losses that respects the hierarchy of claimants under insolvency and does not make the claimants any worse off than they would be under normal insolvency procedures.
4) The method should not reduce the risk that shareholders and those responsible for the losses would otherwise bear, in particular it should not introduce a moral hazard that would encourage institutions to take on increased risk.
5) The method needs to be equitable across financial institutions irrelevant of their size or the sequence in which insolvencies occur.

These characteristics presuppose being able to define what the systemic functions are in addition to giving insured deposit holders uninterrupted access to their funds. It clearly involves ensuring that confidence in the system is maintained as well as the actual avoidance of serious fluctuations. This implies that not merely must financial markets continue to operate, along with the payment and settlement systems but that their structures must be such that people expect them to work in the face of shocks. This confidence comes not just from the systems themselves but from credible commitment of the authorities to step in the event of market failure. Of course, it may very well be that the confidence is misplaced and the authorities cannot or are unwilling to deliver if a problem hits.

There is a clear problem in deciding what is "systemic" in advance. In terms of retail banking, this may simply be in terms of market share. In the New Zealand case, this was straightforward, as there was a clear gap between the smallest of the major banks and the largest of the smaller banks. While a line has to be drawn somewhere, there is no practical difference between two banks with a dollar difference in size. For the proposals suggested here to work, such banks need to be determined in advance and a sufficiently close relationship built up that they could be taken into statutory management or its equivalent at short notice. The authorities in each country need to make careful assessments of the nature of their markets to determine which institutions might be systemic in them. As evidenced by the actions of the UK in expanding the number of banks in the primary market, it may be possible to solve the problem by removing the systemic position of the bank in advance.

However, there is an important distinction between a problem in a single bank when the system is under no other threat and one where the whole system is very fragile and a problem with one could easily bring down many others. In these circumstances, the number of institutions and events that could lead to systemic problems will be greatly increased, thus making prior identification more difficult, as it is context specific. One problem that needs to be addressed with some care is how to be equitable across all the banks during a problem period. Mishkin (2005) suggests allowing the first to fail but intervening to limit the knock on consequences. In the event of a large external shock, this could be rather a lottery and encourage masking of problems to avoid being first in the queue. Perhaps more likely the first will be saved as the total potential call on taxpayers is underestimated initially.

2. Too Big to Fail

One of the main concerns of this chapter is distinguish circumstances where the concern is wider than purely minimizing the loss to the deposit insurer from the concept of "too big to fail". The concept of too big to fail implies that the only technique available to the resolution agency in the event of failure is open bank assistance, namely that the institution has to be kept open and running without a break in business via some form of capital support. The discussion that follows distinguishes keeping the functions of the bank in continuous operation from continuing the ownership and legal personality of the bank. Indeed, the contention is that if the moral hazard is to be avoided and the appropriate pressure put on the bank to resolve its own problems, then the resolution method should involve the owners losing their claim on and control of the bank.[6]

There is, of course, a prior concern articulated clearly by Stern and Feldman (2004) that in a large economy like the United States, it may be

---

[6] It is important not to imply that currently large banks are indeed exhibiting the moral hazard. As Mishkin (2005) points out the evidence in the US tends to suggest that there is little indication. See also Wall (1993).

possible to organize the structure of the financial system in such a way that although most of the economies of scale can be reaped no financial institution is actually essential to the operation of the financial system. They also argue that it is possible to reduce the interdependencies in the system, for payments for example. Hüpkes (2004) takes this further by introducing the idea of "replaceability" — a function is systemic if it cannot be replaced from other sources during the value day. If such replaceability is achieved, any bank could be closed in an ordinary manner without systemic consequences. In most countries, however, internationally competitive banks can readily be large compared to their financial systems and hence too large to close without using methods that take into account their possible systemic impact.[7]

In many respects, the problem is largely that it is difficult to act quickly enough with a large and complex institution (Evanoff and Kaufman, 2005). If the actions could be sorted out in time then the sheer size of the loss may not be the difficulty. However, it is probably mistaken to suggest that problems are likely to be proportionate to the size of the institution. Problems that are of the dimension to affect markets will tend to emerge, whether they are large or small relative to the size of the institution. In one sense, this is reassuring as it also implies that unexpected shocks are less likely to bring down the largest institutions. Where countries are small compared to the size of international banks (as outlined in Hüpkes (2003) for Switzerland in the case of Credit Suisse and UBS) there is a real danger that the banks will be "too big to save" in the sense that neither the fiscal capacity nor the technical capacity exists to avert a disorderly failure and hence financial instability will ensue.

The main difficulty therefore is likely to come from banks that may not necessarily be large from a global point of view but are large compared to some of the markets they operate in.[8] They will indeed be too

---

[7] Stern and Feldman (2006) go further than this and suggest that the authorities should say in advance for each institution that has systemic functions how they propose to handle the insolvency without invoking the idea of "too big to fail". The implication is that either alternative service providers can be lined up so that contracts can be switched or detailed arrangements are in place for how the bank's systems can be handled that they can be permitted to fail as an entity in the manner described in this article.

[8] This article does not consider the problem that some small countries face, that their largest banks could take decisions that are fairly minor for the bank yet have systemic consequences. For example, it is argued that the largest banks operating in Estonia (which are Swedish) could write off their Estonian operations completely and still not make a loss for the parent group in the quarter this occurs. They therefore need tools for avoiding systemic actions by banks in more normal operations, far short of insolvency.

large compared to those markets to be allowed to stop operating but they may be small enough to manage a very rapid resolution without disrupting the market. It is noticeable that the FDIC cites being able to buy time (Reidhill *et al.*, 2005) as an important point in favor of bridge banks. However, the time which needs to be bought has four components:

- time to decide what is the best course of action
- time to establish the condition of all of the parts of the banking group
- time to implement the resolution and reorganisation process
- time to line up buyers for the bank as a whole or in parts.

However, simple delay, as with forbearance does not address the issue. The swift action needs to be final and to provide the confidence to keep trading in place without a rush to exit.

3. The Nature of the Intervention

If the authorities want to keep key activities in a bank operating they have a straightforward range of options available:

(1) They can provide sufficient support to the bank directly to stop the threat of closure, while insisting on strong conditions for action and reorganisation to prevent the losses worsening and start the process of recovery. This would probably involve a change in key staff and the appointment of someone to run the bank in whom the authorities had trust. This would be typical *open bank assistance.*

(2) They can provide sufficient support to enable a competitor to take over either whole bank or at least the functions that the authorities wish to see continue unbroken — *purchase and acquisition*

(3) They can acquire the bank themselves as receivers, conservators or other court appointed agents and continue to keep either the whole bank or the appropriate functions operating. This in itself can take a number of forms. A typical approach is to split the organization into a "good bank" where the healthy and required activities continue and a "bad bank" where the losses are concentrated and where these activities will be terminated and liquidated in the manner normal for an insolvency. The question at issue in the present discussion is the legal form for the continuing bank, whether in whole or in part. The term

bridge bank relates to a particular form used in the US on a number of occasions by the FDIC (Krimminger, 2006; Marino and Shibut, 2005) but this is a generic type and in what follows the discussion is not restricted to the particular characteristics of the US structure. In the scheme described in Mayes *et al.* (2001) and implemented in New Zealand, Switzerland and Norway, *inter alia*, the authorities can step in and reorganize the existing legal institution.

Although the over-riding aim should be some concept of minimizing the loss, the principal driving force of the choice of resolution method is going to be the practicality of what can be done in the time available. However, having a purely ad hoc approach will in itself affect expectations and the moral hazard inherent in the system. The nature of the decision on what is going to be applied needs to be clear in advance and something that will be less desirable for the current owners and managers of the bank in difficulty than the normal sorts of private sector solution, whether or not assisted by the "good offices" of the authorities. One of the other noteworthy features of the US system, which has not been universally adopted, is the concept of Structured Early Intervention and Resolution and within that the idea of Prompt Corrective Action, which is designed to try to prevent problems getting as far as insolvency and direct intervention by the authorities. This entails the early involvement of the resolution agency not just when things are starting to deteriorate but in normal times. This enables the authorities to have in place some of the key ingredients of a successful resolution that can be applied in a hurry. If there has been no preparation, it is rather unlikely that anything could be done to keep a large and complex organization in business other than open bank assistance.

Many countries have powers to act in the way set out under FDICIA in the US, but they do not have the all important compulsion to act in a particular way with only limited opportunity to delay at a series of prescribed benchmarks that trigger actions of increasing firmness. Even fewer have opened a dialogue with their banks to ensure that they know enough about their computer systems, structures and other operating procedures to be able to implement a helpful resolution process in a hurry.

It is still typically assumed that the time for action is the proverbial weekend, with the bank appearing with its problems at the close of business on Friday and everything being sorted out before the markets reopen on Monday morning. This is however an increasingly unrealistic view of the world. The key decisions may very well have to be taken within the course of a day. Knowledge of the problem is likely to leak quickly and turn a problem of manageable proportions into one where the authorities have real difficulty avoiding just the systemic event they are trying to prevent. The emphasis in any of these procedures therefore needs to be on having as much as possible in place that can be done without imposing undue costs on the banks or indeed on the authorities as that could in itself result in something that is not a "loss minimizing" arrangement. The regulatory costs of the system can impose a loss, if they do not act to reduce moral hazard, the risks and the costs in any failures that do occur adequately. It is very difficult to estimate what these parameters are.

The approach of the Reserve Bank of New Zealand, with its "Outsourcing Policy", seems as good a description as any of what might be done. Here, the objective is to try to ensure that whatever operational difficulties a bank may encounter it can be up and operating again before the end of the value day. Insolvency is only one of the things that could act as a trigger, key service providers could fail or a natural disaster could terminate normal operations. In any of these circumstances, the authorities need to be convinced that the bank's vital operations can be restarted promptly without causing harm to the financial system. The outsourcing policy (RBNZ, 2006) is explicit in what the performance should be. The arrangements must be such that:

- The bank's clearing and settlement obligations due on a day can be met on that day;
- The bank's financial risk positions on a day can be identified on that day;
- The bank's financial risk positions can be monitored and managed on the day following any failure and on subsequent days;
- The bank's existing customers can be given access to payments facilities on the day following any failure and on subsequent days.

A statutory manager, the New Zealand term for the official administrator appointed to takeover the running of the institution in the event of failure, must also be able to achieve these objectives. While a bank can only offer simulation evidence that it meets these requirements, it would nevertheless have to satisfy the authorities that its systems were compliant in this regard.

These four provisions cover all of the main aspects that a bank would need to offer to meet the needs of financial stability, namely, that:

- Responsibilities with respect to the rest of the financial system are met in clearing and settlement;
- Customers have access to their accounts;
- It is possible to identify and manage the risks.

What it does not cover explicitly, although it was referred to in the draft, is the ability of the statutory manager to be able to make a summary valuation of the net position of the bank before the end of the value day. If a bank is going to reopen it has to be in a position to offer creditors, depositors and counterparties a credible assurance that they will suffer no further losses and will not be advantaged by attempting to exit their positions rapidly. This requires either recapitalization, a writing down of claims or the issuing of some form of guarantee with state backing.

Kaufman (2007) offers a simple four-point program that has to be met in the case of failure:

(1) Prompt legal closure when the bank's capital declines to some pre-specified and well publicized minimum value greater than zero (legal closure rule);
(2) Prompt estimates of the recovery value and assignment of any credit losses (haircuts) to de jure uninsured bank claimants;
(3) Prompt reopening (e.g., the next business day), particularly of larger banks, with full depositor access to their accounts on their due dates at par value for insured deposits and recovery value for uninsured deposits and full borrower access to their pre-established credit lines; and
(4) Prompt re-privatization and re-capitalization of the bank in whole or in parts at adequate capital levels.

All are characterized by the word "prompt". These requirements are similar in character to the scheme set out in Mayes *et al.* (2001).

The first of his points emphasizes that action needs to occur early, preferably before capital is exhausted. It is preferable that "failure" for a bank be insufficient capital and not insolvency or negative value. Pozdena (1991) emphasizes the virtues of the Danish system that prevailed in the 1980s; see also Mølgaard (2003). Then, despite having the largest stock of non-performing loans of the Nordic countries, Denmark was the one that avoided the financial crisis that swept Finland, Norway and Sweden. It is arguable that their closure policy and associated features of their regulatory system helped in this by making sure that banks did not become highly undercapitalized. They set a floor of 8 percent for capital adequacy. If capital fell below 6 percent then the bank has at most until its next shareholders' meeting to raise at least 75 percent of the shortfall. Closure, in the form of withdrawing the banking license follows almost immediately upon failure. Even above the 8 percent ratio, any bank with a capital ratio below 15 percent had to devote a proportion of its profits to reserves.

On top of that the Danish authorities required mark to market accounting, the writing down of non-performing loans and, for stocks and bonds, a provision for volatility. The experience, which may not be the result of the regime, was that almost all Danish banking problems were solved within the market and troubled banks were bought by larger competitors before the difficulties mounted too far. Only two banks were subject to compulsory closure; one (6th July Bank) was immediately sold, while the other (C&G Banken) liquidated. Pozdena (1991) argues that this was all achieved without imposing any undue burden on the Bank in question. It is worth noting that deposit insurance was only introduced late in the day as a result of a European Union (EU) directive requiring it in all member states, between the two failures. 6th July Bank was closed in March 1987 and C&G Banken the following October. Pozdena suggests that it was only some unusual features of the loan portfolios that prevented these institutions from finding private sector "voluntary" solutions as well.

However, Pozdena conducted his analysis before the main problems erupted in Denmark. Between 1987 and 1995, 122 financial institutions got into difficulty. 102 ceased to exist. Most of the normal resolution methods, merger, capital injection, split into good and bad banks and liquidation were applied. Neither of the two largest "systemic" banks got into serious difficulties. Nevertheless, early action by the authorities kept the problems manageable and avoided a "crisis".

4. Who Should be Responsible?

Although the deposit insurers in the US and Canada, the FDIC and the CDIC, and in some other countries have the responsibility for minimizing losses (to themselves) and hence need to take an active role in ensuring that the risks in the financial system are managed well all of the time — a task that involves them inter alia in the supervision of the institutions holding insured deposits — this is not the norm; see the IADI survey, whose results are discussed in Su (2007). It is more common for deposit insurers to be subservient organizations, often just simple payboxes under the direction of a national supervisor, bankers' association — as is the case in Finland — or other responsible body such as the central bank. In these cases, it is likely that the responsible organization will face a conflict of interest if it is responsible both for the continuing supervision and health of the banking system as well as for resolving problems. The supervising arm will tend to have an interest in seeing the problem resolved without a failure, as will the central bank if it has emergency lending at stake whose collateral may be of doubtful value in the event of a sudden sell-off. Although some of the concern about forbearance is largely theoretical, there are some egregious examples of its use as documented by Mishkin (2005) in the case of the US Savings and Loan crisis. This motivation for forbearance will conflict with the pressure for early intervention and acknowledgement of the problem by an organization responsible for minimizing its losses.

It is relatively difficult — but not impossible — for a single organization to supervise an institution for two purposes at the same time. The resolution agency or arm of the wider organization is interested in understanding the business so it can step in. It is interested in getting reasonable valuations for the assets and liabilities and being able to manage aspects of the computer system in an emergency. This is very different from ensuring compliance. The area of clear overlap is in the assessment of the risks. Having an agency that is well versed in how to handle insolvency step in as soon as the bank encounters any difficulty is likely to make the incentive to achieve a private sector solution much stronger. Mayes and Liuksila (2003) argue that such a resolution agency, even at a European level, does not necessarily have to be heavily staffed if it can draw rapidly on experts who are normally employed elsewhere, as failures are relatively unusual in most western European countries.

5. The Power to Act

Being able to create and run a bridge back or otherwise take a failing institution into a version of public ownership in order to keep functions of systemic importance running implies an appropriate basis in law. It could be applied under normal bankruptcy law by giving appropriate powers to receivers or other administrators of the bankruptcy estate, but in most countries this is not the case. In general, it requires a special bankruptcy law for banks. Even this is not straightforward, as the "owner" of the bank may be a holding company. It may therefore be the owner who is insolvent rather than simply one or more banking components of the group. Other parts of the financial group may not be banks and hence subject to different legislation. Hüpkes (2006) stresses that the legislation needs to enable the banking authorities to act at whatever level of a complex group is appropriate in order to resolve the banking problems. Her conclusion is rather negative: "In view of the limited intervention powers of the lead or coordinating supervisor, there is reason to question whether it would be possible to achieve effective early resolution of a crisis affecting globally active institutions with diverse financial activities carried out through separate legal entities." (p. 25).

To some extent traditions and experience matter in this regard, as both Hadjiemmanuil (2003) and Blowers and Young (2003) argue that the "London approach" of rapid actions through the courts can work when the judiciary well understand the need for speed and accept that errors can be put right or compensated for after the event. The resolution agency needs to be able to act early. Krimminger (2006) reports that Mexico introduced even stronger powers for its deposit insurer Instituto para la Proteccion al Ahorro Bancario (IPAB) in April 2006. Not only can IPAB form a bridge bank, but it can also intervene earlier with a strong effect on the shareholders. Once the capital ratio falls below 8 percent, it can insist on the development of a capital restoration plan, one of whose conditions is that 75 percent of the bank's equity is deposited in a trust for the benefit of IPAB. If the conditions are not met, IPAB can impose losses on the shareholders equivalent to the losses and even gain control of the bank. Once the capital ratio falls to 4 percent, it can implement resolution procedures so that it stands a much better chance of avoiding serious loss. Forming a bridge bank in these circumstances has to offer the prospect of lesser loss than simply closing the bank; such a bridge may only last for a year.

6. The Bridge Bank Approach

A crucial distinction between the "bridge bank" concept and some of the alternatives is that the existing bank is terminated and its banking license withdrawn, and a new institution is created. Under the Swiss system, for example, it is the existing institution that is reorganized (Hüpkes, 2003).

If an appropriate framework is not in place, then the authorities will have no alternative to open bank assistance if they want to avoid the systemic consequences, as the FDIC found in the case of the Continental Illinois failure in 1984 (Reidhill *et al.*, 2005). A bridge bank is likely to be the way the FDIC chooses to handle the failure of bank with systemic implications if only because getting grips with the bank and sorting out the nature of the problems, what can and should be done is likely to take weeks rather than the hours that may be available.

Bridge banks have not been used widely in the US and not at all in the last 12 years, in part because the scale and complexity of failures have been not been such as to necessitate it.[9] They are deliberately a temporary arrangement to allow all or part of a failing institution to continue in operation, for a period of up to two years, extendable in one year increments to five if it has not yet proved possible to sell it or close it in a manner that minimizes the losses. While the FDIC is responsible for creation of the institution and can control it, it does not own it in the sense of holding the common stock or voting shares. The bridge bank is a new national bank, chartered by the Comptroller of the Currency. The ability to create bridge banks was given in the Competitive Equality Banking Act of 1987.

The key feature of the arrangement, which is some respects unique to the US environment, is that it provides the authorities with a means of cutting the bank off from its holding company. In that way, any further assistance given to the bank does not accrue to the shareholders of the holding company or to claimants on the holding company rather than on those with a claim directly on the banking subsidiary. It is a device that puts the failed bank in a form more suitable for its sale to the private sector, in particular by keeping it operating. It enables the FDIC to benefit from the observation that a bank is usually worth more alive than dead even if it is under water (Guttentag and Herring, 1986).

Interestingly, the bridge bank form has been used to put together a whole set of subsidiaries into a single banking entity (40 in the case of First Republic in 1988, 19 in the case of MCorp in 1989 and three in the case of the Bank of New England). However, in the case of First City in 1992, the FDIC decided that the most effective way to proceed was to create

---

[9] They have been used just 10 times in the period between 1988 and 1994. However, the case of Superior Bank, a thrift institution, is functionally similar (Eisenbeis, 2006).

20 individual bridge banks and then it could sell them individually or as a group. Within the 20 subsidiary banks, 16 were formed from the whole deposit base of the failed institution and four only from the insured deposits. Clearly, it may depend upon the circumstances whether all subsidiaries should be treated the same. If there are large outstanding claims before the courts, there may be too much risk in acquiring all the liabilities. It is a difficult judgement in advance to decide whether the subsidiary banks will perform better and be more attractive as a group or individually. No doubt this will be affected be the degree of independence of the various subsidiaries prior to failure. The greater their common systems and synergies from being part of the same holding company then the more sense a joint operation is likely to make. Even if in a sense forming separate bridge banks always leaves the option of recreation of the group open.

First City was not only the last bridge bank to be formed but also the only one after the passing of FDICIA in 1991. Reidhill *et al.* (2005) in their assessment of the usefulness of bridge banks, based on the 10 occasions they have been used is that they help to shorten the period of resolution and that they can be consistent with the least cost resolution requirement. Clearly they buy time, which will enable potential purchasers to complete their investigations and enable the FDIC to restructure the banks to make them more profitable, while meeting the requirements of access by depositors to their funds. They imply that the first choice of immediate sale (at a realistic price) was not available and that simply paying out the depositors and disposing of the assets piecemeal over time as "ordinary" insolvencies did not appear a lower cost route.

Handling a large bank failure is going to be difficult whatever system is used both because of the complexity of the organization and the lack of experience anyone from the outside is going to have in running it or something similar. Thus, while some help will be available from the recently retired in particular, it is inevitable that there will be a heavy reliance on existing staff, some of whom may turn out to be responsible for the problems in the first place. One likely cause of failure is the inability of the previous administration to manage the integration of a previous expensive merger so the systems to be managed may themselves be somewhat in disarray. As Marino and Shibut (2005) point out, the importance of preparedness for the resolution agency is crucial. Techniques can be evaluated on smaller cases and in simulations, but the main source of strength will come from a good understanding of the small number of systemically important institutions that might have to be handled.

7. Alternatives to the Bridge Bank Approach

In Mayes *et al.* (2001) we proposed a scheme that had many of the characteristics of the U.S. scheme, emphasizing the importance of early intervention under a form of Prompt Corrective Action with specific predetermined benchmarks. This entailed a close relationship between a resolution agency and the supervised institutions before there was any concern over the condition of the bank otherwise procedures could not be put in place. It differed from the US arrangements in two main respects. The first was that although we thought it desirable to intervene finally before capital was totally eroded, our interpretation of EU Law was that it would be very difficult for the authorities to intervene before net worth of the institution in mark to market terms reached zero. Otherwise, it would be over-riding the rights of shareholders. In the light of experience since then, including the discussions of the proposal included in Mayes and Liuksila (2003) we have become more convinced that our original idea was correct and that the authorities should seek a change in the law to permit earlier intervention. Simple withdrawal of the banking license might not meet the need, as that would imply a sudden stop to activity and not the smooth resolution we envisaged. The second major difference was in the form of the reorganisation. We did not prescribe the exact method but suggested that the most important issue was to be able to restore the bank to viability in short order so that there would be no break in the business. We saw this entailing four steps:

- The appointment of a receiver, conservator or other form of statutory manager to take over the running of the bank;
- A summary valuation to establish the extent of the deficiency;
- Where insolvency was either not the lowest cost method of resolution or where it would lead to unacceptable financial instability, a writing down of the claims or other restructuring to return the bank to positive net worth in a form that would give confidence to markets;
- We argued that this latter would probably entail a guarantee against any further loss that had government backing.

We argued that the writing down of the claims needed to follow the normal sequence in an insolvency, with the shareholders taking the initial loss, then the subordinated debt holders and then the other creditors in order, with each class being treated equitably. The proposal put forward by Aghion *et al.* (1992) that this take the form of a debt for equity swap with the claimants now having an equity claim on the new institution might be a suitable way to go. If the bank had positive value compensation would have to be paid to the existing shareholders, otherwise this would amount to expropriation.

One of the problems with the FDIC's approach to bridge banks is that involves being able to distinguish clearly between insured and uninsured deposits. The FDIC has no duty to protect uninsured deposits and its proposals suggest they would not be taken into the bridge bank. It is not all clear that unless adequate arrangements are made for such deposits and other claims, so that at least the deposit holders can have immediate access to their written down claims that a loss of access on a large scale might not trigger the systemic problems. Clearly it will help to insist that the deposit insurer can identify the accounts (LaBrosse and Mayes, 2007) and that the banks systems should be transparent and known to the resolution agency in advance as a result of its continuing interaction with the bank in normal circumstances. Banks in the US were not surprisingly rather unenthusiastic about altering their systems to achieve this (Stern and Feldman, 2006) although it is not clear how large the costs might be in practice.

In any case, focusing simply on deposits does not identify the systemic features of the bank's operations. As Hüpkes (2004) points out, these cannot really be "carved out" from the rest of the operation of the bank. They may not be legally or administratively distinct. One could of course require this as a regulator. The area where carve outs do work is in the collateralization of transactions in many markets. In these cases there cannot normally be losses unless collateral values fall so far that they are insufficient to cover the claims.

The Swiss arrangements, set out in Hüpkes (2003), have the advantage of more flexibility than the Mayes *et al.* (2001) proposals, but they require time to implement the reorganisation and apply any reorganisation haircut necessary to bring the new institution to adequate capitalization. Mayes *et al.* suggest that taking the whole organization as it stands is the only thing that can be done in a hurry, even if subsequently it is clear that a reorganisation that involves sale of some of the more profitable parts might maximize a bankruptcy estate. The Swiss scheme can in many ways be thought of as more akin to the later steps in prompt corrective action, and has the advantage that they can be implemented without the agreement of the existing shareholders, although approval of the reorganisation by the courts allows the stakeholders to express their views before the decision is taken. It is a process with considerable merit if it can be implemented before the point of insolvency.

8. Handling the Various Parts of the Business

Hüpkes (2004) helpfully points out that even if one wants to keep a bank open in order to prevent an adverse impact on the financial system this does not imply that all parts of the bank or the wider group need to be kept running if they are a source of actual or potential future losses. Indeed, a degree of shrinkage is likely even if the bank is treated as whole. Peripheral activities may well be sold in order to improve the liquidity of the bank if a fair price can be obtained. New lending is likely to be conducted on a conservative basis etc. Typically, it is necessary to offer (insured) depositors virtually uninterrupted access to their funds. However, where a bank is a key player in financial markets it needs to behave reasonably normally if markets are not going to be disturbed. It is not simply that the bank needs to avoid breaking a whole set of open contracts if its rating and credibility are to be maintained but it needs to offer new contracts on a scale that provides adequate liquidity to the market. This is particularly important where a bank is a key counterparty. Such contracts entail risk, which has to be managed, hence the skilled market players in the bank have to be retained in their posts.

If the restructuring process for the bank requires a haircut or some other means of writing down claims, then the speed at which that has to be done will tend to vary with the time to maturity of the contracts. It is only the transactions that take place on the value day on which the resolution process occurs that have to be handled immediately. However, certainty is required about what will happen to the remaining contracts otherwise the holders of the claims may try to advance them, causing the systemic difficulties it is hoped to avoid.

9. The Cross-Border Issue

While the rapid resolution of a large bank may be possible as described here, it is already more complicated when they are part of a larger group, much of which may be involved in insurance or other non-banking activities.

Not only may they not be covered by the same laws that permit intervention of the authorities before insolvency, but their insolvency also might have much more limited implications for financial stability. Where the bank or group runs across regulatory borders the problem becomes much more complex (Lastra, 2003).

If there are only systemic implications in the country of the parent (home), then the complexity makes resolution more difficult but the spin off problems are largely internalized in the home country, even if the problems causing the insolvency have been incurred in foreign operations. However, once there are systemic implications in more than one country or only in host countries, then the problem becomes a serious threat to systemic stability, as there may be a conflict of interest. The home country may be content see an orderly closure, whereas the host with the systemic problem will want some form of resolution that keeps the business going. It depends on the structure of the group as to whether this can be achieved. If the group is divided neatly into largely free-standing subsidiaries that are locally incorporated and supervised, then having a system where each country can step in and apply its own processes may make sense even if this does not necessarily maximize the recovery value for the group as a whole. However, if the activities themselves run across borders and the banks have branches in other countries that are not freestanding and not locally supervised then this neatness does not apply.

It is this last case that is increasingly applying in the EU,[10] where operation through branches in other member states is actively encouraged in the pursuit of economic integration and the completion of the single market. Operating directly or through branches does not require local approval in the host countries, although local conduct of business rules apply, and supervision (and deposit insurance) remains the responsibility of the home country. Furthermore, under the Winding Up Directive, the parent and branches are supposed to be treated in single proceedings under the insolvency regime of the home country. The host country then does not have control over what will affect its financial stability where the branches are of systemic importance, described as "responsibility without power" in Mayes (2006b). It cannot institute PCA, it cannot intervene before insolvency nor finally afterwards. It has to hope that the home

---

[10] The term EU embraces the wider European Economic Area, that adds Iceland, Liechtenstein and Norway to the 25 EU member states, as they are all governed by EU law in this regard.

country will do that job for it. That might work if the bank were systemic in the home country as well but this is not guaranteed. Mayes *et al.* (2006) offer a way of implementing PCA in such cross-border instances. The home country may choose a resolution approach that does not foster stability in the host. Simply the anticipation that there is going to be a difficult wrangle about "who pays" in the event of a failure would tend to trigger an exit of the smart money from the bank. The current position is clearly unacceptable (Srejber, 2006).

It is highly tempting therefore to follow the approaches applied by the US and New Zealand and cut through the international complexity so that a bank with systemic implications can be treated like a domestic institution whatever the nationality of its ownership (Baxter *et al.* 2004). Thus New Zealand has decided that all banks of systemic importance have to be locally incorporated. Not only that but the New Zealand operation has to be viable in its own right to the extent that a statutory manager can take over something that can be run independently of the parent within the value day as described above.

Since that option is not open in the EU a more collaborative approach is required as set out in Mayes (2006a), for example, where a college of supervisors under the leadership of the home country jointly supervises the financial group and implements SEIR and PCA. Nevertheless there is still a problem in applying a means of resolving an insolvency or unacceptably low capitalization. Losses have to be assigned, guarantees given and even loans advanced. This burden could be too great for the home country and might require joint action by the component countries of the college. This cannot be done at the time. Srejber (2006) argues for a fixed prenegotiated key for burden sharing. However, it seems difficult to see foreign governments being willing to finance something which is largely a concentrated problem even if there would be a theoretical *quid pro quo* in a future crisis.

A likely solution therefore seems to be a supranational organization to handle cross-border banks that are systemically important in at least one member state. This could be done on a case by case basis as the number of such banks is small (between 30 and 50) and the range of countries involved decidedly variable. The alternative is to have a European resolution agency — it could be a European Deposit Insurance Corporation (EDIC) to match the framework of the FDIC, CDIC etc., but it does not need to handle the vast bulk of banks in Europe that are largely national in character and not of systemic importance. Hence, it can be a much smaller organization.

However, this does not solve the problem for such banks that have substantial operations outside the EU. Here, the territoriality approach seems likely to be applied in systemic cases and a New Zealand style approach where rapid intervention along the lines suggested in this chapter is possible seems a sensible way to go. The particular form of the intervention, whether as a bridge bank or another form of reorganization haircut, is less important than simply ensuring that the systemic functions can be continued without a break. Nevertheless, some form of acknowledging the loss and removing the bank from the existing owners seems likely to be both lower cost and more equitable. However, with the current state of preparedness in many countries it is not so likely to be the route chosen. Either some form of open bank assistance or the disorder that results in the systemic problem seem more likely.

References

Aghion, P, O. Hart and J. Moore (1992). The economics of bankruptcy reform. *Journal of Law, Economics and Organization*, 8, 523–546.

Allen, W.A. and G. Wood (2006) Defining and achieving financial stability. *Journal of Financial Stability*, 2(2), 152–172.

Baxter, T.C., J. Hansen and J.H. Sommer (2004). Two cheers for territoriality: An essay on international bank insolvency law. *American Bankruptcy Law Journal*, 78(1), 57–91.

Blowers, B. and G. Young (2003). The economic impact of insolvency law. In *Who Pays For Bank Insolvency?*, D. Mayes and A. Liuksila (eds.), pp. 164–179. Basingstoke: Palgrave-Macmillan.

Diamond, D. and P. Dybvig (1986). Bank runs, liquidity and deposit insurance. *Journal of Political Economy*, 91(3), 401–419.

Eisenbeis, R. (2007). Home country versus cross-border negative externalities in large banking organization failures and how to avoid them. In *International Financial Instability*, Douglas Evanoff, George Kaufman and John Raymond LaBrosse (eds.). Singapore: World Scientific.

Evanoff, D. and G. Kaufman (2005). *Systemic Financial Crises: Resolving Large Bank Insolvencies*. Singapore: World Scientific.

FDIC (2006) Large-bank deposit insurance modernization proposal.

Guttentag, J. and R. Herring, 1986, "Disaster Myopia in International Banking", *Essays in International Finance*, no. 46, Princeton University, September.

Hadjiemmanuil, C. (2003). Bank resolution policy and the organization of bank insolvency proceedings: Critical dilemmas. In *Who Pays For Bank Insolvency?*, D. Mayes and A. Liuksila (eds.), pp. 272–330. Basingstoke: Palgrave-Macmillan.

Harrison, I. (2005). The reserve bank of New Zealand's creditor recapitalization (BCR) project. In *Systemic Financial Crises: Resolving Large Bank Insolvencies*, D. Evanoff and G. Kaufman (eds.), pp. 397–406. Singapore: World Scientific.

Hüpkes, E. (2003) Learning lessons and implementing a new approach to banking insolvency in Switzerland. In *Who Pays For Bank Insolvency?*, D. Mayes and A. Liuksila (eds.), pp. 242–271. Basingstoke: Palgrave-Macmillan.

Hüpkes, E. (2004). Protect functions not institutions. *The Financial Regulator*, 9(3), 43–49.

Hüpkes, E. (2006) Piercing the corporate veil: Managing financial failure in an evolving economic and financial environment. Western Economics Association International Conference, San Diego, 29 June–2 July.

Kaufman, G. (2007) Using efficient bank insolvency resolution to solve the deposit insurance problem. In *Deposit Insurance*, A. Campbell, R. LaBrosse, D. Mayes and D. Singh (eds.), pp. 197–210. Basingstoke: Palgrave-Macmillan.

Krimminger, M. (2006). Controlling moral hazard in bank resolutions: Comparative policies and considerations in system design. Mimeo, FDIC, May.

LaBrosse, J.R. and D.G. Mayes (2007). Promoting financial stability through effective depositor protection: The case for explicit limited deposit insurance. In *Deposit Insurance*, A. Campbell, R. LaBrosse, D. Mayes and D. Singh (eds.), pp. 1–39. Basingstoke: Palgrave-Macmillan.

Lastra, R. (2003). Cross-border bank insolvency: Legal implications in the case of banks operating in different jurisdictions in Latin America. *Journal of International Economic Law*, 79–110.

Marino, J. and L. Shibut (2005). Resolution strategies for large US commercial banks. Mimeo, FDIC, November.

Mayes, D.G. (2006a). Cross-border financial supervision in Europe: Goals and transition paths. *Sveriges Riksbank Economic Review*, 2006/2, 58–89.

Mayes, D.G. (2006b). Responsibility without power: Two solutions to the problem of foreign owned systemic bank branches. *Journal of Banking Regulation*, 8(1), 20–39.

Mayes, D.G., L. Halme and A. Liuksila (2001). *Improving Banking Supervision.* Basingstoke: Palgrave.

Mayes, D.G. and A. Liuksila (2003). *Who Pays For Bank Insolvency?* Basingstoke: Palgrave-Macmillan.

Mayes, D.G., M. Nieto and L. Wall (2006). Multiple safety net regulators and agency problems in the EU: Is prompt corrective action partly the solution? Bank of Spain.

Mishkin, F.S. (2005). How big a problem is too big to fail? NBER working paper 11814, December.

Moe, T.G. (2004). Norway's banking crisis — How Oslo got it right. *The Financial Regulator*, 9(3), 26–33.

Moe, T., J. Solheim and B. Vale (2005). The Norwegian banking crisis. Oslo: Bank of Norway Occasional Paper 33.

Mølgaard, E. (2003). Avoiding a crisis: Lessons from the Danish experience. In *Who Pays For Bank Insolvency?*, D. Mayes and A. Liuksila (eds.), pp. 222–241. Basingstoke: Palgrave-Macmillan.

Murton, A. (2005). Resolving a large bank: The FDIC's perspective. In *Systemic Financial Crises: Resolving Large Bank Insolvencies*, D. Evanoff and G. Kaufman (eds.), pp. 415–420. Singapore: World Scientific.

Pozdena, R.J. (1991). Danish banking: Lessons for deposit insurance reform. *Journal of Financial Services Research*, 5, 289–298.

Reidhill, J., L. Davison and E. Williams (2005). The history of bridge banks in the United States. Washington, DC: FDIC.

Reserve Bank of New Zealand (2006). Outsourcing policy. Document BS11, January, Wellington.

Schnasi, G. (2005). *Safeguarding Financial Stability: Theory and Practice*, Washington, DC: International Monetary Fund.

Srejber, E. (2006). Are we ready to deal with a cross-border banking crisis in Europe? Gdansk, 12 May, available from http://www.riksbank.se.

Stern, G. and R. Feldman (2004). *Too Big To Fail: The Hazards of Bank Bailouts*. Washington, DC: Brookings Institution.

Stern, G. and R. Feldman (2006). Managing too big to fail by reducing systemic risk: Some recent developments. *The Region*, June.

Su, W. (2007). General guidance for the resolution of bank failures. In *Deposit Insurance*, A. Campbell, R. LaBrosse, D. Mayes and D. Singh (eds.), pp. 230–265. Basingstoke: Palgrave-Macmillan.

Wall, L. (1993). Too big to fail after FDICIA. *Federal Reserve Bank of Atlanta Economic Review*, January/February, 1–14.

Prompt Corrective Action: Is There a Case for an International Banking Standard?

María J. Nieto*
Banco de España

Larry D. Wall
Federal Reserve Bank of Atlanta

Benston and Kaufman (1998) proposed a system of predetermined capital/asset ratios that trigger structured actions by supervisors, which they called structured early intervention and resolution (SEIR). SEIR works both by requiring early supervisory intervention as banks become undercapitalized and by requiring that the authorities resolve distressed banks through sale, merger or liquidation at a predetermined minimum regulatory capital ratio. A version of SEIR was first adopted by the US as prompt corrective action (PCA) in the 1991 Federal Deposit Insurance Corporation Improvement Act (FDICIA), and other versions also called PCA were subsequently adopted in Japan, Korea and, more recently, Mexico.

Although the early adopters of PCA were countries that had previously experienced significant distress in their banking system, PCA's positive effect in creating the appropriate incentives for banks, the deposit insurer and the prudential supervisor has lead to proposals to introduce PCA policies in other countries. Goldstein (1997) presents a case for an international banking standard, which includes an incentive compatible

*M. J. Nieto (maria.nieto@bde.es): Banco de España. Alcalá 48, 28014 Madrid (Spain). Larry D. Wall (larry.wall@atl.frb.org): Federal Reserve Bank of Atlanta, 1000 Peachtree Street N.E. Atlanta, Georgia 30309-4470 (USA). The authors thank George Benston, Robert Eisenbeis, Gillian Garcia, Eva Hüpkes, David Mayes, Tokio Morita, Inwon Song and Jan Willem van der Vossen for helpful comments on an earlier draft. The authors also want to thank C. A. E. Goodhart and Rosa M. Lastra as well as the participants in the seminar held at the LSE Financial Markets Group (London, March 2006) and the participants in the Conference on International Financial Instability: Cross-Border Banking and National Regulation organized by the Federal Reserve Bank of Chicago (October 5–6, 2006) for comments on an earlier version. The views expressed here are those of the authors and do not necessarily reflect those of the Banco de España, Federal Reserve Bank of Atlanta or the Federal Reserve System.

safety net and prudential supervision whose principles are inspired in FDCIA-like features. In emerging economies, Goldstein and Turner (1996) propose PCA as a policy aimed at improving incentives for bank owners, managers, and creditors, as well as bank supervisors.

Against the background of the launching of the euro and the expectation of a gradual increase in cross-border banking activity in the European Union (EU), the European Shadow Financial Regulatory Committee (2005) (ESFRC) recommended the establishment of a SEIR regime. Benink and Benston (2005) also propose SEIR as a mechanism to protect deposit insurance funds and taxpayers from losses in the EU. Similarly, Mayes (2005) proposes intervention at prescribed benchmarks as a method to have plausible bank exit policies for systemic risk banks in the EU.

Existing analyses of SEIR/PCA policies have focused on aspects of its economic rationality with little attention paid to implementation issues. However, SEIR was initially designed to address weaknesses in the US supervisory system and, as such, built upon some key features of the then existing US supervisory and deposit insurance systems. Among these key features were that US bank supervisors already had the authority to exercise most of the disciplinary measures authorized in PCA and the US already had an efficient mechanism for resolving failing banks. The primary change brought about by the US adoption of PCA was that of reduced supervisory discretion in exercising forbearance toward undercapitalized banks. Before other countries can adopt an effective version of PCA, their policymakers will need to adopt some institutional feature similar to those found in the US.

The purpose of this article is two-fold: (1) to identify key conceptual approaches and institutional structures needed for PCA to be effective, and (2) identify the changes needed to adopt an effective version of PCA in general and, in particular, in Europe. The first part considers the major conceptual changes that PCA brought to US bank supervision. The second section focuses on the institutional preconditions for a successful implementation of PCA. As a benchmark for current European supervision, this section also considers both the extent to which the preconditions were met in Korea, Japan and Mexico at the time of their adoption of PCA, and the extent to which these preconditions are also called for under the Core Principles for Effective Banking Supervision issued by the Basel Committee on Banking Supervision. The last part provides summary remarks.

1. Conceptual Issues in Adopting PCA

SEIR and PCA are based on a clear philosophy of the role of bank supervisors, i.e. to minimize deposit insurance losses. This philosophy is in many ways different from that which guided the establishment of most bank supervisory authorities. An effective system of PCA may be established without accepting all of the philosophy underlying SEIR. However, in order to have a fully effective system of PCA, the banking supervisory system has to incorporate some key elements of the SEIR/PCA philosophy. The following subsections analyze three key elements of that philosophy: (1) the bank prudential supervisor's primary focus should be on protecting the deposit insurance fund and minimizing government losses, (2) the supervisors should have a clear set of required actions to be taken as a bank becomes progressively more undercapitalized, and (3) that the supervisors should close undercapitalized banks before the economic value of their capital becomes negative. The third element flows from the first two core elements but is sufficiently controversial to merit separate analysis.

1.1 *Should supervisor's goal be to minimize government losses?*

Focusing prudential supervision on limiting government losses has two advantages. First, timely closure reduces the large losses to taxpayers which have occurred in systems that have not followed PCA. Second, timely closure also reduces the resource misallocation that results from the incentive distortions faced by insolvent banks.

Hüpkes *et al.* (2005) note that bank prudential supervisors are often given multiple goals, and indeed, the single goal given to US supervisors in PCA only applies to carrying out PCA's provisions. However, most other goals of prudential supervision could be pursued in ways that do not significantly raise expected losses to the deposit insurer. The one goal that, according to some authors, might be in conflict is that of limiting the damage to the real economy from bank failure. These authors defend that PCA can result in the resolution of a bank that if given sufficient time might recover, thereby avoiding any failure related costs to the real economy.

Benston and Kaufman (1995) argue that the failure of a bank in a system with multiple substitutes is no more costly than the failure of many other types of firms, such as the failure of firms that supplies proprietary information technology that is widely used. This argument is perhaps partially qualified by several papers that have found evidence that the failure of a bank imposes costs on the bank's borrowers, such as that in Brewer *et al.* (2003). The extent to which this qualifies the Benston and Kaufman (1995) claim depends in large part on which borrowers were adversely impacted: (1) good borrowers who were paying a market rate for their loans, and (2) other borrowers that were receiving credit at a below market rate (including bad customers that should not have received loans) because the failed bank was not charging appropriate credit risk premiums. The existing studies do not distinguish between these groups of borrowers.

A longstanding concern is that the failure of a bank could lead to deposit runs at healthy banks, and the resulting panic could lead to the collapse of the banking system. A more recent concern is that some failures could have a substantial adverse impact on the real economy by impairing the payment system. A narrow focus on limiting deposit insurance losses may not be appropriate if such a focused policy were to risk a systemic crisis.

Although a case may be made that systemic concerns should override limiting the losses of the deposit insurer, that case has several weaknesses. First, the analysis of systemic concerns typically takes the risk of bank failure as independent of bank supervisory policies. However, bank supervisory policies that try to prevent bank failure by exercising forbearance toward failing banks and their creditors mute signals of excess risk taking by a bank and may induce increased risk taking by reducing its cost to a bank's owners. Moreover, PCA provides for early intervention to reduce the probability of failure in a variety of ways, including a mandatory requirement that the bank develop and implement an acceptable capital restoration plan.

Secondly, the argument that bank failures are likely to lead to systemic crisis is often overstated according to Kaufman (1988). Moreover, concerns about runs at healthy banks may be mitigated by an active lender of last resort.

Thirdly, allowing insolvent banks to continue in operation runs the risk that they will accumulate even larger losses leading to even greater market disruption when the bank's continued operation is no longer tenable. In contrast, if a bank is required to be closed before its losses exceed the bank's equity and subordinated debt then depositors and other creditors should be exposed to little or no loss. Moreover, prompt resolution reduces the probability that more than one systemically important bank will be insolvent at the same time.

All countries that adopted PCA did it after incurring widespread insolvencies among their depository institutions posing a challenge to prudential supervisors' credibility. In the case of Mexico, the International Monetary Fund (2001, p. 66) explicitly recognizes that the adoption of PCA *"will facilitate remedial action in a timely fashion"* and encourage *"the CNBV to continue working on restoring its credibility by achieving consistency in actions taken toward banks breaching laws and regulations or undertaking unsafe and unsound banking practices"*.

In Europe, although policymakers have not explicitly addressed the relative importance of minimizing deposit insurance losses, the relevant Directive on deposit insurance is fully compatible with such a focus. Directive 94/19/EC of the European Parliament and of the Council of May 30, 1994 (Official Journal of the European Communities L 135, 31st May, 1994) on deposit guarantee schemes harmonizes minimum deposit insurance coverage, but also in its Preamble discourages governments from providing funding to their deposit insurer: *"[T]he cost of financing such schemes must be borne, in principle, by credit institutions themselves."* At the same time, there are limitations, imposed by the EC Treaty, on the ECB and/or the euro area national central banks' lending to governments or institutions (article 101), which limit the possibility of central bank financing of deposit insurance schemes. There are also limitations on the EU Community's ability to "bail out" governments and/or public entities (article 103).

Nonetheless, governments continue to bail out depositors, and even shareholders. A recent survey on forms of intervention by European deposit insurance schemes by De Cesare (2005), finds that 19 percent of interventions involved transfers of assets or other type of assistance in addition to depositors pay-off in the period 1993 to 2003.

1.2 *Should prudential supervisors' discretion to exercise forbearance be reduced?*

A key component of any regulatory and supervisory arrangement is the nature, timing and form of intervention (Llewellyn, 2002). Any supervisory system must determine what discretionary measures may be taken by the supervisors and who has authority to authorize those measures. It must also determine (at least implicitly) whether supervisors should be required to intervene in a prespecified manner at a predetermined point. PCA accepts longstanding US policy that gives the supervisors broad powers to intervene at their own discretion. The key innovation of PCA is that it reduces supervisory discretion to exercise forbearance by requiring supervisory action as a bank's capital falls through a declining set of capital adequacy thresholds.

One argument against mandating supervisory actions in certain circumstances is that retaining supervisory discretion to exercise forbearance increases the probability that a distressed bank will recover. This lack of discretion is particularly criticized with respect to mandatory reorganization which eliminates any prospect that banks with very low capital will recover. The problem with this analysis, as noted above, is that it implicitly assumes that PCA will not affect the probability that a bank will become financially distressed.

The general concept that supervisors should intervene promptly is reflected in three of the four principles in Pillar 2 of the new Capital Accord. Principle 2 of Pillar 2 calls for supervisory evaluation of bank's internal procedures for maintaining adequate capital and take appropriate supervisory action if they are not satisfied. Principle 3 states that supervisors should expect banks to operate above the minimum regulatory capital ratios and should have the ability to require banks to operate above the minimum. Principle 4 establishes that supervisors should intervene at an early stage to prevent individual bank's capital from falling below the minimum requirements and require rapid remedial action. These remedial actions establish the principle of early intervention. However, Pillar 2 contains neither mandatory nor discretionary provisions to replenish capital and turn trouble institutions around before insolvency. Moreover, it does not contain a closure rule.

Principles 2, 3 and 4 of Pillar 2 of the new Basel Accord constitute a step in the right direction but they fall short of a PCA policy. A more structured prudential performance benchmark would make the imposition of sanctions more credible, further discouraging poor agent behavior of prudential supervisors.

1.3 *Should banks be closed with positive regulatory capital?*

Both SEIR and PCA call for timely resolution, which is a policy where banks with sufficiently low but still positive, equity capital are forced into resolution. In the US, resolution is understood to include: (1) the government assuming control of the failed bank, firing the senior managers and eliminating equity holders role in governance, and (2) the government returning the bank's assets to private control through some combination of sale to a healthy bank or banks, new equity issue and liquidation.

Timely resolution provides two important benefits. First, forcing a bank into resolution while it still has positive regulatory capital truncates the value of the deposit insurance put option, reducing the incentive of the bank's shareholders to support excess risk taking. Second, timely resolution is critical to limiting deposit insurance losses.

Timely resolution in the US was perceived by some authors as the government taking private property (Horvitz, 1995). The key argument against the claim that timely resolution involves taking shareholders' property is that PCA provides the shareholders with an opportunity to recapitalize the bank before the bank is forced into resolution. If the shareholders are unwilling to recapitalize the bank and unable to sell it to a healthy bank, that suggests that the owners and other banks agree the bank is no longer financially viable.

Outside the US, Mexico and Korea enforce a closure rule at a level of regulatory capital ratio above 0 percent. In Europe, as highlighted by Mayes *et al.* (2001), with only limited exceptions, supervisors have limited legal powers to intervene if a bank becomes critically under-capitalized.

2. Institutional Preconditions for a Successful PCA

Countries differ in their institutional structures for prudential supervision and mechanisms for resolving insolvent banks. SEIR takes as given some important US institutional structures and some of the structures are critical to the successful implementation of SEIR/PCA. While the other adopters of PCA (Korea, Japan and Mexico) made some institutional changes around the time of their adoption of PCA, their institutions lacked some features that are important to the implementation of PCA. Similarly, many of member states of the EU do not meet all of the preconditions for an effective PCA.

This section considers a number of important prerequisites for PCA to be an effective policy. Our goals are two-fold, first, to explain why the authority or resource is necessary, and second, to show that those preconditions are, in most instances, already called for by the Core Principles for Effective Banking Supervision issued by the Basel Committee, although none of these principles prescribe PCA.

2.1 *Supervisory independence and accountability*

PCA retained US bank supervisors' authority to intervene without prior political or judicial approval in a variety of ways if the bank was violating a specific statute or regulation, or if the supervisors concluded it was being operated in an unsafe or unsound manner. The major change resulting from PCA is that, after its implementation, the supervisors were required to intervene as a bank's regulatory capital ratio deteriorated.

The independence of supervisory action provided to supervisors before PCA is critical to its effective operation. A system that requires the prior approval of political or judicial authorities creates the potential for delay and forbearance in supervisory intervention to the extent that such approval is not automatic and immediate.

The requirement for supervisory independence does not imply that supervisors should be free to operate outside the political and legal system. Indeed, the US version of PCA sought to strengthen that accountability by requiring inspector general reports when a bank failed with material losses to the deposit insurer.[1] The key is that the supervisors should be accountable after supervisory intervention to the judicial system for the legality of their actions and to the political authorities for the appropriateness of their actions.

Korea, Japan and Mexico had issues related to the ability of supervisors to take independent actions at the time they adopted PCA. The International Monetary Fund expressed concern about the lack of budgetary independence for Japan (2003b, p. 38) and Mexico (2001, p. 65). The International Monetary Fund also stated the need for greater legal protection for supervisors in the good faith exercise of their duties for Korea (2003a, p. 35) and Mexico (2001, p. 67). Further, the International Monetary Fund (2003a, p. 36) stated that there was scope for strengthening and clarifying the supervisor's authority to initiate enforcement actions in Korea.

---

[1] For example, the FDIC Office of Inspector General's report on material losses incurred at South Pacific Bank may be found at http://www.fdicig.gov/reports03/03-036-508.shtml. Canada is the only other country in the OECD where the Office of the Auditor General does have similar responsibilities regarding the Superintendent of Financial Institutions (see www.oag-bvg.gc.ca). At the time of writing this article, in the UK, the National Audit Office (NAO) has publicly announced that it will look at the Financial Services Authority (FSA) cost effectiveness management and its role in fighting financial crime in the UK.

The Basel Committee on Banking Supervision recognized the importance of supervisory operational independence by making independence part of its first Core Principle for Effective Bank Supervision.[2]

Nieto and Wall (2006, Table 1) summarize the extent of compliance by various European countries at the time of their respective Financial Sector Stability Assessments. Their results suggest that political independence of European banking supervisors is generally adequate despite concerns in some countries. For example, they note that in some countries, the presence of the government representatives on their supervisory boards could potentially raise the issue of independence from the government. The extent to which the supervisors are able to act independent of the judiciary varies by country. In some countries, such as France, the prudential supervisor is an administrative judiciary authority when imposing sanctions, and its decisions and sanctions can only be challenged before the highest administrative judicial authority. However, in other countries, such as Austria, the legal system puts in some cases the burden of the proof on the supervisors before they can take remedial action. The legal protection of supervisors for their actions taken in good faith in their office also varies from country to country. In Italy, the law does not provide such legal protection to its supervisors against court proceedings.

2.2 *Adequate authority*

PCA requires that the prudential supervisors be given authority to intervene in undercapitalized banks, both as a deterrent to risk taking by healthy banks and as an incentive to try to rebuild capital at undercapitalized banks. If a bank's regulatory capital drops below minimal acceptable levels, PCA requires that the bank be placed in resolution. The need for adequate authority is also recognized by the Basel Committee on Banking Supervision in Core Principle for Effective Bank Supervision 22. The PCA policy applied in the US goes beyond this Core Principle only in that supervisors have direct authority to revoke the license, whereas the Core Principle allows for the possibility that the supervisor may only be able to recommend revocation.

---

[2] The Core Principles were issued by the Basel Committee in September 1997, and endorsed by the international financial community during the annual meeting of the IMF and World Bank in Hong Kong in October, 1997 (http://www.bis.org/publ/bcbs30.pdf).

The International Monetary Fund (2003b) did not point to any inadequacies in the remedial actions that may be taken by Japanese supervisors with respect to PCA. However, the International Monetary Fund (2001, p. 65) noted that the Mexican Ministry of Finance and Public Credit rather than the bank supervisor is responsible for revoking banking licenses. The International Monetary Fund (2003a, p. 36) said that the Korean supervisor had access to the *"full range of remedial measures"* but there was *"scope to strengthen and clarify"* the supervisor's *"powers to initiate enforcement actions"*.

Nieto and Wall (2006, table 1) show that European countries' degree of compliance with this principle varied by country. In a number of countries, the banking law provides supervisors with a wide range of possible corrective actions depending on the severity of the situation. Moreover, if the prudential supervisor does not take immediate action, firms and/or individuals may raise this in a proceeding against them under the general jurisdiction of the courts and Tribunal. In some other countries, such as Finland, Sweden, and Iceland, prudential supervisory powers do not contemplate the ability to restrict asset transfer or to suspend payments to shareholder and/or to purchase banks own shares. In still other countries, such as Italy, Austria and Sweden, legislators do not provide prudential supervisors with authority to bar appointment of individuals from banking once the person has been hired and passed the initial fit and proper test. Although the decision to revoke a bank's license corresponds to the supervisory authority, in a number of countries the government must formally approve the license withdrawal or adoption of specific crisis procedures. Last but not least, in some of the recent entrants in the EU, the ability of the supervisor to address safety and soundness issues in banks is significantly encumbered by its institutional capacity and resources.

2.3 *Adequate resolution procedures*

Confidence in the resolution procedure is critical if bank prudential supervisors are to enforce the timely resolution embedded in PCA. Bank supervisors are likely to resist forcing a bank into resolution if they know it will result in major disruption, such as when the deposit insurer lacks adequate funds to honor its commitments or the resolution procedures were likely to result in severe market disruption.

In the US, the bank insolvency procedure is administered by the Federal Deposit Insurance Corporation (FDIC). If a private sector resolution cannot be worked out, the FDIC places the bank in receivership. As receiver, the FDIC can limit creditors' ability to withdraw funds and can allocate losses in excess of equity to the uninsured creditors. The FDIC typically limits depositors' loss of liquidity by providing insured depositors with immediate access to their funds and uninsured depositors at domestic offices with access to at least part of their funds.

Japan had been refining its framework for resolving failing banks prior to its adoption of PCA, according to the International Monetary Fund (2003b, p. 36), with the report's primary recommendation for improved pre-crisis communication between the Financial Services Authority, the Bank of Japan and the Deposit Insurance Corporation. At the time of adoption, the Korean resolution arrangements were largely based on the procedures needed to address the financial crisis so the International Monetary Fund (2003a, p. 31) called on the Korean authorities to review their resolution arrangements.[3] The International Monetary Fund (2001, p. 18) discussion of Mexico went further calling for the development of *"an adequate framework for closing, resolving and liquidating nonviable banks"*.

European prudential supervisors have a limited set of options in dealing with a distressed bank, albeit there is considerable variation across countries. Some European prudential supervisors (Germany, Italy and Switzerland) can impose a moratorium on debt enforcement prior to the bank being placed into bankruptcy. However, not all supervisors have this power and in countries, such as the United Kingdom, France, Spain and Luxembourg, bank supervisors have to apply to the courts. Such measures are typically accompanied with direct or indirect control by a provisional administrator on bank's management. Hüpkes (2005) describes the suspension and appointment of a provisional administrator as a "quasi-insolvency" procedure, which gives the provisional administrator wide ranging powers to bring about a resolution, including the sale of new stock and the transfer of ownership.

If a bank cannot be made viable under a payments suspension and the appointment of provisional administrator, the alternative is liquidation.

---

[3] The Korean Board of Audit and Inspection recently issued a report alleging that the chief executive of Korean Exchange Bank understated the bank's capital adequacy ratio so that the bank would be deemed to be "troubled" and subject to purchase by a foreign buyer in 2003 according to Santini (2006). The report further alleges that Korean regulators did not adequately check to confirm the bank's condition. These reports taken on added importance as the buyer of the bank, Lone Star Funds, is reselling the bank at a profit of $4.5 billion on an investment of $1.2 billion. This controversy highlights the importance of transparency in supervisory determination of capital and both openness and transparency in the sale of failing banks.

Hüpkes (2005) comes to the conclusion that the administration of bank insolvency proceedings is regarded as a judicial function in most European jurisdictions. In some countries, such as the United Kingdom, the courts rely entirely on general corporate bankruptcy procedures; whereas in other countries, such as Austria, Belgium, Germany, Italy, Luxembourg, the Netherlands and Portugal, special rules or exemptions to the general bankruptcy law are established in the banking law.

Hüpkes (2005) analysis suggests that the existing legal framework offers European prudential supervisors two suboptimal options for addressing an insolvent bank: (1) limited provisional administration, which may not be sufficient to bring about efficient resolution, or (2) turning the problem over to a bankruptcy court.

Not only are failed banks typically resolved through regular corporate bankruptcy proceedings, but the Directive 94/19/EC on deposit guarantee schemes also does not require that depositors will have immediate access to their funds. Estonia, Hungary, Poland and Slovenia are the only European countries whose legislators have set more ambitious timing for the receipt of compensation (Garcia and Nieto, 2005). The potential delay in providing depositors with access to their funds may have macroeconomic consequences that would encourage authorities with responsibility for macroeconomic conditions to promote supervisory forbearance. Dermine (1996, p. 680) stated that:

> The issue is not so much the fear of a domino effect where the failure of a large bank would create the failure of many smaller ones; strict analysis of counterparty exposures has reduced substantially the risk of a domino effect. The fear is rather that the need to close a bank for several months to value its illiquid assets would freeze a large part of deposit and savings, causing a significant negative effect on national consumption.

Although resolution policy has largely been left to its member states, the EU has addressed some of the potential problems with reorganizing and winding up credit institutions that operate across member boundaries. The Reorganization and Winding up Directive for EU Credit Institutions (Directive 2001/24/EC of the European Parliament and of the Council of April 4)[4] has harmonized the rules of private international law applicable to bank collective proceedings with the aim of ensuring the mutual

---

[4] Official Journal of the European Communities L125, May 5, 2001. At the time of writing this article, implementation was pending in four member states: Czech Republic, Greece, Portugal and Sweden.

recognition by member states of the national measures relating to the reorganization and administrative or court-based liquidation of EU banks which have branches in other member states. Hence, the Directive has not harmonized the national banking and bankruptcy laws on those aspects dealing with banks' reorganization and liquidation procedures.

2.4 *Accurate and timely financial information*

Arguably, the biggest weakness of PCA is its reliance on regulatory capital measures of a bank's capital, measures which may significantly deviate from the bank's economic capital. Banks that are threatened by PCA mandated supervisory actions have a strong incentive to report inflated estimates of the value of their portfolios. The extent to which banks are allowed to overestimate their regulatory capital under PCA depends in part on the accounting rules and in part on the enforcement of the rules. In the US, PCA is vulnerable to problems both in the accounting principles and their enforcement. The weakness in the principles is that US generally accepted accounting principles (US GAAP) generally do not permit the revaluation of assets and liabilities for changes in market interest rates, the exception being securities held in a trading account or available for sale account.

The first line of defense in the US for enforcing compliance with accounting rules, especially loan-loss provisioning rules, are the external auditors of a bank. The total impact of external auditors is hard to judge, as there is rarely any public disclosure when a bank changes its asset valuation in response to its external auditor's comments. While Nieto and Wall (2006) survey of the evidence finds some support for external auditor effectiveness, they also find cases where external auditors did not adequately verify the correctness of asset valuations. To the extent that outside auditors are unable or unwilling to force banks to recognize losses in their asset portfolios, PCA depends on the effectiveness of bank examinations by the supervisory agencies. Yet, relying on the supervisors to enforce honest accounting creates a contradiction in PCA. PCA is designed to limit supervisory discretion in enforcing capital adequacy, yet PCA will only be fully effective if the bank supervisors use their discretion in conducting on-site examinations to force timely recognition of declines in portfolio value.

The vulnerability in enforcement is highlighted by Eisenbeis and Wall's (2002) finding that deposit insurance losses at failed banks in the US did not decrease as a proportion of the failed bank's assets after the adoption of PCA, as should have happened if the supervisors were following timely resolution.[5] Their findings suggest that bank supervisors do not always enforce timely recognition of losses.

The respective International Monetary Fund reports prepared shortly after the adoption of PCA, for Korea and Mexico noted opportunities for improving the available information. The International Monetary Fund (2003a, p. 36) highlighted the scope for "strengthening and clarifying comprehensive loan evaluation methodologies and adherence to provisioning criteria" in Korea. In its analysis of Mexico, the International Monetary Fund (2001, p. 66) stated that it was of the "utmost importance to foster greater contribution from the external auditors coupled with the appropriate accountability". The Japanese banking system required substantial recapitalization at the time of the adoption of PCA and many banks would have faced severe disciplinary measures or closure if their reported regulatory capital accurately reflected the resources available to absorb unexpected losses. The International Monetary Fund (2003b, pp. 18–19) expressed particular concern that reported capital overstated the ability to take unexpected losses due to Japanese banks' accounting for tax deferred assets and loan-loss allowances.

The EU is addressing the problems in obtaining accurate and timely information. Although in the EU, member states have traditionally had different supervisory requirements and accounting rules, harmonization has gathered further momentum in the recent years to comply with the International Financial Reporting Standards (IFRS).[6] Most importantly, IFRS requires fair value accounting which takes account of changes in portfolio value due to interest rate changes. With very few exceptions, EU banks are required to present audited financial statements. Most, but not all, EU supervisors also supplement bank auditing with on-site examinations to verify banks' reported financial condition.

One way of reducing the vulnerability of PCA to over-estimates of capital is to supplement regulatory capital ratios with market data in setting the tripwires between different PCA categories. For example, Evanoff and Wall (2002) propose using the spread between the yield on subordinated

---

[5] Note, however, Kane *et al.* (2006) findings that many problem banks have recapitalized themselves (including via sale to another bank) rather than risk being resolved by the FDIC.

[6] Directive 2003/51/CE of the European Parliament and of the Council of 18 June, 2003 (Official Journal of the European Communities L 178/16).

debt and other debt securities of comparable maturity as a trigger for PCA sanctions at the largest US banks.

3. Conclusions

Prompt corrective supervisory action seeks to minimize expected losses to the deposit insurer and taxpayer by limiting supervisors' ability to engage in forbearance. Along with reducing taxpayer losses, PCA should also reduce banks' incentive to engage in moral hazard behavior by reducing or eliminating the subsidy to risk-taking provided by mispriced deposit insurance. These potential benefits from PCA appear to have been recognized, as reflected in the increasing number of recommendations to policymakers to introduce PCA type of provisions in their national legislation. Japan, Korea and, more recently, Mexico have adopted this prudential policy. However, an effective PCA policy requires, on one hand, the acceptance of key aspects of the philosophy underlying SEIR/PCA, and on the other, an institutional framework supportive of supervisors' disciplinary action.

Three aspects of the philosophy underlying SEIR/PCA are critical to its effective operation. First, the primary goal of prudential supervisors should be to minimize deposit insurance losses, a goal which is also likely to result in a reduction in the expected social costs of financial problems. A second part of the SEIR/PCA philosophy is that prudential supervisory discretion to engage in forbearance should be limited. The third critical part of PCA follows from the first two parts; banks should be subject to mandatory closure at positive levels of regulatory capital ratio. This provides an incentive to banks' managers to recapitalize the bank or look for a healthy merger partner and, ultimately, contribute to reduce the cost of deposit insurance.

An institutional framework supportive of prudential supervision disciplinary action is based on four preconditions, which, are in most instances called for by the Core Principles issued by the Basel Committee on Banking Supervision although they do not prescribe PCA.

First, supervisors must have operational independence from the political and judicial systems. Secondly, supervisors must have access to a broad range of supervisory measures to bring about timely corrective action including the license withdrawal requirement. Thirdly, the supervisors must be provided with adequate resolution procedures. Finally, prudential supervisors must have access to accurate and timely financial information on banks' financial condition. The accuracy of banks' financial information depends on both the accounting principles used to measure capital that should reflect the market value of banks' assets and liabilities and the enforcement of those accounting principles.

PCA may be adopted without meeting all of these conditions, as has happened in Korea, Japan and Mexico. However, failure to meet the conditions is likely to result in a less effective implementation of PCA. In the EU, substantial changes would be desirable even if the EU does not adopt PCA, but they are critical to the implementation of a PCA that is as effective as the PCA currently is in the US.

References

Bank for International Settlements (2003). Markets for subordinated debt and equity in Basel Committee member countries. Basel Committee on Banking Supervision, Working Paper No. 12.

Benink, H. and G.J. Benston (2005). The future of banking regulation in developed countries: Lessons from and for Europe. Mimeo.

Benston, G.J. and G.G. Kaufman (1995). Is the banking and payments system fragile?. *Journal of Financial Services Research*, 9, 209–240.

Benston, G.J. and G.G. Kaufman (1998). *Risk and Solvency Regulation of Depositor Institutions: Past Policies and Current Options*. New York: Salomon Brothers Center, Graduate School of Business, New York University.

Brewer, E., H. Genay, W.C. Hunter and G.G. Kaufman (2003). The value of banking relationships during a financial crisis: Evidence from failures of Japanese banks. *Journal of Japanese and International Economies*, 17, 233–262.

Carnell, R.S. (1993). The culture of ad hoc discretion. In *Assessing Bank Reform: FDICIA One Year Later*, G. Kaufman and R. Litan (eds.), pp. 113–121. Washington: The Brookings Institution.

De Cesare, M. (2005). Report on deposit insurance: An international outlook. Working Paper 8, Fondo Interbancario di Tutela dei Depositi.

Dermine, J. (1996). Comment. *Swiss Journal of Economics and Statistics*, 132, 679–682.

Eisenbeis, R.A. and L.D. Wall (2002). The major supervisory initiatives post-FCICIA: Are they based on the goals of PCA? Should they Be? In *Prompt Corrective Action in Banking: 10 Years Later*, G. Kaufman (ed.), pp. 109–142. Volume 14 of Research in Financial Services: Private and Public Policy, JAI.

European Shadow Financial Regulatory Committee (1998). Statement no. 1, Dealing with problem banks in Europe. Center for Economic Policy Studies, 22 June.

European Shadow Financial Regulatory Committee Statement (2005). No. 23, Reforming banking supervision in Europe. 21 November.

Evanoff, D.D. and L.D. Wall (2002). Subordinated debt and prompt corrective regulatory action. In *Prompt Corrective Action in Banking: 10 Years Later*, G. Kaufman (ed.), pp. 53–119. Amsterdam: JAI.

Evanoff, D.D. and L.D. Wall (2002), Sub-debt yield spreads as bank risk measures. *Journal of Banking and Finance*, 26, 989–1009.

Garcia, G. and M.J. Nieto (2005). Banking crisis management in the European Union: Multiple regulators and resolution authorities. *Journal of Banking Regulation*, 6, 206–226.

Goldstein, M. and P. Turner (1996) Banking crises in emerging economies: Origins and policy options. BIS Economic Papers, No. 46 October.

Goldstein, M. (1997). The case for an international banking standard. Policy Analyses in International Economics, No. 47, April. Washington DC: Institute of International Economics.

Horvitz, P.M. (1995). Banking regulation as a solution to financial fragility. *Journal of Financial Services Research*, 9, 369–380.

Hüpkes, E. (2005). Insolvency — Why a special regime for banks? In *Current Developments in Monetary and Financial Law*, Vol.3. Washington DC: International Monetary Fund.

Hüpkes, E., M. Quintyn and M.W. Taylor (2005). The accountability of financial sector supervisors: Principles and practice. IMF Working Paper, March, No. 51.

International Monetary Fund (2001). Mexico financial system assessment program. October, http://www.imf.org/external/pubs/ft/scr/2001/cr01192.pdf

International Monetary Fund (2003a). Republic of Korea financial sector stability assessment. March, http://www.imf.org/external/pubs/ft/scr/2003/cr0381.pdf

International Monetary Fund (2003b). Japan financial sector stability assessment. September http://www.imf.org/external/pubs/ft/scr/2003/cr03287.pdf

Kane, E.J., R.L. Bennett and R. Oshinsky (2006). Evidence of improved monitoring and insolvency resolution under FDICIA. Mimeo.

Kaufman, G.G. (1988) Bank runs: Causes, benefits, and costs. *Cato Journal*, 7, 559–594.

Llewellyn, D.T. (2002). Comment. In *Prompt Corrective Action: Ten Years Later*, G. Kaufman (ed.), pp. 321–333. Amsterdam: JAI.

Mayes, D.G., L. Halme and A. Liuksila (2001). *Improving Banking Supervision*. Basingstoke: Palgrave.

Mayes, D. (2005). Implications of Basel II for the European financial system. Presentation at the Center for European Policy Studies.

Mayes, D.G. M.J. Nieto, and L.D. Wall (2006). Multiple safety net regulators and agency problems in the EU: Is prompt corrective action partly the solution? Mimeo.

Nieto, M.J. and L.D. Wall (2006). Preconditions for a successful implementation of supervisors' prompt corrective action: Is there a case for a banking standard in the EU? *Journal of Banking Regulation*, 17, 191–220.

Santini, L. (2006) Lone star is cleared in probe of KEB deal: Korean board faults former bank officials in 2003 transaction. *Wall Street Journal*, June 20, p. A13.

Insolvency Resolution: Key Issues Raised by the Papers

Peter G. Brierley*
Bank of England

1. Introduction

The three papers in this session raise a number of key issues relating to the optimal resolution of banks, in particular those large banks whose failure is likely to have systemic consequences ("systemic banks"). Maria Nieto and Larry Wall focus mainly on issues relating to domestic banks, with an emphasis on the advantages of the US approach involving prompt corrective action (PCA) and least cost resolution (LCR). They rightly note that early intervention by the banking supervisory authorities, that is, before the bank reaches a state of insolvency, is likely to increase the chances of an orderly resolution of the bank. The use of predefined triggers for intervention is seen as beneficial in terms of promoting greater clarity and reducing the risks of regulatory forbearance. Their paper raises the question of the extent to which banking supervisors should have special powers to initiate and conduct bank resolutions and, even more fundamentally, whether banks should be resolved under a separate regime from that applying to companies in general.

Both Rosa Lastra and David Mayes focus more specifically on the issues that arise in an international context when systemic banks with cross-border operations need to be resolved. Both cover such thorny issues as too-big-to-fail (TBTF) and problems that stem from the structure of international banks or large and complex financial institutions (LCFIs). Rosa Lastra looks at existing international agreements to resolve cross-border systemic banks and the extent to which these may be undermined by different approaches to insolvency, not least those based on universality

*Peter G. Brierley is a special adviser in the financial stability area at the Bank of England. The views expressed represent the author's views and not necessarily those of the Bank of England.

on the one hand and territoriality on the other (the old dichotomy between single- and separate-entity resolution and liquidation). These different approaches can lead to conflicts of interest between home and host authorities, which are investigated in David Mayes' paper. In my own remarks this morning, I will try to cover all these issues in the context of the key theme of the optimal way to resolve systemic banks.

2. The Authorities' Objectives in Bank Resolution

In determining this optimal approach, it is necessary first to specify precisely the main objective of the financial authorities (ministries of finance, central banks and financial regulators). I take this to be to achieve an orderly and efficient resolution of a systemic bank. The insolvency literature postulates that an orderly and efficient resolution is one which achieves the following: (1) it limits as far as possible the systemic risks to financial stability from the bank's failure; (2) it maximizes as far as possible the value of the bank's continuing franchise; (3) it preserves the continuity of the bank's existing contractual commitments; (4) it penalizes managers and shareholders of the bank insofar as they are responsible for the bank's failure; (5) it treats creditors of the bank equitably, maintaining their priority ranking as far as appropriate; and (6) it reimburses insured depositors up to the limit of the deposit insurance scheme as rapidly as possible.

In an ideal world, the various options for resolving banks, whether they be private sector solutions — mergers and acquisitions (M&As) or purchase and assumptions (P&As) — or public sector interventions — bridge banks, some form of nationalization, or liability guarantees — need to be considered against these key *desiderata*. In the real world, of course, things are not so simple. First, in a crisis there may well simply not be enough time to make this evaluation. Second, even if it can be made, it is highly likely that each resolution option will achieve some of the requirements for an orderly and efficient resolution but not others. In some cases, this may reflect a conflict or tension between different objectives. In what follows, I try to illustrate this by looking at some key issues raised by the papers.

3. The Financial Stability–Moral Hazard Trade-Off

Consider first the preservation of financial stability. A crucial issue raised by the failure of a systemic bank is how to balance the need to maintain financial stability with the need to contain moral hazard. The trade-off between these two objectives is not straightforward. Financial stability in the present may best be secured by the provision of support to a failed large bank, but the moral hazard that arises from the perception that this will make future assistance to similarly situated large banks more likely may jeopardize financial stability in future. This issue of too-big-to-fail is emphasized by both Rosa Lastra and David Mayes. The problem arises to the extent that stakeholders of banks deemed TBTF attach less weight to effective monitoring of their activities, thereby encouraging greater risk-taking on the part of such banks. In fact, research carried out at the Bank of England has found little evidence that large banks deemed TBTF necessarily take on more risk than smaller banks, although clearly they have a funding advantage.[1] But this does not negate the significance of the moral hazard issue, since that really relates to whether TBTF banks take on more risk than they would do if they were not deemed TBTF.

4. Constructive Ambiguity versus Transparency

So how best to reduce the moral hazard that arises if market participants believe that systemic banks will inevitably be bailed out? Many approaches rely on "constructive ambiguity", not so much about whether the systemic bank will be resolved in some way rather than liquidated as about the method that will be used and the extent to which it will impose losses on the shareholders, management, subordinated debt holders, uninsured depositors and unsecured creditors of the bank. The alternative to constructive ambiguity is transparency, which is supported strongly in the Nieto–Wall paper. This argues that such transparency is facilitated by the clear and public triggers for intervention in the US PCA approach, which increases the likelihood of early intervention to solve problems experienced by large banks deemed TBTF. On this view, increased transparency in the restructuring process helps to counteract any tendency towards regulatory forbearance. It also arguably provides a degree of accountability that is missing in an ambiguous approach. I would just note in passing that even the very transparent US approach, based on the Federal Deposit Insurance Corporation Improvement Act, PCA and LCR, does not do

---

[1] See F. Soussa, 2000, "Too Big to Fail: Moral Hazard and Unfair Competition", in *Financial Stability and Central Banks: Selected Issues for Financial Safety Nets and Market Discipline*, Bank of England, Center for Central Banking Studies.

away entirely with constructive ambiguity given the existence of the "systemic risk exemption" to the LCR principle (sometimes known, of course, as the TBTF exemption).

5. Avoidance of Insolvency

What the Nieto–Wall paper does highlight, quite rightly in my view, is the importance of avoiding insolvency if at all possible in the systemic bank case. So PCA and structured early intervention and resolution (SEIR) can be regarded as an essential pre-emptive strike against insolvency. As my former colleague at the Bank of England, Charles Goodhart, has emphasized, the first-best solution to dealing with a large bank in financial difficulty is to reorganize it and establish new management before losses accumulate to a level likely to exhaust economic capital.[2] This is one of the strongest arguments in favor of PCA/SEIR.

Several other writers have also made the point that banks whose failure poses a systemic threat should ideally be prevented from ever reaching a formal insolvency procedure.[3] These authors suggest that one means of doing so would be through mechanisms for coordinating a voluntary workout of the bank. A major problem, however, is that this could only succeed on the basis of a full exchange of timely, accurate and consolidated information between relevant market counterparties of the bank, who would need to recognize that it was in their interests to bring about an informal but coordinated resolution. Such "enlightened self-interest" might be more effective than an unrestricted exercise of close-out and collateral rights in returning a distressed large bank to economic viability or at least allowing time for it to be restructured so that it no longer poses a systemic threat. It might perhaps be facilitated by the financial authorities, in much the same way that the Bank of England facilitated the successful restructuring of many UK companies in the 1980s and 1990s under the "London Approach." Such approaches, however, are generally based on

[2] See C. A. E. Goodhart, 2004, "Multiple Regulators and Resolutions", paper presented to Federal Reserve Bank of Chicago Conference on Systemic Financial Crises: Resolving Large Bank Insolvencies, September 30–October 1.

[3] See, for example, R. R. Bliss, 2003, "Resolving Large Complex Financial Organizations", *Federal Reserve Bank of Chicago* and R. A. Eisenbeis, W. Scott Frame, and L. D. Wall, 2004, "Resolving Large Financial Intermediaries: Banks versus Housing Enterprises", Federal Reserve Bank of Atlanta, working paper, No. 2004-23a, October.

consensus, which is much more difficult to achieve for an international bank whose creditors and counterparties are spread around the globe.

One final point, which is noted in the Nieto–Wall paper, is that it is not always straightforward to export certain features of PCA to countries with a tradition of resolving banks using the general (that is, corporate) insolvency law (such as the UK). That law generally prevents companies from entering insolvency proceedings until they are either cash-flow or balance-sheet insolvent. It then puts the onus on specialized insolvency practitioners, working through bankruptcy courts, to resolve the company. Any attempt by the financial authorities, most notably the banking regulators, to bring about an early reorganization of the bank, involving in particular the removal of management and the penalization of shareholders, may well not be possible under insolvency and company law or, at the very least, could lead to legal action being brought against the authorities. A change to this state of affairs would require a fundamental overhaul of insolvency law in those countries.

6. Preserving a Large Bank's Systemic Activities

In practice, an orderly and effective resolution of a systemic bank needs to focus on preserving the bank's systemic functions. The key point here from the viewpoint of moral hazard is that this is not the same as rescuing the bank itself. The work of Eva Hüpkes has been very important in articulating exactly what this does involve: basically identifying the bank's systemic activities — no easy task in itself — and then adopting measures to insulate them from disruption.[4] Hüpkes specifies three main insulation options: replacement of the bank as the provider of all the systemic activities by another large financial institution, dismemberment of the large bank and detachment of the systemic functions; and immunization of the systemic functions from the bank's failure. There are difficulties involved with all these options, especially in a cross-border context, but there can be little doubt that an orderly resolution will need to involve one or more of them.

---

[4] See E. H. G. Hüpkes, 2004, "Too Big to Save — Toward a Functional Approach to Resolving Crises in Global Financial Institutions", paper presented to Federal Reserve Bank of Chicago Conference on Systemic Financial Crises: Resolving Large Bank Insolvencies, September 30–October 1.

7. Exercise of Close-Out/Termination and Collateral Rights

One of the most important issues facing a systemic bank resolution concerns the exercise by market counterparties of their close-out/termination rights and the realization of collateral. The issue here is whether financial stability is best preserved by allowing the full exercise of these rights, on the grounds that they are necessary to the continued smooth functioning of financial markets and the credit intermediation process. This is the approach adopted in most EU countries, where exceptions to insolvency law (and in particular to the automatic moratorium or stay that comes into effect in many insolvency proceedings) to protect these contractual rights have been adopted over the years. Any change to these rights would require substantial amendments not only to domestic law and private sector agreements, but also to EU directives. But the full and unrestricted exercise of these rights may interfere with the ability to transfer good assets to another institution in a P&A or to a bridge bank by undermining the value and integrity of the entity's existing business in any transfer as a going concern. This suggests that there may be a case for, at least, imposing a short temporary limit on the exercise of close-out and termination rights, on the grounds that such a limit may improve the prospects for resolving the bank. The US financial authorities have such a delaying power in bank resolutions and regard it as a crucial precondition for a private sector or bridge bank resolution.

8. A Separate Regime for Bank Insolvency

This difference between the EU and US approaches brings us back to a fundamental issue raised by the Nieto–Wall paper: Should there be a separate insolvency regime for banks? This is the approach adopted not only in the US, but also in Canada, Japan, Australia and Switzerland. Certain other countries, notably Hong Kong and New Zealand, allow financial stability considerations to be prominent in bank resolutions. The main argument for such a separate regime relates to the distinguishing features of a bank failure, in particular the reasons why such a failure may have more widespread consequences than that of a similarly sized nonfinancial company. The World Bank (2003) lists four such reasons: (1) a large bank failure may disrupt the operation of payment and settlement systems; (2) it may cause significant losses to creditor counterparties in the interbank markets; (3) the creditors of a failed bank include large groups of depositors, many of whom are unlikely to be able to mitigate risks or bear losses; and (4) it can trigger a systemic crisis through contagion, jeopardizing otherwise healthy banks and disrupting the intermediation functions of the financial system.[5] The crucial role of confidence, together with the potential for contagion in the banking case, mean that the time available to reach a decision on resolution is likely to be much shorter than in the corporate case.

These factors have motivated the US approach, which involves a combination of a separate insolvency regime for banks with the kind of early intervention emphasized by Maria Nieto and Larry Wall. They see among the advantages of such an approach its greater clarity and its avoidance of any tendency to forbearance on the part of the regulatory authorities. But it also gives vital powers to the financial authorities and banking supervisors, such as the sole right to initiate and conduct insolvency proceedings and the ability to enforce business transfers. In countries with a single (corporate) regime for insolvency, the financial authorities' powers can be circumscribed in various ways: for example, banking supervisors may have to share the right to initiate insolvency proceedings for a bank with the bank's creditors or directors; the conduct of insolvency proceedings may be in the hands of qualified insolvency practitioners, such as private sector administrators or liquidators; and the financial authorities may have limited or no statutory powers to enforce transfers of assets and liabilities. In such a regime, there may be conflicts of interest between the financial authorities and insolvency practitioners, deriving from their very different remits. Such conflicts do not exist in a separate bank insolvency regime administered by the financial authorities.

The advantages of a separate bank insolvency regime do not mean that it can be easily adopted by countries with a different institutional and legal tradition affecting insolvency. We have already noted the difficulty in such countries of initiating a bank resolution before bank capital falls to zero. And their financial authorities' preference for flexibility and constructive ambiguity in the approach to bank resolution may prejudice them against the use of the kind of pre-specified triggers for action that are a feature of PCA. This does not mean that banking supervisors in such countries have no procedures in place for turning

---

[5] See World Bank, 2003, *Global Bank Insolvency Initiative: Legal, Institutional and Regulatory Framework to Deal with Insolvent Banks*.

round underperforming banks. In the UK, for example, although the FSA does not follow a prescribed and pre-announced series of actions as a bank's performance deteriorates, it does aim to pick up any such deterioration in time for appropriate remedial action to be taken. This is done through its risk assessment approach, which seeks to identify, assess and mitigate business and control risks in financial institutions, especially those deemed to be systemic. The risk mitigation part of this process is confirmed in a plan sent to the bank, setting out the issues considered by the FSA to pose a risk to its statutory objectives and proposing actions to address these issues. The FSA then monitors the risk mitigation program to ensure that the required actions are taken by the bank within the timeframe specified.

In countries with this sort of flexible approach to bank resolution and insolvency, there are mixed views on the desirability of shifting to a separate statutory regime for bank insolvency. Switzerland, for example, has recently shifted to a separate regime, although it is interesting to note that this does not include *ex ante* mandatory intervention criteria as capital levels fall, largely reflecting the Swiss banking supervisor's preference for greater flexibility. But in the UK, it could be argued that a separate regime would require further major changes to insolvency law, both at a domestic and EU level, that would be costly and time-consuming to implement. Such changes might not be viewed as a priority given the current very low probability of a major failure at a UK-incorporated systemic bank and recent changes to the insolvency law designed to make it more equitable for creditors.

What then can be done in countries with court-based insolvency procedures emphasizing the equitable treatment of creditors to improve systemic bank resolution processes, without a major legislative overhaul? The answer is probably to move towards a mixed regime in which the general insolvency law is qualified by statutory exceptions that apply to banks and other financial firms. This approach is adopted in a number of countries, including Austria, Belgium, Germany, Italy, Luxembourg, the Netherlands and Portugal. The UK has also made moves in this direction, giving banking supervisors greater rights in insolvency procedures, providing for quicker transfers of banking business (which do not always require the consent of account holders, subject to possible court redress), and providing greater clarity on the scope and timing of automatic stays, and the nature and extent of carve-outs for netting and closeout of financial contracts and the enforcement of collateral.

9. Resolving International Banks: Key Problems

Many of these issues loom even larger in the resolution of systemic banks with cross-border operations. A number of them are discussed in detail in the papers by Rosa Lastra and David Mayes. The first point to make in this context is that the structure of international banks matters crucially in resolution proceedings, because there have to be applied to legal entities. But large and complex international banks are increasingly managed in an integrated fashion (that is, on a group-wide basis) across business or functional lines, with relatively little regard for legal entities or national borders. This makes it very difficult to map the various global lines of business and management structures of such banks into legal entities incorporated in particular jurisdictions, to which insolvency or resolution proceedings can then be applied. And the trend towards integrated group-wide centralized management may mean that local entities lack the in-house senior management, computer facilities, and relevant records and data — in other words, they lack functionality — for their business activities to be easily preserved and reopened quickly on a stand-alone basis.

An important aspect of these structural issues, considered in some detail by Rosa Lastra, concerns the relative treatment of an international bank's foreign subsidiaries and branches in an insolvency. This is especially pertinent in the EU approach to the resolution of EU banks with operations in more than one EU member state. As Lastra notes, this is based on the EU Bank Winding-up and Reorganization Directive of 2001. This applies a universal approach to the resolution of EU-incorporated banks and all their branches throughout the EU, which are subject to a single insolvency proceeding brought in the country of a bank's incorporation. But a crucial unresolved issue is that an EU bank's foreign subsidiaries are not treated in the same manner as its foreign branches elsewhere in the EU. Given that these subsidiaries are separately incorporated in their host countries, the host member states will be able to bring separate insolvency proceedings in respect of such subsidiaries (and indeed their branches). The directive is silent on how such separate proceedings should interact with the resolution of the parent bank.

Lastra's paper also raises the old thorny issue of single-versus separate-entity resolution. Several countries, notably the US, practice separate-entity resolution of foreign banks, usually involving the ring-fencing of local assets. This can undermine an orderly and efficient resolution of a non-US systemic bank with operations in the US, because the US assets

of the failed bank would not be fully consolidated in the insolvency proceeding brought by the insolvency authorities in the bank's country of
incorporation. Although the US approach is designed to protect the creditors of US entities of the foreign bank from the consequences of a failure
that may have originated in poor banking practices or inadequate supervision outside the US, it does so at the expense of creditors of other (non-US)
entities in the group. And I would agree with Lastra's argument that it
appears inconsistent with the US approach to resolving a US bank with
operations abroad, which is based on single-entity principles.

The single/separate entity issue is important because it demonstrates
that improved coordination between insolvency and financial authorities
in different jurisdictions in which a systemic bank has activities — which
most commentators regard as essential to an orderly and efficient resolution of the bank — may face serious obstacles. As David Mayes points out
in his paper, this is essentially because of potential conflicts of interest
between home and host countries. Mayes is surely right that these conflicts may be especially acute if a bank has systemic activities in more
than one country, or if it is of systemic importance in a host country where
it has branches or subsidiaries but not in its home country. In the branch
case, the conflict arises from the host authorities' responsibility for financial stability in the host country and the home authorities' regulatory
responsibility for host country branches. This is a particular issue for the
UK because many European banks concentrate their systemic activities in
their London branches. As Mayes has noted separately, the universal
approach of the EU directive compounds this problem, given that the host
country has to cope with the systemic problems that arise from failure but
cannot control any aspect of the resolution of the bank branch.[6]

I have already covered issues relating to the enforceability of financial contract law and the preservation of financial stability in the context
of resolving domestic systemic banks. These issues are even more difficult to address in international bank resolutions. There will be differences
across countries in the treatment of secured creditors, rights to set-off and
netting, enforcement of collateral and finality of transactions. For example, there is no international convention providing for set-off in one jurisdiction to be recognized elsewhere or which specifies which system of

---

[6] See D. G. Mayes, 2004, "The Role of the Safety Net in Resolving Large Financial
Institutions", in D. D. Evanoff and G. G. Kaufman, eds., *Systemic Financial Crises:
Resolving Large Bank Insolvencies*, Singapore: World Scientific.

law governs parties' rights. And there will be differences in the manner in which different countries seek to preserve financial stability following a systemic bank failure. If that were not enough, all these problems will be compounded in the resolution of LCFIs, whose non-banking activities, as David Mayes points out, may well be subject to completely different insolvency proceedings from those that apply to the banking business.

10. Resolving International Banks: Possible Solutions

So what, if anything, can be done? The literature is full of suggested solutions to the various problems highlighted by the three papers presented in this session. Some of them have indeed been considered in those papers. In evaluating these possible solutions, I would argue against imposing constraints on international banks that are economically inefficient or would inflict an undue regulatory burden on those banks. This rules out, in my view, subsidiarization requirements, which would undermine the efficient use of a bank's worldwide capital. It is also not possible for EU banks under single market legislation — there is unlikely to be a consensus, in my view again, for the necessary wholesale changes to EU directives or national legislation.

I also think that bilateral deals are not really an option. For example, it would be very difficult for the UK financial authorities to negotiate an agreement with the US authorities to resolve on a single entity basis UK banks with operations in the US in return for agreeing a similar treatment for US banks with operations in the UK. Such a deal would only be feasible if both the UK and US authorities regarded resolution by the other country's authorities as offering equivalent protection to domestic creditors of local branches of the other country's banks as would a separate resolution brought under their own rules. The US depositor preference legislation, combined with the predilection of the US authorities for ring-fencing, makes it very unlikely that both sets of authorities would come to that view.

One more interesting potential solution suggested by some commentators, including Mayes in his paper, is some form of supranational authority, for example a body that would take the lead in regulating and resolving LCFIs. The problem with that is that, in the absence of greater harmonization of insolvency law across countries, it is unlikely to be within the realms of practical politics in the foreseeable future.

Harmonization is a long way off, as shown by the fact that even the international agreements that have been negotiated so far, such as the UNCITRAL Model Law and the EU directive, still allow countries to maintain their own approaches to insolvency. Those approaches reflect major differences of view across countries in such vital policy areas as the extent to which the insolvency regime should favor debtors or creditors, as well as very distinct institutional, structural and legal frameworks governing insolvency law. In the light of these different approaches, and the lack of any mechanisms for sharing the burdens arising from the international banking crisis likely to result from an LCFI failure, it must be doubtful whether a sufficient international consensus exists for the establishment of a supranational resolution authority and an agreement on the principles underlying its operation.

In the absence of anything better, therefore, there really is little alternative to continued negotiation of information-sharing and cooperative arrangements between the financial and insolvency authorities across the relevant jurisdictions in which a bank has substantial operations. These will need not only to put in place more effective mechanisms for sharing information on and assessments of distressed international banks, but also to address the conflicts of interest that may arise across jurisdictions in the resolution of those banks.

VII. CROSS-BRODER CRISIS PREVENTION: PUBLIC AND PRIVATE STRATEGIES

Supervisory Arrangements, LOLR, and Crisis Management in a Single European Banking Market

Arnoud W. A. Boot*

University of Amsterdam and Center for Economic Policy Research

1. Introduction

The fragility of the financial system is a key public policy concern. It is widely acknowledged that stability concerns and systemic risks in banking are real and warrant regulatory scrutiny.[1] These issues have become more pertinent with the further integration of financial markets and the increasing cross-border footprint of financial institutions. For the European banking market, Schoenmaker and Oosterloo (2005) document a sizable increase in the cross-border externalities coming from the growing number of banking groups that have a significant cross-border presence. Also, as highlighted in De Nicoló and Tieman (2005), real activities have become more synchronized, exposing European Union (EU) member countries more and more to a common European business cycle.[2] These developments point at the need for an international perspective on regulation and supervision.

The focus in this paper will be on the responsibilities and powers of individual countries vis á vis those at the European level — EU and the European Central Bank (ECB). In this context, various questions will be

---

*Arnoud W. A. Boot is a professor at the University of Amsterdam, Amsterdam Center for Law & Economics (ACLE). He may be contacted at Roetersstraat 11, 1018 WB Amsterdam, The Netherlands, e-mail: a.w.a.boot@uva.nl.

[1] An initial version of this paper was prepared for February 2006 Riksbank (Central Bank of Sweden) meeting on the future regulatory framework for banks in the European Union.
[2] Simultaneously, domestic financial sectors have become more dynamic, less predictable and more exposed to competition. This has ignited a lively debate on the interaction between stability and competitiveness; see Boot and Marinc (2006) for an analysis on the interaction among competitiveness, stability and the effectiveness of regulation.

raised, in particular relating to financial stability and the effectiveness and efficiency of regulatory and supervisory arrangements. My primary focus is on the lender-of-last-resort (LOLR) and the related crisis management structure. However, I will indicate that this role, and the allocation of tasks between the ECB and national central banks, cannot be assessed independently from supervisory arrangements in the EU in general. Both supervisory and LOLR arrangements are fragmented with primary responsibilities at the national level. Key political concerns related to national sovereignty and (too much) concentrated authority at EU and ECB levels could explain this decentralized structure. I will critically evaluate these arrangements. One of my primary conclusions is that a centralization of the LOLR function within the Euro countries is urgent and actually could help facilitate convergence — and ultimately — centralization of prudential supervisory practices.

Some issues I only discuss in passing. One of those issues is the effect that the design of bankruptcy laws has. For example, the divergence between countries in bankruptcy laws and, more in general, the national focus of bankruptcy laws challenge the efficient resolution of a financial crisis involving an internationally active financial institution.[3]

The organization of the paper is as follows. Section 2 provides a characterization of (prudential) supervisory practices in the EU and notes the limited role of the ECB in this area. In Section 3, the focus shifts to the LOLR arrangements. I discuss here three things: the sources of fragility and systemic risks, the allocation of LOLR responsibilities between ECB and national central banks, and the lack of fiscal authority at the EU level. The latter may well complicate the allocation of LOLR and crisis management responsibilities because of the potential budgetary consequences of LOLR support and crisis resolution. Section 4 asks the question whether current arrangements are sustainable and, particularly, what distortions the present decentralized nature of arrangements may induce. In Section 5, I discuss which improvements could be made. Section 6 concludes.

2. A Characterization of ECB and EU Arrangements

The European regulatory architecture is best described as fragmented with primary responsibilities at the level of the individual nation states. Under

---

[3] An important issue is that in some jurisdictions, branches are ring-fenced when the foreign mother institution defaults or is in financial difficulty. Clearly this affects the resolution of financial crises.

the principles of only minimum essential harmonization, home-country control and mutual recognition of supervision embedded in the Second European Banking Directive, prudential supervision remains solidly with the home country (that is, the member state in which the financial institution has been licensed).

At this national level, a diverse assortment of institutional arrangements continues to thrive. If there is a trend, it seems that a domestically centered cross-sector integration of supervision is underway, with the fully integrated Financial Services Authority (FSA) supervisory model in the UK at the extreme. We also observe a "twin peaks" type structure — separating prudential supervision from conduct of business supervision; this structure has also gained popularity. Nevertheless, for now, a wide diversity of arrangements continues to exist. This is further highlighted by the fact that in some countries the central bank is the prudential supervisor, while in other countries — such as in the UK — prudential supervision is the task of an independent supervisory agency.

At the European level, several arrangements are in place to facilitate the supervision of cross-border activities of financial institutions. For example, the European Central Bank has a (limited) coordinating role for the lender-of-last-resort facilities that are placed in the hands of national central banks.[4] Also, various multilateral arrangements exist. Within the ECB, the Banking Supervisory Committee (BSC) brings together banking supervisors of all EU countries to discuss financial stability issues, provide macroprudential oversight, and assess draft EU and national banking legislation.

At the level of the EU, several cooperative arrangements are in place. Up to 2004, these arrangements included the Banking Advisory Committee (BAC) that advises the EU on policy matters related to bank legislation, and the Insurance Committee. In 2004, the European Parliament and the EU Council adopted a "Lamfalussy type" framework (Committee of Wise Men, 2001) based on work by the Economic and Financial Committee (EFC) — a committee advising the Ecofin Council (EFC, 2002). This framework, which initially was designed for streamlining the regulatory and supervisory practices for the European securities markets, was subsequently applied to the financial sector at large. It introduces a structure for

---

[4] The ECB has primarily a facilitating role for systemic issues. For example, its statute points explicitly at its role in promoting the smooth functioning of the payment system (Art. 3.1. and 22 of the statute; see also Art 105(2) of the Maastricht Treaty).

financial sector rulemaking at the European level.[5] In this restructuring and further formalization of the EU regulatory and supervisory framework, both the existing sectoral Bank Advisory Committee (now CEBS) and Insurance Committee (renamed CEIOPS) were being given important roles.[6]

These sectoral committees (banking, insurance and also securities, called CESR) and a separate committee addressing financial conglomerate issues are essentially put under control of the finance ministers and kept at a distance from the ECB and national central banks. Nonsupervisory national central banks and the ECB have observer status, but no voting rights. This effectively gives the ECB no formal role in (micro) prudential supervision.[7]

Some convergence and increasing coordination in supervisory practices is observed. A recent development is the EU Directive on Financial Conglomerates that allocates group-wide supervisory responsibilities to a single coordinator located in the group's home country. The hope is that the Lamfalussy approach at the EU level will lead to a further streamlining and coordination in supervisory and legislative practices, and — ultimately — convergence between member states.[8]

3. Lender of Last Resort

Bagehot's classical motivation for the LOLR was that it would lend freely to solvent but illiquid banks against good collateral at a premium price

[5] The Lamfalussy approach encompasses a four-level regulatory approach: Level 1 involves broad framework principles for legislation; level 2 detailed rules; level 3 aims at cooperation between national regulators, and level 4 addresses enforcement issues (see also Lannoo and Casey, 2005).

[6] These committees have a role at level 2 in the Lamfalussy type four layer framework (see EFC, 2002). Also the existing supervisory oriented Groupe de Contact has a role to play.

[7] The ECB has been careful in defining its role in prudential supervision. While it downplays potential conflicts of interest that may arise in combining central banking and prudential supervision (ECB, 2001), suggesting with that possibly a bigger role for itself, it simultaneously expresses that it is not aiming at a bigger role in supervision but only attempts to broaden cooperation (Duisenberg, 2003).

[8] Other arrangements are in place as well. Various bilateral arrangements, in particular memoranda of understanding (MoUs) between national supervisors, help coordinate cross-border supervision. They further clarify, on a voluntary basis, the cooperation mandated in EU directives regarding information exchange, mutual assistance, establishment procedures, and on-site examinations.

(Rochet, 2004). The reality of LOLR support in various countries in the world has been different in that net infusions of cash in troubled institutions have been quite common, in part because distinguishing between liquidity and solvency problems might be difficult.

This potential confusion and uncertainty about the true nature of illiquidity problems may have worsened over time. In particular, the proliferation of financial markets and the ways in which risks can be shifted through the system undoubtedly complicate the assessment of the fragility of the financial system. For my analysis, an understanding of the sources of fragility and their relative importance is important because it may impact the role that LOLR support plays, and this role might have changed over time. In turn, the assessment of the role of LOLR support in today's financial sector is of preeminent importance for evaluating the present EU arrangements when it comes to LOLR support and crisis management in general.[9] In Subsection 3.1, I will further elaborate on this.

Another important issue is how the LOLR role is organized in the Euro countries. The general principle is one of delegation (subsidiarity) with the LOLR role being given to national central banks. Understanding these arrangements is crucially important for assessing the effectiveness of crisis management in the Euro area. The allocation of responsibilities between national central banks and ECB with respect to LOLR support needs to be evaluated in the broader context of EU supervisory arrangements. In subsection 3.2, I will discuss the present allocation of responsibilities. A brief evaluation is contained in subsection 3.3.

3.1 *Role of lender of last resort (LOLR)*

In the classical interpretation, a financial crisis is directly linked to the notion of bank runs. In a fractional reserve system with long-term illiquid loans financed by (liquid) demandable deposits, runs may come about due to a coordination failure among depositors (Diamond and Dybvig, 1983). Even an adequately capitalized bank could be subjected to a run if the deadweight liquidation costs of assets are substantial. Regulatory interference via LOLR support, deposit insurance and/or suspension of convertibility could all help, and could even fix — in this simple setting — the

---

[9] I will focus on crisis management in the context of systemic concerns. In that case, there is a direct link between the LOLR and crisis management.

inefficiency. Observe that the externalities that a bank failure could create possibly provide a rationale for regulatory interference. These externalities could be directly related to the bank that is subjected to a potential run but also be motivated by potential contagion effects. Many have generalized this simple setting by allowing for asymmetric information and incomplete contracts; see Rochet (2004) for a review. The general conclusion is that fragility is real, and information based runs are plausible.

For the purpose of this paper two observations are important; both are related to the proliferation of financial markets. First, access to financial markets weakens the liquidity insurance feature of demand deposit contracts. To see this, note that the root cause of the fragility in the Diamond–Dybvig world is the underlying demand deposit contract. The rationale for this contract — as brought forward by Diamond and Dybvig (1983) — is the desire for liquidity insurance on the part of risk-averse depositors with uncertainty about future liquidity needs. However, as shown by Von Thadden (1998), the very presence of financial markets allows depositors to withdraw early and invest in the financial market which puts a limit on the degree of liquidity insurance. This is related to the earlier work of Jacklin (1987) who shows that deposit contracts have beneficial liquidity insurance features provided that restricted trading of deposit contracts can be enforced.[10] In any case, these arguments suggest that the proliferation of financial markets weakens that liquidity provision rationale of deposits, which may help explain the lesser importance of deposits for banks.

A second observation is that the proliferation of financial markets may suggest that the LOLR role in providing liquidity loses importance. What I mean is that, in Bagehot tradition, one could ask the question whether the LOLR has a role to play in providing liquidity to liquidity constrained yet solvent institutions when capital markets and interbank markets are well developed. Goodfriend and King (1988) argue that solvent institutions then cannot be illiquid since informed parties in the repo and interbank market would step in. In this spirit, the former ECB board member Tommaso Padoa-Schioppa suggested that the classical bank run may only happen in textbooks since the "width and depth of today's interbank market is such that other institutions would probably replace those which withdraw their funds" (as quoted in Rochet and Vives, 2004).

---

[10] Actually, Jacklin (1987) shows that with the "extreme" Diamond–Dybvig preferences, a dividend-paying equity contract can achieve the same allocations without the possibility of bank runs. However, for basically all other preferences, a demand deposit contract does better provided that trading opportunities are limited.

While these remarks rightfully suggest that the proliferation of financial markets could weaken the need for a LOLR in providing liquidity support, it would go too far to see no role for a LOLR, particularly when information asymmetries are considered. More specifically, an extensive literature on aggregate shocks has moved away from the pure "sunspot" bank run equilibriums, as in Diamond and Dybvig (1983), focusing instead on fundamentals. This literature builds on the empirical evidence in Gorton (1988) showing that banking crises — prior to the creation of the Federal Reserve — were predicted by leading economic indicators. In a recent contribution Rochet and Vives (2004) show that a coordination failure in the interbank market may occur particularly when fundamentals are low, and that this may lead to a need for liquidity support by the LOLR for a solvent institution.[11]

Overall the preceding discussion warrants the conclusion that the proliferation of financial markets (including interbank markets) has improved the risk-sharing opportunities between banks, and possibly has reduced sunspot type bank run problems on individual institutions.[12] But these very same interbank linkages may well have increased systemic risk, that is, the probability of propagation of liquidity and solvency problems to the financial system as a whole. It is therefore at the very least premature to trivialize the need for a LOLR.

Actually, a more market-centered view on systematic risks has gained ground, at the expense of a more institutionally-focused view of systematic risk. The propagation mechanisms for systemic crises have become substantially more complicated and possibly far reaching as well. For example, the revolution in structured finance and securitization may introduce all kinds of systemic issues. The risks in the markets for securitized assets are ill-understood. Once big defaults would occur in this market a meltdown is not excluded, and systemic risks are possibly acute.[13]

---

[11] Another line of research points at asset price bubbles as potential source or cause of fragility and contagion (Allen and Gale, 2000). See Allen (2005) and De Bandt and Hartmann (2002) for surveys on contagion.

[12] Whether total insolvency risk of individual institutions has come down depends on the actual risk taking and capitalization. Evidence in De Nicoló and Tieman (2005) suggests that the insolvency risk of European institutions has more or less remained the same over the last 15 years despite increases in capital over time and a wider geographic range of operations.

[13] Problems include the mighty role of credit rating agencies, the dependence on monoliners, etc.; see Boot *et al.* (2006) for an analysis of the growing importance of credit rating agencies for the functioning of financial markets.

3.2 *LOLR responsibilities in the Euro area*

The ECB has primary stability responsibilities when it comes to the payment system. But the ECB does not have an explicit task of preserving the stability of the financial system in general. This is left to the national central banks. These national central banks also have the LOLR role, and not the ECB. This formal description is of importance, but the practical allocation of tasks in the Eurosystem could deviate considerably, particularly because of the Euro-area-wide consequences of the manifestation of systemic risks.

The practical allocation of tasks and responsibilities as it relates to the LOLR role in the Euro countries between ECB and national central banks only became clear in 1999. At the presentation of the 1998 annual report (October 26, 1999) then ECB president Duisenberg commented that on the part of the ECB "there is a clearly articulated capability and willingness to act if really necessary" (Duisenberg, as reported in Vives, 2001). He added on the procedural issue that "The main guiding principle within the Eurosystem with reference to the provision of emergency liquidity to individual financial institutions is that the competent national central bank would be responsible for providing such assistance to those institutions operating within its jurisdiction". For a general liquidity crisis in the payment system Duisenberg indicated that a direct involvement of the ECB could be expected.[14] The latter is directly in line with the mandate of the ECB that stipulates its role in the smooth functioning of the payment system (Article 105(2) of the Maastricht Treaty).[15]

This interpretation of the LOLR role of the ECB and the national central banks is in line with the rather flexible wording of the role of the ECB in the treaty. The LOLF function is primarily a national responsibility, and the provision of liquidity support is under the responsibility and liability of national central banks. Nevertheless, the ECB also could engage in liquidity support, though it uses stricter collateral requirements. Moreover, the scope of the LOLR involvement at the ECB level is restrained by the lack of fiscal authority at the European level.

---

[14] I am not distinguishing in the text between the European System of Central Banks (ESCB), which is the Eurosystem that Duisenberg is referring to, and the ECB. This simplification is not totally correct because the relevant decision making body at the center is the ESCB, and not the ECB as standalone organization.

[15] See also Schinasi and Teixeira (2005).

3.3 *Evaluation of LOLR arrangements*

The central role of individual national central banks in LOLR activities and the secondary role of the ECB are somewhat curious. Systemic concerns at the EU level, the increasing integration of the EU economies and the introduction of the common currency (euro) would seem to dictate a more well defined LOLR role at the level of the ECB. However, one may argue that national central banks are often better able to assess the immediate liquidity needs of local financial institutions. This may well be valid, but only addresses the practical operational organization of the LOLR role. It does not explain why the responsibility of LOLR support is left to national central banks.

The right way of looking at this is that political considerations have led to these arrangements. In particular, the Maastricht Treaty may have tried to prevent the emergence of an overly powerful ECB at the expense of national central banks. I do not think that there is a much deeper rationale for this, and I am reluctant to put forward more sinister arguments. For example, one could argue that preserving these powers locally serves the desire of national authorities to have better control over their home country financial institutions via the national central bank. This may well be the case. Such local power could help defend these "national interests" when a crisis would occur. This would not be without cost since it would cast doubt on the desired independence of central banks. Nevertheless, I would more readily subscribe to the idea that a desire to protect national sovereignty has prevented national authorities from agreeing to more powerful EU and euro-area institutions.

Also the lack of fiscal powers at the European level is in part, or mostly, motivated by the same balance between national sovereignty and effective EU decision-making. This lack of fiscal authority has made it more complicated for the ECB to assume broader powers in the LOLR role. That is, liquidity support is often provided in circumstances where losses may occur; the question then comes up who is responsible for these losses. A LOLR responsibility organized at the national level "solves" this in that it can fine-tune its actions with the national treasury (Ministry of Finance) that can underwrite those losses.

To complicate this picture even further, the decentralized and fragmented nature of EU-banking supervision, with primary responsibilities at the level of individual member states and only a coordinating and facilitating role at the EU level, in all likelihood further reduces the power of the ECB vis-à-vis the national central banks. National central banks in practice will be a natural partner to the primary local supervisory agencies. Indeed, in many countries the national central bank is also the local supervisory agency. Important in this respect are also the national — home-country — linked deposit insurance arrangements. Again, national authorities are in charge and the national treasury incurs the (contingent) financial obligations.

These contingent financial obligations, combined with the absence of fiscal powers at the EU level, are a strong obstacle for the further centralization of both supervision at the EU level and LOLR responsibilities in the ECB. The well-known motto, "who foots the bill decides", underscores the existing decentralized focus. I see no reason why this would be different here.

4. Are Current Arrangements Sustainable?

The resulting patchwork of national supervision and European-wide coordination has so far upheld itself reasonably well. However, the key questions are how this system will work in crisis situations, and to what extent it accomplishes the efficiency objectives of regulation and supervision in general. In crisis situations, important concerns can be raised about the adequacy of information sharing and cooperation among the various supervisors, the European Central Bank and the national central banks. In particular, in such situations the question about who will be in charge might become very urgent. Potential tensions can easily be envisioned between supervisory agencies, national central banks and the ECB.

Policymakers are aware of these issues. For example, the new Directive on Financial Conglomerates gives the home country supervisor the single coordinating responsibility in all member states for group-wide supervision of the financial conglomerate. Issues of financial stability, however, remain the responsibility of the host countries.

The question is how to coordinate these potentially diverse interests. Particularly in crisis situations, these issues are of paramount importance. The core message of the second Brouwer-report (EFC, 2001) was that no mechanism was in place to coordinate in case of such crisis. For that reason a MoU among virtually all European national central banks and supervisors was formulated that specifies principles and procedures for cooperation in crisis management situations (ECB, 2003).

The fiscal side, in particular the budgetary obligations imposed on member states in case of bailouts, however, also requires the approval of national finance ministries that have to incur the potential financial obligations. In a follow-up MoU, these finance ministries were also included (ECB, 2005).

Several questions can be raised about the efficiency of the arrangements in general. The decentralized structure may give rise to potential conflicts of interest between the national authorities and "outsiders". For example, national authorities might be prone to too-big-to-fail (TBTF) rescues.[16] Alternatively, national authorities may not sufficiently appreciate (that is, internalize) the disrupting consequences that a domestic bank failure could have in other countries. Efficiency might be hampered in other ways as well. For example, the national scope of supervision may help encourage the emergence of "national champions". More fundamentally, the decentralized structure could give rise to level playing field and regulatory arbitrage issues.

Casual observation and reasoning would seem to suggest that integration and further coordination (if not centralization of authority) of both regulation and supervision might yield substantial efficiency gains not only for the supervisory authorities but also, and maybe more importantly, for the supervised financial institutions themselves. There are currently more than 35 supervisory authorities responsible for prudential supervision in the EU, and a typical large financial institution might have to report to more than 20 supervisors (Pearson, 2003).

Yet, practical considerations suggest that a full integration of all regulatory and supervisory functions at the European level may not (yet) be feasible. While it is clear that regulatory and supervisory integration needs to keep pace with the development of the size and the cross-border footprint of the covered banks, the heterogeneity of underlying supervisory systems and the implied costs of integration should not be underestimated. An interesting illustration is the evidence reported by Barth *et al.* (2002) on the variation across the European Union countries in supervisory institutions and practices. Their conclusion is that supervisory arrangements within the EU are as diverse as in the rest of the world. Also, illustrating this point further, the EU countries are current or former standard bearers of all major legal origins. A vast literature now documents

---

[16] One could replace too-big-to-fail with to-big-to-close to emphasize that replacing management, wiping out equity holders, etc., could still be done to mitigate moral hazard.

how legal origin matters for the shape and functioning of the financial system (see La Porta *et al.*, 1998).[17]

While common sense suggests that ultimately a more integrated regulatory and supervisory structure is desirable,[18] the way we would get there is far from clear. The Lamfalussy approach may bring us in the right direction but it does not provide for authority at the pan-European level. Indeed, practical considerations, including political concerns, dictate for now a fragmented structure on which a coordination layer needs to be super-imposed; the lead regulator model is one example of that.[19]

However, the struggle for an efficient pan-European coordination and integration of regulation and supervision is more then just a practical issue that will be sorted out over time. Two things stand out. The first is that the scope of regulation and supervision needs to be contained. Effective supervision and regulation — given the mushrooming cross-sector and cross-border footprint — requires a better demarcation of safety and systemic concerns.[20] The cross-sector integration of financial institutions and the ever more seamless integration of financial markets and institutions have enormously broadened the scope of regulation and the potential sources of systemic risk.

This also relates to the issue of firewalls. For example, does a subsidiary structure reduce systemic concerns? I do not think that an answer is readily available. More generally, what type of constraints, if any, should be put on the corporate structure of financial institutions? While we tend to think of further deregulation in the financial sector possibly leading to even bigger and broader financial institutions, it is far from clear what the future will bring. In any case, changes in the industrial structure of the financial

---

[17] Bank regulation and supervisory practices differ also considerably between civil and common law countries, with a more flexible and responsive approach in the latter.

[18] Actually, some theoretical work points at the potential value of competition between regulators, see also Kane (1988).

[19] An important distinction needs to be made between business conduct regulation and prudential regulation. I have focused on the latter. The former is closer to the functioning of financial markets and lends itself more readily for centralization at the European level. In the context of these financial markets, the "real" Lamfalussy report (Committee of Wise Men, 2001) does not directly propose authority at the EU level but it states that if its proposed approach is not successful the creation of a single EU regulatory authority should be considered.

[20] The earlier discussion on the precise source and propagation mechanism as it relates to systemic risk is actually pointing at the same issue.

sector are of paramount importance for the design and effectiveness of regulation and supervision.[21] If these issues cannot be satisfactorily addressed, I am not very optimistic about the possibilities for effective and efficient pan-European regulation even in the long run.

The second issue is that very little is known about the efficiency and effectiveness of various regulatory and supervisory structures. As Barth *et al.* (2003) put it, "there is very little empirical evidence on how, or indeed whether, the structure, scope or independence of bank supervision affects the banking industry". Their own research suggests that the effect is, at best, marginal but measurement problems are paramount. They conclude from this that we may thus choose to only focus on the effect that regulation has on systemic issues. But here, also, little is known. What this means is that we need much more work that tries to pinpoint the costs and benefits of different regulatory and supervisory arrangements. Obviously, in the context of the widely different national supervisory arrangements, the lack of evidence does not really help in evolving to a harmonized "superior" model.

5. What Should be Done?

It is clear that further improving coordination and cooperation between supervisory bodies makes sense. The EFC (2002) proposals (based on the Lamfalussy approach) and the recent crisis management MoUs (ECB, 2003, 2005) are steps in that direction. Further improvements can be made by harmonizing accounting standards and improving procedures. But this is not enough. Ultimately, more is needed than just good intentions and procedures.[22] The missing command structure in EU arrangements (the various MoUs and the Lamfalussy framework), as well as that with respect to LOLR facilities, needs to be addressed.

As stated already, an EU-wide regulatory and supervisory authority cannot be expected anytime soon. The LOLR function is directly related

---

[21] Earlier, I referred to the concentration in the credit rating business and the importance of ratings for the markets for structured finance (securitization). It is interesting to ask the question what impact a meltdown of one of the main credit rating agencies would have on these markets, and what this in turn would imply for participants in these markets.

[22] Cooperation between a system of dispersed (semi-autonomous) central banks and dispersed and autonomous prudential supervisors is very complicated. Decentralized systemic responsibilities combined with decentralized prudential responsibilities with each involving different bodies offer multiple coordination problems.

to crisis management, and in those circumstances a clear line of control is most important. But accomplishing improvements and particularly changing powers between national authorities and the ECB at the center is — as stated — a political issue. So far, whatever improvements have been made, were predicated by crises. Indeed, crises create urgency. The BCCI crisis was particularly important because this crisis led to willingness to address pan-European coordination failures in supervision. It is then immediately clear that — unless a major crisis would come about soon — there is for the moment no urgency for change. Matters might be even worse. With no crises in sight, complacency could set in.

My own assessment is that current initiatives, including the lead supervisor designation for banking groups, are improvements in the right direction. The Lamfalussy framework I see favorably as well. It will, in my view, indeed improve the efficiency of the legislative and rule-making process, and encourage convergence in regulatory and supervisory practices. Also, the less formalized cooperative initiatives like the Banking Supervisory Committee within the ECB and the widely supported BIS initiatives clearly put us on the path to further improvements and harmonization. These initiatives facilitate a continuous process for improving the supervisory process without having to make highly political and controversial choices. This process I judge very favorably. Nevertheless, a fear for complacency is in order. We need to continue to put improvements in supervisory practices and cooperation among supervisors high on the agenda, and be constantly critical about the speed, efficiency and effectiveness of the process. To speak with Lamfalussy, if the process slows down, more heavy-handed interventions should be considered.[23]

I am much less convinced that the same gradual process should apply to the LOLR structure. The LOLR role is intricately linked to crisis management, and that does not lend itself to a gradual approach or "soft" agreements on cooperation. While the MoUs (ECB, 2003, 2005) help in overcoming some of the lacunae identified in the Brouwer crisis management report (EFC, 2001), I do not think this is a sufficient response. This is not to say that I would criticize these MoUs. Actually, I fully endorse them. The 2005 MoU that addresses cooperation and information

---

[23] These more positive comments on the developments in supervisory arrangements in the EU do no imply that I fully endorse the current state of affairs. One issue that deserves much more attention is how to address TBTF concerns. The US practice, with clear-cut timely interventions, could be particularly helpful in EU banking markets considering the massive domestic consolidation (see Eisenbeis and Kaufman, 2005).

sharing (including views and assessments) among supervisors, central banks and finance ministries is an important document. What it does not do (and does not intend to do) is bring the LOLR responsibility to a more central level. To the contrary, it remains with national central banks which possibly do not, and often cannot, sufficiently take into account the pan-European systemic problems that may have arisen in a crisis situation. This national authority then diffuses the command structure, while the LOLR should be at the heart of crisis management.[24]

In my conversations with some national central bankers in the Euro area, an amazing group feeling and feelings of collective responsibility are expressed. The suggestion is that such a collective feeling of responsibility will effectively guarantee a central command structure at the ECB level because any serious problem with potential Euro-area repercussions would immediately be brought to the ECB, or more correctly the European system of central banks (ESCB). While one should be enthusiastic about the trust in each other and the collective feeling of responsibility that has been created at the ECB level, one has to be careful in trusting such informal approach when it comes to crisis management situations. Those situations are rare, involve novel occurrences that are rather unpredictable, and can have very severe consequences for individual member states. In those situations, national interests may collide with Euro-area-wide responsibilities, and mutual trust might not be sufficient for aligning national interests with Euro-area interests. For this very reason, a clear command structure at the Euro-level is important. This would imply that the ECB should get primary responsibility over the LOLR role.[25]

[24] In my view, the central role given to national central banks is really an artifact of the past when the then rather segmented markets allowed the local central bank to resolve a bank crisis by "forcing" the surviving institutions to take care of the problem. This no longer works because local banks in the increasingly open banking market do no longer feel the same responsibility for resolving problems in their home market. A case in point is the recent failure of a very small Dutch bank with only local Dutch operations (Van Der Hoop). Despite the potential reputation damage to the local financial sector, the (many times bigger) surviving institutions were not willing to step in. A further complicating factor is that due the substantial consolidation in domestic markets, a typical failure might be very difficult to handle for the surviving local institutions.

[25] Let me emphasize that trust and feelings of collective responsibility between national central banks and ECB even then remain important. Much of the information will come from the national level, and trust is needed to facilitate an optimal flow of information. This implies in the broader context of the 2003 and 2005 MoUs as well. Without trust and collective feelings of responsibility, one cannot expect the good intentions with respect to information sharing in those MoUs to be of much value.

But is this feasible without other changes in EU arrangements? In particular, the fragmented domestically centered regulatory and supervisory structures and the lack of fiscal authority at the EU level are problematic. To start with the latter, any more serious role of the ECB in LOLR operations (and crisis management) should go hand in hand with some burden sharing arrangements to cover potential losses in those operations. In my view, this is doable but needs to be arranged. More problematic is the fragmented supervisory arrangement. Several things can be said about this. As already stated, only over time can this be changed. In my view, it is important and absolutely necessary that this is dealt with.[26] But for now this will just not happen for all the reasons given before.

One could then argue is it not logical to also keep the LOLR role for now local? That is, why not keep it close to the local supervisor? Considering, as I have highlighted, the pan-European nature of systemic concerns, a more central authority is needed. Local central banks could however still continue to play an important operational role in LOLR activities. Authority at the ECB level will however give a powerful boost to information sharing, and this could distinctly improve the efficiency and effectiveness of the LOLR operations.

6. Concluding Thoughts

Cross-border banking poses enormous challenges for regulators and supervisors. In the context of the Euro countries, my recommendation is to grant the ECB explicit responsibility over the LLOR function; national central banks would then get a more operational role. This recommendation is not new. Several authors have suggested this (see Lannoo, 2002; and Vives, 2001). As with the centralization of supervisory and regulatory responsibilities in Europe, the political feasibility of a centralized LOLR responsibility remains an issue to be dealt with. I alluded to this earlier.[27]

---

[26] This does not mean that there will not be a role for local supervisors in the future. Local supervisors will always play a role because of the proximity to local institutions which could offer information advantages.

[27] National governments could find LOLR control at the national central banks convenient in the case of a crisis, particularly when financial difficulties threaten large domestic financial institution. This already suggests that national control could worsen TBTF incentives and possibly also compromise the role of national central banks in crisis management (that is, they also would be "forced" to provide LOLR support in the case of solvency problems).

This is also related to the issue of fiscal authority as discussed in subsection 3.3. Burden sharing arrangements are needed for efficient cross-border crisis management.

The EU Treaty does allow for a heavier role of the ECB in LOLR operations,[28] so the true issue might be to get agreement within the decision-making body at the ECB (the European System of Central Banks, ESCB).

An important question is: Is there a downside to a more centralized LOLR responsibility? Would this compromise the independence of the ECB? For example, political pressure (also via Ecofin) to provide liquidity support in the case of a bank crisis might become more intense. One could argue that this type of pressure has always been present in central banking and is actually much more intense for national central banks. A related concern is that the heavier LOLR role could intensify the potential conflict between financial stability and monetary policy objectives within the ECB. It is hard to assess the importance of this argument. The current arrangement already has this potential conflict (and one could argue about the importance of this conflict between objectives; see Issing, 2003).

On the positive side — apart from the benefits related to a more central command structure (see Section 5) — I see several other potential advantages:

1. More prudent use of the LOLR facility (see Vives, 2001; and Lannoo, 2002).
2. Extra urgency on communication between the ECB on the one hand and national central banks and supervisory agencies on the other. National authorities could be more willing to share information with the ECB (only then support can be expected). Thus, self interest may facilitate the information exchange.
3. It might be a catalyst for further reforms in pan-European supervision. In particular, a stronger position of the ECB could induce the EU (and Ecofin) to strengthen the role of the EU in supervision to "counter" the enhanced power of the ECB. This would probably be positive because it would reduce the fragmentation in supervision, speed up convergence and enhance coordination. In a sense, it would add urgency to the Lamfalussy process.

---

[28] Also, the ECB statute allows for a more dominant role of the ECB with respect to the LOLR function.

The latter benefit might at first blush sound tangential, but actually be a very important one. We need a catalyst for further European regulatory and supervisory integration for the financial sector. Expanding the powers of the ECB could be such catalyst.

Obviously cross-border banking goes beyond the borders of the EU and Euro countries. So, even accomplishing a fully coordinated and efficient EU crisis management structure is not sufficient. The international orientation and mix of activities of many banks asks for an efficient world-wide crisis coordination mechanism. Since this involves different currency-areas, the feasibility of LOLR resort centralization is limited. International harmonization and integration of regulatory and supervisory practices is needed.

Whatever path chosen, the integration of financial supervision and regulation will be far from easy. Resolving the fundamental issues related to the scope of regulation and, to a lesser extent, our understanding about the costs and benefits of different arrangements (see the previous section) would help. Being pragmatic is important in this debate; first-best-choices are not in sight.

References

Allen, F. (2005). Modeling financial instability. *National Institute Economic Review*, 192, 57–67.

Allen, F. and D. Gale (2000). Financial contagion. *Journal of Political Economy*, 108, 1–33.

Bart, J.R., D.E. Nolle, T. Phumiwasana and G. Yago (2003). A cross-country analysis of the bank supervisory framework and bank performance. *Financial Markets, Institutions & Instruments*, 12(2), 67–120.

Barth, J.R., G. Caprio and R. Levine (2002). Bank regulation and supervision: What works best? Working paper, World Bank.

Bhattacharya, S., A.W.A. Boot and A.V. Thakor (1998). The economics of bank regulation. *Journal of Money, Credit and Banking*, 30(4), 745–770.

Bhattacharya, S., A.W.A. Boot and A.V. Thakor (eds.) (2004). *Credit Intermediation and the Macro Economy*. Oxford, UK: Oxford University Press.

Boot, A.W.A. and M. Marinc (2006). Competition and entry in banking: Implications for capital regulation. Discussion paper University of Amsterdam, April.

Boot, A.W.A., T.T. Milbourn and A. Schmeits (2006). Credit ratings as coordination mechanisms. *Review of Financial Studies*, 19(1), 81–118.

Committee of Wise Men (2001). Final report of the Committee of Wise Men on the regulation of the European securities markets. Lamfalussy Report, Brussels, February 15.

De Bandt, O. and P. Hartmann (2002). Systemic risk: A survey. In *Financial Crises, Contagion and the Lender of Last Resort*, C. Goodhart and G. Illing (eds.). Oxford, UK: Oxford University Press.

De Nicoló, G. and A. Tieman (2005). Economic integration and financial stability: A European perspective. Working paper, IMF.

ECB (2003). Memorandum of understanding on high-level principles of cooperation. Press release, March 10.

ECB (2005). Memorandum of understanding on cooperation between the banking supervisors. Central Banks and Finance Ministries of the European Union in Financial Crises Situations, press release, May 18.

EFC (2001). Report on financial crisis management. Brouwer report, document from the Economic and Financial Committee, EFC/ECFIN/251/01.

EFC (2002). Financial regulation, supervision and stability. Document from the Economic and Financial Committee, EF76/ECOFIN 324, October 10.

Eisenbeis, R.A. and G. Kaufman (2005). Bank crises resolution and foreign-owned banks. *Economic Review*, 90(4), 1–18.

Freixas, X (2003). Crises management in Europe. In *Financial Supervision in Europe*, J. Kremer, D. Schoenmaker and P. Wierts (eds.). Cheltenham, UK: Edward Elgar.

Goodfriend, M. and R. King (1988). Financial deregulation, monetary policy and central banking. In *AEI Studies*, W. Haraf and R.M. Kushmeider (eds.). No. 481, UPA, Lanham, MD.

Goodhart, C. (ed.) (2000). *Which Lender of Last Resort for Europe?* Central Banking Publications.

Goodhart, C., P. Hartmann, D. Llewellyn, L. Rojas-Suarez and S. Weisbrod (1998). *Financial Regulation*, Routledge, London.

Hartman, P., A. Maddaloni, and S. Manganelli (2003). The Euro area financial system: Structure, integration and policy initiatives. ECB Working Paper, no. 230.

Issing, O. (2003). Monetary and financial stability: Is there a trade-off. Presentation for the *Conference on Monetary Stability, Financial Stability and the Business Cycle*. Basle, March 28–29.

Jacklin, C.J. (1987). Demand deposits, trading restrictions, and risk sharing. In *Financial Intermediation and Intertemporal Trade*, E. Prescott and N. Wallace (eds.). Minneapolis: University of Minnesota Press.

Kane, E.J. (1988). How market forces influence the structure of financial regulation. In *Restructuring Banking and Financial Services in America*, W.S. Haraf and R.M. Kushmeider (eds.), pp. 343–382. Washington DC: American Enterprise Institute.

Lannoo, K. (2002). Supervising the European financial system. Working paper.

Lannoo, K. and J.P. Casey (2005). EU financial regulation and supervision beyond 2005. CEPS Task Force Report No. 54.

Lastra, R. (2002). The governance structure for financial regulation in Europe. Special Paper 133, Financial Markets Group, LSE.

La Porta, R., F. Lopes-de-Silanes, A. Shleifer and R.W. Vishny (1998). Law and finance. *Journal of Political Economy*, 106, 113–1155.

Pearson (2002). Comment. In *Financial Supervision in Europe*, J. Kremer, D. Schoenmaker and P. Wierts (eds.). Cheltenham, UK: Edward Elgar.

Rochet, J.C. (2004). Bank runs and financial crises: A discussion. In *Credit Intermediation and the Macro Economy*, S. Bhattacharya, A.W.A. Boot and A.V. Thakor (eds.). Oxford, UK: Oxford University Press.

Rochet, J.C. and X. Vives (2004). Coordination failures and the lender of last resort: Was Bagehot right after all? Working paper.

Schinasi, G.J. and P.G. Teixeira (2005). The lender of last resort in the European single financial market. Working paper IMF and ECB, December 12.

Schoenmaker, D. and S. Oosterloo (2005). Financial supervision in an integrating Europe: Measuring cross-border externalities. *International Finance*, 8(1), 1–27.

Vives, X. (2001). Restructuring financial regulation in the European Monetary Union. *Journal of Financial Services Research*, 19, 57–82.

Regulation and Crisis Prevention in the Evolving Global Market

David S. Hoelscher*
International Monetary Fund

David C. Parker
International Monetary Fund

1. Introduction

National regulatory systems are not keeping up with the evolving nature of cross-border financial firms. Regulatory systems remain locally bound, with laws and regulations designed to ensure national financial stability and to limit the national costs from the failure of financial institutions operating in the country. However, cross-border financial firms that organize their business activities on a global or regional basis are emerging. Location of business lines in such firms increasingly is determined by global risk management concerns and by the regulatory systems in host countries.

Policy initiatives are needed, both at the national and multilateral levels, to adapt regulatory systems to the changing global and regional markets. The European Union (EU) has already made important progress in ensuring adequate information exchange across supervisory regimes. Initial steps have also been made in identifying needed reforms in the broader crisis management framework. Outside the EU, however, progress in addressing these issues is limited. Information exchange among supervisors is largely ad hoc and little progress has been made in harmonizing

*David S. Hoelscher is chief of the Systemic Issues Division, Monetary and Financial Systems Department and David C. Parker is on staff, both at the International Monetary Fund. The authors would like to thank Jonathan Fiechter, Michael Taylor and Jan Willem van der Vossen, as well as participants in the conference sponsored by Federal Reserve Bank of Chicago and International Association of Deposit Insurers, for helpful comments on earlier drafts. The views reflected in this paper are personal and do not necessarily reflect the views of the International Monetary Fund.

regulatory and supervisory regimes or identifying differences in crisis management techniques.

If policy initiatives are insufficient, host authorities will be led to impose increasingly stricter controls on cross-border firms aimed at ensuring stability of the domestic financial system. Some host supervisors are already considering alternatives to ensure that both branches and subsidiaries can be treated as stand alone financial institutions. Cross-border financial firms may face a multitude of capital regimes and regulatory structures that increase the cost and could limit the efficiency of financial intermediation. Crisis resolution in this environment could also be more inefficient and costly than if more efficient means of crisis resolution are developed.

The role for international institutions is modest. National regimes are responsible for financial stability and countries will not accept changes that undermine their ability to meet that responsibility. International institutions can help identify pertinent differences among countries and provide a forum for discussion on harmonization. Multilateral institutions may be well placed to run desktop exercises simulating the failure of a cross-border financial firm and helping participants draw conclusions about possible weaknesses in existing crisis management frameworks. Progress in resolving these differences or developing mechanisms for managing crises, however, rest ultimately with the national policy makers and their constituents.

This paper is organized in three sections. The first section discusses the evolving nature of both global markets and regulatory structures. The second section examines alternative directions available for regulatory structures and the role of multilateral institutions in maintaining financial stability. The last section offers some conclusions.

2. Evolving Character of Financial Intermediation

2.1 *Evolving cross border financial firms*

The global financial market is evolving at a rapid pace. Spurred by technological change, the costs of international transactions have fallen, the range of services and products considered tradable has expanded, and the time required to make transactions has fallen.[1] The flow of information

---

[1] Ben Bernanke, "Economic Integration, What's New and What's Not?" speech at Jackson Hole, WY, August 29, 2006.

has allowed cross-border firms — both financial and nonfinancial — to take advantage of cross country cost differentials, enhancing profits and increasing efficiency.

Cross-border financial firms are adjusting to this evolving environment. Three aspects of this adjustment stand out. First, the pace of credit extension has accelerated as cross-border firms enter new markets and offer new products. Second, cross-border firms are taking advantage of the ease of communication to manage the firm's activities on a global basis. The distinction between branches and subsidiaries is being blurred and financial functions for the cross-border firm are being concentrated in specific locations. The third aspect of adjustment reflects the role of foreign firms in host countries. The expansion of foreign firms brings important benefits to the host countries in terms of experience, access to international markets, and funding sources. At the same time, however, such entities can come to have a systemic importance in the host country while being relatively unimportant in the cross-border firm.

The cross-border credit flows have expanded rapidly. BIS data point to rapid increases in cross-border claims (Table 1). Between 2000 and 2005, cross-border firms with parents located in the UK, France and Spain have increased by over 100 percent, while such claims in Germany, Japan and the US have grown by around 50 percent. On an aggregate basis, the growth in foreign claims to developed world outpaced the growth of such claims to the developing world. In part, this may reflect

Table1. Consolidated foreign claims of reporting banks

	Total	Growth Rate 2000–2005					
		Germany	**UK**	**Japan**	**French**	**US**	**Spain**
All countries	95.9	49.4	131.9	42.1	125.2	38.6	139.0
Developed countries	103.2	49.4	151.8	39.9	133.6	31.1	280.4
Developing countries	66.9	26.5	163.1	22.8	82.3	52.1	22.9
Africa & Middle East	95.8	19.6	294.4	10.9	84.8	25.3	32.6
Asia & Pacific	96.1	23.6	199.4	19.6	53.3	115.5	−36.9
Europe	128.0	55.6	120.8	177.4	284.7	55.8	132.5
Latin America/ Caribbean	14.5	−24.1	35.9	−13.1	−10.0	18.4	22.2

the expansion of European firms within Europe and the rebound of the Japanese banking system.

Information on the extent to which this rapid increase in foreign claims is channeled through branches and subsidiaries is limited. The Bank for International Settlements (BIS) data does not distinguish between credit extended by the parent to foreign residents and credit extended by branches and subsidiaries to foreign residents. For Europe, Schoenmaker and Oosterloo (2005) show that only a small number of the 30 largest banks in Europe are sufficiently cross border to generate home-host problems. In a more recent study, Schoenmaker and van Laecke (2006) found significant cross-border activities to be unevenly distributed across regions. Using a transnationality index, they found cross-border business significant (about 25 percent) of European banks' business but only modest importance (10 percent of business) for American and Asian Pacific banks. For the US, available data suggests that the growth of credit through branches and subsidiaries is rising at a faster pace than overall credit (Table 2).

Table 2. Cross border activities of US banks

	Percentage change	Distribution[a]	
		2000	**2005**
All Cross Border Claims	38.6%	100.0%	100.0%
Developed	31.1%	62.7%	59.3%
Developing	52.1%	27.8%	30.5%
Africa	25.3%	2.0%	1.8%
Asia	115.5%	8.5%	13.2%
Europe	55.8%	2.7%	3.0%
Latin America	18.4%	14.6%	12.5%
Other	48.4%	9.5%	10.2%
Branches and Subsidiaries	54.6%	56.9%	63.5%
Developed	54.6%	39.0%	43.5%
Developing	22.6%	12.7%	11.3%
Africa	81.8%	0.3%	0.4%
Asia	115.2%	3.5%	5.5%
Europe	117.4%	0.6%	1.0%
Latin America	−25.5%	8.3%	4.5%
Other	134.2%	5.1%	8.7%

[a] As percent of total cross-border claims

A second area where firms are changing is the evolving role of subsidiaries and branches in the cross-border firm. The distinction between branches and subsidiaries is beginning to blur as cross-border firms use communication and technological innovations to allocate capital and risk on a global basis. The traditional country-based model is being replaced by a more sophisticated business line model with global integration of both management functions. Kuritzkes *et al.* (2003) provide some evidence of this development, describing a so-called "hub and spoke" organizational model. In this model, the hub is responsible for the allocation of balance sheet items, liquidity and capital within the group. The business units (spokes) manage their own risks using the methodology directed by the center. Management is specialized, with branches or subsidiaries specializing in functions, such as risk management, internal controls, treasury operations (including liquidity management and funding) and compliance. This development reflects the adaptation of the global firm to profit maximizing possibilities provided by the integrated global markets.

A third area is the growing importance of cross-border firms in host country financial systems. In some host countries, cross-border firms' subsidiaries dominate host countries' financial systems. The newly emerging European countries, for example, have opened their financial systems to investments by large European firms. In some emerging European economies, virtually the entire financial system is in the hands of foreign banks. This trend is not limited to the emerging European countries. Many emerging market countries have opened their markets to foreign investments, gaining access to international markets, but found that foreign firms have come to dominate their financial systems.

2.2 *Evolving supervisory and regulatory frameworks*

Countries are trying to modify their supervisory and regulatory frameworks to meet the challenges posed by cross-border financial firms. Methods of implementing the original framework, embodied in the Basel Concordant of 1988, have been revised and a new framework, Basel II, is under development. Notwithstanding advances, significant challenges remain for the monitoring and supervision of cross-border firms, as well as for the resolution of cross-border financial firms.

One of the earlier efforts at cross-border supervision was outlined in the Basel Concordat.[2] That agreement lays out two overarching principles: (1) the host authority should confirm that cross-border bank entities (subsidiary or branch) be subjected to effective consolidated supervision by the home authority; and (2) the home authority should be able to obtain from the cross-border bank entity all the information it needs for effective supervision. Under this framework, the activities of cross-border banks are consolidated and supervised as part of the whole financial group by the home supervisor. Supervision of branches is the responsibility of the home supervisor. The supervision of subsidiaries of cross-border firms is more complex. Subsidiaries are licensed and supervised by the host countries. At the same time, accounts are consolidated and included in the supervision of the consolidated cross-border firm so home supervisors have a full picture of risk management within the consolidated entity.

Basel II is being introduced to shift supervision away from a detailed check-the-box approach to compliance with a more judgmental assessment of the effectiveness of risk management systems. The framework introduces a more risk-sensitive approach to capital adequacy, underlines banks' responsibility for ensuring adequate capital, and provides a stronger basis for the role of markets.[3] Concerning cross-border activities of cross-border banks, Basel II assigns responsibility for monitoring the risk management of the consolidated group to the home supervisor. For many of the cross-border firms, such risk management will use highly

---

[2] The Concordate was published in 1988. A set of minimum standards, as well as recommendations for more effective implementation, was issued by Basel Committee of Banking Supervision (1992 and 1996). Additional principles for the cross-border implementation of the New Capital Accord (Basel II) were formulated in Basel Committee of Banking Supervision (2003b and 2004). Finally, some of the principles and guidelines prepared by The Joint Forum on Financial Conglomerates (1999a, b) are applicable to cross-border issues.

[3] Specifically, Basel II identifies three pillars. Pillar 1 aligns the 1988 Accord's guidelines by aligning the minimum capital requirements more closely to each bank's actual risk of economic loss. Pillar 2 requires supervisors to review banks' internal assessments of their overall risks and capital needs to determine whether additional capital is needed. Pillar 3 enhances the degree of transparency in bank's public reporting to encourage market discipline. Moreover, Pillar 1 permits a "simple standardized approach", broadly based on the Basel I Accord of 1988, a "standardized approach", using external credit ratings to establish capital adequacy charges, and an "advanced internal ratings-based approach". The latter two methodologies are based on probability of default and other components of credit risk derived from banks' own internal risk analysis systems.

sophisticated techniques for evaluating the risk profile of the consolidated group.

The effectiveness of supervisory frameworks may be undermined by the trends in the global markets described above — the expansion of cross-border banking activities and the specialization of functions within such firms. The existing supervisory framework does not address potential conflicts of interest between home and host authorities, nor does it establish an international basis for the cross-border cooperation. Specifically, the following problems exist:

- Differences in rules, regulations and legal frameworks make it difficult for supervisors to evaluate the institution's financial statements.
- Differences in regulation can lead to regulatory/supervisory arbitrage, with the cross-border firm allocating activities to jurisdictions where regulation is relatively lax.
- With different regimes, the responsibility for acting may be diluted or unclear. When several authorities are included, the flow of information may be slow or inadequate.
- Triggers for corrective action or, in the case of failure, intervention, may be different and, therefore, prevent timely supervisory action.
- Home country supervision may face a loss of "host country proximity" to the activities of the branches and subsidiaries.
- Host country supervision may not have adequate information to understand the group's risk-adjusted capital position.

In advanced markets, recognition of these limitations has led to innovations in supervisory practices. The Basel Committee on Bank Supervision has established the Basel Accord Implementation Group — a voluntary coordinating group of supervisors — to improve coordination and cooperation among supervisors. Moreover, the EU has moved toward (1) community-wide legal and regulatory harmonization; (2) elimination of formal, legal barriers to information sharing among supervisors; and (3) a network of communication and coordination procedures to facilitate cooperation. These efforts have been reinforced by the establishment of colleges of supervisors that ensure cooperation between the lead supervisor and local supervisors. The lead supervisor would regularly inform the college of the situation of the group. At the same time, the college would act as a forum for an information exchange between the supervisors involved, and discuss local supervisors' proposals. In case of a crisis, the college would become a "management team" where the lead supervisor acts as primus inter pares.

While these efforts have been used in the EU, harmonization of supervisory regimes and cooperative supervision are less common outside the EU. Regional markets, as seen above, face emerging regional firms that pose the same issues but harmonization of practices and supervisory cooperation is less developed. In a crisis, national authorities may be unable to comply with MoUs on shared responsibility signed under more stable times. In addition, there is the problem of coordinating the actions of the home-country authorities with those of the host-country central bank when emergency liquidity is required. The fact that the EU countries have not been able to agree on such rules, in spite of the obvious potential risks in their absence, highlights the difficulty of balancing conflicting interests among more diverse countries.

2.3 *Other safety net features*

A country's safety net is broader than just bank supervision and includes insolvency regimes, deposit insurance systems, and emergency lending facilities. All of these functions — supervision, liquidity support, bank resolution and deposit insurance — are essential features of an adequate framework for a successful safety net. While some progress has been seen in supervisory framework, unfortunately very little has been done to adapt the remaining elements of a country's safety net to the challenges posed by cross-border financial intermediations.

Resolution of a failed bank is a legal procedure, codified in local law. As seen in the resolution of cross-border banks such as BCCI, jurisdictional difference can complicate the resolution process. Some jurisdictions have a single insolvency framework for both financial and nonfinancial institutions while others have separate legal regimes. Differences can exist in the powers and responsibilities of receivers, in the ability of the receiver to cancel or modify existing contracts, and in the tools available when the bank is considered systemically important. Both the IMF and the World Bank have sought to identify the range of issues that can exist in insolvency regimes.[4] While no effort is made to reconcile such differences, acknowledging the wide range of

---

[4] See the General Bank Insolvency Initiative.

differences points to a potential difficulty when involving two or more legal jurisdictions.

Deposit insurance systems, another feature of a country's safety net, are strictly local in nature and few efforts have been made to cast deposit insurance in a global context. Local depositors are generally protected by locally financed deposit insurance systems. In the context of the failure of a cross-border firm, generally depositors in branches are covered by the home country deposit insurance system and depositors in subsidiaries are covered by the host system. This structure leads to some important anomalies. In the event of a truly cross-border firm with an elaborate branch network, the home country deposit insurance system may be unable to meet the funding demands in the face of a failure. Even if funds were available, public officials may object to paying out a significant portion of deposits held outside the home country. This concern has been raised in the case of Nordea, for example. Nordea is considering changing all its foreign subsidiaries to branches. In the event of a failure of Nordea, the home authorities would then be responsible for repayment of more deposits held throughout the region. The political issues involving such a resolution are unclear. Some countries, including Switzerland and the US, explicitly exclude deposits held in branches outside the home country, treating them, instead, as general creditors of the failed institution.

3. The Way Forward

3.1 *Framework for financial stability in a global environment*

The current regulatory system, while evolving to meet these challenges of the changing global market place, is not yet fully adequate. This framework is likely to evolve in one of two directions. One direction involves more rapid and effective harmonization of regulatory and legal regimes together with institutional and regulatory arrangements that allow for managing the risks of cross-border firms. Agreements on burden sharing or establishment of unified supervisory framework could be part of this effort. The other direction the framework may take, possibly the "default option" in case the first does not occur, is for the authority of host supervision to expand, covering branches of cross-border firms and the requirement that all foreign operations of cross-border firms meet minimum standards within the local financial system.

One alternative is for countries to seek further regulatory and legal harmonization, forgoing national oversight of their financial systems and adopting a unified regulatory framework. The EU is moving in this direction, by harmonizing supervisory rules and regulations. However, to be effective, harmonization should be expanded to include legal systems and other features of the financial safety net. Such harmonization could be complimented by a single regulatory body with responsibility for supervision and resolution of all financial firms. Alternatively, countries could design and adapt a binding legal and regulatory system for supervisor and failure resolution. An intermediate format could also envision the establishment of a regional banking license, whereby a regional bank would be licensed jointly by the host countries. The process of joint licensing would establish rules for the joint supervision and resolution of the institution.[5]

The other alternative is for host authorities to take over full control of all oversight and supervision functions of both branches and subsidiaries of cross-border firms. This approach takes the view that it is "imprudent for a host authority to rely on the home authority to protect the host financial system" and, instead, implement a framework for the supervision of foreign banks.[6] This model, potentially, sacrifices group-level efficiency for the sake of a more even distribution of risks and crisis management capacity between the home and the host jurisdiction. It may discourage economically efficient cross-border integration of banking markets but clarify the role and accountability of authorities in a crisis.

Countries will choose one of these directions based on domestic views about the relative importance of two issues: the importance of regional harmonization and the role of foreign entities in financial intermediation. Different weights to these two concerns influences the regulatory and legal frameworks adapted by country authorities. While the EU has opted for continued harmonization, other regions are more concerns about recognizing and controlling the systemic importance of foreign firms. These two alternatives can be combined to highlight the implications of alternative approaches. Different combinations of

---

[5] While such a regional license does not exist in the European context, a similar arrangement does exist in the United States where nationally chartered banks operate side by side with state chartered banks.

[6] See, for example, Kane (2006).

		Low	High
Stability	Low	Home/Host	Enhanced supervision
concerns	High	Strong local autonomy	Unified supervision

Figure 1. Degree of legal/regulatory harmonization

regulatory harmonization and impact of branches/subsidiaries on financial stability suggest different approaches to supervision. Specifically, see Figure 1.

If countries opt for greater harmonization and integration of financial system, supervisory regimes will have to be based on more formal, cooperative agreements based in law and regulations. When low levels of integration exist, informal agreements on information sharing can be effective. Countries may negotiate multilateral Memoranda of Understanding (MoUs) outlining intensions. As integration increases, the benefits of such informal arrangements diminish. Stronger agreements are necessary that are consistent with each country's legal framework. The Nordic countries, for example, have signed legally binding, detailed MoUs that go beyond information exchange and detail how to handle foreign branch supervision.[7]

If a country has a foreign branches or subsidiary with systemic importance in the local financial system, host controls will tend to intensify. In the absence of a multilateral framework for supervision and crisis resolution, the host authorities will have to ensure that they have sufficient authority over the activities of the foreign firm. Countries may require that both local subsidiaries and branches can be treated as a stand alone entity. Local authorities may require that a significant role be given to local minority shareholders or that shares of the local institution be traded in local capital markets. Such requirement may be imposed even if they limit the ability of the cross-border financial firm to operate the firm on a global basis.

Different countries have followed different approaches to managing cross-border firms. While the EU has moved efficiently towards

---

[7] The MoUs detail the cause of action for both host and home supervisors when a branch of a foreign financial institution is established in a country. It establishes explicitly who informs whom, when and which information will be provided at a minimum. In addition, it lays out the principles for cooperation in the supervision of those branches, including on-site inspections.

		Low	High
Stability concerns	Low	Home /Host	EU
	High	New Zealand	Nordea

Figure 2.   Degree of legal/regulatory harmonization

greater harmonization and coordinated action, other regions have only begun to coordinate their actions. As the global market is evolving rapidly, greater host control may become increasingly the norm. An illustrative but by no means exhaustive approach, Figure 1 could be re-written emphasizing the supervisory arrangements currently applied in a variety of countries. Future work could be to systemically examine the different approaches taken in the management of cross-border firms, see Figure 2.

3.2 *Options for multilateral institutions*

The role for multilateral institutions in helping guide these developments are modest. At the country level, international institutions can assist the authorities plan and develop the policy stance appropriate for ensuring a stable and sound financial system. In this context, there may be scope for identifying incompatibilities between safety net features among trading partners and assisting in the identification of economic policies necessary to ensure stability in the presence of a significant exposure to foreign firms.

Beyond the direct, bilateral contacts, multilateral institutions may also assist in coordinating regional activities. Three areas of coordination stand out. First, international organizations may be well placed to collect and disseminate information of cross-border flows. As discussed earlier, information on the developments in cross-border financial flows are limited and, across regions, inconsistent in definitions. Countries could benefit from a better understanding of the degree and intensity of the issue. Second, multilateral efforts could help more clearly identify the extent to which safety nets within a region differ. Third, multilateral institutions could facilitate the conduct of regional table top exercises, simulating the regional impact of a regional cross-border failure. Such simulations help identify critical inconsistencies of approach across countries and point the way to future work on policy coordination and policy harmonization.

Multilateral institutions could also provide a forum for countries to consider different paths towards reconciling their legal and supervisory frameworks. Multilateral agencies could help authorities identify areas of conflict and facilitate coordination efforts. Replicating, in part, the work done within the EU, other regional groups could be established to assist in the identification of broad principles, implement agreement on decision making and, possibly, begin the more difficult task of identifying mechanisms for burden sharing in a crisis. Such a discussion could begin with:

- definitions of what costs should be included in burden sharing agreements,
- how to evaluate the systemic costs of a failure, and
- criteria for allocating burden.

4. Conclusions

Cross-border transactions are a growing phenomenon in today's world. The expansion of trade is being mirrored in expansion of financial services. The integration of Europe explains an important portion of the growth in cross-border activities but certainly not all of it. With the exception of Africa, all regions in the world have seen an increase in cross-border activities, with particularly sharp increases in Latin America. British, US, and Spanish banks have seen the most rapid increase in cross-border activities. This development reflects the efforts of firms to take advantage of the benefits of specialization, more efficient resource management and more modern risk management techniques.

Cross-border activities pose particular challenges to national supervisory authorities. Differences in the legal and institutional environment can inhibit adequate cross-border bank supervision. Supervisors of the cross-border institution may face a bewildering range of rules, regulations, and legal approaches to the supervision and resolution of failed institutions. These differences may mask the true financial conditions of the cross-border institution, make regulatory intervention more complex, and, provide incentives for regulatory arbitrage. A second set of challenges arise when a foreign branch or subsidiary is of systemic importance to the financial system in the host country. The host authorities are responsible first and foremost to maintain their country's financial stability. This challenge would point to an important role for the national authorities in supervising and controlling subsidiaries and branches.

Multilateral arrangements could assist countries maximize benefits from cross-border financial flows. But options for multilateral institutions in this environment are modest. On a bilateral basis, multilateral institutions can assist authorities consider alternative policy stances. Multinational institutions might complement bilateral contacts with efforts to facilitate regional activities. Information could be collected and disseminated. Regional table top exercises or simulations of cross-border financial failures could be organized that would identify critical inconsistencies of approach across countries and point the way to future work. Finally, multilateral institutions could provide a forum for countries to consider different paths towards reconciling their legal and supervisory frameworks.

If progress in harmonizing and coordination policy responses does not keep up with changes in the global market, country authorities will instead adopt policy frameworks that ensure the stability of their own financial system. Where concerns about financial stability predominate, countries have sought to strengthen the host country's oversight of branches and subsidiaries. Some countries have required local affiliates of foreign firms — both subsidiaries and branches — to be able to can stand alone as a financial institution. In the case of a failure, the authorities would ringfence the financial entities and resolve then domestically. In the absence of greater progress in harmonization and coordination, growing host controls on financial flows could be expected.

References

Kane, E. (2006). Confronting divergent conceptual interests in cross border regulatory arrangements. In *Cross Border Banking: Regulatory Challenges*, G. Caprio, D. Evanoff, and G. Kaufman (eds.). Singapore: World Scientific.

Kuritzkes, A., T. Schuermann and S. Weiner (2003). Risk measurement, risk management and capital adequacy of financial conglomerates. *Brookings-Wharton Papers in Financial Services*, 141–194.

Schoenmaker, D. and S. Oosterloo (2005). Financial supervision in an integrated Europe: Measuring cross-border externalities. *International Finance*, 8, 1–27.

Schoenmaker, D. and C. van Laecke (2006). Current state of cross-border banking. Presented at the International Banking Conference, Federal Reserve of Chicago, October 5–6.

Derivatives Governance and Financial Stability

David Mengle*

International Swaps and Derivatives Association, Inc.

Financial stability and crisis prevention are generally considered to be public sector responsibilities. Regulatory agencies, for example, seek to detect incipient crises and forestall them in the course of their prudential activities. Further, central banks seek to promote financial stability by means of acting as providers of liquidity in a crisis. Finally, multinational organizations specifically include financial stability as organizational objectives. The Bank for International Settlements, for example, sponsors a Financial Stability Forum and a Financial Stability Institute, both that bring together officials from various jurisdictions to address matters related to crisis detection and prevention. The International Monetary Fund lists preventing and resolving crises among its primary missions and publishes a semiannual Financial Stability Report.

As suggested above, private sector organizations also perform an important function in preventing and alleviating crises. Private efforts can take both explicit and implicit forms. In connection with derivatives activity, perhaps the best known private sector financial stability effort was the Group of Thirty derivatives study that culminated in the publication in 1993 of *Derivatives: Practices and Principles*. The objective of the study was to explain the role of OTC derivatives and to assess the state of OTC derivatives risk management. The result was a set of 24 recommendations that reflected current risk management practices among dealers and end-users. The study set a pattern that later efforts would follow, namely, to describe current practices in a way that was sufficiently flexible to be adapted to different corporate cultures without turning into a "checklist" to be imposed mechanically on all.

Another explicit effort was the 1999 Counterparty Risk Management Policy Group (CRMPG) study, Improving Counterparty Risk Management

*David Mengle is head of research at the International Swaps and Derivatives Association, Inc.

Practices, which was initiated by major financial institutions in the wake of the 1998 hedge fund crisis. The study focused on credit and market risk management issues that became especially critical with the increasing role of hedge funds, and emphasized liquidity, leverage, stress testing and risk disclosure.

Most recently, major financial firms, both sell-side and buy-side, undertook an update of the CRMPG study, entitled "Toward Greater Financial Stability: A Private Sector Perspective" but known more commonly as Counterparty Risk Management Policy Group II. The primary objective of the study, which was published in 2005, was to evaluate the state of counterparty risk management following the original study. The study went beyond the original, however, by emphasizing the documentation and operational infrastructure and by making specific recommendations for the automation of back office systems for structured financial products, especially credit derivatives.

The above private sector efforts have in common the explicit objective of promoting financial stability. But there are other private sector efforts that effectively promote financial stability without explicitly seeking to do so; these efforts are arguably the first line of defense against financial crises. The stated objective of such "implicit" financial stability efforts is typically not crisis avoidance, but rather something of more immediate and private benefit such as development of infrastructure or of industry standards. The result is nonetheless enhanced stability, lower crisis incidence, and alleviation of the effects of crises if and when they occur.

Fundamentally, the most important guarantors of financial stability are the risk management activities performed by individual firms; in particular, the increasing use of OTC derivatives to manage risk is arguably an important stabilizing factor. But individual activity has its limits; at some level, collective efforts are necessary to address problems. The following sections focus on implicit private sector collective efforts — which have been characterized as "private interbank discipline"[1] — with respect to over-the-counter derivatives. OTC derivatives are a particularly appropriate example because they operate across legal and regulatory boundaries under a largely informal yet effective governance structure. The following section describes OTC derivatives and their governance, with particular attention to the role of the International Swaps and Derivatives Association.

---

[1] David Oedel, 1993, "Private Interbank Discipline", *Harvard Journal of Law and Public Policy* 16, pp. 327–409.

1. OTC Derivatives and ISDA

Over-the-counter (OTC) derivatives are customized, privately negotiated bilateral agreements designed explicitly to shift risk from one party to another. They differ substantially from futures contracts, which are standardized, exchange-traded derivatives subject to automatic risk control procedures and covered by a uniform regulatory framework. Although OTC derivatives commonly employ risk management procedures that are economically similar to those used for futures, such procedures are not required but are subject to negotiation between the contracting parties.

OTC derivatives, which most agree date from the beginning of the 1980s, fall into three main product categories. *Forward contracts* involve the agreement on the trade date to an exchange at agreed terms on an agreed date. *Swaps* are essentially sequences of forwards: They involve the agreement on the trade date to a series of exchanges of cash flows at agreed terms on an agreed series of payment dates. The most common form of swap obligates one party to pay a fixed interest rate and the other to pay a floating interest rate calculated on a notional principal. Finally, *options* give one party (buyer), who pays a premium to the other party (seller or writer), the right but not the obligation to buy or sell an agreed amount of an underlying asset at an agreed price on or until an agreed date. Most OTC derivative product variations involve various configurations or combinations of forwards, swap, and options. Underlying risks include interest rates, currencies, commodity and equity prices, and credit.

Credit derivatives are relatively new derivative products, and come in two main types. *Total return swaps* are agreements in which one party passes the total economic performance — both credit and market risk — to the other party, who in return pays a money market interest rate plus a negotiated spread. *Credit default swaps* are agreements in which one party pays a fixed periodic fee to the other party for protection against default by a third party. The difference between the two is that credit default swaps transfer only credit risk, while total return swaps transfer both credit and market risk. According to the British Bankers Association, credit default swaps were about 94 percent of credit derivatives outstanding as of 2006.[2]

OTC derivatives governance. Regulatory regimes generally recognize that the bilateral and customized nature of OTC derivatives make them unsuitable for traditional financial regulatory regimes; indeed, OTC

---

[2] British Bankers Association, 2006, "BBA Credit Derivatives Report 2006".

derivatives are explicitly exempt from regulation as futures in the United States and they are typically not regulated as securities in most major jurisdictions.[3] Because OTC derivatives are not regulated as a separate category of products as are securities or futures, they are sometimes described as unregulated products. Such a characterization is inaccurate, however; OTC derivatives are subject to a diverse set of regulatory influences along with an informal yet effective governance structure.[4]

First, the vast majority of derivatives dealers are subject to some form of official regulation, most commonly as banks or securities firms. In the European Union, where a large proportion of derivatives activity takes place, derivatives participants are explicitly subject to regulation as a condition of receiving the Single Passport.[5] Hedge funds are a major category of market participant and often not directly regulated, but they do not act as dealers. Given the diverse regulatory environment spanning a wide variety of jurisdictions, the private interbank discipline that characterizes OTC derivatives governance is by necessity highly adaptable to different regulatory regimes.

Second, the OTC derivative governance framework places great emphasis on the underlying legal infrastructure within which market participants conduct business rather on specific rules governing activity. As a general matter, significant OTC derivatives activity takes place only in jurisdictions in which contracts and property rights are respected and enforceable. The primary means of strengthening the legal infrastructure is to increase legal certainty across diverse jurisdictions. The International Swaps and Derivatives Association, Inc. (ISDA), for example, has worked with a variety of jurisdictions to achieve enhancements to bankruptcy codes in order to facilitate the posting of collateral, to permit the early termination of swap contracts, and to recognize the enforceability of close-out netting of obligations.

Finally, swaps activity proceeds under the presumption of market discipline — in which firms are accountable for and will bear the losses that result from their decisions — as opposed to compliance with a detailed set

---

[3] Oedel, 1993.

[4] This discussion draws on David Mengle, 2003, "Regulatory Origins of Risk Management", in *Modern Risk Management: A History*, London: Risk Books, Chapter 27. Wikipedia defines governance as "the use of institutions, structures of authority and even collaboration to allocate resources and coordinate or control activity in society or the economy."

[5] European Parliament, Directive 2004/39/EC.

of restrictions on conduct. The difference between a regime based on market discipline and one based on regulatory compliance shows up in the relative diversity of governance structures for OTC derivatives compared with compliance structures for securities and other formally regulated products. Compliance departments, on the one hand, are designed to respond to a specific set of requirements that are uniform across institutions, and the structure of such departments is likely to be dictated by the nature of the rules to be enforced; one would expect compliance structures to be somewhat uniform across firms. OTC derivatives, on the other hand, are monitored by control and reporting functions structured to fit a particular corporate organization and control culture; one would expect that, because firms differ, so would risk management departments that monitor OTC derivatives activity.

ISDA plays a major role in the governance of OTC derivatives activity as described above. Yet, ISDA has no explicit regulatory role; all of its efforts are voluntary in nature. The following section describes the role ISDA plays in swaps governance.

Role of ISDA. The International Swaps and Derivatives Association is the international trade association for OTC derivatives market participants. ISDA's origins lie in the early 1980s as a project of eleven major dealers interested in imposing order on a new market. A major problem at the time was that each dealer had its own documentation, and disputes over terms of transactions gave rise to frequent and costly disputes; the initial objective of the project was to create a common documentation infrastructure.[6] ISDA was chartered in 1985 as the International Swap Dealers Association; since that time, ISDA expanded its membership to include non-dealer derivatives participants, and changed its name to the current version in 1993. As of mid-September 2006, a total of 742 organizations were ISDA members. Of that total, 219 were Primary Members (dealers); 270 were Subscriber Members (end-users such as corporations, government and multinational entities, and hedge funds); and 253 were Associate Member (service providers such as law firms, rating agencies, data providers and brokers).

ISDA is not a self-regulatory organization. It has (and seeks) no explicit regulatory mandate from any jurisdiction, and its decisions are not

---

[6] Sean Flanagan, 2001, "The Rise of a Trade Association: Group Interactions within the International Swaps and Derivatives Association", *Harvard Negotiation Law Review* 6, pp. 211–264.

binding on its members. As mentioned above, all efforts are voluntary, and focus primarily on the legal and operational infrastructure that underpins OTC derivatives activity.

ISDA functions by means of a board of directors, consisting mostly of senior managers of derivatives businesses at primary member firms; and committees, consisting of employees of member organizations and facilitated by ISDA staff. The ISDA committee structure is the central element of ISDA's functioning. Some committees address a particular component of the derivatives infrastructure such as documentation, operations, or collateral; other committees are concerned with specific products such as credit derivatives, equity derivatives, or energy and emerging products; others address policy matters such as regulation, accounting or tax; and still others focus on a geographical region such as Canada, Asia-Pacific, or Central and Eastern Europe.

ISDA is best known for the ISDA Master Agreement, which serves as standard form documentation for most OTC derivatives activity. The ISDA Master Agreement is negotiated by two parties, ideally prior to entering actual transactions, and sets the terms of the bilateral relationship between the parties. The Agreement enables the contracting parties to pre-negotiate the so-called "non-economic" terms of transactions, such as representations and warranties, events of default and governing law, so that a specific transaction need only involve negotiation of "economic" terms such as price or rate, notional amount, and maturity. The most significant function, however, is the *single agreement structure* under which the ISDA Master Agreement serves as the contract between the two parties and individual deals are incorporated by reference into the Agreement. In other words, individual OTC transactions are not legally separate contracts, but instead part of the contract known as the Master Agreement.

The ISDA Master Agreement consists of several components. First, the ISDA Master Agreement proper is a standard form document developed jointly by ISDA committee members, legal counsel and ISDA staff; the most recent version was issued in 2002. The contracting parties do not typically alter the Agreement itself. The second component is the Schedule to the Agreement, in which parties specify any terms that deviate from the standard terms of the Master Agreement itself. Such terms result from negotiation between the parties prior to execution, and could include additional termination events such as downgrade or net asset value thresholds. The third component is the Credit Support Annex, which facilitates credit exposure management by specifying the terms under which the parties engage in risk management activities such as collateral; a schedule to the CSA contains any deviations from the standard form itself.

The fourth component of the Master Agreement is the Confirmation, which the parties produce each time they transact and which serves as evidence of an individual deal. New or unusual transactions are documented under a Long-form Confirmation, which allows for detailed specification of transaction terms. In contrast, established types of transactions such as interest rate swaps and credit default swaps are documented under a Short-form Confirmation, which is linked to various sets of definitions developed and updated periodically by ISDA. Finally, ISDA occasionally develops protocols that amend provisions of the ISDA Master Agreements to address industry-wide events such as the introduction of the euro. While not explicitly part of the ISDA Master Agreement, protocols add to industry efficiency by eliminating the need for bilateral negotiations to amend the terms of an agreement.

An important feature of the ISDA Master Agreement is that it includes specific provisions that help manage and limit credit losses in the event of counterparty default. The first provision is for *early termination* of contracts if an event of default occurs. When such an event takes place, the non-defaulting party closes out and accelerates (terminates) all existing transactions under the Agreement, and calculates a net present value to obtain a closeout amount. The second provision is for *closeout netting*, which — if legally enforceable in the defaulting party's jurisdiction — combines offsetting obligations between the two parties into a single net payable or receivable. Finally, the Credit Support Annex facilitates collateralization in order to limit losses if a default occurs. All of the above attract considerable interest from regulators; close-out netting and collateralization, by limiting credit exposure on derivatives, can reduce required regulatory capital for institutions subject to capital regulation. In order to increase the level of certainty, ISDA commissions legal opinions regarding netting and collateral protection for various jurisdictions and makes them available to member firms.

In addition to the documentation infrastructure, ISDA is concerned with the operational and risk management infrastructure, including trade processing, confirmation, settlement, as well as collateralization and other credit support. ISDA committees do not impose binding standards, but serve as means of cooperation in developing voluntary standards and sharing information regarding current and emerging practices. ISDA also conducts annual surveys to assess the state of infrastructure development: The Operations Benchmarking Survey collects and publishes information about the efficiency, accuracy, and level of automation of reporting firms' operations functions; and the Margin Survey collects and publishes information about the extent of collateral use and coverage in reporting firms' OTC derivatives activity.

Finally, ISDA acts as an advocate for OTC derivatives internationally in a variety of ways. First, ISDA actively encourages national governments to enact legislation that facilitates derivatives activity by authorizing early termination and by making closeout netting enforceable in bankruptcy. Second, ISDA committees and representatives track and seek to influence legislative and regulatory matters that affect OTC derivatives, with particular attention to legal certainty. Recent examples include the Commodity Futures Modernization Act of 2000 in the United States, and, currently, the Markets in Financial Instruments Directive (MiFID) in the European Union. Third, ISDA has been active in addressing the provisions of the new risk-based capital standards (Basel II) that affect OTC derivatives. And finally, ISDA committees have provided feedback to the Financial Accounting Standards Board in the United States and the International Accounting Standards Committee on their accounting standards for derivatives.

The above ISDA activities do not claim to be crisis avoidance measures; all appear to be motivated by member firms' self-interest. Yet they promote financial stability in two ways. First, they promote a sound and workable infrastructure for derivatives activity and thereby reduce the vulnerability of OTC derivatives to systemic shocks. And second, by creating an infrastructure that facilitates the use of derivatives to manage risks, they contribute to the stability of world financial markets.[7] The next section presents the development of credit derivatives and their infrastructure as a case study in private sector efforts that promote financial stability.

---

[7] Alan Greenspan, 2005, "Risk Transfer and Financial Stability", Federal Reserve Bank of Chicago, Conference on Bank Structure; and Jesse Eisinger, "Long & Short: On Hold for Five Years, 9/11 Drag May Begin to Emerge in Economy", *Wall Street Journal*, September 13, 2006.

2. Implicit Financial Stability Efforts in Practice: Credit Derivatives

Credit derivatives are privately negotiated agreements that explicitly transfer credit risk from one party to another. As mentioned earlier, the most common type of credit derivative is the credit default swap (CDS). In a CDS, one party (protection buyer) pays a fixed periodic fee to the other (protection seller) for protection against default by a third party (reference entity) in an agreed amount. The reference entity is most commonly a single corporation or sovereign entity (name), a basket of names, or a diversified index of names; a recent innovation is a CDS referencing an asset backed security issue or index. The fee (CDS spread) paid by the buyer is fixed on the trade date, and is an annual percent of the underlying amount paid on a quarterly basis; the CDS spread is a function of the market's estimate of the reference entity's expected default loss. If a default event occurs, the seller compensates the buyer in one of two ways. In *physical settlement*, the buyer delivers to the seller an obligation such as a bond of the reference entity; in return the seller pays the par value of the obligation. In *cash settlement*, the seller pays the buyer the loss amount, which is normally the par value minus the post-default value of the obligation. Physical settlement is the standard settlement method, although that is likely to change in the near future as described below.

Credit default swaps were developed in the 1990s in response to two problems faced by financial institutions. The first problem was that financial institutions had no means of hedging credit risk; put differently, banks could not take a short position in credit.[8] Given that credit risk was and continues to be the most significant risk faced by banks, hedging could be quite useful. A second problem was that diversification of credit risk was difficult to accomplish. Banks were consequently prone to concentration of credit exposures. If a solution could be found to the first problem, the solution could help address the second problem. Credit derivatives were the solution. The British Bankers Association first surveyed credit derivatives in 1997; reported notional amount outstanding was $180 billion. According to ISDA, which began surveying credit default swaps in 2001, notional amount outstanding as of June 2006 was $26.0 trillion.[9] One estimate places single-name CDS at 60 percent of total volume and index

---

[8] Shorting a corporate bond is generally infeasible in practice.
[9] British Bankers Association, 2006; ISDA Market Survey, Mid-Year 2006.

CDS at 25 percent; the remainder includes such products as basket CDS, tranched index products and synthetic securitization products.[10]

Operational infrastructure. ISDA has been active in industry efforts to address operational challenges posed by credit derivatives. ISDA has also promoted efforts to spur liquidity in the credit derivatives market. An example is the adoption of standard settlement dates: Unless specifically negotiated otherwise, CDS payment dates occur on only four days of the year: March 20, June 20, September 20, and December 20. The standard dates were chosen with the explicit goal of making CDS more liquid by channeling trading to a limited number of settlement and maturity dates.

Another challenge has been the growth of index CDS, which has led to concerns that purchased CDS protection is now several orders of magnitude greater than the supply of underlying reference entity bonds. If a default were to occur and market participants were to attempt physical settlement, the resulting liquidity pressure on the underlying bonds could be so substantial as to reduce the effective default protection and to make settlement impossible by threatening bond market liquidity. In order to avoid such difficulties, ISDA developed a series of CDS Index Protocols to substitute cash settlement, which involves direct compensation for loss, for physical settlement. The primary task of these protocols is to facilitate cash settlement by establishing an auction procedure for determining post-default bond value. The first such protocol addressed the March 2005 bankruptcy of Collins & Aikman Products Co. Subsequent protocols have covered credit events involving Delta Air Lines and Northwest Airlines, Delphi Corporation, Calpine Corporation and Dana Corporation. ISDA is nearing completion of a permanent solution in which cash settlement is the standard and physical settlement is an option.

Documentation infrastructure. Prior to 1999, credit default swaps were documented under a Long-form Confirmation because of the lack of a standard set of definitions. ISDA's first contribution was a Long-form Confirmation template issued in 1998; ISDA issued the first set of credit derivative definitions in the following year. As CDS activity grew, the CDS documentation generally held up well; major defaults of Enron and WorldCom settled smoothly and posed few problems. Still, problems inevitably rise that test the applicability of the ISDA documents and definitions. Once the relevant committee has developed a solution, ISDA

---

[10] CRMPG II, p. A-4.

issues supplements to the definitions as an interim fix. Once the solutions develop critical mass, ISDA develops and issues a new set of definitions that embody the lessons learned and enable market participants to benefit. The process by which ISDA documentation adapts to changing circumstances and to unanticipated challenges can be seen in the way ISDA dealt with challenges that arose over the last few years.

One such problem was restructuring. The 1999 Definitions included debt restructuring — that is, actions such as lowering coupon or extending maturity — as a credit event triggering payment under a CDS. The definition was put to the test with the restructuring in 2000 of loans to Conseco. Banks agreed to extend the maturity of Conseco's senior secured loans in return for higher coupon and collateral; protection was thereby triggered on about $2 billion of CDS. Protection buyers then took advantage of an embedded "cheapest to deliver" option in CDS by delivering long-dated senior unsecured bonds, which were deeply discounted — worth about 40 cents on the dollar — relative to the restructured loans — worth over 90 cents on the dollar. Protection sellers ended up absorbing losses that were greater than those incurred by protection buyers, which led many sellers to question the workability of including restructuring. The problem was complicated further by the insistence by some regulators that CDS cover restructuring in order for a CDS hedge to qualify for capital relief. The result, arrived at through the committee process, was a set of modifications to the definition of restructuring that placed some limits on deliverable bond maturity and therefore on the cheapest to deliver option.

Another problem involved apportioning credit protection when a reference entity de-merges or spins off part of its activities into new entities. The problem arose in the United Kingdom in 2000, when National Power de-merged into two companies, one of which inherited 56 percent of National Power's obligations and the other held the rest. The problem was to determine the new reference entity for CDS referencing National Power, but the 1999 Definitions did not provide sufficient guidance to assure the market that courts would agree on the outcome. The result was to develop a set of detailed "Successor" provisions, which provided quantitative thresholds for such cases.

Yet another problem was debt moratoria or repudiations in emerging markets. During the Argentine debt crisis of 2002, there were several changes of government, involving a succession of officials that made threats regarding debt repudiation. The problem arose that, under the 1999

Definitions, it might be possible to declare a repudiation credit event following a statement by a government official even if in the end the government did not fail to pay its obligations. In order to reduce the risk of declaring a credit event prematurely, ISDA developed more stringent criteria for such an event.

These three solutions were developed by ISDA and promulgated at first by means of supplements to the 1999 Definitions. These solutions were considered sufficient to merit a new set of definitions. The result was the 2003 Credit Derivative Definitions, which embodied the new changes along with various minor amendments.

3. Limits to Implicit Financial Stability Efforts:
Credit Derivatives and Novations

The entry of hedge funds and other investors into credit derivatives has been an important factor in the development of CDS market liquidity and efficiency. Such investors enter primarily to take positions. If an investor believes protection on a reference entity to be underpriced, for example, it buys protection; if the view turns out to be correct, the fund reverses the transaction at a profit. Similarly, a fund that believes that a distressed credit's prospects will improve could sell protection in the hope of unwinding at a profit if the improvement occurs. Although such speculative activity has attracted some official concern, it is generally recognized as beneficial because it contributes to market liquidity.[11]

In order to understand the novations problem, it is necessary to understand how OTC derivatives trade. OTC derivatives do not trade in the same way as securities, that is, by means of transfer of ownership. Instead, they trade "synthetically" by three different means, each of which involves payment by one party to the other of a transaction's mark-to-market value. First, the parties can agree to a *termination*, under which they agree to extinguish the original obligation following payment. Second, one party can enter into an *offsetting transaction*, which leaves the original transaction in place but cancels out its economic effect. Finally, one party can enter into a *novation*, also known as an *assignment*, under which the party (transferer) transfers its rights and obligations under the transaction to a third party (transferee) in exchange

---

[11] International Monetary Fund, 2006, "Global Financial Stability Report", April, Chapter II.

for a payment. The ISDA Master Agreement requires a transferor to obtain prior written consent from the remaining party before a novation takes place.

Until relatively recently, novations were relatively infrequent; the usual method of exiting a transaction was an offsetting transaction. As hedge funds became more active in CDS, however, novations became increasingly common. Investors, and especially hedge funds, tend to prefer unwind through novation to unwind through offset because they are reluctant to incur additional credit exposure in the form of an offsetting swap. And they generally prefer novation to termination because termination limits unwind possibilities to the original counterparty and has the potential of providing insights into trading strategies to the counterparty. The result was an increase in novations, especially as index trading grew; one estimate placed novations at 40 percent of trade volume.[12]

Novations became a problem because of the failure of participants to follow established procedure. First, an investor wishing to step out of a transaction via novation might not obtain prior consent from the remaining party. Second, the transferee might not verify that the transferor had obtained clearance. Finally, the remaining party, which might not have been aware of the novation until the first payment date following, might later on back-date its books to the novation date and simply change the counterparty name. The finger pointing went further: When dealers complained that investors failed to obtain consent, investors countered that remaining parties might give consent but fail to transmit the necessary information to the back office in a timely manner. Although novations in such cases did not typically lead to significant adverse credit exposures for dealers — transferees are virtually always dealers and therefore better capitalized than the hedge fund transferors — they did present substantial operational problems in the form of confirmation backlogs.

The industry was aware of the problem. ISDA addressed the issue in 2002 by developing novation definitions, a standard novation confirmation, and a best practices statement. Regulators were also aware of the problem, and in some cases expressed concern publicly. Further, the large number of counterparties involved made it difficult to solve the problem by means of bilateral negotiations. In order to break the impasse, ISDA decided in the spring of 2005 to pursue a protocol

---

[12] CRMPG II, p. 115.

approach, under which ISDA would draft specific procedures to which counterparties can agree to adhere when undertaking novations. Once a counterparty agrees to adhere to the protocol, any dealings with other adhering counterparties.

A solution did not ensue, however, because of competitive pressures and the lack of incentive to act alone. On the one hand, dealers were aware of the problem and would benefit if all parties to novations followed established procedures as developed in the protocol. But on the other hand, refusing to agree to novations if procedures were not followed would lead to losing potentially profitable business to those dealers that did not insist on proper procedures. The industry consequently found itself in a Prisoners' Dilemma situation in which each party would benefit from adhering to proper procedures but had no means of knowing whether other parties would do so as well. The result was no change, and confirmation backlogs increased.

During August 2005, however, Federal Reserve Bank of New York President Timothy Geithner invited fourteen major credit derivative dealers to a meeting to discuss CDS operations issues, with particular attention to confirmation backlogs. At the meeting, which occurred the following month, the dealers agreed to reduce backlogs and to report their progress periodically. Although all participants are ISDA members, ISDA is not a direct participant in the industry meetings.

The effort to reduce backlogs led to increased interest in pursuing ISDA's proposed protocol solution in a way that was acceptable both to dealers and hedge funds. The result, known as the ISDA Novation Protocol, was announced just before the New York Fed meeting in September.[13] The protocol entailed extensive negotiation between dealers, hedge funds, and other participants, and specified a set of explicit duties for the parties to a novation. Under the protocol, parties wishing to act as transferees are required to obtain prior consent, but are now able to do so electronically. If the remaining party provides consent prior to 6pm New York time, the novation is complete; the remaining party can respond by email. If the remaining party does not provide consent prior to 6pm, the transferor and transferee enter into an offsetting transaction that obtains a similar economic result to the novation.

---

[13] Kenneth Raisler and Lauren Teigland-Hunt, 2006, "How ISDA Took on the Confirmations Backlog", *International Financial Law Review*, February. The protocol is published at http://www.isda.org/isdanovationprotII/isdanovationprotII.html.

Market participants were given a deadline to sign on to the ISDA Novation Protocol; dealers agreed not to transact novations with parties that did not agree. In order to provide assurance that remaining parties would not respond promptly to novation requests, dealers committed to specific standards for responding by the deadlines in the protocol. The result has been considered a success: 2,000 parties signed on to the original Novation Protocol, and almost 190 entities have signed on to a version designed for new participants. Initial assessments of the protocol have been favorable. These assessments have corresponded to reports that the industry has made considerable progress in reducing confirmation backlogs, which by June 2006 had been reduced 80 percent from their September 2005 levels, and increasing overall operational efficiency.[14]

The case of novations demonstrates that collective action problems can threaten the feasibility of private sector efforts, but that thoughtful regulatory action can facilitate a solution. Although all parties had an interest in a solution, none believed the other side was willing to take the necessary steps. Further, competitive considerations made dealers reluctant to exert pressure on one of their most active client groups. The regulatory intervention provided sufficient cover for dealers to insist on adherence by their clients. In this case, a relatively light touch by a regulator was sufficient to bring about a solution.

4. Conclusion

Few would deny the importance of the role played by public sector organizations, both at the national and multinational level, in preventing crises and promoting financial stability. Yet on a day-to-day basis, private organizations associated with private, profit-seeking activities might play an even more fundamental role than public organizations. In the case of OTC derivatives, which from their inception have operated across borders, a governance structure evolved that arguably compensates for the lack of cross-border regulatory authority.

OTC derivatives operate in an infrastructure designed to allow market participants to anticipate problems before they occur and to develop solutions when problems do occur. Although OTC derivatives do not fit well

---

[14] Paul Davies, "Dealers Cut Down Derivative Backlog", *Financial Times*, July 20, 2006.

into customary forms of financial regulation, they have proven themselves to be compatible with a diverse set of regulatory regimes. Even when collective action reaches its limits, the novations issue has shown the potential for private and public organizations to operate in a complementary manner.

Cross-Border Crisis Prevention: Public and Private Strategies

Gerard Caprio, Jr.*
Williams College

First, let me begin by thanking the organizers for an outstanding agenda. Related to that, just the theme for this session is unusual — public and private strategies. Most conferences on regulation deal only with the former (guess who organizes these) or the latter (organized only by the private sector). So, the Chicago Fed deserves particular congratulations for understanding that both public and private sector entities need to be involved if we are to make progress in preventing, or mitigating the costs of, cross-border crises.

After the earlier papers in this conference, and certainly from Arnoud Boot's paper, it is difficult to be anything but pessimistic that cross-border crises will long be prevented. As he notes, we are still waiting for a lender of last resort (LOLR) to emerge in Europe, as the national central banks, rather than the European Central Bank (ECB), have this power. All that can comfort those worried about a cross-border bank leading to troubles, which in Europe should be termed Banco Ambrosiano risk, is existence of a web of memoranda of understanding (MoUs) to sort out difficulties. However, if such an "organizational structure", if it can be called that, could effectively manage a crisis, then one might believe that the World Bank, with its decentralized management style, would do at least as good a job in handling crises as the International Monetary Fund (IMF). However, the international community decided a while ago that it actually knew better, and that for handling a crisis, centralized decision-making was the key to rapid and effective response. Strangely, many in Europe acknowledge this point and yet apparently remain willing to accept the present uncertainty when it comes to a cross-border systemic issue. Thus, it is not a problem of ignorance, but rather one of decision-making,

*Gerard Caprio, Jr. is a professor of economics at Williams College.

perhaps coupled with a sense of complaisance. Although this was not a reason for concern 20 years ago, it is today, and increasingly will become more important, as Europe finally reduces its barriers to cross-border competition.

What is perhaps most discouraging about the European inability to decide on a single LOLR is that it raises the legitimate fear — if "they" cannot coordinate among what still is a relatively smaller group, what hope is there that a larger and more diverse international group will be able to settle this issue? And if "they" cannot, does anyone seriously believe that domestic authorities, out of the goodness of their hearts, will cover depositors in other territories? I certainly would not expect to see such generosity, particularly as it would violate the fiduciary duty that local authorities have to home country taxpayers.

To be sure, we could of course turn to the IMF. However, the failure to reach an agreement on LOLR issues internationally would of course be replicated on their board, in all likelihood. Given the difficulty in deciding on incremental quotas for member countries at the most recent Bank-Fund Annual Meetings, it is hard to believe that much progress would be made in deciding on a role for the Fund. Indeed, a good part of David Hoelscher's paper is labeled "Options for going forward". Fewer options and more certainty are needed for an international LOLR.

If public sector agreement is not forthcoming, one then asks whether the private sector can cope. David Mengle provides an optimistic take on this in his paper on derivatives governance, with an informative contribution. I would like to believe that private sector groups would play a positive role. My own research in banking (Barth *et al.*, 2006) shows that neither capital requirements nor supervision has a significantly positive impact on the banking system, whereas private monitoring fosters the development and efficiency of the sector, as well as reducing the degree of corruption in banking. However, that work does not find a significant impact of market discipline on systemic bank stability. Instead, what works to enhance stability is greater diversification in banking, better incentives to curb excessive risk-taking (reducing the generosity of deposit insurance, for example), and fewer limits on bank activities.

We conclude from that study that it is important to focus on increased disclosure and on a supportive role for supervision — to verify the information disclosed, to administer penalties when disclosure is faulty, and to close failing banks, using market signals to identified those needing closure. Market discipline alone might not do the job. In the derivatives area, while Mengle's examples are noteworthy contributions, at the same time that I was reading his paper I had picked up a copy of *Traders, Guns, and Money* (Das, 2006), which talks about the "underside" of derivatives. If even 10 percent of the author's story is accurate, it suggests that derivatives and the hedge funds (and banks) that heavily utilize them will be closer to the cause of a future crisis than to its prevention. Garry Schinasi, in his comments, raised the issue of increasing disclosure requirements for hedge funds, a suggestion that was met with some resistance in the discussion. Here I have to note that previous attempts to increase disclosure, such as in England in the 19th century and the US during the depression, both in securities markets, were followed by a significant expansion in those markets (see Sylla, 1997). So, it may be that the industry is overstating the dangers of greater disclosure.

Lastly, I have to conclude that while the contributions of the authors to this session were commendable, the state of agreement decidedly is not. If a movie were to be made about the conference, its title would be from the 1940s classic, *A Wing and A Prayer*. For that is about all that we have to avoid a crisis from cross-border finance — much hope, but not much else.

References

Barth, J., G. Caprio and R. Levine (2006). *Rethinking Bank Regulation: Till Angels Govern*. New York and London: Cambridge University Press.

Das, S. (2006). *Traders, Guns, and Money, Knowns and Unknowns in the Dazzling World of Derivatives*. London: FT/Prentice Hall.

Sylla, R. (1997). The rise of securities markets: What can government do? In *Reforming Financial Systems: Historical Implications for Policy*, G. Caprio and D. Vittas (eds.). New York and London: Cambridge University Press.

VIII. WHERE TO FROM HERE: POLICY PANEL

Cross-Border Banking: Where to from Here?

Mutsuo Hatano*

Deposit Insurance Corporation of Japan

I am very much honored to have this opportunity to speak to you about my viewpoint on the cross border issues. Today, I am going to look at cross border issues from the Japanese perspective, focusing on one of our organization's concerns. But first, I would like to look at the current design of the Japanese deposit insurance system.

The Japanese deposit insurance scheme has been designed for a relatively "closed" system with little consideration of cross-border issues. One of the characteristics of the Japanese deposit insurance system, for example, is that there is no coverage for deposits accepted by foreign banks' branches in Japan. Neither does our system cover deposits placed with foreign branches of Japanese banks. This "no-coverage of foreign banks" policy came out from the fact that it is difficult to supervise foreign banks at the same level as that for domestic banks. Besides, the impact is very limited as the share of retail banking held by foreign banks is relatively low. Only about 3 percent of total deposits is held by foreign banks. Also the "no-coverage of outside territory" policy resulted from the fact that the Japanese deposit insurance system originally was designed to protect the small depositors in Japan. Also, the amount of deposits accepted by Japanese bank's foreign branches has been pretty small, so the impact has been very limited.

Our system, accordingly, has been somewhat isolated from the outside and less vulnerable to cross-border issues in terms of its design. Thus, if the Japanese system would have remained as a pure "paybox" type of deposit insurance system, the cross-border issue would not be an urgent issue for the Deposit Insurance Corporation of Japan (DICJ). However, due to the deregulation of financial markets and advances in

*Mutsuo Hatano is deputy governor at the Deposit Insurance Corporation of Japan.

financial technologies, money can now easily cross borders. The DICJ has been assigned several functions and mandates, in addition to the paybox type functions, that it cannot ignore the trend of borderless money transaction.

In addition to the basic functions, such as "premium collection" and reimbursement to depositors, the DICJ has several other functions. I would like to talk today about some of our newer functions namely, "purchase and recovery of nonperforming loans (NPLs)" and "pursuit of legal liabilities" related to bank failures. We execute these operations through our 100 percent subsidiary, the Resolution and Collection Corporation (RCC).

Assume a bank's debtor in Japan had fallen in default and is suspected of hiding assets by sending the money to a neighboring country, pretending as if it was an investment in, or a loan to, a certain company in that country. The debtor had run a business of small-sized hotels especially for couples and lovers in Japan. The debtor, at the end of a boom economy in 1990, borrowed a large amount of money from banks to invest in a large-scale project to expand his business. For a time, the business went well. But Company A gradually had a worsening of its profitability and eventually it fell in default. The DICJ had purchased the claims on Company A, with the value of 2.4 billion yen, approximately US$20 million, from the banks concerned. Then, we received a request for write-offs with the final payment of 130 million yen from the debtor, Company A.

However, as a result of our asset investigation of the debtor in Japan, we found that the debtor might have invested 12 billion yen and loaned 300 million yen to a certain Company B in the neighboring country. In fact, the debtor and his family own 77 percent of Company B. We then faced the obstacle of cross-border issues. We must have something concrete on the flow of money, whether the money was received by the Company B or not, in order to prove the legitimacy of the claim.

Naturally, the DICJ cannot exercise its investigative right or power abroad, which is delegated to us in our own country. Accordingly, the DICJ cannot obtain any absolute proof of the money flow and may need some help from the neighboring authorities in this case. This case is only one example of potential issues in cross-border banking.

Mutual cooperation with deposit insurance organizations and authorities of foreign countries in regard to this kind of investigation is one of the most difficult problems to be solved in the cross border issues.

However, solving the problem should be crucial to secure the social justice and fairness and to minimize the social cost.

The DICJ has a group of legal experts in-house to deal with this kind of international matter. However, there are several complicated and difficult problems when dealing with international legal affairs. Bilateral agreements for maintenance of confidentiality between deposit insurance organizations and authorities may be one of the options. And it may need to include a debt collection company or asset management company. In this case, some documentation of the agreement, such as a Memorandum of Understanding, may be of a great help to deal with this kind of problem.

Having bilateral agreements requires mutual understanding, and any adjustment to both legal systems may take a great deal of time and money. The rule of maintenance of confidentiality should fit in well with the international norm when trying to solve cross border problem within two or more different jurisdictions, although things would be more complicated and difficult. In that sense, a multilateral agreement or a multilateral MoU is, at least, desirable to solve the problem.

I assume that a multilateral organization of the area could help in setting up such an international norm. We have some precedents in International Organization of Securities Commissions (IOSCO) and the Financial Action Task Force (FATF) on Monetary Laundering.

In the area of deposit insurance, I think we also need such a framework for international cooperation in the area of the cross border issues. In fact, International Association of Deposit Insurers (IADI) is planning a workshop on cross-border issues in May 2007. This is a positive step toward the future. I hope that IADI, as the most broad-based international organization of deposit insurers, will play a key role in the area of cross-border issues affecting deposit insurance.

Remarks on Deposit Insurance Policy

Andrey Melnikov*
Deposit Insurance Association, Russia

It is my pleasure to participate on this panel and deliver some remarks based on what we have learned over the past two days.

I represent an agency engaged in deposit insurance and bank liquidation. Therefore, I will focus on issues well known to me — cross-border regulation in these areas.

The current session objective is to summarize key conference presentations.

The first conclusion is that the majority of countries are well aware of the financial markets' cross-border issues. Otherwise, we would not be sitting in this room. This is an obvious outcome of globalization.

The second conclusion — expanding banks' cross-border operations — gives rise to some important issues. Among them the interaction and refinement of relations among various countries' supervisors.

Major issues arise when one country allows the opening up of branches of other countries' banks. Therefore, home/host supervisory arrangements must be put into place. This process is not always free of conflicts. But it is ongoing.

However, in the area of deposit insurance these approaches are only in the initial stage of development. There are disputes and differences with regard to definitions of what is an insured deposit, how best to protect depositors' rights, and so on.

How should we move forward?

My proposal is as follows. We have to start developing a unified approach to deposit insurance respecting cross-border banks' operations. This is necessary to ensure transparency in legal and economic relationship. Depositors, banks and legislators will need this as well. We all have to be prepared to deal in a pragmatic way, particularly in crisis situations.

*Andrey Melnikov is the deputy general director of the Deposit Insurance Agency, Russia.

Thus, what kind of unified approach could be used, if a country's legislation allows for the opening up foreign banks' branches on its territory? Let's review two possible scenarios involving countries A and B. Branches of a bank from Country A start operation on B's territory.

The first question — whose deposit insurance system should guarantee depositor protection in such branches? In my opinion, it should be A.

The second question — what should be done if the deposit coverage is higher in Country B? To resolve the issue, Country A bank's branch should be allowed to participate in the deposit insurance system of Country B. This should be done to guarantee indemnity for the difference in coverage levels.

In this way, we will ensure unified competitive conditions and consumer protection rules.

The third question: the opposite situation — what should be done if coverage is lower in Country B? In this case it would not be appropriate to obligate Country A bank's branch participate in the local deposit insurance system. Moreover, it would be the right thing to restrict the coverage for branch's depositors by Country B limit.

I consider the above three rules to be optimal and reasonable.

The fourth condition may be more difficult. We want financial markets to develop freely. For this, we should be able ensure equal opportunity for owners of deposits denominated in national or foreign currencies. This would be the same with residents and non-residents. In the Russian Federation, we decided to follow this plan.

This morning, we discussed issues related to insolvent banks' resolution. The issue is critical for a deposit insurer as it is directly linked with reimbursement of depositors. In 2002, the Bank for International Settlements issued a paper "Supervisory Guidance of Dealing with Weak Banks". Unfortunately, it did not cover issues of banks' liquidation and settlements with their creditors.

I would like to draw your attention to another outstanding paper. It is "General Guidance for the Resolution of Bank Failures", developed by the International Association of Deposit Insurers (IADI). That paper was completed at the end of 2005. It contains information from a survey of 34 countries' experience in the area of banks' resolution.

I would like you to consider the fact that among countries included in the survey only three had legislation covering cross-border banks' resolution procedures. Therefore, a new IADI project headed by the Federal Deposit Insurance Corporation deserves overall support. The project is called "Cross-Border Issues".

There is another project of intellectual importance. It is a joint undertaking of The World Bank, the International Monetary Fund (IMF), and the Bank for International Settlements within the "Global Bank Insolvency Initiative" project. Its main goal is to progressively create an international consensus regarding the framework, including best practices and alternatives to deal with bank insolvency. I propose that the World Bank and IMF include IADI representatives in preparation of the addendum called "Cross-Border Aspects of Bank Insolvency".

Now I would like to say a few words about what approaches might be used when our views on cross-border banks' resolution are drawing closer. The approaches are based on my personal experience in liquidating cross-border banks.

For example, we had insolvency cases for banks with branches located in other countries, specifically in Cyprus. We had to deal with situations when bank's creditors took into custody its branch's property or appointed a separate branch liquidator.

This principle — "ring fencing" — is used in other countries as well, specifically in the US. It would prevent banks' creditors who are not branch's creditors from claiming assets located in this particular branch. The bank's liquidator is unable to include these assets in single bankruptcy estate. As a result, he is unable to distribute their value on fair basis among all creditors.

In my opinion, such practice is contradictory to the interests of cross-border banking development. It is outdated and would require actions aimed at matching with current reality.

I consider the following approach to be fair: All insolvent banks' assets, including its branches' assets located overseas, should be included in a single entity estate. Funds obtained as a result of asset disposition should be distributed among depositors and other creditors in accordance with unified rules and regulations.

I understand it may sound too optimistic, and even categorical, but we are discussing which direction we should be moving. It is a harmonization of approaches, a sharing of best practices, and a mutual recognition of law and awards of the court. That should be set as key goals to fulfill in the near future.

Thus, to sum up, to successfully handle issues related to cross-border financial instability, it is necessary to stick to the following:

* Trace and identify potential conflict zones and seek ways to resolve them beforehand;

- Follow harmonization of legislation and practices in the area of financial markets regulation and institutional restructuring;
- Establish mutual interests in the infrastructure among safety net participants on international basis.

We will have to work hard in order to implement the most valuable ideas and proposals developed internationally and those we heard during discussions yesterday and today.

The Importance of Planning for Large Bank Insolvencies

Arthur J. Murton*

Federal Deposit Insurance Corporation

I want to add my congratulations to the organizers of this conference. Once again, they have put together two days of thought-provoking and relevant panels. I always enjoy coming to the Federal Reserve Bank of Chicago. Every time I get out of the taxicab here, I look across the street to the building that once housed Continental Illinois, a bank that starred in one of the most important chapters in the history of the Federal Deposit Insurance Corporation (FDIC). It was the failure of Continental that brought prominence to the term "too-big-to-fail".

When I enter this building, I am always struck by the impressive atrium and massive pillars which bring to mind the importance of the Federal Reserve System in preserving the stability of our financial system. I am reminded then of the building where I work. The FDIC headquarters are located a block from the White House, with a wonderful view of the Washington Monument and the mall that surrounds it. While I believe this location speaks to the importance of the FDIC as a federal agency, I have to acknowledge that it may also reflect the fact that several decades ago, Washington was a sleepier city and prime real estate was available when the FDIC needed to relocate its offices.

In 1963, at the dedication of the FDIC headquarters, the Chairman of the House Banking and Currency Committee, Wright Patman, stated that:

> ... I think we should have more bank failures. The record of the last several years of almost no failures and, finally last year, no bank failures at all, is to me a danger signal that we have gone too far in the direction of bank safety.

---

*Arthur J. Murton is the director of the Division of Insurance and Research at the Federal Deposit Insurance Corporation.

Twenty years later, his concerns were more than addressed by a decade with the most bank failures since the creation of the FDIC.

The first paper of this conference pointed out that cross-border banking crises have actually been quite rare. It crossed my mind that Doug Evanoff was rather bold to arrange a conference where the focal point is a problem that occurs less frequently than we might imagine. Think of the alternative — call it a Patman Equilibrium — a world in which banking crises are frequent. While this would provide more data and experiences to fuel conferences such as these, most would agree that the costs would outweigh the benefits. Instead, we prefer a world — a Prompt Corrective Action (PCA) equilibrium — in which bank crises are rare. This limits the availability of data and experience, but it does not limit the value of this conference.

The discussions over the past two days have pointed out the challenges that could arise if a large multi-national financial institution were to face significant capital or liquidity problems. An earlier speaker pointed out that safety net arrangements are falling behind market developments and that, in fact, market realities are far ahead of regulatory frameworks designed to address cross-border financial crises. Such a state of affairs could lead to a condition where people throw up their hands and take the position that it is too difficult to prepare, so it is better to wait and react when problems emerge.

But these issues are worth thinking about and grappling with. If I could digress for a moment I would like to provide an example of why this is the case. Consider the following equation:

$$X^{X^{X^{X^{\cdots}}}} = 2 \, .$$

What does X equal? This problem was given to my daughter's seventh grade class the first week of school last year; in other words, to a group of children who up to that point had been exposed only to elementary school math. While the solution may be obvious to the sophisticated audience we have here today, one would expect this problem to present quite a challenge to a group of 12-year-old children.

The teacher who presented this problem, Mr. Vern Williams of Fairfax County, Virginia, is renowned throughout our region for developing students with extraordinary love of and proficiency in mathematics. Each week he presents problems such as these. His point, of course, is that it is worthwhile for his students to grapple with problems they may not be able to solve. There is value in exploring different paths to the solution and the insights the students gain are useful when they are faced with problems they are expected to solve.

This leads me back to this conference. As Mr. Williams does for his students, this conference presents us with questions that are difficult to answer, but the past two days have shown that there is value in discussing them. Not only is the dialog itself beneficial, but bringing together the interested parties can lead to the kind of cooperation and coordination that is necessary to solve cross-border problems when they arise.

As Chairman Bair mentioned yesterday in her remarks, deposit insurers from around the world have made great strides in recent years to create vehicles for collaboration such as the International Association of Deposit Insurers (IADI) and the European Forum of Deposit Insurers (EFDI). The FDIC actively supports such efforts while also recognizing, as the attendance at this conference points out, the need for dialog across a much broader community.

While deposit insurance is just one piece of the cross-border regulatory puzzle, it is an important piece. The role of deposit insurance varies significantly across countries. In some jurisdictions, deposit insurance is not simply about protecting the savings of small depositors. In the US, for example, the deposit insurance system features a bankruptcy mechanism for banks that is separate and distinct from the bankruptcy mechanism for all other financial and non-financial businesses. This obviously has important implications for how an insolvent bank is handled and how its creditors, borrowers, counterparties and investors are treated.

I want to talk now about something else Chairman Bair mentioned yesterday: what the FDIC is doing to enhance its ability to handle the failure of a large bank. While such an event is highly unlikely, the FDIC must plan and prepare for it. This advance work is particularly important because in all likelihood time would be at a premium if such an event occurred.

The FDIC has resolved over 1,600 failed banks in the last 25 years. The typical failure involves a bank closing on a Friday afternoon and re-opening the following Monday morning, providing depositors with uninterrupted access to their funds.

There are two points worth noting about this experience. The first is that the vast majority of these failures occurred prior to the passage of the FDIC Improvement Act of 1991 and thus were not subject to the least-cost test. This meant that the FDIC had the discretion, which it typically exercised, to resolve the failure in a way that allowed all depositors to be protected. It was not necessary to separate the insured and uninsured deposits.

The second point is that these failures were not large by today's standards. The largest of these, Continental Illinois, First Republic, and Bank of New England, approached $40 billion in assets; while large at the time, a bank of that size would not rank in the top forty today.

If a large bank were to fail today, the first major decision would be whether to invoke the "systemic-risk exception". This exception would allow the FDIC to forgo imposing losses on uninsured depositors. The systemic-risk exception may be used if a least-cost transaction "would have serious adverse effects on economic conditions or financial stability". Congress intended that this course of action not be undertaken lightly. Thus, a systemic risk determination can only be made by the Secretary of the Treasury, after it is approved by two-thirds majorities of the FDIC Board and the Federal Reserve Board and after consultation with the President.

At the time that a large bank is on the brink of failure, policymakers will need to consider a number of significant factors in deciding whether to adhere to a least-cost resolution or to invoke a system-risk exception. One factor could be the extent to which the operational aspects of the resolution itself could exacerbate potential "serious adverse effects". A goal of the FDIC is to ensure that decision-makers are able to make the policy choice free of operational considerations.

Operational readiness requires planning and preparation in a number of areas. There are at least three aspects of a large bank failure that could present significant operational challenges under a least-cost resolution. First, there is a need to separate insured deposits from uninsured deposits in a timely manner. Second, the failure may involve qualifying financial contracts (QFCs), such as derivative transactions. The special provisions in the law that govern the handling of QFCs will require quick decision-making with what will likely be limited information. Finally, the failure could involve foreign operations which could create logistical and jurisdictional challenges.

The FDIC has been preparing for these and other challenges of a least-cost resolution. The FDIC has a high-level committee to review and direct these efforts and we work closely with other federal agencies. In particular, the FDIC has done a great deal of work to enhance our ability to separate insured and uninsured deposits — what we refer to as the claims administration process.

In the event of a large bank failure, the FDIC expects to establish a bridge bank to provide for as much continuity of banking operations as possible. The bridge bank would be a national bank owned by the FDIC. The bridge bank would presumably open the next business day under new management selected by the FDIC. The FDIC would be preparing to divest itself of the ownership and return the resulting bank to the private sector.

A critical early step in the process would be deciding which claims are transferred to the bridge bank and which claims are left behind in the receivership created by the failure. This is not a simple matter, for two reasons. The first is that the rules for deposit insurance coverage are complicated. The second is that the deposit systems of most, if not all, banks are not designed to track the insured amounts of deposit accounts. This is the case because banks see little business value in knowing the insured status of accounts and regulators have not required them to keep such records.

In December 2005, the FDIC issued a Notice of Proposed Rulemaking (ANPR) to seek comments on ways to improve the claims administration process. The ANPR proposed several options that would require certain banks to alter their deposit systems. Not surprisingly, many of the comments we received focused on the cost-benefit tradeoff. The FDIC reviewed the comments, continued discussions with industry representatives, and refined our thinking as to how best to proceed. It is likely that the FDIC will seek further comment from the industry on the best way to approach these issues through another ANPR later this year.

It has been more than two years since an FDIC-insured bank failed — the longest hiatus in the history of the FDIC. In benign times such as these, it is tempting to discount the probability of banking problems and potential instability. The FDIC is resisting this temptation and is using this time to plan and prepare for what we hope will not happen. As I said earlier, the organizers of this conference should be commended for providing a forum for all of us to focus on the challenges that may lie ahead.

Where to from Here: Policy Panel

Guy Saint-Pierre*

Canada Deposit Insurance Corporation

I would like to begin by extending a warm "thank you" to Michael Moskow, president and chief executive officer (CEO) of the Chicago Fed and to J. P. Sabourin, chair of the Executive Council of IADI for hosting such an excellent conference. My congratulations go out as well to the excellent speakers we have heard over the past two days.

As you all know, the phenomena of cross-border banking and national financial regulation, and how they meet, is not only a question for academics but for practitioners as well. Today, I would like to address "… where to from here …" from the practical perspective of a deposit insurer and give you my views on how to improve the way we deal with cross-border bank failures.

Let me start by saying that the previous conference speakers have done an excellent job highlighting the problems we face with cross-border banking including such issues as the use of lender of last resort facilities, insolvency regimes, home versus host country supervision, and information sharing and coordination activities. These are all serious matters deserving serious attention and of particular importance for deposit insurers, central banks and others who typically end up on the hook in the event of a cross-border failure.

At the Canada Deposit Insurance Corporation (CDIC), we have not had a great deal of experience with cross-border banking failures — just one and that was the Bank of Credit and Commerce International (BCCI) in 1991. Although it was our only real cross-border failure, we learned some valuable lessons which I would like to convey to you.

First of all, the failure of BCCI was a surprise to us. At CDIC, we heard about the failure of the parent of our member institution — the Bank of Credit and Commerce Canada (BCCC) — at the last minute. The news

* Guy Saint-Pierre is president and chief executive officer of the Canada Deposit Insurance Corporation.

came on a Friday, and we had to locate our CEO on the golf course. We then rushed immediately to meet with our fellow financial safety net participants (the Superintendent of Financial Institutions, the Bank of Canada, and the Ministry of Finance) to deal with the proposed take-over of the Canadian bank subsidiary by the Superintendent. I recall our CEO showed up without a jacket and tie.

However, not having a jacket and tie turned out to be the least of his worries.

Due to the lack of early warning and the legal complexities of how BCCI was taken over, we had numerous problems winding up this institution. For example, it took us over six months to effectively close this bank because our laws at the time did not provide us with sufficient grounds for winding up the affairs of BCCI's Canadian bank subsidiary. Our rules then only allowed for the winding up of a member institution in the case of the member's insolvency. At the time, the Canadian BCCI subsidiary was solvent but the parent had failed. In the aftermath of BCCI, our insolvency laws were expanded to allow for the winding up of a CDIC member institution based upon the Superintendent having taken control of the institution.

The lack of early warning also lead to delays in reimbursing insured depositors. The CDIC could not undertake early preparatory examinations of our BCCI member and it consequently took us over a month to reimburse depositors. Depositor reimbursement should have taken, at the very most, a week with this type and size of institution under normal circumstances.

The speakers over the last two days have commented on the importance of good information sharing and cooperation among safety net players. We have heard about developing memoranda of understanding (memoranda of understanding can be very important for outlining the terms of information sharing — domestically, among safety net organizations and, internationally, between home and host supervisors and deposit insurers). Obviously, the existence of more effective information sharing and coordination agreements would have been very helpful for us in the BCCI failure.

But as a practitioner, I believe there is a need for even stronger mechanisms, such as bilateral and multilateral legal agreements such as treaties. To start with I would like to suggest that, every time an international bank wants to enter into another country, the host country should only allow this if a bilateral agreement is in place between itself and the home country regulatory authorities and deposit insurer. What you will find is that the banking industry will quickly push all parties involved to adopt multilateral international agreements.

This brings to an end my closing comments on where we go from here. I thank you all for your kind attention and for your time. I'd be delighted to answer any questions you have.

Some Private-Sector Thoughts on Home/Host-Country Supervisory Issues

Lawrence R. Uhlick*

Institute of International Bankers

1. Introduction

I am pleased to have this opportunity to offer some private-sector thoughts on home/host country supervisory issues. Of course, no thoughtful member of the private sector would question the need for robust supervision of financial institutions. Problems do arise, however, when global entities operating in multiple jurisdictions are subject to conflicting guidance and burdensome duplication of supervisory efforts. This is not merely a concern of internationally headquartered banking organizations operating in the US; it is also very much a concern of US banking groups with large international operations, such as Citigroup and JPMorgan Chase.

To be sure, there has been tremendous progress in international coordination and cooperation among global supervisors. And some home/host problems often can be ameliorated by the efforts of international coordination groups such as the Basel Committee and through such meetings as those involving derivative market participants and their domestic and international regulators. But as Tim Geithner, Sir Callum McCarthy and Annette Nazareth pointed out late last month in a joint article published in the *Financial Times*, even more cooperation among supervisors will be needed to pursue "borderless solutions" to the many complex problems in today's global market.[1]

*Lawrence R. Uhlick is chief executive officer of the Institute of International Bankers, which represents the interests of the international banking community in the United States. The views expressed in this paper are the personal views of Mr. Uhlick and do not necessarily represent the views of the Institute.

[1] See Timothy Geithner, Callum McCarthy and Annette Nazareth, 2006, "A Safer Strategy for the Credit Products Explosion", *Financial Times*, September 28.

Against this backdrop, it seems clear that regulation by sovereign countries of global banking organizations will be with us for quite a while. Indeed, the prospect of a global regulator is extremely remote — even if one assumes it is a good idea. Therefore, internationally active banks will experience home/host-country coordination issues for the foreseeable future. These issues are particularly prevalent with regard to cross-border branches and agencies, but there are also home/host problems with regard to Basel II implementation for subsidiaries and in relation to umbrella supervision by both home and host country supervisory authorities.

2. Cross Border Branches and Agencies

Let us start with cross-border branches and agencies and begin by acknowledging that there really has been a sea change with regard to the amount and depth of communications and coordination between home and host country supervisors during the last 10 years with respect to international banking institutions. This can be contrasted to the periodic meetings at international regulatory conferences that focused on general principles such as the Basel I agreement in 1988. There is now extensive ongoing discussion among home/host regulators of internationally active banking institutions. And not just during some sort of crisis situation. For example, they coordinate in the context of periodic examinations that they each conduct, as well as through periodic discussions of risk controls, capital strength and a whole variety of individual developments and concerns. This increased coordination has helped reduce inconsistent guidelines and to some degree the unnecessary duplication of supervisory review. Indeed, it must be conceded that you hear less frequently about private-sector concerns with differing home/host perspectives on market risk computations and controls, which occurred a fair amount in the 1990s.

Having said that, there is still room for greater cooperation and sharing of supervisory responsibilities with regard to examinations and oversight, and the potential for less duplication of efforts in these areas. For example, some large internationally headquartered banking institutions operating in the US have multiple on-site regulators from the Federal Reserve and state banking agencies in addition to the extensive global consolidated oversight they receive by home country authorities. The overseas operations of many internationally active US banks are subject to similar overlapping supervisory review. As I have pointed out on prior occasions, including my remarks at the Chicago Fed conference in May 1999, do the Financial Services Authority (FSA) and US banking authorities both have to supervise Barclays and Citigroup as large complex banking organizations in their respective jurisdictions.[2] While the private sector accepts the safety and soundness responsibility of the host country regulator, we believe host country regulators could achieve much greater efficiency in the process were they to team up or partner with home country regulators in carrying out their responsibilities.

The Basel II process does not exacerbate the situation regarding cross-border branches — at least not among the Group of Twenty (G20) countries — because they are subject to home country — not host country — Basel requirements. But in the US, branches of nondomestic banks are not home free. Under the landmark Gramm-Leach-Bliley Act, the Federal Reserve looks at a bank's global capital in making a determination whether to grant it financial holding company status — and thus become eligible to conduct a broader range of securities, insurance and merchant banking activities. To the Fed's credit, it generally uses home-country computations since it would be an extreme step to require banks to recalculate separate Basel computations on a global basis in accordance with host country standards. Accordingly, there is a big difference between a host country's review of an international bank's capital, in accordance with its home country capital standards, and the concentrated supervisory attention that an international bank's branches and other US operations actually experience on a continuing basis under existing US host-country examination and supervision of an internationally headquartered institution.

3. Cross-Border Subsidiaries

Where Basel II is having an impact on home/host relations applies more in connection with subsidiaries. The traditional thinking regarding subsidiaries was that the host country had pretty free rein with a separately capitalized entity incorporated in the host jurisdiction. Even the European Union's (EU) Second Banking Directive, whose "passport" system permits

---

[2] Lawrence Uhlick, 1999, "Meeting the Challenges of Supervising Banking Organizations' Cross-Border Activities", *Proceedings of a Conference on Bank Structure and Competition*, Federal Reserve Bank of Chicago, May.

European-wide branches to operate subject only to home country super-vision, took a different approach with regard to bank subsidiaries in Europe. In many respects, the subsidiary is expected to fully conform to all regulatory and supervisory requirements similar to domestically head-quartered institutions in the same jurisdiction. This was certainly true under Basel I. The expectations of the private sector regarding Basel II were much higher with regard to the consistent application of the Basel framework not only on a consolidated basis but as applied to various legal entities around the world. For example, it was anticipated that validation of sophisticated risk models used under the advanced internal ratings based methodology could essentially be performed by home-country reg-ulators and accepted by host-country regulators for various subsidiaries. Duplication of this process seems highly unnecessary, at least to private sector participants. This is especially the case with respect to the treatment of intermediate holding companies established to rationalize the structure of an international bank's operations in a host country. Subjecting these entities to host country Basel II requirements, as is contemplated in the United States, is both unjustified and unnecessary.

However, with regard to other aspects of the Basel II regime the situ-ation is, in fact, a lot more complex. For example, it is worth considering whether validation regarding some retail portfolios should reflect host country conditions and might more appropriately be conducted by host country authorities and be accepted by home country authorities. Similar considerations might apply to commercial real estate portfolios. However, it would appear that for wholesale corporate portfolios validation by home country consolidated regulators of the model would be highly appropriate. And there is strong sentiment that risk regarding transnational corporate borrowers should not be treated differently in the home and host country jurisdictions. Likewise, validation of the treatment of securitization port-folios under Basel II would appear to be a matter more appropriately addressed by home country supervisory authorities.

This problem of different treatment of the same corporate borrower is exacerbated by the differences in the definition of default, as for example under the European Commission's Capital Requirements Directive (CRD) and the US Basel II notice of proposed rulemaking (NPR). Private banks are concerned that differing definitions of default would necessitate main-tenance of separate home/host databases to facilitate home/host computa-tions, which would entail considerable additional costs and burdens.

Concerns regarding needless duplication of supervisory effort also have arisen with regard to the Basel II Pillar 2 review process, where one would expect host countries, to a significant extent, to be able to utilize and rely upon home country efforts in order to reduce the duplication and burden on domestic subsidiaries.

I want to emphasize that the "college of regulators" approach developed by the Basel Committee's Accord Implementation Group (AIG) is encouraging practical solutions to many of these problems so as to minimize burdens resulting from home/host implementation of Basel II advanced methodologies. And I should also point out that the private sector gives high marks to AIG Chairman Nick Le Pan for a highly commendable effort to explore these concerns and seek consensus solutions by home/host country supervisors to minimize unnecessary burdens.

In addition, the Committee of European Banking Supervisors has proposed a system of solving these issues among home/host regulators in Europe with respect to parents and subsidiaries operating there. It will need to be left to future meetings to see whether these collective efforts are successful in ameliorating the burdens that otherwise would be incurred in implementing Basel II on a global basis.

4. Umbrella Supervision

There are also home/host issues in relation to umbrella supervision. Non-US banks that have branches or subsidiaries in the US are subject to Federal Reserve holding company — or umbrella — supervision despite home country umbrella supervision of their global operations. These arrangements have been in place with regard to branches since the International Banking Act of 1978, and previously with regard to ownership of bank subsidiaries, and have generally worked reasonably well. However, it is interesting to contrast the arrangements under the EU conglomerates directive, whereby financial institutions headquartered in the US and other non-EU countries are not subject to European-wide umbrella supervision if there is "equivalent" umbrella supervision by their home country supervisors. Under this arrangement, the EU determined that the SEC provides "equivalent" umbrella supervision to US securities firms under the Securities and Exchange Commission's (SEC) Consolidated Supervised Entity (CSE) regulation. It should be recognized that prior to this SEC regulation, the major securities firms in the US and their affiliates were not subject to holding company or umbrella supervision by the SEC. In fact, the regulation depends on a securities firm group volunteering to be subject to SEC umbrella supervision in order to be eligible for the favorable risk-base Alternative Net Capital rule for the registered broker-dealer.

International banks have questioned the appropriateness of being required to submit to a third layer of umbrella supervision of their global operations to be eligible for the favorable SEC net capital rule rather than qualifying on the basis of the equivalent umbrella supervision provided by their home country regulators. In effect, the favorable effort by the EU to avoid duplicating equivalent umbrella supervision by third countries is not being followed by the SEC with respect to international banking groups that are already subject to extensive umbrella supervision that meets international standards. International banks continue to believe that they should be eligible for the favorable risk-based alternative net capital rule because they are already subject to equivalent home country umbrella supervision.

It should be noted that American bank holding companies that are regulated by the Federal Reserve Board would also be subject to duplication of umbrella supervision under the SEC rule. However, there are reports that Citigroup is applying to the SEC (and conferring with the Federal Reserve) to be eligible for the favorable risk-based capital treatment of its securities affiliate and that the issue of duplicative umbrella supervision that is mandated by the SEC's CSE regulation could be revised in the future. In this context, internationally headquartered banks would like to receive comparable treatment since they too receive extensive umbrella supervision by both the Federal Reserve and their home country regulators. Such a favorable change would be consistent with the treatment of American securities firms under the EU Conglomerates Directive.

5. Conclusion

Tensions between home/host regulatory and supervisory requirements and expectations are an inherent feature of the modern international banking system, especially in view of the broad territorial reach and far-ranging operational complexity and interdependence that characterize banks' cross-border activities. Managing this tension and determining the appropriate degree of home/host division of supervisory responsibility remain the principal challenges to achieving a properly balanced and efficient international supervisory regime. And while I recognize the paramount concern of international regulators will be to avoid cross-border financial disruptions, there is nevertheless an understandable interest on the part of private-sector institutions to minimize unnecessary burdens and to have as much consistency as possible in home/host supervision of their global operations in order to avoid any undue negative impact on financial results and shareholder value.

Conference Agenda

Thursday, October 5

9:00 am   Registration

9:40 am   Welcoming Remarks
Michael H. Moskow, President and Chief Executive Officer, Federal Reserve Bank of Chicago
J. P. Sabourin, Chair, Executive Council, International Association of Deposit Insurers

10:00 am   Session I: Landscape of International Banking and Financial Crises
Moderator: Douglas D. Evanoff, Federal Reserve Bank of Chicago

Current State of Cross-Border Banking
Dirk Schoenmaker, Ministry of Finance, The Netherlands

Actual and Near-Miss Cross-Border Crises
Carl-Johan Lindgren, Economic Consultant

Review of Country Financial Stability Reports
Sander Oosterloo, Ministry of Finance, The Netherlands
Discussant: Luc Laeven, International Monetary Fund

12:00 pm   Luncheon and Keynote Address
Moderator: Gordon Werkema, First Vice President and Chief Operating Officer, Federal Reserve Bank of Chicago
Speaker: Stefan Ingves, Governor, Bank of Sweden (Riksbank)

2:00 pm	Session II: Causes and Conditions for Cross-Border Instability Transmission and Threats to Stability *Moderator: Craig H. Furfine, Federal Reserve Bank of Chicago*

Contagion Links
Bent Vale, Bank of Norway (Norges Bank)

Cross-Border Currency Crises
Jon Danielsson, London School of Economics, and Gabriele Galati, Bank for International Settlements

Hedge Funds and Other Nonbanks
Glenn Yago and James R. Barth, Milken Institute
Discussant: Garry J. Schinasi, International Monetary Fund

3:45 pm   Break

4:00 pm   Session III: Prudential Supervision
Moderator: Dalvinder Singh, Journal of Banking Regulation and Oxford Brookes University

Home Country/Cross-Border Externalities
Robert Eisenbeis, Federal Reserve Bank of Atlanta

Home–Host Country Conflicts
Richard J. Herring, University of Pennsylvania

Nonbank Supervision
Paul Wright, Financial Services Authority, United Kingdom
Discussant: Eric Rosengren, Federal Reserve Bank of Boston

6:00 pm   Reception

6:45 pm   Dinner and Keynote Address
Moderator: Michael H. Moskow, President and Chief Executive Officer, Federal Reserve Bank of Chicago
Speaker: Sheila C. Bair, Chairman, Federal Deposit Insurance Corporation

Friday, October 6

7:30 am   Continental Breakfast

8:15 am   Session IV: Government Safety Net
                 Moderator: David K. Walker, Canada Deposit
                 Insurance Corporation

                 Lender of Last Resort across Borders
                 Vitor Gaspar, Banco de Portugal

                 Deposit Insurance across Borders
                 Michael H. Krimminger, Federal Deposit Insurance
                 Corporation

                 Intercountry Conflicts
                 Andrew P. Powell, Inter-American Development
                 Bank, and Giovanni Majnoni, World Bank
                 Discussant: Thorsten Beck, World Bank

10:00 am   Break

10:15 am   Session V: Insolvency Resolution
                 Moderator: Ray LaBrosse, International Association
                 of Deposit Insurers

                 Cross-Border Resolution Conflicts
                 Rosa Maria Lastra, Queen Mary, University
                 of London

                 Bridge Banks and Too Big to Fail/Systemic Risk
                 Exemption
                 David G. Mayes, Bank of Finland

                 Prompt Corrective Action/Structured Early
                 Intervention and Resolution
                 María J. Nieto, Banco de España, and Larry Wall,
                 Federal Reserve Bank of Atlanta
                 Discussant: Peter G. Brierley, Bank of England

12:15 pm   Luncheon and Keynote Address
                    Moderator: Charles L. Evans, Federal Reserve Bank
                    of Chicago
                    Speaker: Raghuram G. Rajan, International Monetary
                    Fund

2:15 pm   Session VI: Cross-Border Crisis Prevention: Public
                    and Private Strategies
                    Moderator: Richard J. Rosen, Federal Reserve Bank
                    of Chicago

                    Multinational Cooperation and Lead Supervisor
                    Arnoud W. A. Boot, University of Amsterdam

                    Multinational/Transnational Organizations
                    David S. Hoelscher and David Parker, International
                    Monetary Fund

                    Private Organizations
                    David Mengle, International Swap and Derivatives
                    Association
                    Discussant: Gerard Caprio, Jr., Williams College

4:00 pm   Break

4:15 pm   Session VII: Where to from Here: Policy Panel
                    Moderator: George G. Kaufman, Loyola University
                    Chicago and Federal Reserve Bank of Chicago
                    Mutsuo Hatano, Deposit Insurance Corporation
                    of Japan
                    Andrey G. Melnikov, Deposit Insurance Agency
                    (Russian Federation)
                    Arthur J. Murton, Federal Deposit Insurance
                    Corporation
                    Guy Saint-Pierre, Canada Deposit Insurance
                    Corporation
                    Lawrence R. Uhlick, Institute for International
                    Bankers

6:00 pm   Reception

6:45 pm   Dinner and Keynote Address
Moderator: Ray LaBrosse, International Association of Deposit Insurers
Speaker: J. P. Sabourin, Chair, Executive Council, International Association of Deposit Insurers

Index